# Artificial Intelligence

# Artificial Intelligence
## Applications in Healthcare Delivery

Edited by
## Sandeep Reddy

Routledge
Taylor & Francis Group
A PRODUCTIVITY PRESS BOOK

First published 2021
by Routledge
600 Broken Sound Parkway #300, Boca Raton FL, 33487

and by Routledge
2 Park Square, Milton Park, Abingdon, Oxon, OX14 4RN

Routledge is an imprint of the Taylor & Francis Group, an informa business

Library of Congress Control Number: 2020941574

ISBN: 9780367321512 (hbk)
ISBN: 9780429317415 (ebk)

Typeset in Garamond
by codeMantra

# Contents

# Foreword

Artificial intelligence (AI) provokes us to reimagine healthcare. The very substrate of clinical practice is expertise, and the machinery that transforms that knowledge into care is decision-making. For decades, we have imagined ways of doing things better for our patients – better drugs, better surgeries, better procedures and, always, better decisions.

Computational methods that capture clinical knowledge and automate reasoning have been with us for decades. We are witnessing now a renaissance in the field of AI, driven in part by better methods for learning and making decisions by machine. This rebirth is also driven by the steady digitization of healthcare. The more we measure practice and make those measures machine readable, the more readily can we embed AI into clinical practice.

This embedding of AI into healthcare is the focus of this book. No matter how accurate or efficient a machine process is, if it cannot be well embedded into real-world applications, then it will not achieve what we expect of it. The application of AI to real-world problems is sometimes considered mere 'engineering' work, but the task of application is actually a scientific challenge at least as complex as that of creating reasoning machines.

Implementation science is the discipline that seeks to understand how we embed tools and practices into the complex network of people, processes and tools that come together to create our human systems. Healthcare is amongst the most complex of human industries, and we know that embedding technology into healthcare is a complex process in of itself. What works well in one place may not work so well elsewhere. What is important in one place is not so in another.

The application of AI into healthcare then is not so much the creation of a medicine driven by algorithms, but a medicine which is practised as a partnership between human and machine, each bringing their complementary strengths. That partnership is then embedded in a complex network of relationships and constraints that profoundly shape how well they perform.

The challenge before us is to deeply understand what makes AI work in some healthcare settings and not others. We must understand which elements of application context shape the outcomes of application and how we design the partnership that will be formed between human and machine – each bringing unique strengths to the task of providing patient care. When we are finished, we will have profoundly reshaped healthcare and for the better.

**Professor Enrico Coiera**
*Director, Centre for Health Informatics*
*Australian Institute of Health Innovation*
*Macquarie University*

# Editor

**Associate Professor Sandeep Reddy** is an artificial intelligence (AI) in healthcare researcher based at the Deakin School of Medicine, Geelong, Australia, besides being the founder/chairman of Medi-AI, a globally focused AI company. He also functions as a certified health informatician and is a Fellow of the Australasian Institute of Digital Health and a World Health Organisation-recognised digital health expert.

He has a medical and healthcare management background and has completed machine learning/health informatics training from various sources. He is currently engaged in research about the safety, quality and explainability of the application of AI in healthcare delivery in addition to developing AI models to treat and manage chronic diseases. Also, he has authored several articles and books about the use of AI in medicine. Further, he has set up local and international forums to promote the use of AI in healthcare in addition to sitting on various international committees focusing on AI in healthcare.

# Technical Reviewers

## Primary Technical Reviewer

**Dr Bhushan Garware** works as a senior data scientist at Persistent Systems. He heads Deep Vision Group at Persistent Systems with special interest in medical imaging. He holds a Ph.D. degree and has three patents in his name. He has conducted many workshops and tutorial sessions on machine learning in several industries, academia and research institutes. He has published his work on applications of deep learning for CT, MRI, X-ray and microscopic images in reputed international conferences. His current areas of research interest are explainable AI and assistive intelligence.

## Secondary Technical Reviewer

**Ravi Kiran Bhaskar** is a software professional with over 20 years of experience, currently working as a Technical Architect at *The Washington Post*. He has an M.S. in Electrical Engineering from George Mason University, Fairfax, VA, USA, and B.E. in Electronics Engineering from Nagpur University, India. His career spanned across multiple disciplines ranging from satellite communications, mobile networking, security, web development, web services, system administration, search engineering and supervised/

unsupervised learning. He specialises in natural language processing, search technologies and algorithm development, and is passionate about disruptive technologies in the fields of machine learning, artificial intelligence and high-performance computing.

# Contributors

**Hamid Abdi**
School of Engineering
Deakin University
Geelong, Australia

**Uwe Aickelin**
School of Computing and
    Information Technology
University of Melbourne
Melbourne, Australia

**Arash Keshavarzi Arshadi**
Computational Biotechnology
University of Central Florida
Orlando, Florida

**Ramanath Bhandari**
Department of Opthalmology
Springfield Clinic
Springfield, Illinois

**Balaji Bikshandi**
Faculty of Science & Technology
University of Canberra
Canberra, Australia

**Uli K. Chettipally**
Society of Physician Entrepreneurs,
    San Francisco Bay Area chapter
InnovatorMD
San Francisco, California

**James Condon**
University of Adelaide,
Adelaide, Australia

**Ricardo Correa**
Department of Endocrinology
University of Arizona College of
    Medicine, Phoenix and Phoenix
    VAMC
Tucson, Arizona

**Fernando A. Crespo**
DAiTA LAb, Facultad de Estudios
    Interdisciplinarios
Universidad Mayor
Santiago, Chile

**Juan Luis Cruz**
Hospital Universitario 12 de Octubre
Madrid, Spain

**Jacek B. Cywinski**
Anesthesiology Institute
Cleveland Clinic
Cleveland, Ohio

**Neha Deo**
Mayo Clinic Alix School of
    Medicine
Mayo Clinic
Rochester, Minnesota

**Zobaida Edib**
School of Computing and
    Information Technology
University of Melbourne
Melbourne, Australia

**Daniel J. Fox**
Department of Clinical Research
Springfield Clinic
Springfield, Illinois

**Anna Fragkoudi**
Outcome Health
Melbourne, Australia

**Vishnu Vardhan Garla**
Department of Endocrinology
University of Mississippi Medical
    Center
Jackson, Mississippi

**Deepak Kumar Gopalakrishnan**
School of Engineering
Deakin University
Geelong, Australia

**Gonzalo Hernández**
Centro Científico y Tecnológico
    de Valparaíso
Valparaíso, Chile

**Rahul Kashyap**
Department of Anesthesiology/
    Critical Care Medicine
Mayo Clinic
Rochester, Minnesota

**Hadi Akbarzadeh Khorshidi**
School of Computing and
    Information Technology
University of Melbourne
Melbourne, Australia

**Dinesh Kumar**
Faculty of Science & Technology
University of Canberra
Canberra, Australia

**Stefanie Lip**
Institute of Cardiovascular and
    Medical Sciences
University of Glasgow
Glasgow, United Kingdom

**Vidur Mahajan**
Mahajan Imaging
New Delhi, India

**Dwarikanath Mahapatra**
Inception Institute of Artificial
    Intelligence
Abu Dhabi, United Arab Emirates

**Chaitanya Mamillapalli**
Department of Endocrinology
Springfield Clinic
Springfield, Illinois

**Piyush Mathur**
Anesthesiology Institute
Cleveland Clinic
Cleveland, Ohio

**Adam McLeod**
Outcome Health
Melbourne, Australia

**Ernestina Menasalvas**
Universidad Politécnica de
    Madrid
Madrid, Spain

**Sandosh Padmanabhan**
Institute of Cardiovascular and
    Medical Sciences
University of Glasgow
Glasgow, United Kingdom

**Lyle Palmer**
University of Adelaide
Adelaide, Australia

**Francis A. Papay**
Cleveland Clinic Lerner College of
    Medicine
Case Western Reserve University
Cleveland, Ohio
and
Dermatology and Plastic Surgery
    Institute
Cleveland Clinic
Cleveland, Ohio

**Christopher Pearce**
Outcome Health
Melbourne, Australia

**Michelle Peate**
School of Computing and
    Information Technology
University of Melbourne
Melbourne, Australia

**Mariano Provencio**
Department of Oncology
Puerta de Hierro University
    Hospital and
Universidad Autónoma de Madrid
Madrid, Spain

**Aditya Ravishankar**
School of Engineering
Deakin University
Geelong, Australia

**Natalie Rinehart**
Outcome Health
Melbourne, Australia
and
Case Western Reserve University
Cleveland, Ohio

**Milad Salem**
Computational Biotechnology
University of Central Florida
Orlando, Florida

**Dharmendra Sharma**
Faculty of Science & Technology
University of Canberra
Canberra, Australia

**Johnson Thomas**
Department of Endocrinology
Mercy
Springfield, Missouri

**Mark R. Traill**
Metro Health
University of Michigan
Wyoming, Michigan

**Vasanth Venugopal**
Mahajan Imaging
New Delhi, India

**Shyam Visweswaran**
Department of Biomedical
    Informatics
University of Pittsburgh
Pittsburgh, Pennsylvania

**Xuetong Wu**
School of Computing and
    Information Technology
University of Melbourne
Melbourne, Australia

# Chapter 1

# Algorithmic Medicine

Sandeep Reddy
*Deakin University*

## Contents

## 1.1 Introduction

For long health services have faced several challenges, chief among them being rising expenditure and workforce shortages without clear solutions in sight (Topol, 2019). At the same time, there has been an unprecedented generation of medical data ranging from sources such as electronic health records, medical imaging and laboratory units (Sidey-Gibbons & Sidey-Gibbons, 2019). Clinicians have for long relied on computers to analyse such data as the analysis of such complex, and large datasets exceed their human capacity. In this context, the emergence of artificial intelligence (AI) with its ability to significantly enhance the data analysis process has presented an opportunity for clinicians and healthcare administrators to gain better insights (Reddy, 2018). An opportunity to optimise care delivery, reduce healthcare delivery costs and support a stretched workforce.

Of the various AI approaches, the most pertinent to analysing data is machine learning (ML), which comprises aspects of mathematics, statistics and computational science (Sidey-Gibbons & Sidey-Gibbons, 2019). ML is the core of changes occurring in medicine because of AI. Unlike non-AI methods and software, which rely mainly on traditional statistical approaches, ML software utilises pattern detection and probabilistic approaches to predict medical outcomes (Reddy, 2018). This utilisation of ML algorithms and other AI approaches to deliver medical care is what can be termed as *algorithmic medicine*. The ability to predict crucial medical outcomes through AI algorithms can make healthcare more precise and efficient. Beyond medical care, AI can also support healthcare administration, drug discovery, population health screening and social assistance (Reddy, 2018), thus expanding the scope of algorithmic medicine beyond the confines of clinical care, i.e. direct clinician to patient care. This ability and promise have ignited the interest of governments and other healthcare stakeholders to consider incorporation of AI in healthcare administration and delivery seriously. This chapter outlines what would be involved for this to occur and what the impact will be.

## 1.2  AI in Medicine – A History

Before we define AI and describe its techniques, it will be pertinent to review the history of AI in healthcare. The concept of intelligent machines is not new and in fact can be traced to Ramon Llull's theory of reasoning machine in the 14th century (Reddy, 2018). However, modern AI can be tracked back to the past 70 years with the term originating from the workshop organised by John McCarthy at Dartmouth College in 1956 (AAIH, 2019). In the following decade, the availability of faster and cheaper computers allowed experimentation with AI models particularly in the areas of problem-solving and interpretation of spoken language (Anyoha, 2017). However, as work progressed in these areas, the lack of requisite computational power and the limitations of the then algorithmic models came to fore. In the 1980s, there was a revival of interest in AI particularly so in expert systems, which were modelled to mimic the decision-making process of a human expert (Figure 1.1). However, again these types of models fell short of expectations, and interest in AI in both academia and industry

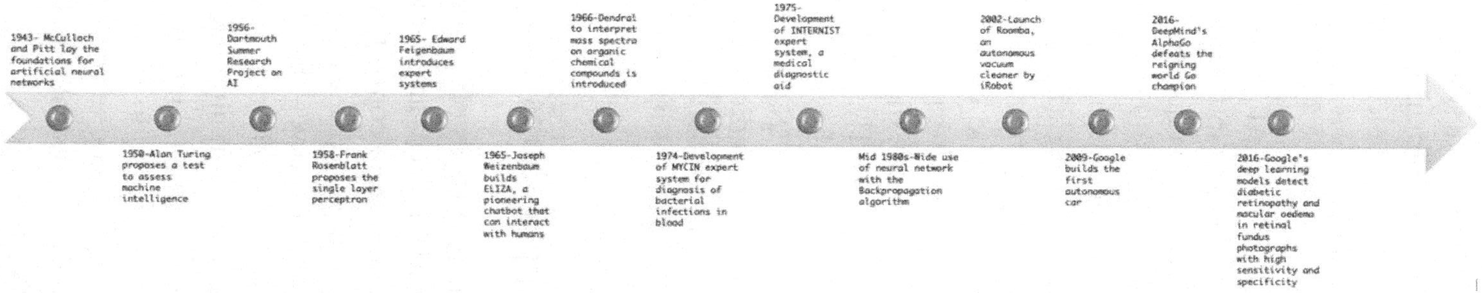

**Figure 1.1 History of AI and its use in medicine.**

waned. Commencing in the mid-2000s, the availability of suitable technical hardware and emergence of neural networks, an advanced form of ML, coupled with their demonstrable performance in image and speech recognition once again brought AI back to the limelight. Since then, significant funding and interest has led to further advances in algorithms, hardware, infrastructure, and research.

Paralleling the general history of AI, its use in medicine formally commenced with the DENDRAL project in the 1960s, which was an early expert system with an objective to define organic compound structures by investigating their mass spectra (AAIH, 2019). The development of this system required new theories and programming. This was followed by MYCIN in the 1970s, which was aimed at identifying infections and recommending appropriate treatment. The learning from MYCIN was extrapolated to develop the CADUSEUS system in the 1980s. This system was then hyped as the most knowledgeable medical expert system in existence. In line with the general history of expert system, the application of expert systems in medicine fell short of expectations. The sophistication of neural networks and availability of hardware to run these algorithms presented a new opportunity for the use of AI in medicine (Naylor, 2018; Reddy, 2018). Since then, increasing evidence has been detailed of what AI models can do in terms of medical imaging interpretation, support for clinical diagnosis, drug discovery and clinical natural language processing.

## 1.3 AI Types and Applications

Before we discuss the different types of AI and its applications, it is important to define what AI is? There are numerous definitions of AI in the literature, but this one derived from computer science describes AI as "the study of intelligent agents and systems, exhibiting the ability to accomplish complex goals" (AAIH, 2019). However, this definition is oriented to an academic perspective. From an application and industry perspective, AI can be best described as "machines assuming intelligence". Now that we have defined AI, it is pertinent to mention here two levels of AI: *General* and *Narrow AI.* General AI, also referred to as Artificial General Intelligence, is when AI exhibits "a full range of cognitive abilities or general intelligence actions by an intelligent agent or system" (AAIH, 2019), while Narrow AI, also referred to as Weak AI, is where AI is specified to address a singular or limited task.

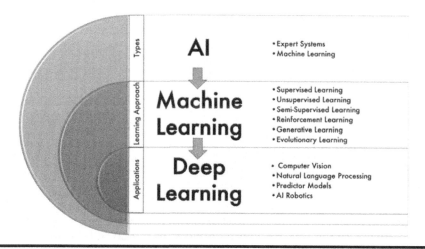

**Figure 1.2   AI types, learning approaches and applications.**

The predominant approach of AI, currently, is ML (Figure 1.2). This approach involves performing tasks without explicit instructions relying mainly on patterns and relationships in the training data and environment (AAIH, 2019). To develop ML models, you will need to define the necessary features, i.e. dependent and independent or input and target variables, and develop datasets including the features. Further to this, you split up the dataset into training and test datasets to allow for internal validation. Following this, the datasets are trained or tested with relevant ML algorithms. If the training dataset contains the input data and the appropriate output/target variable, then it is termed *supervised learning* (El Morr & Ali-Hassan, 2019). However, if there is no known output and the algorithm is left to detect hidden patterns or structures within the dataset, then this is *unsupervised learning*. In recent years, a hybrid form where the training set has a mix of labelled and unlabelled data and the expectation is that a function predicting the target variable is arrived at, which is termed *semi-supervised learning* (El Morr & Ali-Hassan, 2019).

ML algorithm development does not necessarily have to adopt the training approach described above. *Reinforcement learning*, a relatively newer form of ML, involves a process of maximising reward function based on the actions taken by the agent (AAIH, 2019). A trial-and-error approach is adopted to eventually arrive at optimal decision-making by the agent. In *generative learning*, the model development involves creating new examples from the same distribution as the training set and in certain instances with a particular label. The *evolutionary algorithm* model builds on this approach where initially developed algorithms are tested for their fitness, similar to an

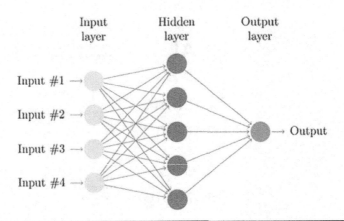

**Figure 1.3  Representation of the neural network architecture (Creative Commons License).**

evolutionary process, until peak performing algorithms are identified and no more progress in fitness of the group can be derived (AAIH, 2019).

While there are numerous ML algorithms in use, a couple of commonly used algorithms in medicine are linear regression, logistic regression, decision trees, random forest and support vector machines (SVMs). An advanced form of ML that excels at analysing complex patterns between variables in datasets is *deep learning* (DL) (Topol, 2019). This approach is inspired by the architecture and ability of human brains whereby learning and complex analysis is achieved through interconnected neurons and their synapses. This is computationally simulated through many layers of artificial neurons between the input and output variables. These artificial neurons through a hierarchical and interconnected process are programmed to detect complex features and the model depending on complexity of data adds necessary number of layers (auto-didactic quality) (Topol, 2019). Sandwiched between the input and output layers are the hidden layers (see Figure 1.3), which adds to the feature optimisation and model performance but also creates opacity about the decision-making process of the model.

While there are myriad ways as to how neural networks and AI are in use in healthcare, three applications where they are mostly used or have most promise are profiled: *computer vision, natural language processing* and *robotics.*

## 1.3.1 Computer Vision

Computer Vision (CV) is where computers assist in image and video recognition and interpretation (Howarth & Jaokar, 2019). Increasingly DL has

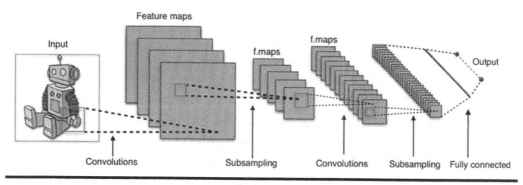

**Figure 1.4 Architecture of a CNN (Creative Commons License).**

become central to the operation of CV. This is due to DL's many layers useful for identifying and modelling the different aspects of an image. In particular, *convolutional neural networks* (CNNs), a form of DL, involve a series of convolutions and max-pooling layers (see Figure 1.4) as its underlying architecture has been found to be very useful in image classification (AAIH, 2019; Erickson, 2019). CNNs are credited for reviving interest in neural networks in recent years. The way the CNNs work is by commencing with low-level features in the image and progress to higher-level features that represent the more complex components of the image. For example, the first layers will identify points, lines and edges, and the latter layers will combine these to identify the target class. An early example of CNN was AlexNet, an image classification model (AAIH, 2019). More recent versions are CNNs with specialised layers including ResNet, ResNeXt and region-based CNN (Erickson, 2019).

CNNs are increasingly being applied in medical image interpretation (Erickson, 2019): for example, to classify chest X-rays that have malignant nodules and those that haven't. Here, a set of labelled or annotated chest X-rays are used to train the neural networks to compute features that are reliable indicators of malignancy or lack. CNNs can be used for segmentation too where the class of interest is delineated from the remaining area of non-interest. However, CNNs are not restricted to analysing chest X-rays and have also been used to interpret CT, MRI, fundoscopy, histopathology and other images (Erickson, 2019; Reddy, 2018; Reddy, Fox, & Purohit, 2019).

## *1.3.2 Natural Language Processing*

Natural language processing (NLP) is a process of computationally representing, transforming and utilising different forms of human language, i.e. text or speech (Wu et al., 2020). Unlike other data, computing human language is not straightforward as there is a lot of imprecision in human language (Chen, 2020). Also, the unit component of language is not necessarily conducive to computation. To address this natural language must be initially reencoded into a logical construct before it can be administered for information extraction or translation. For many years, NLP reliant on traditional ML approaches like SVM and logistic regression, which were trained on very high dimensional and sparse features, yielded shallow models (Friedman, Rindflesch, & Corn, 2013). However, the advent of DL and its use in NLP has resulted in better performing models. This is because DL enables multi-level automatic feature representational learning.

An important reason for the success of DL in NLP is because of *distributed representation*, which describes the similar data features athwart multiple scalable and interdependent layers (Young, Hazarika, Poria, & Cambria, 2018). Examples of distributed representation include word embeddings, word2vec and character embeddings. These examples follow the distributional hypothesis, where it is assumed that words with similar meanings tend to occur in a similar context. Thus, the models aim to capture the characteristics of the neighbours of a word to predict meaning. DL has also been useful in Automatic Speech Recognition (ASR), sometimes referred to as speech-to-text (Chen, 2020). Recurrent neural networks have been demonstrated to work well for ASR by lending the algorithm tolerance to complex language conditions such as accents, speed and background noise.

Clinical use of NLP has extended to the vector representation of clinical documents such as clinical guidelines, extracting clinical concepts from electronic medical records or discharge summaries through named entity recognition, mapping clinical ideas and diagnoses with codified guidelines, and developing human-to-machine instructions (Rangasamy, Nadenichek, Rayasam, & Sozdatelev, 2018). NLP can also be potentially used for non-clinical healthcare purposes such as efficient billing and accurate prior authorisation approval through the extraction of information from unstructured physician notes or electronic health records. Further uses of NLP include transcription and chatbot services (Reddy, Fox, et al., 2019).

### 1.3.3 Robotics

Robots are machines that can carry out complex action and can be programmed by computers (Ben-Ari & Mondada, 2017). Not all robots are programmed by computers and are purely mechanical in nature.

However, for this chapter, we will review those robots that are programmable by a robot. Robots can be of two categories: fixed and mobile, depending on the environment they operate. Fixed robots like industrial robots operate in a well-defined environment, while mobile robots move and perform activities in poorly defined and uncertain environments. Algorithms work in robots through embedded computers that run on pseudocode utilising a mix of natural language, mathematics and programming structures.

In healthcare, robots are used in various ways, including in surgery, hospitals and aged care (Pee, Pan, & Cui, 2019; Reddy, 2018). One such application that has become popular in recent years is robotic-assisted surgery (Svoboda, 2019). In this format, surgeons control multiple robotic arms through a hand-operated console (Figure 1.5). This application enables surgeons' greater vision and dexterity to operate in hard-to-reach areas.

Yet, this is not AI robotics which is about robots operating in an automated or semi-automated fashion. In this regard, trials are being held to allow for independent operation of surgical procedures (Svoboda, 2019). More straightforward or repetitive tasks like suturing and valve repair lend themselves to surgical automation, while complex surgical tasks may take many more years to be automated. Elsewhere, robotic assistants have been used either to support the elderly as social companions or to guide them with medications, appointments and in unfamiliar environments. As AI-enabled robots attain more autonomous functionality through intelligent algorithms, their use in various areas of healthcare is only to increase (Reddy, 2018; Reddy, Fox, et al., 2019).

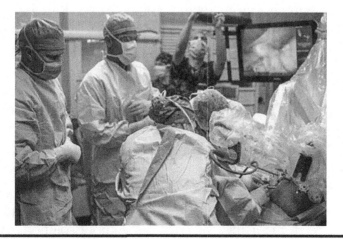

**Figure 1.5   Robotic-assisted surgery (Creative Commons License).**

As AI algorithms and models evolve, there will be broader applicability of them in healthcare to drive efficiency and improved patient outcomes. Demonstrable evidence in the areas of CV, NLP, AI robotics and predictor models will enable adoption and broader use of AI within healthcare broadly and specifically within clinical care models.

## 1.4 Challenges and Solutions

While AI has enabled unprecedented sophistication and performance in medicine that very few technologies can match, it has also presented significant challenges in its implementation (Reddy, Allan, Coghlan, & Cooper, 2019). While medical data are abundant, they all are not necessarily structured or standardised to train AI models (Wang, Casalino, & Khullar, 2018). While the human brain is capable of inferring patterns from heterogeneous and noisy data, AI models are less so. Utilisation of incorrect and non-representative data can have several implications in the context of healthcare delivery, including the introduction or affirmation of biases and exacerbation of health disparities. Also, in a clinical setting, reliance on a model trained on inaccurate data can have medico-legal repercussions (Reddy, Allan, et al., 2019). Another issue that has emerged specifically with the use of DL models is the opacity of decision-making that is intrinsic to these models. When trained on large datasets, DL models use their many layers to simulate complicated regularities in the data. However, the layered non-linear feature learning makes it impractical to interpret the learning process (Hinton, 2018). The inability to clearly explain the DL model's conclusion basis presents an obstacle to its use in clinical medicine. For example, if a DL model were to make a clinical recommendation or diagnosis without a clear rationale, it will find little acceptance amongst clinicians. Further to this, the training of ML models involves several parameters (rules) (Beam, Manrai, & Ghassemi, 2019). Because of the use of randomness in training many ML models, there are different possibility parameters arrived at each time the model is retrained, thus limiting reproducibility of the models. Finally, the mathematical accuracy of AI models means nothing if there is no impact on patient outcomes. Currently, very few studies have presented evidence of the downstream benefit of AI models in medicine.

While these are relatively significant challenges for the adoption and applicability of AI in medicine, they are not without solutions. Most medical DL models are relatively small and focused on medical image interpretation, which has fewer issues in terms of structure and reproducibility (Beam et al., 2019). Increasingly, medical researchers are utilising shared or open-source datasets to train their models and providing open access to the code used for the training. These measures allow for transparency and reproducibility of AI models. Also, academic and transdisciplinary collaborations present an opportunity to test and embed AI models in routine clinical care (Sendak, Gao, Nichols, Lin, & Balu, 2019). To address bias or safety and quality issues that may arise from the use of AI models, a governance model that incorporates *fairness, transparency, trustworthiness* and *accountability* has been proposed (Figure 1.6) (Reddy, Allan, et al., 2019).

*Fairness* requires representation from the community at which the AI medical application is aimed at in determining how the software developer uses data (Reddy, Allan, et al., 2019). The representation could be at a data governance panel that reviews datasets used for training such AI medical applications. While it is not feasible for all software developers to constitute such panels, they could potentially draw advice from a government-instituted committee. Information from the group can contribute to less discriminatory or less biased AI models being developed. *Transparency* stresses the explainability of medical AI models. Where possible, algorithms that lend themselves to explainability are to be utilised, and when DL types of algorithms are necessary, functional understanding of the model conveyed through interpretable frameworks. Also, in clinical practice, informed consent is obtained from patients before use of AI medical applications in the treatment and management of their medical conditions. These initiatives

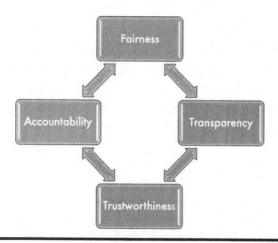

**Figure 1.6 Components of an AI in healthcare governance framework. (Adapted from Reddy, Allan et al. (2019).)**

are also required to ensuring *trustworthiness* of AI medical applications in addition to educating clinicians and the general community about AI and its use and limitations. Through this education and subsequent understanding, AI stands a better chance of being accepted by the medical and patient populations. Finally, accountability is about ensuring the safety and quality of AI medical application through appropriate regulatory and clinical governance processes. This requires input and involvement from a range of governmental and non-governmental bodies. Further to this, legal frameworks and guidance need to be constituted as to who becomes responsible if there were AI-related medical errors or mishaps. In essence, accountability is extending beyond the AI medical application to cover a range of players (Reddy, Allan, et al., 2019). This is necessary to ensure the appropriate and safe use of AI in medicine.

## 1.5  The Future

As costs of running healthcare, the volume of medical data, the time required to train and deploy work-ready medical workforce and complexity of medical delivery increase, it is inevitable for stakeholders to explore an increased role for AI. The rate and extent at which AI gets adopted in routine clinical care delivery are not guaranteed. However, based on current evidence, one can speculate where AI can contribute to and benefit clinical care. AI can replace some of the mundane or repetitive tasks that clinicians engage with leaving them more time to engage with patients in a meaningful manner. Also, areas which require analysis of complex or voluminous data may benefit from AI's ability to infer patterns from the data contributing to an augmented medicine model. Further, the progression of research and trials in AI robotic systems can eventuate in the automation of certain aspects of surgery, aged care and hospital logistics (Pee et al., 2019; Svoboda, 2019). All these developments herald an era of *algorithmic medicine*.

## References

AAIH. (2019). Artificial intelligence in healthcare: a technical introduction. *Alliance for Artificial Intelligence in Healthcare (AAIH) White Paper*, (September), 1–45. Retrieved from https://www.theaaih.org/pdf/1571334853.pdf.

Anyoha, R. (2017). The history of artificial intelligence. Retrieved February 23, 2020, from http://sitn.hms.harvard.edu/flash/2017/history-artificial-intelligence/.

Beam, A. L., Manrai, A. K., & Ghassemi, M. (2019). Challenges to the reproducibility of machine learning models in health care. *JAMA – Journal of the American Medical Association*, 6–7. doi: 10.1001/jama.2019.20866.

Ben-Ari, M., & Mondada, F. (2017). Elements of robotics. *Elements of Robotics*, 1–308. doi: 10.1007/978-3-319-62533-1.

Chen, P. H. (2020). Essential elements of natural language processing: what the radiologist should know. *Academic Radiology*, *27*(1), 6–12. doi: 10.1016/j.acra.2019.08.010.

El Morr, C., & Ali-Hassan, H. (2019). *Analytics in Healthcare: A Practical Introduction*. SpringerBriefs in Health Care Management and Economics. doi: 10.1007/978-3-030-04506-7.

Erickson, B. J. (2019). Deep learning and machine learning in imaging: basic principles. *Artificial Intelligence in Medical Imaging*, 39–46. doi: 10.1007/978-3-319-94878-2_4.

Friedman, C., Rindflesch, T. C., & Corn, M. (2013). Natural language processing: state of the art and prospects for significant progress, a workshop sponsored by the National Library of Medicine. *Journal of Biomedical Informatics*, *46*(5), 765–773. doi: 10.1016/j.jbi.2013.06.004.

Hinton, G. (2018). Deep learning-a technology with the potential to transform health care. *JAMA – Journal of the American Medical Association*, *320*(11), 1101–1102. doi: 10.1001/jama.2018.11100.

Howarth, D., & Jaokar, A. (2019). *Deep Learning and Computer Vision with CNNs*. Data Science Central. doi: 10.1017/CBO9781107415324.004.

Naylor, C. D. (2018). On the Prospects for a (Deep) Learning Health Care System. *JAMA*, *320*(11), 1099–1100. doi: 10.1001/jama.2018.11103.

Pee, L. G., Pan, S. L., & Cui, L. (2019). Artificial intelligence in healthcare robots: a social informatics study of knowledge embodiment. *Journal of the Association for Information Science and Technology*, *70*(4), 351–369. doi: 10.1002/asi.24145.

Rangasamy, S., Nadenichek, R., Rayasam, M., & Sozdatelev, A. (2018). Natural language processing in healthcare.

Reddy, S. (2018). Use of Artificial Intelligence in Healthcare Delivery. *EHealth – Making Health Care Smarter*. doi: 10.5772/intechopen.74714.

Reddy, S., Allan, S., Coghlan, S., & Cooper, P. (2019). A governance model for the application of AI in health care. *Journal of the American Medical Informatics Association*, *0*(0), 1–7. doi: 10.1093/jamia/ocz192.

Reddy, S., Fox, J., & Purohit, M. P. (2019). Artificial intelligence-enabled healthcare delivery. *Journal of the Royal Society of Medicine*, *112*(1), 22–28. doi: 10.1177/0141076818815510.

Sendak, M., Gao, M., Nichols, M., Lin, A., & Balu, S. (2019). Machine learning in health care: a critical appraisal of challenges and opportunities. *EGEMs (Generating Evidence & Methods to Improve Patient Outcomes)*, *7*(1), 1. doi: 10.5334/egems.287.

Sidey-Gibbons, J. A. M., & Sidey-Gibbons, C. J. (2019). Machine learning in medicine: a practical introduction. *BMC Medical Research Methodology*, *19*(1), 1–18. doi: 10.1186/s12874-019-0681-4.

Svoboda, E. (2019). Your robot will see you now. *Nature, 573*(6), 110–111. doi: 10.1097/01.nnn.0000550481.89594.cd.

Topol, E. J. (2019). High-performance medicine: the convergence of human and artificial intelligence. *Nature Medicine, 25*(1), 44–56. doi: 10.1038/s41591-018-0300-7.

Wang, F., Casalino, L. P., & Khullar, D. (2018). Deep learning in medicine-promise, progress, and challenges. *JAMA Internal Medicine*, E1–E2. doi: 10.1038/nature21056.

Wu, S., Roberts, K., Datta, S., Du, J., Ji, Z., Si, Y., … Xu, H. (2020). Deep learning in clinical natural language processing: a methodical review. *Journal of the American Medical Informatics Association : JAMIA, 27*(3), 457–470. doi: 10.1093/jamia/ocz200.

Young, T., Hazarika, D., Poria, S., & Cambria, E. (2018). Recent trends in deep learning based natural language processing [Review Article]. *IEEE Computational Intelligence Magazine, 13*(3), 55–75. doi: 10.1109/MCI.2018.2840738.

# Chapter 2

# Use of Artificial Intelligence in the Screening and Treatment of Chronic Diseases

Chaitanya Mamillapalli, Daniel J. Fox, and Ramanath Bhandari
*Springfield Clinic*

Ricardo Correa
*University of Arizona College of Medicine Phoenix and Phoenix VAMC*

Vishnu Vardhan Garla
*University of Mississippi Medical Center*

Rahul Kashyap
*Mayo Clinic*

## Contents

## 2.1  Introduction

Chronic health diseases are physical or mental conditions that last more than one year and cause functional restrictions that require monitoring and treatment (Hajat and Stein, 2018). Patients with multiple chronic conditions experience frequent hospitalizations, die prematurely, require consultation with multiple specialists, and accrue high healthcare utilization rates (Navickas et al., 2016). They are also on multiple medications with complex drug interactions and have difficulty adhering to treatment that adversely impacts the quality of life and outcomes (Navickas et al., 2016). A significant proportion of the aging population (patients >65 years of age) is at higher risks of these chronic health diseases, with incidence impacting almost one-third of the world's population and rates of patients experiencing greater than four chronic diseases at a time expected to double between 2015 and 2035 (Marengoni et al., 2011; Kingston et al., 2018).

As a result of its increasing prevalence, a 2015 Global Burden of Disease report correlates 70% of deaths to chronic disease complications (Global Burden of Disease Study 2015, 2016).

In addition to high morbidity and mortality, managing chronic disease complications results in high economic costs and significant productivity losses to communities. In 2016, chronic diseases cost the United States 1.1 trillion dollars and placed substantial burdens on health systems nationwide (The Costs of Chronic Disease in the U.S., 2019). The World Health Organization (WHO) anticipates a shortage of approximately 12.9 million healthcare providers globally by 2035 (Kingston et al., 2018).

The complexities of chronic disease management, coupled with primary care physician time limitations and worldwide healthcare provider shortages, contribute to suboptimal treatment for patients (approximately 46.3% of patients with chronic diseases do not receive care per the recommended guidelines) (McGlynn et al., 2003). Further, current chronic disease management strategies are not equipped to address unique patient complexities.

The healthcare industry's current infrastructure suffers from workforce shortages, underfunded systems, increases in demands, and an explosion of chronic disease prevalence and increased cost. Novel healthcare delivery models are urgently needed to address the complexities and multimorbidities that result from increasing chronic disease prevalence (Navickas et al., 2016). AI is a combination of promising technologies that may play a crucial role in future healthcare model success. This chapter will focus on AI's potential role in successful healthcare delivery, its implications for three chronic health diseases (diabetes, cardiovascular disease or CVD, and dementia), the challenges and considerations for AI technologies in the healthcare environment, and its practical applications.

## 2.2 Role of Artificial Intelligence in Chronic Disease

Machine learning (ML) is a subset of AI that utilizes computer algorithms to analyze data and correlate relationships between risk factors (variates) and health conditions (result variables or covariates). ML models provide scalable solutions that may address the global burden of increased chronic disease prevalence. They may also be used to evaluate unstructured datasets and synthesize disease predictions to provide personalized and patient-specific healthcare recommendations. Contrary to traditional statistical modeling, ML processes potentially improve predictions and classifications because they are not dependent on preconceived variable assumptions. Healthcare systems already have key elements to enhance chronic healthcare delivery: electronic medical records (EMRs) with rich data, evidence-based guidelines, and infrastructures with computing power.

ML promises significant improvements to care compared to current risk score utilization. Physicians routinely use risk scores to make healthcare management decisions. However, these risk scores use limited numbers of clinical variables with modest predictive accuracy in individual subjects. ML leverages big data, recognizes complex patterns, and refines predictive accuracies via repetition and adjustment. Utilizing analytical data methods with patient data and evidence-based guidelines may allow healthcare providers to instantaneously tailor patient-specific recommendations to promote appropriate preventative and therapeutic personalized medicine strategies.

Personalized medicine's primary objective is to utilize patient insights and features to derive patient-specific risk factors and subsequently customize treatment options based on the individualized risk profile (Redekop and Mladsi, 2013). ML models may play a vital role in personalized medicine by helping to merge diverse healthcare datasets, electronic health records (EHRs), imaging data, genetic data, biomarker analyses, and data from mobile sensors (Rumsfeld et al., 2016). Deploying ML systems may foster personalized medicine, predict the risk of disease/complications, and therefore recommend actionable interventions and prevent acute events. Technological advances offer healthcare providers with countless tools to fully understand their individual patients' needs and provide the best possible care. The explosive use of digital health and mobile apps creates patient habit and activity datasets that can be merged with EMR data. Using these data sources, ML models may analyze real-time patient needs and guide healthcare providers to enhance the management of chronic diseases such as diabetes, CVD, and dementia.

## 2.3 Machine Learning in Diabetes

Diabetes is a glucoregulatory dysfunctional disease manifested by hyperglycemia and broadly categorized two subtypes (type 1 and type 2 diabetes). Type 1 diabetes has an absolute deficiency of insulin secretion, whereas type 2 diabetes is characterized by relative insulin deficiency and insulin resistance (Diagnosis and Classification of Diabetes Mellitus, 2009). Type 2 diabetes is more common, accounts for 90% (~425 million) of diabetes cases worldwide, and is projected to increase exponentially in the upcoming years (IDF diabetes atlas, 2017). ML studies in diabetes can be categorized into the following four groups:

1. Prediction and diagnosis of type 2 diabetes
2. Blood glucose management
3. Diabetes phenotyping
4. Early detection of diabetic complications.

## 2.3.1 Prediction and Diagnosis of Type 2 Diabetes

Currently recommended diabetes laboratory screening tests comprise fasting blood glucose, hemoglobin A1c, and oral glucose tolerance tests. A diabetes diagnosis is confirmed by a 2-hour glucose tolerance test measuring >200 mg/dl or A1c≥6.5% or fasting glucose levels >126 mg/dl. Prediabetes is a precursor for diabetes with glucose levels above normal levels but less than the defined thresholds for diabetes (2-hour glucose levels at 140–200 mg/dl, A1c 5.7%–6.5%, and fasting glucose at 100–126 mg/dl) (Bowen et al., 2018). Approximately 37%–70% of patients with prediabetes progress into type 2 diabetic status within four years of onset at an overall rate of 10%/year (Nathan et al., 2007).

Universal prediabetes and diabetes screening are not recommended due to the lack of mortality benefit. Rather, opportunistic/selective screening is recommended for patients with high-risk factors. The screening models encounter major practical limitations because they are time-consuming and require data that are not always readily available (Bowen et al., 2018). Diabetes screening rates in high-risk patients are continually below 50% in some series despite the availability of multiple guidelines and risk scores. Several factors contribute to low diabetes screening rates, including heterogeneity among screening recommendations, lack of familiarity with validated diabetes risk factors among healthcare providers, and limited access to risk factor data at the time of patient encounters (Bowen et al., 2018).

An alarming 90% (~77.4 million US patients) of the projected prediabetic population remains undiagnosed (ADA statistics about diabetes). Type 2 diabetes may also be present 4–6 years prior to clinical diagnosis and consequently exposing the patients to micro- and macrovascular complications (Porta et al., 2014). Accurate and timely identification of prediabetes and diabetes is critical for the effective implementation of diabetes prevention programs. ML models may provide scalable and sustainable solutions to evaluate diabetes risk at the population level to facilitate selective prediabetes and diabetes screening and provide evidence-based prevention and treatments to high-risk subjects. Such models may be implemented at a population level without additional tests, screening, or chart reviews beyond what is freely available in health records and administrative data. Studies have already developed and demonstrated ML models as diabetes prediction tools in clinical settings (Figure 2.1; Table 2.1).

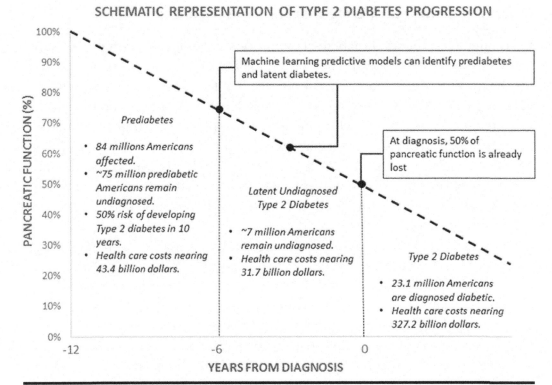

SCHEMATIC REPRESENTATION OF TYPE 2 DIABETES PROGRESSION

**Figure 2.1** **Type 2 diabetes disease progression and latency between disease onset and diagnosis. ML models may be utilized to predict type 2 diabetes diagnoses years before their clinical discovery and well before patients lose half of their pancreatic function.**

**Table 2.1** **Studies That Have Developed and Demonstrated ML Models as Diabetes Prediction Tools**

| Study Description | ML Methods | Results |
|---|---|---|
| **Mani et al.**<br>Retrospective study<br>3,375 subjects<br>EMR-based diabetes<br>forecasting study at<br>Vanderbilt University<br>medical center<br>17 attributes were<br>studied | Gaussian Naïve<br>  Bayes<br>Logistic regression<br>K-nearest neighbor<br>CART<br>Random Forests<br>Support vector<br>  machine (SVM) | Predicted diabetes 180 days and<br>  365 days prior to diagnosis<br>Random Forest was the best<br>  performing model with<br>The area under the curve (AUC)<br>  0.803<br>Sensitivity 0.759<br>Specificity 0.731<br>Positive predictive value (PPV) 0.24 |

*(Continued)*

**Table 2.1 (*Continued*)   Studies That Have Developed and Demonstrated ML Models as Diabetes Prediction Tools**

| Study Description | ML Methods | Results |
|---|---|---|
| **Zou et al.** Retrospective study 68,994 healthy people and 68,994 diabetic patients Hospital physical examination data from Luzhou, China 14 attributes (Demographic, Physical exam and lab data) | Decision tree Random Forest Neural network | Diabetes detection: Random Forest Accuracy (ACC) 0.8084 Sensitivity 0.84 Specificity 0.76 ACC fasting glucose: 0.76 |
| **Razavian et al.** Retrospective study 697,500 subjects Administrative claims cohort of 4.1 million individuals (Independence Blue Cross, Pennsylvania) | Dual Coordinate Descent Two models *Parsimonious model used* 21 diabetes risk factors with traditional logistic regression ML-based *Enhanced model* used 538 variables | Predicted diabetes 2 years in advance Parsimonious model AUC 0.75 Enhanced model AUC 0.800 |
| **Mamillapalli et al.** Retrospective study 85,719 subjects EHR data from a large multi-specialty clinic in the United States Nine attributes (demographic, physical exam and lab data) | Supervised Jungle binary classifier | Diabetes detection: PPV 0.686 Negative predictive values (NPV) 0.88 AUC 0.72 F-score 0.77 |

*(Continued)*

**Table 2.1 (*Continued*)    Studies That Have Developed and Demonstrated ML Models as Diabetes Prediction Tools**

| Study Description | ML Methods | Results |
|---|---|---|
| **Hall et al.** prospective study CGM data on 57 healthy volunteers | Complexity-invariant dynamic time warping (CID-DTW) | Patients with normoglycemia and prediabetes were categorized into three glucotypes: <br>• Low variability (L) glucotype <br>• Moderate variability (M) glucotype <br>• Severe variability (S) glucotype <br>24% of the normoglycemic patients have glucose excursions similar to diabetics <br>Authors hypothesize glucose variability is the initial manifestation of dysglycemia and may represent an earlier stage of prediabetes |

## 2.3.2 Blood Glucose Management

Approximately 30%–50% of the United States' diabetic patient population does not meet the personalized target for blood pressure, glucose, and lipid parameters (Ali et al., 2013). The underlying reasons for uncontrolled diabetes are multifactorial:

1. Patients on insulin treatment need adjustment based on blood glucose levels, carbohydrate counting, and activity level.
2. Non-adherence to the treatment regimens.
3. Treatment and regimen complexities.
4. Disease burden.
5. Hypoglycemia is a major rate-limiting issue in reaching glycemic targets, especially in patients with type 1 diabetes mellitus (T1DM).

Improvement in diabetes control is associated with a decrease in complications and healthcare cost burden (Lafeuille et al., 2014; UK Prospective Diabetes Study (UKPDS) Group, 1998). ML models and clinical decision support systems (DSSs) have successfully leveraged large datasets generated by continuous glucose monitor (CGM) devices and sensor-augmented insulin pumps and have improved glycemic outcomes (Table 2.2). The combination of glucose sensors and closed-loop control algorithm insulin infusion

**Table 2.2 Studies That Have Developed and Demonstrated ML Models as Clinical Decision Support Systems to Control Blood Glucose Levels**

| Study Description | ML Methods | Results | Clinical Application |
|---|---|---|---|
| **Bergenstal et al.** Prospective study. 124 patients with type 1 diabetes. MiniMed 670G is an integrated insulin pump systems with hybrid closed loop. | Proportional-integral derivative (PID) algorithm controls insulin dosing that responds to glucose level. | Improvement in HbA1c from 7.4% to 6.9%. Improvement in the rate of hypoglycemia. | Medtronic 670G is the first FDA-approved hybrid closed-loop insulin pump. |
| **Gregory et al.** Multicenter, randomized controlled crossover outpatient pivotal trial. Tandem X2 insulin pump is an integrated insulin pump system. | Simple linear regression algorithm that predicts glucose levels. Predictive low glucose suspends (PLGS) algorithm use the recent four CGM sensor glucose values to calculate glucose levels 30 minutes in advance. Insulin delivery is stopped if predicted glucose level is <80 mg/dl or if observed glucose concentrations fall below 70 mg/dl. | 31% relative reduction in hypoglycemia without worsening of hyperglycemia. | Tandem X2 insulin pump with PLGS is available. |

*(Continued)*

**Table 2.2 (*Continued*) Studies That Have Developed and Demonstrated ML Models as Clinical Decision Support Systems to Control Blood Glucose Levels**

| Study Description | ML Methods | Results | Clinical Application |
|---|---|---|---|
| **Nimri et al.**<br>24 patients with type 1 diabetes. Physicians' adjustments of insulin pump settings based on CGM were compared to the automated algorithm, the Advisor Pro (DreaMed Diabetes Ltd., Israel). | Advisor Pro algorithm. ML method not specified. | Automated recommendation of insulin treatment with Advisor Pro performed in par with the advice given by expert physicians. | DreaMed Advisor Pro was approved by the FDA on June 12, 2018. An automated decision support system to adjust insulin pump settings in patients with type 1 diabetes. |
| **Goldner et al.**<br>One Drop mobile app collected 1,923,416 blood glucose measurements from 14,706 patients with noninsulin treated T2DM. | ML method not specified. | 91% of ML model predictions were within 50 mg/dl of the actual value. Mean absolute error of predictions was 21.3 mg/dl. | Forward prediction of blood glucose levels can help patients with modifying their behavior to help with the prevention of blood glucose value. |

devices is the foundation for hybrid closed-loop systems (artificial pancreas) which imitates islet physiology and auto-adjusts insulin delivery based on glucose levels (Weaver and Hirsch, 2018).

CGM and integrated insulin pump devices help to improve quality of life, glycemic control, and reduce comorbidities associated with diabetes. Healthcare organizations are however experiencing several challenges with these systems primarily because they require substantial patient and provider engagement and high-resource utilization (required for non-reimbursed healthcare provider time to interface with new technologies) (Weaver and Hirsch, 2018).

### 2.3.3 Diabetes Phenotyping

Type 2 diabetes is a heterogeneous disease with diverse phenotypes and varying risks of diabetes-related complications. Phenotype identification via ML models helps to target high-risk groups for intensive disease management (Table 2.3).

### 2.3.4 Early Detection of Diabetes Complications

Uncontrolled diabetes is associated with the risk of micro- and macrovascular complications (cardiovascular, renal, peripheral vascular, ophthalmic) (Chawla et al., 2016). Diabetic retinopathy (DR) is the most common microvascular complication of diabetes. Early diagnosis and treatment of DR are important to prevent vision loss in diabetic patients. Despite the American Diabetes Association (ADA) recommendations for annual eye exams, compliance rates for retinal screenings remain low near 50% even in developed countries (Liu et al., 2018). IDX-DR, an ML algorithm for detection of diabetic retinopathy, was evaluated in the primary care setting, demonstrated a sensitivity of 87.2%, specificity of 90.7%, and an imageability rate of 96.1% (Abràmoff et al., 2018). IDX-DR obtained FDA approval for the autonomous diagnostic system for detecting diabetic retinopathy. This technology's implementation potentially improves DR screening rates and decreases the incidence of diabetes-induced blindness.

**Table 2.3  A Study That Has Developed and Demonstrated ML Models to Predict Diabetic Phenotyping**

| Description of the Study | ML Methods | Results | Clinical Application |
|---|---|---|---|
| **Li et al.** 11,210 individuals. EMRs and genotype data from Mount Sinai Medical Center in New York. | Topological data analysis. | T2DM group identified three new T2DM subtypes on the basis of distinct patterns of clinical characteristics and disease comorbidities. Subtype 1: Young patients Classical T2DM with high BMI. Kidney disease and eye disease. Higher HbA1c. Subtype 2: Lower weight. Malignancy and CVDs. Subtype3: CVDs, neurological diseases, allergies, and HIV infections. Specific genes unique to the subtypes were identified. | Identify T2DM patient homogenous subgroup phenotypes with distinct clinical and genetic characteristics. This approach can be deployed to study other chronic diseases. |

# 2.4 Machine Learning in Cardiovascular Disease

CVDs are diseases that affect the heart or blood vessels and include hypertension, coronary heart disease, heart failure, atrial fibrillation, and stroke. CVD is one of the leading causes of mortality or morbidity and accounts for one-third of the deaths worldwide (Eckel et al., 2014; Alwan, 2011). About 102 million (41.5%) US adults currently have at least one cardiovascular condition, and ~131 million (45%) are projected to suffer from CVD by 2035. CVD's estimated annual 2014–2015 cost was 555 billion dollars in the United States, and it is projected to double by 2035 to 1.1 trillion dollars.

Age-adjusted cardiovascular mortalities have reduced significantly over the past 50 years. Despite its significant incidence decline, CVD remains to be the leading cause of death (McClellan et al., 2019). Contributing factors for recent flattening cardiovascular mortality rate reduction include (McClellan et al., 2019)

1. Patients fail to make risk factors modifications.
2. Patients do not adhere to recommended treatments.
3. Failure to diagnose.
4. Failure to use evidence-based medication regimens.

Additionally, significant cardiovascular mortality disparities are present across different groups by race, sex, and ethnicity. These may result from patient difficulties to comply with CVD risk factor modification treatments, socio-economic variables, and behavioral factors (McClellan et al., 2019). AI may provide solutions to alleviate some of these CVD treatment challenges by personalizing treatment, targeting high-risk patients, and potentially decreasing cardiovascular outcome disparities. Current cardiology ML studies are categorized in the following four groups:

1. Cardiovascular risk prediction
2. Phenotypic and prognostic studies
3. ECG and diagnostic accuracy improvement
4. Imaging and diagnostic accuracy improvement.

## 2.4.1 Cardiovascular Risk Prediction

Failure to diagnose and prevent CVD remains problematic. A significant proportion of apparently healthy subjects without prior symptoms continue to die suddenly (Naghavi et al., 2006). Traditional CVD risk prediction models such as the Framingham risk score assesses only at the population level with discriminatory accuracy at the individual level remaining suboptimal (75%). As a result, individual patients experience overtreatment or under treatment with related morbidity and economic costs (Wilson Peter et al., 1998; Detrano et al., 2008).

Traditional CVD risk prediction models are limited in predictive performance because they adopt restrictive modeling methods with limited numbers of variables. Identifying asymptomatic patients who are at high risk of CVD and starting on intense preventive treatment is a major ongoing challenge, particularly with traditional CVD risk models (Franco et al., 2011). Comprehensive tools with improved accuracy are needed to address these challenges. ML models may provide solutions to CVD risk prediction by identifying current and new CVD risk factors, evaluating patient variables comprehensively, and potentially discovering new CVD therapeutic strategies (Table 2.4).

## 2.4.2 Identification of Novel Cardiovascular Disease Phenotypes

ML models have helped to classify novel heart disease genotypes and phenotypes by identifying therapeutically homogeneous patient subgroups within heterogeneous diseases such as heart failure preserved ejection fraction (HFpEF), pulmonary hypertension, and coronary artery disease (Krittanawong et al., 2017). As a result, these models may assist patients and healthcare providers with prognostic and therapeutic decisions, active and informed decision-making about invasive procedures, and efficient resource utilization (Table 2.5).

## 2.4.3 ECG and Diagnostic Accuracy Improvement

ML methods may be utilized to improve ECG accuracy and, combined with sensors, instantaneously and automatically detect cardiac arrhythmias (Tables 2.6 and 2.7).

**Table 2.4 Studies That Have Developed and Demonstrated ML Models to Improve CVD Risk Prediction**

| Author Description of the Study | ML Methods | Outcomes | Clinical Application |
|---|---|---|---|
| **Alaa et al.** Retrospective analysis of prospective cohort. 423,604 participants in UK Biobank (No CVD at baseline). 473 variables. | Linear SVMs. Random Forest. Neural networks. AdaBoost. Gradient boosting. | Risk prediction of CVD Auto Prognosis model: AUC 0.774 Framingham score: AUC 0.724 Cox PH model with conventional risk factors AUC 0.734 Cox PH model with all UK Biobank 473 variables AUC 0.758 4,801 CVD cases were reported at 5 years and Auto Prognosis was able to accurately predict 368 more cases than Framingham risk score. | Improved performance of CVD risk prediction. Auto Prognosis model using non-laboratory variables about lifestyle and medical history can be used in developing countries (when lab values are not available) to predict CVD. |

(Continued)

**Table 2.4 (Continued)  Studies That Have Developed and Demonstrated ML Models to Improve CVD Risk Prediction**

| Author Description of the Study | ML Methods | Outcomes | Clinical Application |
|---|---|---|---|
| **Bannister et al.** Retrospective analysis of prospective cohort. 3,873 patients from the symptomatic CVD from the Second Manifestations of Arterial Disease (SMART) study cohort. The composite endpoint was cardiovascular death, non-fatal stroke, and myocardial infarction. 25 risk factors associated with CVD. | Genetic programming (GP). | GP machine model has a comparable predictive ability to that of manually tuned Cox regression in determining the risk of a cardiovascular event. At 3 years: GP: C-Statistic 0.69 Cox regression: C-Statistic 0.7 | The GP model can be used for clinical prediction modeling and prognostication of CVD. |
| **Weng et al.** Retrospective analysis of prospective cohort. Clinical data of 378,256 patients from UK family practices. 22 risk factors associated with CVD. | Random Forest. Logistic regression. Gradient boosting machines. Neural networks. | The ML algorithm performed superior to the American College of Cardiology and American Heart Association risk algorithm. Neural networks achieved the best performance: Sensitivity 67.5%, PPV 18.4% Specificity 70.7% NPV 95.7% An extra +7.6% more patients were identified accurately with CVD compared to traditional algorithms. | Improved performance of risk prediction of CVD. |

*(Continued)*

**Table 2.4 (Continued)  Studies That Have Developed and Demonstrated ML Models to Improve CVD Risk Prediction**

| *Author*<br>*Description of the Study* | *ML Methods* | *Outcomes* | *Clinical Application* |
|---|---|---|---|
| **Ambale-Venkatesh et al.** Retrospective analysis of a prospective cohort. 6,814 participants from Multi-Ethnic Study of Atherosclerosis (MESA) cohort. (extensively phenotyped population with no CVD at baseline). 735 variables imaging and non-invasive tests, questionnaires and biomarker panels were screened, and the top 20 predictors were identified. | Random survival forest. | Random survival forest showed greater predictive power than established risk scores in risk prediction of death, stroke, heart failure, and atrial fibrillation Risk prediction of coronary heart disease at 12 years: *Random survival forest* Concordance Index (C-index) 0.81 Brier score (BS) 0.067 *ACC/AHA ASCVD* C-index: 0.73, BS: 0.11 *Framingham risk score* C-index: 0.73, BS: 0.089 (Higher C-index and lower BS denote better predictive accuracy). | Improved performance of CVD risk prediction. |

*(Continued)*

**Table 2.4 (*Continued*)  Studies That Have Developed and Demonstrated ML Models to Improve CVD Risk Prediction**

| Author / Description of the Study | ML Methods | Outcomes | Clinical Application |
|---|---|---|---|
| **Kakadiaris et al.** Retrospective analysis of a prospective cohort. 6,459 participants from the MESA cohort. Validation was done on the FLEMENGHO study (Flemish Study on Environment, Genes and Health Outcomes). Same variables as in ACC/AHA risk calculator. | SVM | Risk prediction of CVD: ACC/AHA Risk Calculator. Sensitivity 0.76, specificity 0.56, and AUC 0.71 ACC/AHA Risk Calculator recommended statin treatment in 46.0% of the patients; despite the high proportion of patients on statin treatment, 24% of cardiac events occurred in patients not on statin treatment. ML Risk Calculator Sensitivity 0.86, specificity 0.95, and AUC 0.92. ML Risk Calculator recommended statin treatment in 11.4% of the patients; only 14.4% of cardiac events occurred in patients not taking statin treatment. ML Risk Calculator outperformed ACC/AHA risk calculator in risk prediction of CVD; selected fewer patients for statin treatment yet missing fewer cardiac events. | Evidence from randomized clinical trials and meta-analysis strongly support statin treatment for primary prevention of CVD. (Taylor et al., 2013) Improved the performance of CVD risk prediction and identification of appropriate patients for statin treatment. |

**Table 2.5  Studies That Have Developed and Demonstrated ML Models to Identify CVD Phenotypes**

| *Author*<br>*Description of the Study* | *ML Methods* | *Outcomes* | *Clinical Application* |
|---|---|---|---|
| **Shah et al.**<br>Retrospective analysis of a prospective cohort of 397 patients with HFpEF from Northwestern University.<br>Echocardiogram imaging and clinical variables for the classification and prediction of outcomes in patients with HFpEF. | Agglomerative hierarchical clustering.<br>Model-based clustering.<br>SVM | New phenotypic classification of patients with heart failure and preserved ejection fraction.<br>Phenotype1: younger patients with lower B-type natriuretic peptide levels (BNP).<br>Phenotype 2: High prevalence of obesity and diabetes mellitus, COPD.<br>Phenotype3: oldest patients with chronic kidney disease, highest BNP, and Meta-Analysis Global Group in Chronic Heart Failure (MAGGIC) risk scores.<br>Substantial differences in outcomes of cardiovascular hospitalization or death. | HFpEF is a heterogeneous disorder; phenotyping will help with classification and categorization and may guide the development of new targeted treatments. |

*(Continued)*

**Table 2.5 (*Continued*)  Studies That Have Developed and Demonstrated ML Models to Identify CVD Phenotypes**

| Author Description of the Study | ML Methods | Outcomes | Clinical Application |
|---|---|---|---|
| **Cikes et al.** Retrospective analysis of a prospective cohort. 1,106 heart failure patients from the Multicenter Automatic Defibrillator Implantation Trial with Cardiac Resynchronization Therapy (MADIT-CRT) cohort. Echocardiographic data and clinical parameters. Identify patients with a beneficial response to cardiac resynchronization therapy (CRT). | Multiple kernel learning. Clustering (K-means). | Four distinct phenogroups were identified. Two phenogroups had significantly better CRT treatment responses; Phenogroup 1: Hazard ratio (HR) 0.35. Phenogroup 3: HR 0.36. | Phenogrouping of heart failure patients using echo and clinical parameters and identification of patients suitable for CRT treatment. |
| **Dawes et al.** Retrospective analysis of a prospective cohort. Cardiac MRI (CMR) has become a gold standard to assess cardiac mass and volume (Ripley et al., 2016). CMR images of 256 patients with newly diagnosed pulmonary hypertension. CMR imaging-based algorithm of three-dimensional patterns of systolic cardiac motion. | Supervised the ML method (specific ML method not specified). | ML method can classify patients into specific prognosis classes. The difference in the median survival of high risk and low risk group was 13.8 years and 10.7 years, respectively. Survival prediction: ML method: AUC 0.73 Conventional imaging: AUC 0.60 | Determine prognostic risk in individual patients and guide management in patients with pulmonary hypertension. |

(*Continued*)

**Table 2.5 (*Continued*)   Studies That Have Developed and Demonstrated ML Models to Identify CVD Phenotypes**

| *Author*<br>*Description of the Study* | *ML Methods* | *Outcomes* | *Clinical Application* |
|---|---|---|---|
| **Motwani et al.**<br>Retrospective analysis of a prospective cohort.<br>10,030 patients with suspected coronary artery disease from the Coronary CT Angiography Evaluation for Clinical Outcomes: An International Multicenter Registry.<br>Cardiac CT has a lot of variables affecting risk, and it can be challenging for clinicians to calculate the individual risk.<br>69 clinical variables | Boosted ensemble algorithm.<br>10-fold stratified cross-validation. | 5-year all-cause mortality.<br>LogitBoost model<br>AUC 0.79<br>Framingham risk score:<br>AUC 0.61<br>Segment stenosis score:<br>AUC 0.64<br>Segment involvement score:<br>AUC 0.64<br>Duke index:<br>AUC 0.62. | Prediction of all-cause mortality in individual patients with suspected coronary artery disease. |

**Table 2.6  Studies That Have Developed and Demonstrated ML Models to Improve ECG and Diagnostic Accuracy**

| Author / Description of the Study | ML Methods | Outcomes | Clinical Application |
|---|---|---|---|
| **Bumgarner** Prospective, non-randomized, and adjudicator-blinded study. Kardia Band (KB) enables to record ECG using an Apple smartwatch. KB algorithm for atrial fibrillation as compared to 12 lead ECGs for atrial fibrillation interpretation. | Specific ML method not specified. | KB interpretations were compared to physician-reviewed ECGs. 77% of the patients were interpreted automatically by KB: • Sensitivity 93%, • Specificity 84% • K coefficient 0.77. 33% of the ECGs from KB were uninterpretable, Physician interpretation of these KB recordings: • Sensitivity 99% • Specificity 83% • K coefficient of 0.83. | KB is cleared by the FDA to detect bradycardia, tachycardia or AFib. The patient can record rhythm strip instantaneously with smartwatch and can be interpreted by an algorithm as atrial fibrillation or sinus rhythm. |
| **Hannun et al.** 91,232 single-lead ECGs from 53,549 patients who used a single-lead ambulatory ECG monitoring device. Validated on 2017 PhysioNet Challenge data. | Deep neural network (DNN) | Classify ten different arrhythmias. ML model performance was compared to cardiologists: AUC 0.97. $F_1$ score 0.837. Average cardiologist F1 score 0.780. | Improve the diagnostic accuracy, efficiency and scalability of computerized ECG interpretations. |

## 2.4.4 Imaging and Diagnostic Accuracy Improvement

**Table 2.7  Studies That Have Developed and Demonstrated ML Models to Improve Imaging and Diagnostic Accuracy**

| Author Description of the Study | ML Methods | Outcomes | Clinical Application |
|---|---|---|---|
| **Bai et al.** Retrospective analysis of a prospective cohort. 4,875 subjects with 93,500 images UK Biobank dataset, annotated by clinical experts. Presently measurements of volume and mass for tracing the cardiac MRI are done manually. The cardiologist may need to spend about 20 minutes to analyze images. This is a time-consuming and tedious process that can lead to subjective errors. | Fully convolutional network (FCN) | ML model achieved high performance on par with human experts in evaluating the cardiac dimensions. DICE metric: Left atrium cavity 0.93. Right atrium cavity 0.96. Left ventricular cavity 0.94. Right ventricular cavity 0.90. | ML models can automate clinical measures of cardiac images and can aid clinicians in CMR image analysis and diagnosis. |

*(Continued)*

**Table 2.7 (*Continued*) Studies That Have Developed and Demonstrated ML Models to Improve Imaging and Diagnostic Accuracy**

| Author<br>Description of the Study | ML Methods | Outcomes | Clinical Application |
|---|---|---|---|
| **Nakajima et al.**<br>Retrospective analysis of a prospective cohort.<br>Japanese multicenter study of 12 institutions. | Artificial neural networks (ANNs). | Performance of ANN diagnostic model of Myocardial perfusion SPECT image compared against conventional quantification.<br>ANN:<br>AUC Stress defect 0.92.<br>AUC Rest defects 0.93.<br>AUC Ischemia 0.9.<br>Conventional quantification method:<br>AUC Stress defect 0.82.<br>AUC Rest defects 0.86.<br>AUC Ischemia 0.75.<br>Diagnostic ability of cardiac ischemia was comparable to human experts and superior to conventional semi-quantitative methods. | May help with interpretation of myocardial perfusion scan and/or function as a second opinion for the interpreting physician. |

# 2.5 Machine Learning in Dementia

Dementia is a neurodegenerative disorder that causes severe cognitive impairment and resultant severe disabilities (Hugo and Ganguli, 2014). About 50 million people have dementia worldwide, and the WHO estimates 10 million new cases occur each year. Alzheimer's dementia (AD) is the most common type of cognitive impairment, accounting for 70% of new cases (https://www.who.int/news-room/fact-sheets/detail/dementia). The total medical care and long-term care cost burden incurred due to dementia in 2015 were 818 billion dollars, and costs are expected to spike to 2 trillion dollars by 2050 (https://www.who.int/news-room/fact-sheets/detail/dementia). ML models may provide solutions to dementia-induced healthcare demands. Current studies using ML for dementia are broadly categorized as follows:

1. Early dementia prediction
2. Dementia phenotyping.

## 2.5.1 Early Dementia Prediction

Underdiagnosis of dementia remains a significant problem, with up to half of dementia patients remaining undiagnosed or with a delayed diagnosis for up to 2.5 years (Purandare, 2009). A dementia diagnosis is challenging due to the heterogeneous nature of the disease, and its clinical presentation often mimics other conditions such as depression.

Early dementia diagnosis ensures potential patients receive appropriate treatment and access to participating in clinical trials. They also offer better access to services that improve the quality of life and provide patient families with sufficient time to plan for long-term care needs.

Dementia screening methods are critical to achieving early dementia diagnosis; however, screening for dementia in primary care settings is not routinely recommended because its effectiveness has not been validated (Recommendation against national dementia screening, 2015). Dementia risk scores require additional data collection from patients that are not clinically routine, and even after additional data collection, they do not recognize patients who may have undiagnosed dementia (Walters et al., 2016, Barnes and Lee, 2011). Thus, dementia screening methods are not widely used because of their limited applicability in general practice. ML model development and deployment may assist in screening large groups of people and identifying patients at high risk for dementia for targeted screening (Table 2.8).

**Table 2.8 Studies That Have Developed and Demonstrated ML Models to Improve Dementia Prediction**

| Author / Description of the Study | ML Methods | Outcomes | Clinical Application |
|---|---|---|---|
| **Jammeh et al.**<br>Retrospective study.<br>24,858 patients. (850 patients with dementia).<br>Case-controlled design.<br>18 general practices in the UK over 2 years.<br>Routinely collected read codes data which has information regarding diagnosis, risk factors and behaviors. | SVM.<br>Naïve Bayes.<br>Random Forest.<br>Logistic regression. | Detected undiagnosed dementia, from the routinely collected read codes in the practice. Naïve Bayer classifier was the best model:<br>Sensitivity 84.47.<br>Specificity 86.67.<br>AUC 0.869. | Early identification of dementia using routinely collected data. |
| **So et al.**<br>Retrospective study.<br>14,000 patients (9,799 in the normal group and 4,201 in the cognitive decline group).<br>Patients who presented for dementia screening from the Gangbuk-Gu center for dementia in the Republic of Korea.<br><u>Two-stage model</u><br>The first stage was for a screening test to categorize as normal or abnormal group using Mini-Mental State Examination Korean version (MMSE-KC) data.<br>The second stage was to categorize as MCI or dementia using Consortium to Establish a Registry for Alzheimer's Disease Korean version (CERAD-K) data. | Naïve Bayes. Bayes Network.<br>Logistic Regression.<br>Random Forest.<br>SVM.<br>Multilayer perceptron (MLP). | Diagnosis of dementia:<br><u>First stage:</u><br>MLP had higher accuracy with 97.2%.<br><u>Second stage</u><br>SVM has the best performance for predicting dementia with 74% accuracy. | Early diagnosis of dementia using neuropsychological and demographic data. |

*(Continued)*

**Table 2.8 (*Continued*) Studies That Have Developed and Demonstrated ML Models to Improve Dementia Prediction**

| Author<br>Description of the Study | ML Methods | Outcomes | Clinical Application |
|---|---|---|---|
| **Zhang et al.**<br>Retrospective study.<br>416 subjects.<br>Dataset of 3D MR images from Open Access Series of Imaging Studies (OASIS). | SVM.<br>Radial basis function kernel (RBF-SVM).<br>Polynomial kernel (POL-SVM). | Early detection of dementia.<br>POL-KSVM<br>Accuracy 92.36%.<br>Sensitivity 83.48%.<br>Specificity 94.90%. | A classification system for the development of computer-aided diagnosis (CAD) system for the early detection of dementia. |
| **Nori et al.**<br>Retrospective study.<br>OptumLabs Data Warehouse.<br>US national de-identified dataset of more than 125 million privately insured individuals.<br>50 clinical variables. | Lasso logistic regression algorithm. | ML model was able to forecast new cases of dementia four or five years before the onset of symptoms.<br>AUC 64.3%.<br>Sensitivity 31.9%.<br>Specificity 86.4%.<br>Lift 1.9. | Early diagnosis of dementia. |

**Table 2.9  Studies That Have Developed and Demonstrated ML Models to Dementia Phenotyping**

| a. Author<br>b. Description of the Study | ML Methods | Outcomes | Clinical Application |
|---|---|---|---|
| **Gamberger et al.** Prospective design. 562 subjects with mild cognitive impairment (MCI). Alzheimer's Disease Neuroimaging Initiative (ADNI) study with 5-year longitudinal outcomes and biomarker data. | Multi-layer clustering algorithm. | Identified two homogenous clusters of slow decliners and rapid decliners. The subgroup of rapid decliners compared to the slow decliners had A. Five times the rate of progression to dementia. B. Two-fold atrophy in the brain. | Classification of dementia into homogenous MCI subgroups • Can help with a new understanding of dementia disease mechanisms and development of novel treatments. • Accurate prognostication can help patients and clinicians; reassurance can be offered at very low risk for progression. |

## 2.5.2 Dementia Phenotyping

Alzheimer's dementia (AD) is a heterogeneous disease with varying degrees of symptoms, rates of decline, and ages of onset. Clinical drug trials have failed at a 99% rate over the past two decades. These negative results represent the research field's incomplete understanding of dementia's pathophysiology and prognosis (Cummings et al., 2019).

ML models may assist researchers to identify patient subgroups with mild cognitive dysfunction and a high risk of dementia progression; this may help to develop novel disease-modifying dementia therapies (Table 2.9).

# 2.6 Challenges in the Implementation of AI in Chronic Disease Management

## 2.6.1 Methodical Challenges

AI's capacity to enhance and improve healthcare is not without its challenges (Challen et al., 2019). ML model bias and clinical safety concerns specific to chronic healthcare management are referenced and addressed as follows:

■ Most AI models are based on retrospective studies, demonstrate association, and do not prove causation (Thiese, 2014; Yu et al., 2018). Random data variations without a real biological basis may be erroneously classified as a phenotype (Ascent of machine learning in medicine, 2019). The solution for this is methods that incorporate causal discovery algorithms or hybrid approaches which are combinations of probabilistic and causal discovery methods (Glymour et al., 2019). Further prospective controlled studies are needed to assess these ML models in a real-world clinical setting (Yu and Kohane, 2019).

■ Models are only as good as the data they are trained on. Even perfect models are restricted by training datasets, dataset quality, and degrees of the signal. Further, most ML studies are trained on databases that comprise a specific population, which harbors the potential for "distribution shift" (Amodei et al., 2016) and may hamper a model's general applicability to diverse population groups. "Out-of-sample inputs" is a mismatching condition between training and operational data that may result from either training data inadequacies or incorrect trained model application to an unanticipated patient situation (Amodei et al., 2016). Different outcome definitions are used during the ML model development, which may also cause additional reproducibility problems.

■ Excessive learning by neural networks also creates models that are prone to overfitting, which reduces data applicability to real-world scenarios (Nagpal, 2017). Regularization is a process that is used to reduce over-fitting; however, its role remains to be tested and utilized for model applicability across a wider general population (Nagpal, 2017).

■ Prediction drift is a mismatching phenomenon between training and operational data because of changes in disease patterns over time. It may affect a model's accuracy (Davis et al., 2017). Dichotomization is performed in models to classify patients into discrete categories. Inappropriate dichotomization, however, may reduce a model's predictive precision (Johnson et al., 2018).

■ Unsupervised ML models may perform as a "black box" with unexplained decision-making rationale that is opaque to interpretation (Yu et al., 2018). This lack of transparency in a new technology decreases healthcare providers' and patients' trust in such algorithms and may contribute to lower adoption rates.

■ Reporting standardization is not yet established for ML model accuracy (Forman and Scholz, 2010; Lobo et al., 2008).

- ML models adoption may lead to "automation bias", which is a phenomenon of clinicians accepting the decision from the algorithms without confirmatory investigations (Parasuraman and Manzey, 2010; Tsai et al., 2003).
- Concerns regarding the possibility of bias against minorities in underlying datasets, which will be inadvertently learned by the ML models and will influence the output (Romei and Ruggieri, 2013).

## 2.6.2 Practical Challenges

AI technologies have successfully integrated themselves into healthcare fields such as fundus imaging, chest X-ray interpretation, histopathology, evaluation of skin lesions, ECG monitoring, and hybrid closed-loop insulin pumps to name a few. AI use in chronic disease management is evolving; however, many challenges remain to be addressed prior to its industry-wide adoption:

- Data Quality – High-quality training dataset availability is currently limited. End-to-end ML model development needs large-scale data collection procedures that require data sharing. Sharing patient health records is highly regulated, and patient data privacy for ML method development remains a point of contention (Yu et al., 2018).
- Cost – ML model research requires high development costs and expertise. Significant resources are needed to extract and normalize data and customize models to suit organizational requirements. Further, short-term financial investment benefits have not yet been realized, and only indirect society benefits via potential early diagnoses and improved patient quality of life have been demonstrated. AI researchers have not yet performed large outcome studies that demonstrate improved outcomes and lower healthcare costs, and therefore have not established or determined a quantifiable value to chronic disease management (Rumsfeld et al., 2016).
- Clinical Integration – AI models require integration into clinical workflow to demonstrate their full beneficial potential. AI integration, however, is hampered by current EHR infrastructure limitations. Execution of the computational environment for collecting, storing, and sharing confidential health data has its challenges (Yu et al., 2018).
- Interoperability – Third-party application interoperation with EHR systems is not often successful; however, there are some on the horizon with the development of interoperability frameworks such as

FHIR (Fast Healthcare Interoperability Resources) that can help with AI integration in clinical DSSs (Yu et al., 2018). Framework design standards are also crucial for AI implementation in clinical practice; however, they are not yet available (Middleton et al., 2013).

■ Leadership – Healthcare executives do not currently possess in-depth knowledge about ML model capabilities, challenges, and limitations for chronic disease management.

■ Legal – Current legal and ethical frameworks do not address direct or indirect discrimination, liabilities, and responsibilities to regulate AI management for chronic disease (Romei and Ruggieri, 2013).

## 2.6.3 Solutions

AI models used for chronic disease management may have unintentional harmful consequences to patient care if their challenges and limitations are not addressed. To address these challenges, healthcare providers, developers, AI researchers, and administrators need to collaborate to develop high-impact AI applications and infrastructure required for successful utilization. Successful AI model development will require correct study design determination, adequate sample sizes, appropriate variable use, and development of complete data protocols. Models must also have abundant and easily accessible data to adequately serve diverse population demographics. AI model validation should be performed ideally through randomized clinical trials in diverse settings to ensure result reproducibility and model generalizability to various clinical settings and patient population. Researchers should ensure diversity in age, ethnicity, and gender in model validation and training datasets to develop widely applicable models. Deployed models must also be continuously refined and trained with real-time patient data.

Successful AI model utilization requires industry adoption and regulatory infrastructure development. Physicians should champion AI adoption, serve as subject medical experts to healthcare systems, and play leading roles in model development, validation, and implementation. Regulatory agencies should establish diagnostic standards and legal and ethical frameworks to ensure comprehensive model performance and security evaluation in real-life clinical situations. ML model regulations have already initiated with the FDA's "pre-certification" announcement in April 2018, which will intend to give certification to the technology developer rather than the product itself (Transforming FDA's Approach to Digital Health, 2019).

## 2.7 Real-Life Clinical Practice Applicability

AI-based systems have already made significant contributions to specific chronic disease management facets (e.g., management of diabetes with the use of insulin pump treatments). Significant potential already exists for clinical DSSs that may be implemented in EMRs to assist with prescription medications and adhere to protocols and guidelines. ML models may also work in the background of EHRs to automatically collect variables and permit immediate risk score computations (Figure 2.2).

ML models integrated into EHR systems may serve as physician aids at the point of care. ML-based predictive tools can help immensely with chronic health disease evaluation, early diagnoses, and optimal treatment, thereby enabling access equality and democratization of health care. With future development, chronic disease management will become more effective, personalized, convenient, and efficient to pave the way for personalized medicine.

The healthcare industry is beginning to respond to AI's promising business potential. Multiple startup companies have claimed interests in the business space:

■ "Medial Early Sign" risk prediction algorithms were used in a 645,000-prediabetes cohort and identified the top 20% high-risk population. Of the subjects identified, 64% became diabetic within 12 months (Prediabetes to Diabetes Progression, 2017).

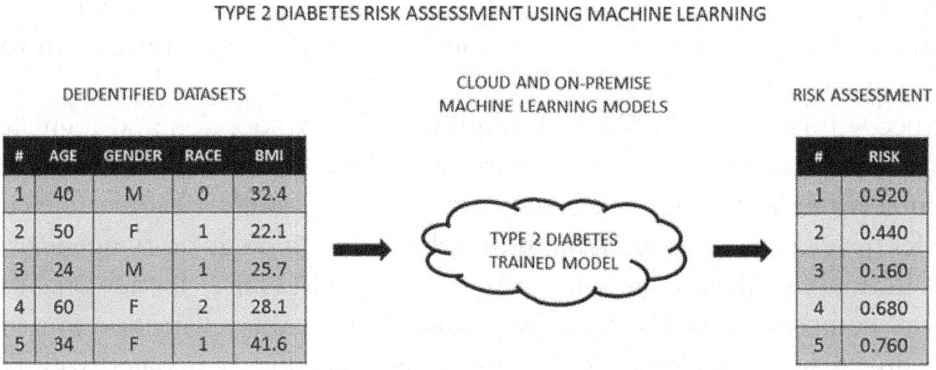

TYPE 2 DIABETES RISK ASSESSMENT USING MACHINE LEARNING

DEIDENTIFIED DATASETS

CLOUD AND ON-PREMISE
MACHINE LEARNING MODELS

RISK ASSESSMENT

| # | AGE | GENDER | RACE | BMI |
|---|-----|--------|------|-----|
| 1 | 40 | M | 0 | 32.4 |
| 2 | 50 | F | 1 | 22.1 |
| 3 | 24 | M | 1 | 25.7 |
| 4 | 60 | F | 2 | 28.1 |
| 5 | 34 | F | 1 | 41.6 |

TYPE 2 DIABETES
TRAINED MODEL

| # | RISK |
|---|------|
| 1 | 0.920 |
| 2 | 0.440 |
| 3 | 0.160 |
| 4 | 0.680 |
| 5 | 0.760 |

**Figure 2.2 Diagrammatic representation of a diabetes prediction model that may be used with EHR systems to implement diabetes ML. These models may alert physicians to screen patients for diabetes based on individual risk probability.**

- "Base Health" is a population health software that analyzes at-risk population and identifies individuals at risk for chronic or acute medical conditions. The software claims to accurately predict the probability of 42 common health conditions (Basehealth – Platform).
- Mayo Clinic has announced a 10-year partnership with Google with the aim of developing new healthcare delivery models using AI. Such collaboration between global leaders in healthcare and technology is a promising development and may accelerate the adoption of AI in solving the challenge of managing patients with chronic disease (Mayo Clinic selects Google as strategic partner for healthcare innovation, cloud computing – Mayo Clinic News Network).

## 2.8 Conclusions

AI technology in healthcare settings has made tremendous advancements to predict chronic health condition diagnosis and prognosis. They also have the potential to improve patient care by aiding physicians to rapidly understand large amounts of data for time-sensitive decisions. AI models will not replace physicians; however, they may improve physician performance for patients by augmenting accurate diagnosis, decreasing medical errors, saving fiscal and time resources, and improving the overall patient–doctor relationship. Despite the rapid pace of innovation and the hype of the benefits that AI technology offers, concerns remain regarding the ML system accuracy and reproducibility. Rigorous standards are required to address accuracy, bias, and safety concerns prior to ML's industry-wide healthcare system implementation. Healthcare organizations, insurance providers, and government agencies should also maintain realistic perspectives about the risk-to-benefit ratios of ML system implementation. If authorities incentivize the development and deployment of AI systems in the industry, its benefits may help immensely to improve patient outcomes, expand patient access, and reduce recurrent health expenditures

## References

Abràmoff, M. D., Lavin, P. T., Birch, M., Shah, N., & Folk, J. C. (2018). Pivotal trial of an autonomous AI-based diagnostic system for detection of diabetic retinopathy in primary care offices. *NPJ Digital Medicine, 1*, 39. doi: 10.1038/s41746-018-0040-6.

Alaa, A. M., Bolton, T., Di Angelantonio, E., Rudd, J. H. F., & van der Schaar, M. (2019). Cardiovascular disease risk prediction using automated machine learning: A prospective study of 423,604 UK Biobank participants. *PloS One, 14*(5), e0213653. doi: 10.1371/journal.pone.0213653.

Ali, M. K., Bullard, K. M., Saaddine, J. B., Cowie, C. C., Imperatore, G., & Gregg, E. W. (2013). Achievement of goals in U.S. diabetes care, 1999-2010. *The New England Journal of Medicine, 368*(17), 1613–1624. doi: 10.1056/NEJMsa1213829.

Alwan, A. *Global Status Report on Noncommunicable Diseases 2010*. Geneva: World Health Organization, 2011.

Ambale-Venkatesh, B., Yang, X., Wu, C. O., Liu, K., Hundley, W. G., McClelland, R., … Lima, J. A. C. (2017). Cardiovascular event prediction by machine learning: The multi-ethnic study of atherosclerosis. *Circulation Research, 121*(9), 1092–1101. doi: org/10.1161/CIRCRESAHA.117.311312.

Amodei, D., Olah, C., Steinhardt, J., Christiano, P., Schulman, J., & Mané, D. (2016). Concrete problems in AI safety. *ArXiv:1606.06565 [Cs]*. Retrieved from http://arxiv.org/abs/1606.06565.

Ascent of machine learning in medicine | Nature Materials. (n.d.). Retrieved September 28, 2019, from https://www.nature.com/articles/s41563-019-0360-1.

Bai, W., Sinclair, M., Tarroni, G., Oktay, O., Rajchl, M., Vaillant, G., … Rueckert, D. (2018). Automated cardiovascular magnetic resonance image analysis with fully convolutional networks. *Journal of Cardiovascular Magnetic Resonance: Official Journal of the Society for Cardiovascular Magnetic Resonance, 20*(1), 65. doi: 10.1186/s12968-018-0471-x.

Bannister, C. A., Halcox, J. P., Currie, C. J., Preece, A., & Spasić, I. (2018). A genetic programming approach to development of clinical prediction models: A case study in symptomatic cardiovascular disease. *PLoS One, 13*(9), e0202685. doi: org/10.1371/journal.pone.0202685.

Barnes, D. E., & Lee, S. J. (2011). Predicting Alzheimer's risk: Why and how? *Alzheimer's Research & Therapy, 3*(6), 33. doi: 10.1186/alzrt95.

Basehealth - Platform. (n.d.). Retrieved September 30, 2019, from https://www.basehealth.com/platform.html.

Bergenstal RM, Bailey CJ, Kendall DM. *Type 2 diabetes: assessing the relative risks and benefits of glucose-lowering medications. Am J Med 2010;123:374*, e9–374.e18.

Bowen, M. E., Schmittdiel, J. A., Kullgren, J. T., Ackermann, R. T., & O'Brien, M. J. (2018). Building toward a population-based approach to diabetes screening and prevention for US adults. *Current Diabetes Reports, 18*(11), 104. doi: org/10.1007/s11892-018-1090-5.

Bumgarner, J. M., Lambert, C. T., Hussein, A. A., Cantillon, D. J., Baranowski, B., Wolski, K., … Tarakji, K. G. (2018). Smartwatch algorithm for automated detection of atrial fibrillation. *Journal of the American College of Cardiology, 71*(21), 2381–2388. doi: 10.1016/j.jacc.2018.03.003.

Challen, R., Denny, J., Pitt, M., Gompels, L., Edwards, T., & Tsaneva-Atanasova, K. (2019). Artificial intelligence, bias and clinical safety. *BMJ Quality & Safety, 28*(3), 231–237. doi: 10.1136/bmjqs-2018-008370.

Chawla, A., Chawla, R., & Jaggi, S. (2016). Microvasular and macrovascular complications in diabetes mellitus: Distinct or continuum? *Indian Journal of Endocrinology and Metabolism, 20*(4), 546–551. doi: 10.4103/2230–8210.183480.

Cikes, M., Sanchez-Martinez, S., Claggett, B., Duchateau, N., Piella, G., Butakoff, C., … Bijnens, B. (2019). Machine learning-based phenogrouping in heart failure to identify responders to cardiac resynchronization therapy. *European Journal of Heart Failure, 21*(1), 74–85. doi: 10.1002/ejhf.1333.

Cummings, J. L., Morstorf, T., & Zhong, K. (2014). Alzheimer's disease drug-development pipeline: Few candidates, frequent failures. *Alzheimer's Research & Therapy, 6*(4), 37. doi: 10.1186/alzrt269.

Davis, S. E., Lasko, T. A., Chen, G., Siew, E. D., & Matheny, M. E. (2017). Calibration drift in regression and machine learning models for acute kidney injury. *Journal of the American Medical Informatics Association: JAMIA, 24*(6), 1052–1061. doi: 10.1093/jamia/ocx030.

Dawes, T. J. W., de Marvao, A., Shi, W., Fletcher, T., Watson, G. M. J., Wharton, J., … O'Regan, D. P. (2017). Machine learning of three-dimensional right ventricular motion enables outcome prediction in pulmonary hypertension: A cardiac MR imaging study. *Radiology, 283*(2), 381–390. doi: 10.1148/radiol.2016161315.

Detrano, R., Guerci, A. D., Carr, J. J., Bild, D. E., Burke, G., Folsom, A. R., … Kronmal, R. A. (2008). Coronary calcium as a predictor of coronary events in four racial or ethnic groups. *The New England Journal of Medicine, 358*(13), 1336–1345. doi: 10.1056/NEJMoa072100.

Diagnosis and Classification of Diabetes Mellitus. (2009). *Diabetes Care, 32*(Suppl 1), S62–S67. doi: 10.2337/dc09-S062.

Eckel, R. H., Jakicic, J. M., Ard, J. D., de Jesus, J. M., Miller, N. H., Hubbard, V. S., … Nonas, C. A. (2014). 2013 AHA/ACC guideline on lifestyle management to reduce cardiovascular risk: A report of the American College of Cardiology/American Heart Association Task Force on Practice Guidelines. *Circulation, 129*(Suppl 2), S76–S99.

Forman, G., & Scholz, M. Apples-to-apples in cross-validation studies: Pitfalls in classifier performance measurement. ACM SIGKDD Explorations Newsletter Published Online First, 2010.

Franco, M., Cooper, R. S., Bilal, U., & Fuster, V. (2011). Challenges and opportunities for cardiovascular disease prevention. *The American Journal of Medicine, 124*(2), 95–102. doi: 10.1016/j.amjmed.2010.08.015.

Gamberger, D., Lavrač, N., Srivatsa, S., Tanzi, R. E., & Doraiswamy, P. M. (2017). Identification of clusters of rapid and slow decliners among subjects at risk for Alzheimer's disease. *Scientific Reports, 7*(1), 6763. doi: 10.1038/s41598-017-06624-y.

Global, regional, and national life expectancy, all-cause mortality, and cause-specific mortality for 249 causes of death, 1980–2015: A systematic analysis for the Global Burden of Disease Study 2015. (2016). *Lancet (London, England), 388*(10053), 1459–1544. doi: 10.1016/S0140-6736(16)31012-1.

Glymour, C., Zhang, K., & Spirtes, P. (2019). Review of causal discovery methods based on graphical models. *Frontiers in Genetics, 10*. doi: 10.3389/fgene.2019.00524.

Hajat, C., & Stein, E. (2018). The global burden of multiple chronic conditions: A narrative review. *Preventive Medicine Reports, 12*, 284–293. doi: 10.1016/j.pmedr.2018.10.008.

Hall, H., Perelman, D., Breschi, A., Limcaoco, P., Kellogg, R., McLaughlin, T., & Snyder, M. (2018). Glucotypes reveal new patterns of glucose dysregulation. *PLoS Biology, 16*(7), e2005143. doi: 10.1371/journal.pbio.2005143.

Hannun, A. Y., Rajpurkar, P., Haghpanahi, M., Tison, G. H., Bourn, C., Turakhia, M. P., & Ng, A. Y. (2019). Cardiologist-level arrhythmia detection and classification in ambulatory electrocardiograms using a deep neural network. *Nature Medicine, 25*(1), 65–69. doi: 10.1038/s41591-018-0268-3.

Hugo, J., & Ganguli, M. (2014). Dementia and cognitive impairment: Epidemiology, diagnosis, and treatment. *Clinics in Geriatric Medicine, 30*(3), 421–442. doi: 10.1016/j.cger.2014.04.001.

IDF diabetes atlas – 2017 atlas. (n.d.). Retrieved September 28, 2019, from https://diabetesatlas.org/resources/2017-atlas.html.

Jammeh, E. A., Carroll, C. B., Pearson, S. W., Escudero, J., Anastasiou, A., Zhao, P., … Ifeachor, E. (2018). Machine-learning based identification of undiagnosed dementia in primary care: A feasibility study. *BJGP Open, 2*(2). doi: 10.3399/bjgpopen18X101589.

Johnson, K. W., Torres Soto, J., Glicksberg, B. S., Shameer, K., Miotto, R., Ali, M., … Dudley, J. T. (2018). Artificial intelligence in cardiology. *Journal of the American College of Cardiology, 71*(23), 2668–2679. doi: 10.1016/j.jacc.2018.03.521.

Kakadiaris, I. A., Vrigkas, M., Yen, A. A., Kuznetsova, T., Budoff, M., & Naghavi, M. (2018). Machine learning outperforms ACC/AHA CVD risk calculator in MESA. *Journal of the American Heart Association: Cardiovascular and Cerebrovascular Disease, 7*(22). doi: 10.1161/JAHA.118.009476.

Kingston, A., Robinson, L., Booth, H., Knapp, M., Jagger, C., & MODEM project. (2018). Projections of multi-morbidity in the older population in England to 2035: Estimates from the Population Ageing and Care Simulation (PACSim) model. *Age and Ageing, 47*(3), 374–380. doi: 10.1093/ageing/afx201.

Krittanawong, C., Zhang, H., Wang, Z., Aydar, M., & Kitai, T. (2017). Artificial intelligence in precision cardiovascular medicine. *Journal of the American College of Cardiology, 69*(21), 2657–2664. doi: 10.1016/j.jacc.2017.03.571.

Lafeuille, M.-H., Grittner, A. M., Gravel, J., Bailey, R. A., Martin, S., Garber, L., … Lefebvre, P. (2014). Quality measure attainment in patients with type 2 diabetes mellitus. *The American Journal of Managed Care, 20*(1 Suppl), s5–s15.

Li, L., Cheng, W.-Y., Glicksberg, B. S., Gottesman, O., Tamler, R., Chen, R., … Dudley, J. T. (2015). Identification of type 2 diabetes subgroups through topological analysis of patient similarity. *Science Translational Medicine, 7*(311), 311ra174. doi: 10.1126/scitranslmed.aaa9364.

Liu, Y., Zupan, N. J., Shiyanbola, O. O., Swearingen, R., Carlson, J. N., Jacobson, N. A., … Smith, M. A. (2018). Factors influencing patient adherence with diabetic eye screening in rural communities: A qualitative study. *PLoS One, 13*(11). doi: 10.1371/journal.pone.0206742.

Lobo, J. M., Jiménez-Valverde, A., & Real, R. (2008). AUC: A misleading measure of the performance of predictive distribution models. *Glob Ecology Biogeography, 17*, 145–151.

Mani, S., Chen, Y., Elasy, T., Clayton, W., & Denny, J. (2012). Type 2 diabetes risk forecasting from EMR data using machine learning. *AMIA Annual Symposium Proceedings, 2012*, 606–615. Retrieved from https://www.ncbi.nlm.nih.gov/pmc/articles/PMC3540444/.

Marengoni, A., Angleman, S., Melis, R., Mangialasche, F., Karp, A., Garmen, A., … Fratiglioni, L. (2011). Aging with multimorbidity: A systematic review of the literature. *Ageing Research Reviews, 10*(4), 430–439. doi: 10.1016/j.arr.2011.03.003.

Mayo Clinic selects Google as strategic partner for health care innovation, cloud computing – Mayo Clinic News Network. (n.d.). Retrieved September 28, 2019, from https://newsnetwork.mayoclinic.org/discussion/mayo-clinic-selects-google-as-strategic-partner-for-health-care-innovation-cloud-computing/.

McClellan, M., Brown, N., Califf, R. M., & Warner, J. J. (2019). Call to action: Urgent challenges in cardiovascular disease: A presidential advisory from the American Heart Association. *Circulation, 139*(9), e44–e54. doi: 10.1161/CIR.0000000000000652.

McGlynn, E. A., Asch, S. M., Adams, J., Keesey, J., Hicks, J., DeCristofaro, A., & Kerr, E. A. (2003). The quality of health care delivered to adults in the United States. *The New England Journal of Medicine, 348*(26), 2635–2645. doi: 10.1056/NEJMsa022615.

Middleton, B., Bloomrosen, M., Dente, M. A., Hashmat, B., Koppel, R., Overhage, J. M., … American Medical Informatics Association. (2013). Enhancing patient safety and quality of care by improving the usability of electronic health record systems: Recommendations from AMIA. *Journal of the American Medical Informatics Association: JAMIA, 20*(e1), e2–e8. doi: 10.1136/amiajnl-2012-001458.

Motwani, M., Dey, D., Berman, D. S., Germano, G., Achenbach, S., Al-Mallah, M. H., … Slomka, P. J. (2017). Machine learning for prediction of all-cause mortality in patients with suspected coronary artery disease: A 5-year multicentre prospective registry analysis. *European Heart Journal, 38*(7), 500–507. doi: 10.1093/eurheartj/ehw188.

Naghavi, M., Falk, E., Hecht, H. S., Jamieson, M. J., Kaul, S., Berman, D., … SHAPE Task Force. (2006). From vulnerable plaque to vulnerable patient – Part III: Executive summary of the Screening for Heart Attack Prevention and Education (SHAPE) task force report. *The American Journal of Cardiology, 98*(2A), 2H–15H. doi: 10.1016/j.amjcard.2006.03.002.

Nagpal, A. (2017, October 13). Over-fitting and regularization. Retrieved September 28, 2019, from https://towardsdatascience.com/over-fitting-and-regularization-64d16100f45c.

Nakajima, K., Kudo, T., Nakata, T., Kiso, K., Kasai, T., Taniguchi, Y., ... Edenbrandt, L. (2017). Diagnostic accuracy of an artificial neural network compared with statistical quantitation of myocardial perfusion images: A Japanese multicenter study. *European Journal of Nuclear Medicine and Molecular Imaging*, *44*(13), 2280–2289. doi: 10.1007/s00259-017-3834-x.

Nathan, D. M., Davidson, M. B., DeFronzo, R. A., Heine, R. J., Henry, R. R., Pratley, R., ... American Diabetes Association. (2007). Impaired fasting glucose and impaired glucose tolerance: Implications for care. *Diabetes Care*, *30*(3), 753–759. doi: 10.2337/dc07-9920.

Navickas, R., Petric, V.-K., Feigl, A. B., & Seychell, M. (2016). Multimorbidity: What do we know? What should we do? *Journal of Comorbidity*, *6*(1), 4–11. doi: 10.15256/joc.2016.6.72.

Nimri, R., Dassau, E., Segall, T., Muller, I., Bratina, N., Kordonouri, O., ... Phillip, M. (2018). Adjusting insulin doses in patients with type 1 diabetes who use insulin pump and continuous glucose monitoring: Variations among countries and physicians. *Diabetes, Obesity & Metabolism*, *20*(10), 2458–2466. doi: 10.1111/dom.13408.

Nori, V. S., Hane, C. A., Martin, D. C., Kravetz, A. D., & Sanghavi, D. M. (2019). Identifying incident dementia by applying machine learning to a very large administrative claims dataset. *PloS One*, *14*(7), e0203246. doi: 10.1371/journal.pone.0203246.

Parasuraman, R., & Manzey, D. H. (2010). Complacency and bias in human use of automation: An attentional integration. *Human Factors*, *52*(3), 381–410. doi: 10.1177/0018720810376055.

Porta, M., Curletto, G., Cipullo, D., Rigault de la Longrais, R., Trento, M., Passera, P., ... Cavallo, F. (2014). Estimating the delay between onset and diagnosis of type 2 diabetes from the time course of retinopathy prevalence. *Diabetes Care*, *37*(6), 1668–1674. doi: 10.2337/dc13-2101.

Purandare, N. (2009). Preventing dementia: Role of vascular risk factors and cerebral emboli. *British Medical Bulletin*, *91*, 49–59. doi: 10.1093/bmb/ldp020.

Razavian, N., Blecker, S., Schmidt, A. M., Smith-McLallen, A., Nigam, S., & Sontag, D. (2015). Population-level prediction of type 2 diabetes from claims data and analysis of risk factors. *Big Data*, *3*(4), 277–287. doi: 10.1089/big.2015.0020.

Recommendation against national dementia screening. (n.d.). Retrieved September 28, 2019, from https://www.gov.uk/government/news/recommendation-against-national-dementia-screening.

Redekop, W. K., & Mladsi, D. (2013). The faces of personalized medicine: A framework for understanding its meaning and scope. *Value in Health: The Journal of the International Society for Pharmacoeconomics and Outcomes Research*, *16*(6 Supp), S4–S9.

Ripley, D. P., Musa, T. A., Dobson, L. E., Plein, S., & Greenwood, J. P. (2016). Cardiovascular magnetic resonance imaging: What the general cardiologist should know. *Heart (British Cardiac Society)*, *102*(19), 1589–1603. doi: 10.1136/heartjnl-2015-307896.

Romei, A. & Ruggieri, S. (2013). Discrimination data analysis: A multi-disciplinary bibliography. In *Discrimination and Privacy in the Information Society: Data Mining and Profiling in Large Databases*, Custers, B., Calders, T., Schermer, B. & Zarsky, T. (eds.). Springer Berlin Heidelberg, 109–135. doi: 10.1007/978-3-642-30487-3_6.

Rumsfeld, J. S., Joynt, K. E., & Maddox, T. M. (2016). Big data analytics to improve cardiovascular care: Promise and challenges. *Nature Reviews. Cardiology*, *13*(6), 350–359. doi: 10.1038/nrcardio.2016.42.

Shah, S. J., Katz, D. H., Selvaraj, S., Burke, M. A., Yancy, C. W., Gheorghiade, M., … Deo, R. C. (2015). Phenomapping for novel classification of heart failure with preserved ejection fraction. *Circulation*, *131*(3), 269–279. doi: 10.1161/CIRCULATIONAHA.114.010637.

So, A., Hooshyar, D., Park, K. W., & Lim, H. S. (2017). Early diagnosis of dementia from clinical data by machine learning techniques. *Applied Sciences*, *7*(7), 651. https://doi.org/10.3390/app7070651

Statistics About Diabetes | ADA. (n.d.). Retrieved September 28, 2019, from https://www.diabetes.org/resources/statistics/statistics-about-diabetes.

Taylor, F., Huffman, M. D., Macedo, A. F., Moore, T. H., Burke, M., Davey Smith, G., … Ebrahim, S. (2013). Statins for the primary prevention of cardiovascular disease. *The Cochrane Database of Systematic Reviews*, *2013*(1), CD004816. doi: 10.1002/14651858.CD004816.pub5.

The Costs of Chronic Disease in the U.S. | Milken Institute. (n.d.). Retrieved September 28, 2019, from http://www.milkeninstitute.org/reports/costs-chronic-disease-us.

Thiese, M. S. (2014). Observational and interventional study design types; an overview. *Biochemia Medica*, *24*(2), 199–210. doi: 10.11613/BM.2014.022.

Tsai, T. L., Fridsma, D. B., & Gatti, G. (2003). Computer decision support as a source of interpretation error: The case of electrocardiograms. *Journal of the American Medical Informatics Association: JAMIA*, *10*(5), 478–483. doi: 10.1197/jamia.M1279.

UK Prospective Diabetes Study (UKPDS) Group. (1998). Intensive blood-glucose control with sulphonylureas or insulin compared with conventional treatment and risk of complications in patients with type 2 diabetes (UKPDS 33). *Lancet (London, England)*, *352*(9131), 837–853.

Walters, K., Hardoon, S., Petersen, I., Iliffe, S., Omar, R. Z., Nazareth, I., & Rait, G. (2016). Predicting dementia risk in primary care: Development and validation of the dementia risk score using routinely collected data. *BMC Medicine*, *14*. doi: 10.1186/s12916-016-0549-y.

Weaver, K. W., & Hirsch, I. B. (2018). The hybrid closed-loop system: Evolution and practical applications. *Diabetes Technology & Therapeutics*, *20*(S2), S216–S223. doi: 10.1089/dia.2018.0091.

Weng, S. F., Reps, J., Kai, J., Garibaldi, J. M., & Qureshi, N. (2017). Can machine-learning improve cardiovascular risk prediction using routine clinical data? *PLoS One*, *12*(4), e0174944. doi: 10.1371/journal.pone.0174944.

Wilson Peter, W. F., D'Agostino Ralph, B., Levy, D., Belanger, A. M., Silbershatz, H., & Kannel, W. B. (1998). Prediction of coronary heart disease using risk factor categories. *Circulation, 97*(18), 1837–1847. doi: 10.1161/01.CIR.97.18.1837.

Yu, K., Beam, A., & Kohane, I. (2018). Artificial intelligence in healthcare. *Nature Biomedical Engineering, 2*(10), 719–731.

Yu, K.-H. & Kohane, I. S. (2019). Framing the challenges of artificial intelligence in medicine. *BMJ Quality and Safety, 28*, 238–241.

Zhang, Y., Dong, Z., Phillips, P., Wang, S., Ji, G., Yang, J., & Yuan, T.-F. (2015). Detection of subjects and brain regions related to Alzheimer's disease using 3D MRI scans based on eigenbrain and machine learning. *Frontiers in Computational Neuroscience, 9*, 66. doi: 10.3389/fncom.2015.00066.

Zou, Q., Qu, K., Luo, Y., Yin, D., Ju, Y., & Tang, H. (2018). Predicting diabetes mellitus with machine learning techniques. *Frontiers in Genetics, 9*. doi: 10.3389/fgene.2018.00515.

*Chapter 3*

# AI and Drug Discovery

## Arash Keshavarzi Arshadi and Milad Salem
*University of Central Florida*

## Contents

## 3.1 Introduction

Drug discovery's history goes back thousands of years (Ji, Li, and Zhang 2009). Since the early civilizations, people learned to combat diseases with plants, animals or inorganic natural resources. Using Artemisia annua in old Chinese medicine for treating fever, using rose oil for aromatherapeutic treatments of heart conditions in traditional Persian medicine and leveraging opium to relieve the pain in ancient Greece medicine are among the well-known examples of understanding miraculous power of natural-based resources (Willcox and Bodeker 2004; Mohebitabar et al. 2017; Norn, Kruse, and Kruse 2005). Through advances in chemistry, biology and physics, people started to understand the real effective elements (small molecules and peptides) in those natural products which has been the basis of modern drug discovery (Eder, Sedrani, and Wiesmann 2014). Quinine extraction from the cinchona tree, penicillin extraction from *Penicillium fungi*, Artemisinin extraction from wormwood tree and morphine extraction from Poppy plants are some big discoveries of small molecules for medical purposes (Gaynes 2017; Willcox and Bodeker 2004). However, the trial-and-error-based research for discovering these molecules has not satisfied the high demand for drug candidates.

## 3.2 High-Throughput Screening (HTS)

With advances in automation and new explorations in biotechnology and pharmaceutical sciences, drug discovery has entered a new era. Robots are able to screen thousands of compounds every day to find potent scaffolds (Li and Vederas 2009). Through more advances in chemical synthesis and high-throughput screening (HTS), synthetic compounds are being considered to replace natural product-based ones for many reasons; first, natural product-based compounds are very unfriendly to HTS. Second, their quantities and concentrations do not reach the limit for automated screening. Third, they put animals and plants under extinction pressure. Moreover, synthesizing their structure is hard due to their high structural complexity. Lastly, they are cheaper to provide for early drug discovery. Therefore, companies and laboratories are switching to the screening of millions of synthetic compounds instead (Amirkia and Heinrich 2015; Koehn and Carter 2005).

However, switching to synthetic HTS has adverse effects, which has led to transferring small molecule drug discovery to a non-profitable industry. Synthetic libraries lack diversity and complexity; consequently, their hit rates have been relatively low (hit is a candidate active compound). Second, the whole process is very time-consuming, labor-intensive and expensive (Li and Vederas 2009). Early-stage drug discovery would take up to 5 years which is frustrating and expensive (Strovel et al. 2004). Finally, there has been a real urge for new technologies to predict or generate new active molecules (Kennedy et al. 2008). Computer-aided drug discovery (CADD) has been a very popular area that has no need for actual cell or enzyme-based assays and is able to find potent hits using algorithm-based models. This method decreases the time and money dedicated to potent hit discovery. The real challenge in this field would be the level of unfamiliarity that chemists and biologists have with computational sciences. Based on the size of the data generated in biomedical sciences every day, there will be a lot of unexplored potentials.

## 3.3 Virtual Screening (VS)

One important branch of CADD is virtual screening (VS). VS is a process to predict the potency of the compounds in inhibition of micro-organism or a molecule-based target like an enzyme (Rollinger, Stuppner, and Langer 2008). Target-based (rational) VS and non-target-based (irrational) VS are two main fields of VS (Lionta et al. 2014; Ripphausen, Nisius, and Bajorath 2011). Each of Target-based approach includes at least two main subsections: structural-based virtual screening (SBVS) and ligand-based virtual screening (LBVS) (Ripphausen et al. 2011). SBVS consists of any type of computer-aided prediction for compounds' activity through inhibiting a molecular target with known 3D structure. Molecular docking is a popular example of SBVS (Huang, Shoichet, and Irwin 2006). It mostly consists of determining the binding affinity of the target and the ligand. The target would be any kind of biomolecule such as lipid, DNA and protein. The model can work with the simulation of interactions or complementary surface. On the other hand, LBVS mostly predicts compounds' potency minimally by understanding the molecular patterns in the hits with mostly considering no information about the cell of interest. Cluster analysis (CA) would be a good example of the LBVS. Determining the similarity of the compounds is the basis of CA (Abramyan et al. 2016).

Both SBVS and LBVS have two important subsections: supervised and unsupervised approaches. If an approach needs specific labels with the data to use them for its simulation, it is supervised. On the other hand, some approaches do not need the data to be labeled. For instance, CA does not need any information regarding the target cell; instead, it works just with molecules structures and finds their level of similarity (Lo et al. 2018).

At its core, VS uses a model to predict the interaction or properties of compounds. Similar to most of the predictive processes, two tasks need to be completed in order to make predictions from the input: feature extraction and decision-making. At the feature extraction stage, the input is converted into feature vectors that can be high dimensional and/or large in size. The feature vectors are representatives of the input and describe the input within an n-dimensional domain. Having done so, a model learns to discriminate between the inputs based on their features to predict the desired properties and conclude the decision-making stage. While VS is often categorized into LVBS and SBVS groups based on the existence of targets, it is useful to study how different VS processes handle the feature extraction and decision-making stages. In the following sections, this comparison is shown by explaining two types of VS: fingerprint-based and deep feature-based VS.

## 3.4 Fingerprint-Based Virtual Screening

Molecular fingerprints are numeric arrays representing chemical compounds and structures. The first fingerprints were created to aid in searching chemical databases and were afterwards used in clustering and similarity searching between molecules. They also proved useful in activity classification and VS; in fact, the predominant approach of extracting features from molecules is creating fingerprints. Fingerprints encode structural properties (such as connections and bond type), physical features (such as shape) and other expert-defined characteristics (such as electrostatics). Many variants of fingerprints exist with a vast literature on how to define or modify them, with extended-connectivity fingerprint (ECFP) being one of the most commonly used fingerprints (Rogers and Hahn 2010). ECFP finds a sub-graph within the molecule and extracts features from the presence or absence of that sub-graph. The resulting fingerprint is easily interpretable as the existence of a specific section of the input molecule can be linked to its predicted activity, aiding in the identification of useful scaffolds. ECFP results in the same fingerprint for a given molecule regardless of the order of the atoms; this order invariance is a common characteristic of fingerprints. ECFP combines Morgan algorithm with a fast hashing scheme, resulting in a fingerprint that is rapidly computed in a short time, changing based on the given dataset, and contains a representation of sub-structures' presence.

Using ECFP for VS, fingerprints of molecules are used as descriptors and then fed to a classifier. It is highly important to note that this results in dividing the feature extraction (creating fingerprints) and decision-making (prediction bioactivity) stages. In the next section, the combination of two stages in deep learning is discussed.

# 3.5 Automatic Feature Extraction via Deep Learning

For many years, artificial intelligence (AI) has been assisting with problem-solving in the real world. The first generation of AI algorithms involved hard-coded instructions guiding the machine in making decisions. This was an attempt to force the machine to follow humans' knowledge, resulting in an exponential increase in the number of needed instructions as the tasks became more complex. The following generation of AI tools abandoned instructing the machine and allowed the machine to learn to make decisions. This era resulted in "machine learning" algorithms that excelled at being trained on featured datasets or structured data and learned to predict the outcome. However, the human was still in the loop with these algorithms, extracting useful features from the data for the machine to learn from. Naturally, this involved human knowledge akin to human instructing the machine, controlling what the machine can learn from.

The latest generation of AI tools discards the featurization of the data and gives the task of feature extraction to the machine. This resulted in "deep learning" algorithms that simultaneously perform feature extraction and decision-making via training on raw data. Through learning, the machine is incentivized to learn features that are representations of the patterns existing in the data. While these features are similar to human-defined features in their descriptive form, they are more abstract and often harder to interpret. This complexity also comes with an advantage; the machine-leaned features often have a higher descriptive power. Evidently, given enough data, the machine can observe patterns within the data that humans are not able to identify, giving the machine an advantage in the given narrow task.

The changes in the AI algorithms and feature extraction affected the many fields that leveraged applied AI. The most noticeable change comes within the image domain, where the community collectively moved towards using deep learning's autonomous feature extraction instead of hand-made features. The ImageNet Large-Scale Visual Recognition Challenge (ILSVRC) has been an arena for the imaging community to illustrate the most accurate model in image recognition. In 2012, the first deep learning model submitted to ILSVRC, AlexNet (Krizhevsky, Sutskever, and Hinton 2012), had the lowest error in identifying the image in its top-five predictions using deep learning, with a large gap in performance compared to the runner-up which used man-made features. This difference in performance gained the attention of the imaging community, resulting in nearly all the entries for the next year (2013) to be deep learning-based models.

## 3.6 Deep Learning-Based Virtual Screening

While fingerprint-based VS is highly interpretable, it isolates feature extraction from classification. ECFP mimics the knowledge of human experts in the manner they view and describe the molecules: absence or existence of sub-graphs. This manner of feature extraction is similar to that of the imaging community before adopting deep learning. On the other hand, deep learning has been used to automatically extract features from the input molecules (Figure 13.1).

In recent years, new architectures and methods have emerged that propose learning of molecule representations during training. These approaches use different deep learning models to automatically extract features from the input molecules, as seen in Figure 3.2. Deep learning approaches offer the privilege of highly non-linear features, i.e., "deep features". These features encode molecules different from the traditional fingerprint approaches, which are often not interpretable. Nevertheless, it has been shown that these features can result in better classification and generalization. Since molecules are inherently structured like graphs, graph convolutional neural networks (GCNNs) have been a dominant tool in that regard. A molecule is similar to a graph with atoms being nodes and bonds being the edges in the graph.

The authors in Duvenaud et al. (2015) trained a GCNN to learn fingerprints similar to the ECFP concept during training. Kearnes et al. (2016) were able to extend graph convolutions via improving the input featurization stage. In the input featurization step, the molecules are converted to graphs, with two arrays recording the atoms and the bonds, respectively. Deep features might be perceived as a drastic step away from expert-defined fingerprints; however, the subject matter expertise is still involved in the input

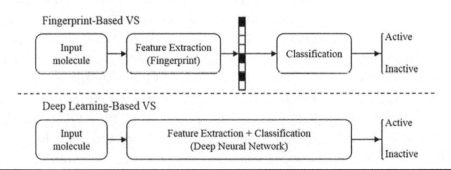

**Figure 3.1 Typical pipelines for VS using fingerprints versus using deep learning automatic feature extraction. (In deep learning models, feature representations and decision-making for classification are learned simultaneously during training.)**

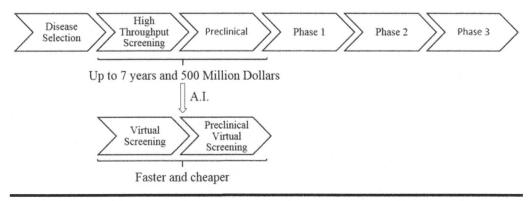

**Figure 3.2 Drug discovery – an expensive and tedious process. (Early drug discovery, excluding FDA approval, when companies, laboratories find hits and optimize them to the non-toxic, potent and stable leads. This process can cost up to $500 million. AI would decrease most of the costs including screening for potency, selectivity, microsomal stability, etc. Also, developing algorithms is way faster than wet lab screening.)**

featurization stage and in creating the inputs for the deep learning model. One successful collection of deep learning tools would be the DeepChem repository (Ramsundar et al. 2019).

Allowing the deep learning models to derive information from the data also opens the possibility of using multiple datasets during training. One approach would be pretraining (Hu et al. 2019), using different datasets to train the network before the network is trained on a specific task. Pretraining allows the patterns and knowledge within the other dataset to be leveraged when learning from the main dataset. Another approach would be multitask learning, in which multiple tasks can be learnt at once. Since different tasks might rely on the same patterns within the molecules, multitask training can be helpful in finding those patterns simultaneously for a different task and may raise accuracy and generalization (Ramsundar et al. 2015).

## 3.7 Successful Examples

Since the last decade, many companies started using AI and many start-ups have been founded based on related algorithms. The first example is Insilico Medicine, a newly founded company by developing drug discovery engines. Their areas of interest are de novo drug design, AI applications in extending longevity, etc. (Zhavoronkov et al. 2019; Zhavoronkov and Mamoshina 2019). The second example is ReviveMed, a company that developed a machine learning-based algorithm to analyze the metabolomic data. They assert that uncovering the dysregulated metabolites is very important for understanding most of the diseases, and they develop their platform using AI and data from proteins, genes, drugs, etc. (Pirhaji et al. 2016). Other companies like Cyclica and Atomwise are mostly focused on structure-based drug discovery. Cyclica has developed many AI-based platforms such as Ligand Express and Ligand Design to accelerate drug discovery at many levels (May 2019). The last example would be the model capable of predicting tuberculosis resistance to the ten first-line drugs. This model, which is developed in the Harvard University, is faster and more precise than old resistance detectors (Chen et al. 2019). AI applications in drug discovery would not be limited to biotech start-ups and companies. Academic laboratories would be the most suitable places for exploiting these tools. As it was asserted, the drug discovery process is very time-consuming and expensive. AI-based models would be the best alternative for those expensive approaches due to the financial restrictions in academia. These algorithms are cheap, rapid and easy to use.

## 3.8 The Impact of AI in Drug Discovery, Future Perspective

Considering the efforts made in these areas, VS is not the first line for early drug discovery, and HTS is still the preferred approach to find the hits in spite of using VS as a helper. One reason would be the low accuracy of the mentioned models. Knowing that some of the revolutionary scaffolds would be missed using the computational approaches, few would put it in the first place. Therefore, new computational technologies and approaches are required to revolutionize the lagging field of CADD.

Based on many disciplines that have incorporated deep learning, it seems inevitable that drug discovery's future will be influenced by deep learning too. One of the main challenges faced by deep learning in this field is the existence of a minimal number of publicly available datasets (Pérez-Sianes, Pérez-Sánchez, and Díaz 2016). The appearance of organized datasets for molecules such as MoleculeNet (Wu et al. 2018) provides hope this issue can be addressed. As we discussed, there are many known applications of AI in drug discovery such as target- or non-target-based VS, de novo drug design, metabolomics, and system biology. The pertinent aspect will be whether the actual question is solved by the use of AI. New and innovative approaches/

algorithms such as transfer learning, unsupervised learning and GAN. Drug repurposing, drug interactions, the toxicity of molecules, microsomal activity, resistance emergence and target identification provide a good base for the appropriate questions to be addressed.

# References

Abramyan, T. M., J. A. Snyder, A. A. Thyparambil, S. J. Stuart, and R. A. Latour. 2016. "Cluster analysis of molecular simulation trajectories for systems where both conformation and orientation of the sampled states are important." *Journal of Computational Chemistry* 37 (21): 1973–1982. doi: 10.1002/jcc.24416.

Amirkia, V., and M. Heinrich. 2015. "Natural products and drug discovery: a survey of stakeholders in industry and academia." *Frontiers in Pharmacology* 6 (October): 1–8. doi: 10.3389/fphar.2015.00237.

Chen, M. L., A. Doddi, J. Royer, L. Freschi, M. Schito, M. Ezewudo, I. S. Kohane, A. Beam, and M. Farhat. 2019. "Beyond multidrug resistance: leveraging rare variants with machine and statistical learning models in mycobacterium tuberculosis resistance prediction." *EBioMedicine* 43 (May): 356–369. doi: 10.1016/j.ebiom.2019.04.016.

Duvenaud, D., D. Maclaurin, J. Aguilera-Iparraguirre, R. Gómez-Bombarelli, T. Hirzel, A. Aspuru-Guzik, and R. P. Adams. 2015. "Convolutional networks on graphs for learning molecular fingerprints." In NIPS'15 Proceedings of the 28th International Conference on Neural Information Processing Systems - Volume 2, 2224–2232.

Eder, J., R. Sedrani, and C. Wiesmann. 2014. "The discovery of first-in-class drugs: origins and evolution." *Nature Reviews Drug Discovery* 13 (8): 577–587. doi: 10.1038/nrd4336.

Gaynes, R. 2017. "The discovery of penicillin—new insights after more than 75 years of clinical use." *Emerging Infectious Diseases* 23 (5): 849–853. doi: 10.3201/eid2305.161556.

Hu, W., B. Liu, J. Gomes, M. Zitnik, P. Liang, V. Pande, and J. Leskovec. 2019. "Pre-training graph neural networks." May. ArXiv, abs/1905.12265.

Huang, N., B. K. Shoichet, and J. J. Irwin. 2006. "Benchmarking sets for molecular docking." doi: 10.1021/JM0608356.

Ji, H.-F., X.-J. Li, and H.-Y. Zhang. 2009. "Natural products and drug discovery. Can thousands of years of ancient medical knowledge lead us to new and powerful drug combinations in the fight against cancer and dementia?" *EMBO Reports* 10 (3): 194–200. doi: 10.1038/embor.2009.12.

Kearnes, S., K. McCloskey, M. Berndl, V. Pande, and P. Riley. 2016. "Molecular graph convolutions: moving beyond fingerprints." *Journal of Computer-Aided Molecular Design* 30 (8): 595–608. doi: 10.1007/s10822-016-9938-8.

Kennedy, J. P., L. Williams, T. M. Bridges, R. N. Daniels, D. Weaver, and C. W. Lindsley. 2008. "Application of combinatorial chemistry science on modern drug discovery." *Journal of Combinatorial Chemistry* 10 (3): 345–54. doi: 10.1021/cc700187t.

Koehn, F. E., and G. T. Carter. 2005. "The evolving role of natural products in drug discovery." *Nature Reviews Drug Discovery* 4 (3): 206–220. doi: 10.1038/nrd1657.

Krizhevsky, A., I. Sutskever, and G. E. Hinton. 2012. "ImageNet classification with deep convolutional neural networks."

Li, J. W.-H., and J. C. Vederas. 2009. "Drug discovery and natural products: end of an era or an endless frontier?" *Science* 325 (5937): 161–165. doi: 10.1126/science.1168243.

Lionta, E., G. Spyrou, D. K. Vassilatis, and Z. Cournia. 2014. "Structure-based virtual screening for drug discovery: principles, applications and recent advances." *Current Topics in Medicinal Chemistry* 14 (16): 1923–1938. doi: 10.2174/1568026 614666140929124445.

Lo, Y. C., S. E. Rensi, W. Torng, and R. B. Altman. 2018. "Machine learning in chemoinformatics and drug discovery." *Drug Discovery Today* 23 (8): 1538–1546. doi: 10.1016/j.drudis.2018.05.010.

May, M. 2019. "When there's more than one way to target a cancer." *Nature Medicine* 25 (8): 1181–1182. doi: 10.1038/d41591-019-00016-7.

Mohebitabar, S., M. Shirazi, S. Bioos, R. Rahimi, F. Malekshahi, and F. Nejatbakhsh. 2017. "Therapeutic efficacy of rose oil: a comprehensive review of clinical evidence." *Avicenna Journal of Phytomedicine* 7 (3): 206–213. http://www.ncbi.nlm.nih.gov/pubmed/28748167.

Norn, S., P. R. Kruse, and E. Kruse. 2005. "History of opium poppy and morphine." *Dansk Medicinhistorisk Arbog* 33: 171–184. http://www.ncbi.nlm.nih.gov/pubmed/17152761.

Pérez-Sianes, J., H. Pérez-Sánchez, and F. Díaz. 2016. "Virtual screening: a challenge for deep learning." In, 13–22. Springer, Cham. doi: 10.1007/978-3-319-40126-3_2.

Pirhaji, L., P. Milani, M. Leidl, T. Curran, J. Avila-Pacheco, C. B. Clish, F. M. White, A. Saghatelian, and E. Fraenkel. 2016. "Revealing disease-associated pathways by network integration of untargeted metabolomics." *Nature Methods* 13 (9): 770–776. doi: 10.1038/nmeth.3940.

Ramsundar, B., P. Eastman, P. Walters, and V. Pande. n.d. *Deep Learning for the Life Sciences: Applying Deep Learning to Genomics, Microscopy, Drug Discovery, and More.* O'Reilly Media, Inc., Sebastopol, CA.

Ramsundar, B., S. Kearnes, P. Riley, D. Webster, D. Konerding, and V. Pande. 2015. "Massively multitask networks for drug discovery." February. ArXiv, abs/1502.02072.

Ripphausen, P., B. Nisius, and J. Bajorath. 2011. "State-of-the-art in ligand-based virtual screening." *Drug Discovery Today* 16 (9–10): 372–376. doi: 10.1016/J.DRUDIS.2011.02.011.

Rogers, D., and M. Hahn. 2010. "Extended-connectivity fingerprints." *Journal of Chemical Information and Modeling* 50 (5): 742–754. doi: 10.1021/ci100050t.

Rollinger, J. M., H. Stuppner, and T. Langer. 2008. "Virtual screening for the discovery of bioactive natural products." In *Natural Compounds as Drugs Volume I*, 211–249. Birkhäuser, Basel. doi: 10.1007/978-3-7643-8117-2_6.

Strovel, J., S. Sittampalam, N. P. Coussens, M. Hughes, J. Inglese, A. Kurtz, A. Andalibi, et al. 2004. *Early Drug Discovery and Development Guidelines: For Academic Researchers, Collaborators, and Start-Up Companies. Assay Guidance Manual.* Eli Lilly & Company and the National Center for Advancing Translational Sciences. http://www.ncbi.nlm.nih.gov/pubmed/22553881.

Willcox, M. L., and G. Bodeker. 2004. "Clinical review traditional herbal medicines for malaria." doi: 10.1136/bmj.329.7475.1156.

Wu, Z., B. Ramsundar, E. N. Feinberg, J. Gomes, C. Geniesse, A. S. Pappu, K. Leswing, and V. Pande. 2018. "MoleculeNet: a benchmark for molecular machine learning." *Chemical Science* 9 (2): 513–530. doi: 10.1039/C7SC02664A.

Zhavoronkov, A., Y. A. Ivanenkov, A. Aliper, M. S. Veselov, V. A. Aladinskiy, A. V. Aladinskaya, V. A. Terentiev, et al. 2019. "Deep learning enables rapid identification of potent DDR1 kinase inhibitors." *Nature Biotechnology* 37 (9): 1038–1040. doi: 10.1038/s41587-019-0224-x.

Zhavoronkov, A., and P. Mamoshina. 2019. "Deep aging clocks: the emergence of AI-based biomarkers of aging and longevity." *Trends in Pharmacological Sciences* 40 (8): 546–549. doi: 10.1016/J.TIPS.2019.05.004.

## Chapter 4

# Mammographic Screening and Breast Cancer Management – Part 1

James Condon and Lyle Palmer
*University of Adelaide*

## Contents

## 4.1 Introduction

This chapter will introduce important epidemiology and principles of breast cancer and provide some background to screening mammography and its historical relationship with computation. Selected applications of artificial intelligence to screening mammography are then summarized before discussing challenges and possible future applications, including the improved assessment of prognosis and potential for robust predictive models.

## 4.2 Breast Cancer

'Breast cancer' denotes a common and important group of diseases which represent about one in four cancer deaths in women worldwide (BreastScreen Australia monitoring report, 2014–2015). Approximately one in eight women will be diagnosed with breast cancer at some point in their lives. The lifetime risk of developing breast cancer for a woman with a faulty BRCA1 or BRCA2 gene is approximately 70% (Cancer Australia, 2019). Comprehensive information on breast cancer risk factors (see Table 4.1) and their supporting evidence are available at Cancer Australia (2019). Early detection and treatment of breast cancer, when smaller and less likely to have spread to other parts of the body, is associated with longer survival (Saadatmand et al., n.d.). Delays in diagnosis and treatment are associated with worse outcomes (Rossi et al., 1990). More advanced cancers generally require more intensive treatments, and therapies for advanced cancer are associated with decreased quality of life (Paraskevi, 2012).

'Breast cancer' in fact represents a heterogeneous group of disorders. Not only can the breast cancer of one person be very different from that of another, but the cellular features and extent of one person's cancer can vary over space and time (Pareja et al., 2017). There is a wide variation in patient age, comorbidities, overall general health, preferences, and priorities. The treatment options and prognosis also vary considerably between patients. A multidisciplinary team of surgeons, medical oncologists, radiation oncologists, radiologists, cancer nurses, and others devise treatment options to offer a given patient after considering and discussing all factors known to affect prognosis and treatment. Specifically, the risk of metastases and local cancer recurrence are considered. In addition, hormonal status, evidence of cancer in axillary lymph nodes, and numerous histological features are examined to classify cancer and predict prognosis and treatment response.

**Table 4.1  Risk Factors for Invasive Breast Cancer (Cancer Australia, 2019)**

| |
|---|
| Age |
| Genetic factors (e.g., BRCA mutations) |
| Being overweight and obese |
| Alcohol |
| Smoking |
| Mammographically dense breasts |
| Higher socioeconomic status |
| Younger age of the first menstrual period |
| Later age when the first child was born |
| Not having had children |
| Later age menopause |
| Hormone replacement therapy |
| Ductal carcinoma in situ (DCIS) |
| Radiation therapy to the chest (for the previous cancer treatment) |

Ultimately, patients choose combinations of treatment options based on the likely impact their cancer and the treatment will have on their quality of life and life expectancy, after advice from their treating team. For non-metastatic breast cancer, surgery remains the primary treatment for the majority of patients. Many patients choose to conserve as much healthy breast tissue as possible. Treatment must balance conserving healthy breast tissue and avoiding unnecessary intervention with removing all cancer and the associated risk of recurrence (Gradishar et al., 2018). 'Adjuvant therapy' refers to additional treatment(s) given after the removal of diseased tissue by surgery. Adjuvant therapies used to treat breast cancer include chemotherapy, radiotherapy, and targeted therapy (e.g., Trastuzumab), and these are increasingly personalized (Chan et al., 2017).

# 4.3 Mammography and Population Screening

Mammography, from the Latin prefix 'mamma-' for female breasts and '-graphy' meaning something written or represented in a specific way, is the use of X-rays to image breasts and identify abnormalities, especially cancer. It was first developed as a technique for mastectomy specimens in 1913 (Gold et al., 1990). Today, mammography is used to screen asymptomatic women for breast cancer in many countries as well as to further assess screen-detected and symptomatic abnormalities. Typically, eligible women are invited to screen every 2 years. One examination consists of two different views per breast (see Figure 4.1). The first trial of screening asymptomatic women for breast cancer with physical examination and mammography started in 1956 (Gershon-Cohen, 1961), detecting 92 benign lesions and 23 malignancies (including six non-palpable cancers) after screening 1,312 women. This demonstrated that screening could reveal asymptomatic cancers, allowing earlier treatment. At the time, some of these cancers were undetectable by any other method. Debate continues on the effectiveness of mammographic screening programs (Autier & Boniol, 2018). Largely citing observational and cohort studies, some authors examine the impact of screening programs on incidence and question whether reductions in rates of advanced breast cancer and rates of breast cancer deaths over time are more attributable to improvements in treatment and population demography (Møller et al., 2019). However, numerous randomized controlled trials have demonstrated significant reductions in breast cancer mortality for women aged 50–69 years (Strax et al., 1973; Tabár et al., 2011; Nyström et al., 2002; Bjurstam et al., 2003) and in women from age 40 (Moss et al., 2015). This

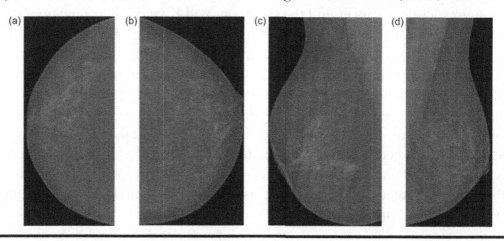

**Figure 4.1 Four images demonstrating mammography views and appearance of cancer. Images reproduced with permission from Ines Domingues. (a) Right craniocaudal (CC) view in a patient who went on to have further investigation and biopsy-proven cancer. (b) Left CC view in a separate patient assessed as normal, for routine follow-up. (c) Right mediolateral oblique (MLO) view in another patient with biopsy-proven cancer. (d) Left MLO of normal breast (separate patient). (Images reproduced from the INbreast database with permission from Ines Domingues).**

relative reduction in the risk of dying from breast cancer is on the order of 20%–30% over various follow-up periods ranging from 3 to 29 years (Tabár et al., 2011; Nyström et al., 2002; Bjurstam et al., 2003)). It is possible that longer studies may demonstrate a larger reduction over time. The World Health Organisation (WHO) has methodically examined the evidence of harms and benefits for organized population-based screening mammography and made recommendations relative to the availability of resources and quality of the screening program, and by age group (WHO, 2019). For women aged 50–69 in well-resourced settings, WHO recommends population-based screening (with conditions regarding cost, quality and assurance, shared decision-making, and respect for patient values and preferences, among others). Likewise, for women aged 40–49 and 70–75 with the proviso that the screening be in the context of rigorous research, monitoring and evaluation (WHO, 2019). The benefits of mammography screening programs include diagnosis of asymptomatic breast cancer, reduction in the risk of dying from breast cancer, and reduced risk of progressing to advanced breast cancer (Broeders et al., 2018; Moss et al., 2015). Benefits outweigh disadvantages including rates of overdiagnosis due to screening mammography and the anxiety of recall due to an abnormal examination (Moss et al., 2015). Estimates of number-needed-to-treat and relative risk reduction vary but can be approximated as follows. In women aged 50–74, eight deaths are prevented for every 1,000 women screened every 2 years. Two to four episodes of screening in women aged 40–74 can reduce the risk of breast cancer death by 25%–31% (Tabár et al., 1985; Shapiro et al., 1985).

Abnormalities on mammograms often constitute a very small portion of the total image, approximately 2% of pixels. Around 0.5%–1% of asymptomatic women attending screening programs are found to have breast cancer (Lehman et al., 2017). The detection of cancer from screening mammography therefore is a doubly imbalanced problem (rare in the cohort, rare in the image) and requires years of specialty training for human detection. The appearance of abnormalities representing cancer can be very subtle (see Figure 4.1a). Some cancers are mammographically occult, with no visible abnormalities at all. These can currently only be detected by other imaging modalities (e.g., ultrasound, magnetic resonance imaging) and comprised 13.2% of all cancers in one study (Wu et al., 2019). The contour of masses found on mammography is highly correlated with the underlying pathology, with clearly defined, well-circumscribed masses associated with benign abnormalities and indistinct or spiculated contours often representing cancer (Berment et al., 2014).

Assessment of human radiologists' performances for detecting signs of breast cancer varies widely in methodology and results (Carney et al., 2010) and is confounded by myriad variables. The experience of the radiologist likely affects performance metrics, with some data suggesting that sub-specialist breast fellowship radiologists are more sensitive but less specific (Elmore et al., 2009). Barlow et al. (2004) in contrast found that neither a greater volume of examinations nor experience at interpreting mammograms was associated with improved performance. Studies assessing human performance may exclude radiologists that do not meet an arbitrary threshold of volume of examinations (Lehman et al., 2017) and this, while necessary for adequate statistical power, may bias studies towards more experienced readers (when in actuality, other less experienced radiologists are assessing mammograms). Other assessments have relied on participation of breast radiologists, which may also select for more confident, experienced radiologists (Carney et al., 2010). The number and qualifications of readers differs geographically (USA single reader, Europe double reader) and effects screening performance. The incidence of abnormalities in the given population affects the cancer detection rate (Evans et al., 2013).

The reported sensitivity of screening mammography for breast cancer detection ranges widely from 51.5% (Duijm et al., 2009) to 92.5% with specificity generally >88% up to 99.5% and significant interobserver variability (Elmore et al., 2009; Hofvind et al., 2012). The most comprehensive estimated performance metrics are consistent with these ranges (see Table 4.2).

**Table 4.2  Estimates of Human Screening Performance**

| | |
|---|---|
| Abnormal interpretation rate (AIR) | 11.6% |
| CDR (/1,000 exams) | 5.1 |
| Sensitivity | 86.9% |
| Specificity | 88.9% |
| False negative rate (/1,000 exams) | 0.8 |
| PPV (any abnormal interpretation, recommended for further evaluation) | 4.4% |
| PPV (where findings were suspicious or highly suggestive of malignancy and biopsy recommended) | 25.6% |
| PPV (biopsy performed) | 28.6% |

Examinations conducted 2007–2013 (Lehman et al., 2017).

**Table 4.3  Patient Characteristics Affecting Mammographic Appearance (Boyd et al., 2002; Stomper et al., 1996)**

| |
|---|
| Age |
| Habitus |
| Hormone replacement therapy |
| Stage in menstrual cycle and menopausal status |
| Previous pregnancies |
| Past abnormalities and past surgery |

Variability in cancer detection performance ultimately influences the ability of screening programs to reduce breast cancer mortality (Carney et al., 2010). Regarding image characteristics, the mammography system vendor and the specifications of the reading station introduce variability into the appearance of a mammogram. Patient characteristics bring a source of variation to the mammographic appearance of breasts (see Table 4.3). Variables such as the type, contrast, and lighting of the radiologists' monitors and details of ambient light are stipulated in screening protocols.

# 4.4  Artificial Intelligence and Mammography

Artificial intelligence has significant applications to breast cancer screening for numerous reasons:

- Large total number of mammograms.
- Difficult, digitized visual detection task.
- Visual abnormalities can be classified based on their features.
- Variable human performance.
- Shortage of radiologists and breast radiologists.
- Early detection of breast cancer improves morbidity and mortality.

Many countries have national breast cancer screening programs that invite healthy middle-aged women without any breast symptoms to periodically undergo mammography. Mammograms, relative to other imaging modalities, therefore, constitute a large volume of images, and when developing classifiers with machine learning, the total number ($n$) of examples available for each given class is generally proportional to classifier performance. The technique of acquiring mammograms transitioned from one requiring physical film to a digital technique around 2005, with about half of all images in the USA national screening program digitized by 2010 (Van Ravesteyn et al., 2015).

Considering mammograms and how they are acquired and interpreted, we have a task that:

- Is inherently digital.
- Consumes significant resources (financial, expertise, time, etc.).
- Has a large number of historical examples with ground truth supervision.
- Requires the identification of visual features.
- Ultimately requires a binary patient-wise decision to either
  a. Recall for further investigation.
  b. Continue screening at recommended interval.
- Is a classification decision and estimate of cancer probability significantly based on visual features (like shape and contour) of any abnormalities present.
- Is subject to variable human performance.
- Contributes significantly to the timely diagnosis of breast cancer and therefore the associated morbidity and mortality.

It is therefore no surprise that screening mammography has been the subject of computational research for decades.

## 4.5 History of Computer-Aided Mammographic Screening

Winsberg was the first to take a computational approach to the detection of breast cancer in 1967 (see Figure 4.2) (Winsberg et al., 1967), and there have been hundreds of scientific studies since. Artificial neural networks have been utilized for this task since at least 1993 (Wu et al., 1993). While some suggest more than 20 layers to a CNN qualifies as 'deep learning' (Teare et al., 2017), there is not always a clear separation from older machine learning techniques. Studies relating to computer-aided diagnosis (CADx) and detection (CADe) in mammography and those using deep learning are heterogeneous in methodology and focus on different combinations of deep learning, fully automated and more traditional machine learning and hand-crafted approaches. As a result, the large volume of studies on

**Figure 4.2   Three hundred and seventy kilogram Control Data Corporation (CDC) 12-bit computer from the 160 series used in the early 1960s computational mammography (Winsberg et al., 1967). (This image, which was originally posted to Flickr, was uploaded to commons using Flickr upload bot on 9 May 2012, 11:59 by Arnold Reinhold. On that date, it was confirmed to be licensed under the terms of the license indicated. This file is licensed under the Creative Commons Attribution 2.0 Generic license.)**

computer-based methods for interpreting mammograms, either independently or in conjunction with a human radiologist, cannot easily be separated into traditional computer CADe/x and higher throughput machine and deep learning. It is clear, however, that DL methods are increasingly applied to the analysis of mammograms and have progressed computational mammography significantly in recent years. There are a large volume of studies since 2017 alone. A comprehensive analysis of all applicable literature since 1967 is beyond the scope of this chapter.

Computer-aided detection (CADe) refers to software designed to assist radiologists in identifying and locating abnormalities on medical images (Jalalian et al., 2013). In mammography, computer-assisted diagnosis (CADx) refers to systems that assist radiologists in assigning significance to either individual abnormalities or the whole image (Jalalian et al., 2013). These can be combined into a clinical workflow: mammographic images serve as input, abnormalities like masses and microcalcifications are detected, the likelihood of malignancy is estimated, and areas of concern are visually flagged for the interpreter. Some systems serve as a whole-image checker, whereas others notate specific, abnormal areas. In the USA, the FDA-approved CAD in 1998 and its use has been reimbursable since 2002. Seventy-four percent of US mammography interpretations involved CADx by 2010 (Kohli & Jha, 2018). These traditional CADe/x methods, which rely on *a posteriori* knowledge of appearance or combinations of features for the assessment of abnormality and estimation of malignancy, are largely regarded as unsuccessful (Kohli & Jha, 2018). This failure has been attributed to impractical computational cost, the large number of false positives (i.e., poor sensitivity) that cause the user to disregard all markings, and generally poor efficacy (Kohli & Jha, 2018), as well as negatively impacting radiologist reading time and introducing bias into their decision-making process.

> ...We believe CAD failed because of insufficient processing power and supervised learning.
>
> Its widespread implementation unmasked the lack of its effectiveness.
>
> **(Kohli & Jha, 2018)**

## 4.6 Deep Learning for Screening Mammography

### 4.6.1 Current State of the Art

Deep learning has been applied to screening mammography, with a rapidly growing body of scientific literature that suggests the field is on the cusp of prospective, clinical use. These applications can broadly be categorized into the following overlapping groups:

- Triage systems
- Cancer and abnormality detection
- Density and cancer risk assessment.

### 4.6.2 Triage

Around 99% of women who undergo screening mammography do not have malignant breast cancer. The vast majority of mammograms do not warrant any further investigation or change to the routine screening frequency

(2 – yearly in most countries) (Lehman et al., 2017). The following studies used deep learning to classify mammograms as effectively normal and cancer-free, and address the large total number and associated human workload of reviewing these mammograms. Importantly, any such triage system will have subsequent effects on the distribution of normal to abnormal images in the remaining mammograms and potentially on radiologists' cancer detection rate, which warrant further study. Apart from reducing workload and burden on cancer screening services, a synthetically increased incidence of cancer in radiologist-reviewed datasets may increase the cancer detection rate (Evans et al., 2013).

Rodriguez-Ruiz et al. (2019b) used a proprietary deep learning model to assign a score from 1 to 10 representing risk of malignancy, iteratively testing each score as a cut-off point for exclusion from human interpretation. They acknowledge that such a triage system requires further validation and balances reducing workload with risk of increasing false negatives relative to the chosen threshold for exclusion. Such a threshold could be chosen based on local practices and incidence of breast cancer, and could be integrated into a system where mammograms pre-screened as normal are single-read and others are double-read. The most feasible result was a cut-off score of two which resulted in a 17% workload reduction and exclusion of 1% of exams containing cancer (Rodriguez-Ruiz et al., 2019b).

Yala et al. (2019a) simulated the use of a deep learning model to triage screening mammograms as cancer-free, also with a preset probability threshold, and subsequent diversion from radiologist assessment. They demonstrated a human workload reduction of 19%, improved specificity, and non-inferior sensitivity. The authors recognized the limitations of their work, which included the use of data from a single institution and scanner manufacturer and the need for prospective external validation (Yala et al., 2019a).

## 4.6.3 Cancer Detection

A large number of studies have been published on the ability of deep learning models to classify mammograms into 'cancer' or 'cancer-free', although for some women, this is potentially an oversimplification of tumor biology (see the 'Differentiating Ductal Carcinoma In Situ and Invasive Breast Cancer' section). Regardless, diagnosis of cancer with a view to definitive treatment when suitable is obviously important. Broadly, deep learning approaches to cancer detection can be grouped into image-level classification (or classifying entire images) and object detection (or classifying abnormal image features within an image) or a combination of the two (Wu et al., 2019; Bionetworks, 2019). Some papers exclusively address 'mass' detection. Masses represent a subset of the mammograms of women with cancer, others having more subtle signs such as architectural distortion or clustered microcalcifications or no mammographically visible findings at all. Caution should be taken when comparing results across different datasets and given the variable attention to locating particular findings (like masses or architectural distortion). Also, stand-alone deep learning models are typically assessed with Area Under the Receiver Operating Characteristic Curve (AUROC), and human performance with sensitivity and specificity, which can be compared only by extrapolating one or more human metrics to a Receiver Operating Characteristic Curve (ROC) or selecting a specific operating point for a deep learning model.

Wu et al. (2019), using a database of over 1 million mammography images, found that deep learning improves radiologists' performance at breast cancer screening, when simulated retrospectively. They initially trained a fine-grained, auxiliary $256 \times 256$ patch-level classifier on pixel-level annotations with ImageNet pre-trained weights and a DenseNet-121 architecture. This model was then inferred on full images to create separate heatmaps for benign and malignant lesions, then forming input channels on full image and patient-level classifiers. Image-level classifiers were based on a ResNet architecture variously combined into breast-level and patient-level models (see Wu et al. (2019) for further details). Tested on over 14,000 screening episodes with an unadjusted incidence of abnormalities, their model was approximately as accurate as an experienced radiologist in detecting malignancy, with an AUC of 0.895. Importantly, they showed that the average of cancer probability of a human radiologist and of their deep learning model was superior to either method alone, the first research to demonstrate this. They extrapolate that radiologists and their deep learning model had learnt somewhat different aspects of mammographic cancer detection and that such a model could be used as a complementary secondary reader (Wu et al., 2019). Their model is available publicly (Nyukat, 2019).

Rodriguez-Ruiz et al. collected digital mammograms from nine datasets and seven countries across Europe and the USA, totaling 2,652 screening exams. Of these, 653 exams contained malignancies. The cumulative dataset consisted of mammography images, the assessment of a total of 101 radiologists, and the presence or absence of malignancy, as determined by either biopsy or at least 1 year of follow-up. For five of the nine datasets, radiologists' assessments were a probability of malignancy (from 1 to 100), with the remainder as a Breast Imaging Reporting and Data System (BI-RADS) score (American College of Radiology, 2013) (see Table 4.4). These were converted to a ROC by averaging each reader's nonparametric curves along lines perpendicular to the chance line. For each dataset, sensitivity and specificity of radiologists assessment for malignant cancer were calculated with a recall threshold of BI-RADS score 3 (probably benign (American College of Radiology, 2013)) or higher. Radiologists and AI system sensitivities were compared with two-modality analysis of variance (ANOVA) at the same specificity level. With this methodology, demonstrating the challenges in comparing AI with human performance, the human AUC was 0.814, and proprietary AI system was 0.840 (Rodriguez-Ruiz et al., 2019).

**Table 4.4 Breast Imaging Reporting and Data System (BI-RADS), American College of Radiology (Ribli et al., 2018)**

| Assessment | Management | Likelihood of Cancer |
|---|---|---|
| Category 0: Incomplete – need additional imaging evaluation and/or prior mammograms for comparison | Recall for additional imaging and/or comparison with prior examination(s) | N/A |
| Category 1: Negative | Routine mammography screening | Essentially 0% likelihood of malignancy |
| Category 2: Benign | Routine mammography screening | Essentially 0% likelihood of malignancy |
| Category 3: Probably benign | Short-interval (6-month) follow-up or continued surveillance mammography | >0% but ≤2% likelihood of malignancy |
| Category 4: Suspicious Category 4A: Low suspicion for malignancy Category 4B: Moderate suspicion for malignancy Category 4C: High suspicion for malignancy | Tissue diagnosis (biopsy) | > 2% but < 95% likelihood of malignancy > 2% to ≤ 10% likelihood of malignancy > 10% to ≤ 50% likelihood of malignancy > 50% to < 95% likelihood of malignancy |
| Category 5: Highly suggestive of malignancy | Tissue diagnosis | ≥95% likelihood of malignancy |
| Category 6: Known biopsy-proven malignancy | Surgical excision when clinically appropriate | N/A |

Kim et al. (2018) aimed to develop an algorithm that could discriminate cancer from normal cases based on raw images without annotation. They analyzed a total of 29,107 digital screening episodes, each consisting of four standard views. Of these, 4,399 cases or 14.9% had pathology-confirmed cancers. There were 3,101 cancer cases versus 23,530 normal cases in the training set (13.2% cancer). Equal numbers of cancer and non-cancer cases were used for cross-validation and test sets. Women with mammograms assigned a BI-RADS score of 2 through five (including 'probably benign', 'suspicious', and 'highly suspicious for malignancy'), where pathology was non-cancerous, were excluded. The training, validation, and test datasets were evenly distributed in age, breast density, manufacturer, cancer type (invasive, non-invasive), feature, and mass size ($\geq$ or $<20\,mm$) to control for selection bias. Cancerous features were mass (54%) and microcalcifications (45%), focal asymmetry (10.7% of cancers), and distortion (2.3% of cancers). Results were a test-set AUC for cancer/non-cancer of 0.906 and F1 score of 0.81. Sensitivity was not affected by density (with statistical significance – $p = 0.3$); however, specificity and accuracy decreased with increasing density ($p<0.06$ and 0.02). Importantly, they demonstrate statistically differing model sensitivity and specificity per manufacturer (see Table 4.5), despite random perturbation of pixel intensity contrast and brightness ($\pm10\%$) during training, indicating that the distribution of manufacturers in any training set may affect diagnostic performance.

As part of a DREAM challenge, Nikulin first trained a $224\times224$ patch-level model using five labels on Digital Database for Screening Mammography (DDSM (Lee et al., 2017)) data:

- 0 – healthy tissue, the patch is randomly selected from a healthy breast image.
- 1 – calcification benign.
- 2 – mass benign.

**Table 4.5   Kim et al. (2018) Deep Learning Differentiation of Normal versus Cancerous Mammograms; Test Set Results by Vendor**

| Manufacturer | Sensitivity (%) | Specificity (%) | Accuracy (%) | AUC |
|---|---|---|---|---|
| GE | 74.6 | 89.1 | 81.9 | 0.910 |
| Hologic | 67.0 | 92.1 | 82.4 | 0.880 |
| Siemens | 88.8 | 61.7 | 83.0 | 0.888 |

- 3 – calcification malignant.
- 4 – mass malignant.

This model was then incorporated into an image-level classifier and fine-tuned (additional training of parameters). With ground truth based on a tissue biopsy within 1 year of the given screening exam, their result in classifying exams into cancer or cancer-free in the challenge was an AUC of 0.874. Nikulin concludes that depth (or the number of layers of a neural network) is better than width (or the nodes per layer) and identifies that, compared to problems generating much of the theory and practice of computer vision like ImageNet, objects for detection in screening mammography are much smaller and have less components (Bionetworks, 2019).

Ribli et al. published an independent model trained on both INBreast and DDSM, and achieved the second place in the DREAM mammography challenge. Their model was pre-trained on ImageNet and re-trained on DDSM and their own Semmelweis University dataset of 11,300 images. Results were an AUC on INBreast of 0.95 and an AUC of 0.85 on the dream dataset (Ribli et al., 2018). A demonstration version of this model is available at GitHub (https://github.com/riblidezso/frcnn_cad).

Kyono et al. (2019) present a model primarily for cancer detection, that is also capable of and tested as a triage system. They utilize multi-task learning, whereby additional labels (target variables or) were used in addition to the binary outcome of core biopsy or surgical specimen-proven cancer to assist network regularization and overall performance. There were five auxiliary labels: 'sign', 'suspicion', 'conspicuity', breast density (per radiologist-assessed percent density), and age (where 'sign' was the abnormal finding, e.g., 'spiculated', 'microcalcification'; suspicion was one of 'normal', 'benign', 'probably benign', 'suspicious', and 'malignant'; and 'conspicuity' was one of 'not visible', 'barely visible', 'visible, not clear', and 'clearly visible'). Using four views from 1,000 randomly held out test set, their model achieved an AUROC of 0.791 for cancer detection. They demonstrated that multi-task labels, test-time augmentation, and multiview inputs all improved performance. As a triage system, their model was able to reduce radiologist examinations by 42.8% while improving the overall diagnostic accuracy (Kyono et al., 2019).

All methodological issues and difficulties comparing human and machine performance considered, deep learning appears to currently achieve retrospective results at least approximating human performance. For further overview of the use of artificial intelligence including deep learning for mammography, the reader is referred to reviews by Hamidinekoo et al.

(2018), Houssami et al. (2019), Abdelhafiz et al. (2019), Gao et al. (2019), Harvey et al. (2019), and Geras et al. (2019).

### 4.6.4 Density and Cancer Risk

Breast density is associated with higher risk of breast cancer, although the degree of relative risk increase varies across the literature. Assessment of density is variable across computational methods, human radiologist assessment, and its correlation with breast cancer (Destounis et al., 2017). Screening programs may or may not notify women with high density, with 38 states in the USA recently legislating mandatory notification (Keating & Pace, 2019). Density is thought to confer increased risk via two mechanisms:

1. Dense breast tissue can have the effect of masking cancerous lesions.
2. Women with dense breasts have relatively more tissue from which cancer can generate (Kerlikowske & Vachon, 2016).

There is currently limited evidence about the most appropriate screening interval or course of action given a Gaussian distribution of breast density (Keating & Pace, 2019).

Yala et al. (2019b) compared image-only and an image plus traditional risk factors (hybrid) deep learning models with logistic regression of traditional risk factors and the Tyrer-Cuzick (TC) model using 39,558 women. These risk factors included breast density, age, weight, height, age at first menstrual period, menopausal status, hormone replacement therapy, BRCA gene status, past history of ovarian cancer and breast biopsy, family history, and Ashkenazi inheritance. Data included 1,821 patients with a diagnosis of invasive breast cancer or DCIS within 5 years from baseline imaging. They found superior performance of the hybrid model with an AUC of 0.70 (95% CI 0.66–0.75). An image-only model resulted in an AUC of 0.68 (95% CI 0.64–0.73). Traditional risk factor logistic regression and the Tyrer-Cuzick model were performed at AUCs of 0.67 (95% CI 0.62–0.72) and 0.62 (95% CI 0.57–0.66), respectively.

## 4.7 Challenges and Future Possibilities

The direct comparison of different machine learning-based models for screening mammography is difficult due to heterogeneity in the datasets used to train the models, image sizes, architecture of the neural network, and variation in 'ground truths' used to develop and test them, as well as variation in mammogram acquisition and the prior incidence of cancer. Some models attempt to classify at an image level and some at a patient level with or without methods to detect regions of interest for various abnormalities (e.g., masses or architectural distortion). Some studies apply these techniques to relatively small public datasets and others to large private datasets, all with variation in mammography system vendors, which contribute fundamentally to image acquisition. There is diversity in preprocessing methods, integration of the four views (and where in the model this occurs), and use of non-imaging demographic features. There is also variability in the use of screen film versus digital mammograms during training and validation although some studies successfully apply models trained on film mammograms to full-field digital mammograms with fine-tuning (Bionetworks, 2019; Shen et al., 2019).

Currently, most published literature in the field relies on supervised methodologies, those with a definitive 'label' ('target' or '*y*'). These are typically in the forms of human assessment of likelihood of malignancy from mammograms (BI-RADS score (American College of Radiology, 2013) – see Table 4.4) or other images, or pathological examination (macroscopic and microscopic). In practice, some cancerous tissue is required to confirm the presence of cancer with microscopy and staining and tissue processing techniques. This tissue may be obtained with various biopsy methods including a fine-needle aspiration, core biopsy, and open biopsy by a surgeon.

A biopsy specimen can be a subsample of the whole population of tumor cells and the tumor microenvironment which may be significantly different to non-biopsied tumor foci (Sinha & Piwnica-Worms, 2018). Non-invasive image-based analysis of tumor prognostic features would be especially useful for multifocal and heterogeneous tumors and metastases, which are only partly sampled with biopsy (Lubner, 2019). In addition to intratumoral heterogeneity, the accuracy and precision of hormone receptor assays may vary depending on the cancerous tissue specimen (core biopsy, open biopsy, mastectomy) and its preparation (Arber 2002; Goldstein et al., 2003; Wood et al., 2007; Mann et al., 2005

Given variability in both pathological and radiological assessments, 'ground truths' incompletely capture the complexity of tumor features, some of which may be important for prognostication (e.g., differentiation of DCIS and IBC). Models that map inputs to these 'ground truths' may have a degree of dependency on local idiosyncratic data, features and their distributions, and potentially, limited generalizability rather than comprehensive coverage of true biological signal.

Due to this heterogeneity, the field has struggled with replication. The effect that local variables have on generalizability to external validation datasets and the magnitude of accuracy increases with larger multi-institutional datasets are areas in need of further research.

# 4.8 Prognosis and Treatment Response

With accumulating retrospective data, AI has the potential to reduce the financial and clinician strain on screening programs, more accurately predict breast cancer prognosis and treatment response, and, in doing so, lead to better health outcomes and reduce healthcare costs. Accurately predicting risk of cancer recurrence, for example, is of great need. More accurate information about prognosis enables better selection of therapies and avoidance of unwarranted treatment complications and toxicities. There is a growing body of literature around predicting prognosis or prognostically important features with AI. Some authors suggest that the combination of patient genome and phenotypic data might be used for calculating risk of recurrence (Crivelli et al., 2018). Studies have examined the ability of machine learning to predict response to neoadjuvant chemotherapy and axillary lymph node metastases (Cain 2019, Dihge 2019, Wu 2014, Ha 2018).

## 4.8.1 Differentiating Ductal Carcinoma In Situ and Invasive Breast Cancer

There is considerable scientific literature addressing the potential for overdiagnosis in mammography screening (Autier et al., 2017 and Welch 2016). Since the advent of population-based screening, ductal carcinoma in situ (DCIS), a non-obligate precursor to invasive breast cancer, has comprised an increasing portion of screen-detected lesions (Sinha & Piwnica-Worms, 2018). Reflecting some uncertainty around potential for invasion, patients with screen-detected DCIS receive a wide range of primary and adjuvant treatments that vary according to the treating clinician and locality (Francis et al., 2015b). Estimates are that up to 85% of women with DCIS and no components of invasive breast cancer will never progress to an invasive form (Cowell et al., 2013; Elshof et al., 2015). There are several ongoing trials aiming to assess outcomes in women with DCIS treated with monitoring and adjuvant therapy versus those treated surgically (Elshof et al., 2015; Francis et al., 2015a), (Youngwirth et al., 2017). Choosing no treatment for DCIS may be completely appropriate for a 90-year-old woman and entirely inappropriate for a 30-year-old woman. The ideal, therefore, is to accurately differentiate pure DCIS (which might be safely monitored) and invasive breast cancer, which needs treatment and can be potentially fatal (Toss et al., 2017). This is difficult for several reasons; the underlying lesion may have a complex distribution of invasive and in situ components (see Figure 4.3), and biopsies can be challenging (when the tumor cannot be palpated, relying on image guidance) and sample a finite amount of the tumor, which may not contain the invasive component. About 25% of women with a biopsy showing DCIS go on to have a mastectomy that contains invasive breast cancer. There is a potential role for convolutional neural networks in predicting which patients have pure DCIS and which have DCIS with invasion (Mutasa et al., 2019). The diagnostic differentiation of pure DCIS from a tumor with any form of invasion is crucial for accurate prognosis. This differentiation already has significant impact on treatment decisions and may be even more significant, depending on the results of ongoing trials, (Youngwirth et al., 2017). If deep learning models can realize more accurate differentiation of pure DCIS compared to invasive breast cancer, in concert with longitudinal studies, this could help reduce any over-investigation and overdiagnosis associated with screening mammography.

## 4.9 AI for Breast Cancer Care

The holy grail in artificially intelligent breast cancer informatics is a hospital- or district-wide system that takes as preoperative input, for each patient, a variable length and mix of genotypic and phenotypic data (potentially including demographics, history, multiple imaging modalities, and histo-pathological images and results) and outputs computed probabilities of hormone receptor status, histological subtype, axillary disease, recurrent surgery, long-term tumor recurrence, metastases, response to various treatments, and overall and disease-free survival. The metrics of these risks could then be updated with intra- and post-treatment data. Such a system would be somewhat dependent on casemix and volume of retrospective patient data, based on current methodologies, and there are therefore challenges with the external validation of these models as well as the application of supervised machine learning techniques to brand-new therapies. The performance of such a multimodal deep learning model, in terms of calibration

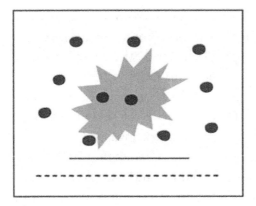

3a. Single focus of invasive carcinoma associated with DCIS

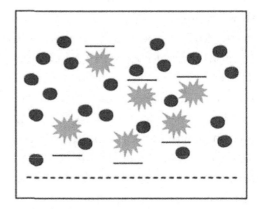

3b. Predominantly DCIS but with multiple, separate, microscopic foci of invasive carcinoma. These often represent foci of microinvasive carcinoma (see text).

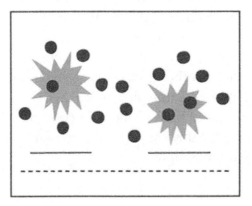

3c. More than one invasive carcinoma but arising in a single area of DCIS

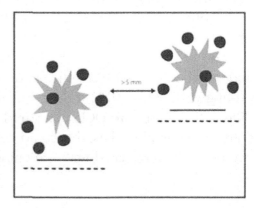

3d. More than one invasive carcinoma but arising in separate (non-confluent) areas of DCIS

Invasive carcinoma

DCIS

Size of invasive carcinoma

Size of whole lesion

**Figure 4.3   Schematic representation of potential spatial relationships between synchronous DCIS and invasive carcinoma. This information is reproduced with the permission of Cancer Australia.**

with outcome predictions, could be monitored over time and re-trained as needed. The technical, human resource, and IT infrastructure requirements for such a persistent, multimodal model are considerable.

# 4.10 Multi-Institutional Model Training

A large mammography dataset by current standards (e.g., 1 million uncompressed, high-resolution full-field digital mammographic images) can require in the order of 50 TB of hard-drive storage. Previous work has demonstrated that best cancer classification results are achieved with full high-resolution images, in contrast to non-medical image classification where objects ('dog', 'cat', 'car', etc.) are relatively coarse and images are routinely downscaled for computational efficiency (Geras et al., 2017). Therefore, computational capacity and data storage can become significant limitations, but potentially mean that better results are to come, with larger datasets at original resolution. Any one institution has a finite population and number of annual mammographic examinations. There is a low incidence in screening populations, and large volumes of cancerous examples are required to train deep learning models. More data generally confers more accurate models. Given this, a single institution will have a finite number of cancerous examples and models may improve accuracy with larger effective training dataset sizes. With the advent of distributed or federated training platforms (Getting started with distributed data parallel, 2019), multiple institutions could synchronously train a collective deep CNN, each using their own data, with periodic weight updates set every $n$ epochs (Chang et al., 2018). In this way, institutions contribute data to model training, without data ever having to leave the institution (providing adequate computational resources). This leaves data in the hands of custodians and avoids issues around security and patient privacy. The technical challenges of such a project including the overhead and runtime impact of weight updates and the context of large images (20 million pixels) are significant. Sound planning and integration of distributed deep learning software could lay the path for future re-training and calibration. At the time of writing, the only example of this applied to mammography, in our knowledge, is a simulation study (Chang et al., 2018), rather than real-world, multi-institutional collaboration. Alternatively, images themselves could be collaboratively stored in some central data warehouse for subsequent model training. With such aggregation, the noise of idiosyncrasies like scanner manufacturer and subtle acquisition artifacts could be 'learnt' better, theoretically enabling greater accuracy and detection of 'true' cancer biology signal. High vendor noise could be critical, for example, in the event that a screening service adopts predictions of a model sensitive to vendor noise and then changes vendors. Regardless, the asymptotic accuracy of deep learning cancer detection with mammography would be limited by the absence of visual features in a significant portion of cancers (in the order of 13.2% in one reader study including DCIS (Wu et al., 2019)).

## 4.11 Interpretability

> We do not wish to penalize the machine for its inability to shine in beauty competitions, nor to penalize a man for losing in a race against an aero plane.

**Alan Turing, Computing Machinery and Intelligence (1950)**

The black-box problem of deep learning is increasingly described and refers to the difficulty in rationalizing model output with human-readable explanations (Ribeiro et al., 2016). Some degree of interpretability may be important for trust and is important for adoption of deep learning models, but complete interpretability assumes no gap between what is human-readable and machine-readable. Having already developed models superior to humans in multiple tasks, we may continue to do so beyond human cognitive capacity and develop models not able to be completely interpreted by one human. Understanding and explanation are not binary. If AI models can safely improve sensitivity and specificity with transparent development and consideration for patient privacy and ethics, then our capacity to entirely introspect and comprehend their millions of parameters may be inconsequential. However, solutions and new approaches to the black-box problem continue to improve our ability to interpret models, and these have been useful in mammography. Various saliency maps and visualization techniques have been used to highlight areas of the image that are important for classification (Geras et al., 2019), some successfully incorporating region of interest-level heatmaps into model input. Some suggest that as interpretability improves, trained models may be used as knowledge discovery tools able to learn and potentially communicate (or 'teach') features correlated with diagnoses or prognoses to their human users (Geras et al., 2019).

## References

Abdelhafiz, D Yang C, Ammar R, Nabavi S. Deep convolutional neural networks for mammography: Advances, challenges and applications. *BMC Bioinform.* 2019 June 6;20(Suppl 11):281.

American College of Radiology. ACR BI-RADS Atlas: Breast imaging reporting and data system; mammography, ultrasound, magnetic resonance imaging, follow-up and outcome monitoring, data dictionary. 2013.

Arber DA. Effect of prolonged formalin fixation on the immunohistochemical reactivity of breast markers [Internet]. *Appl Immunohistochem Mol Morphol.* 2002;10: 183–186. doi: 10.1097/00129039-200206000-00015.

Autier P, Boniol M. Mammography screening: A major issue in medicine. *Eur J Cancer.* 2018 February;90:34–62.

Autier P, Boniol M, Koechlin A, Pizot C, Boniol M. Effectiveness of and overdiagnosis from mammography screening in the Netherlands: Population based study. *BMJ.* 2017 December 5;359:j5224.

Barlow WE, Chi C, Carney PA, Taplin SH, D'Orsi C, Cutter G, et al. Accuracy of screening mammography interpretation by characteristics of radiologists. *J Natl Cancer Inst.* 2004 December 15;96(24):1840–1850.

Berment H, Becette V, Mohallem M, Ferreira F, Chérel P. Masses in mammography: What are the underlying anatomopathological lesions? *Diagn Interv Imaging.* 2014 February;95(2):124–133.

Bionetworks S. Synapse | Sage Bionetworks [Internet]. [cited 2019 August 14]. Available from: https://www.synapse.org/#!Synapse:syn9773040/wiki/426908.

Bjurstam N, Björneld L, Warwick J, Sala E, Duffy SW, Nyström L, et al. The Gothenburg breast screening trial [Internet]. *Cancer.* 2003;97:2387–2396. doi: 10.1002/cncr.11361.

Boyd NF, Dite GS, Stone J, Gunasekara A, English DR, McCredie MRE, et al. Heritability of mammographic density, a risk factor for breast cancer. *N Engl J Med.* 2002 September 19;347(12):886–894.

BreastScreen Australia monitoring report 2014–2015, table of contents - Australian Institute of Health and Welfare [Internet]. Australian Institute of Health and Welfare. [cited 2019 June 30]. Available from: https://www.aihw.gov.au/reports/cancer-screening/breastscreen-australia-monitoring-2014-15/contents/table-of-contents.

Broeders MJM, Allgood P, Duffy SW, Hofvind S, Nagtegaal ID, Paci E, et al. The impact of mammography screening programmes on incidence of advanced breast cancer in Europe: A literature review. *BMC Cancer.* 2018 September 3; 18(1):860.

Cain EH, Saha A, Harowicz MR, Marks JR, Marcom PK, Mazurowski MA. Multivariate machine learning models for prediction of pathologic response to neoadjuvant therapy in breast cancer using MRI features: A study using an independent validation set. *Breast Cancer Res Treat.* 2019 January;173(2):455–463.

Carney PA, Sickles EA, Monsees BS, Bassett LW, Brenner RJ, Feig SA, et al. Identifying minimally acceptable interpretive performance criteria for screening mammography. *Radiology.* 2010 May;255(2):354–361.

Chan CWH, Law BMH, So WKW, Chow KM, Waye MMY. Novel Strategies on Personalized Medicine for Breast Cancer Treatment: An Update [Internet]. *Int J Mol Sci.* 2017 November 15;18(11). doi: 10.3390/ijms18112423.

Chang K, Balachandar N, Lam C, Yi D, Brown J, Beers A, et al. Distributed deep learning networks among institutions for medical imaging. *J Am Med Inform Assoc*. 2018 August 1;25(8):945–954.

Chougrad H, Zouaki H, Alheyane O. Deep convolutional neural networks for breast cancer screening. *Comput Methods Programs Biomed*. 2018 April;157:19–30.

Cowell CF, Weigelt B, Sakr RA, Ng CKY, Hicks J, King TA, et al. Progression from ductal carcinoma in situ to invasive breast cancer: Revisited. *Mol Oncol*. 2013 October;7(5):859–869.

Crivelli P, Ledda RE, Parascandolo N, Fara A, Soro D, Conti M. A new challenge for radiologists: Radiomics in breast cancer. *Biomed Res Int*. 2018 October 8;2018:6120703.

Destounis S, Arieno A, Morgan R, Roberts C, Chan A. Qualitative versus quantitative mammographic breast density assessment: Applications for the US and abroad [Internet]. *Diagnostics (Basel)*. 2017 May 31;7(2). doi: 10.3390/diagnostics7020030.

Dihge L, Ohlsson M, Edén P, Bendahl P-O, Rydén L. Artificial neural network models to predict nodal status in clinically node-negative breast cancer. *BMC Cancer*. 2019 June 21;19(1):610.

Duijm LEM, Louwman MWJ, Groenewoud JH, van de Poll-Franse LV, Fracheboud J, Coebergh JW. Inter-observer variability in mammography screening and effect of type and number of readers on screening outcome. *Br J Cancer*. 2009 Mar 24;100(6):901–907.

Elmore JG, Jackson SL, Abraham L, Miglioretti DL, Carney PA, Geller BM, et al. Variability in interpretive performance at screening mammography and radiologists' characteristics associated with accuracy. *Radiology*. 2009 December;253(3):641–651.

Elshof LE, Tryfonidis K, Slaets L, van Leeuwen-Stok AE, Skinner VP, Dif N, et al. Feasibility of a prospective, randomised, open-label, international multicentre, phase III, non-inferiority trial to assess the safety of active surveillance for low risk ductal carcinoma in situ – The LORD study. *Eur J Cancer*. 2015 August;51(12):1497–1510.

Evans KK, Birdwell RL, Wolfe JM. If you don't find it often, you often don't find it: Why some cancers are missed in breast cancer screening. *PLoS One*. 2013 May 30;8(5):e64366.

Francis A, Fallowfield L, Rea D. The LORIS trial: Addressing overtreatment of ductal carcinoma in situ [Internet]. *Clin Oncol*. 2015a;27:6–8. doi: 10.1016/j.clon.2014.09.015.

Francis A, Thomas J, Fallowfield L, Wallis M, Bartlett JMS, Brookes C, et al. Addressing overtreatment of screen detected DCIS; the LORIS trial. *Eur J Cancer*. 2015b November;51(16):2296–2303.

Gao Y, Geras KJ, Lewin AA, Moy L. New frontiers: An update on computer-aided diagnosis for breast imaging in the age of artificial intelligence [Internet]. *Am J Roentgenol*. 2019;212:300–307. doi: 10.2214/ajr.18.20392.

Geras KJ, Mann RM, Moy L. Artificial intelligence for mammography and digital breast tomosynthesis: Current concepts and future perspectives. *Radiology.* 2019 September 24;293:246–259.

Geras KJ, Wolfson S, Shen Y, Wu N, Kim SG, Kim E, et al. High-resolution breast cancer screening with multi-view deep convolutional neural networks [Internet]. 2017 [cited 2019 September 29]. Available from: http://arxiv.org/abs/1703.07047.

Gershon-Cohen J. Detection of breast cancer by periodic x-ray examinations [Internet]. *JAMA.* 1961;176:1114. doi: 10.1001/jama.1961.63040260015013a.

Getting started with distributed data parallel — PyTorch Tutorials 1.2.0 documentation [Internet]. [cited 2019 Sep 28]. Available from: https://pytorch.org/tutorials/intermediate/ddp_tutorial.html.

Giger ML, Karssemeijer N, Schnabel JA. Breast image analysis for risk assessment, detection, diagnosis, and treatment of cancer. *Annu Rev Biomed Eng.* 2013 May 13;15:327–357.

Gold RH, Bassett LW, Widoff BE. Highlights from the history of mammography [Internet]. *RadioGraphics.* 1990;10:1111–1131. doi: 10.1148/radiographics.10.6.2259767.

Goldstein NS, Ferkowicz M, Odish E, Mani A, Hastah F. Minimum formalin fixation time for consistent estrogen receptor immunohistochemical staining of invasive breast carcinoma [Internet]. *Am J Clin Pathol.* 2003;120:86–92. doi: 10.1309/qphdrb00qxgmuq9n.

Gradishar WJ, Anderson BO, Balassanian R, Blair SL, Burstein HJ, Cyr A, et al. Breast cancer, version 4.2017, NCCN clinical practice guidelines in oncology. *J Natl Compr Canc Netw.* 2018 March;16(3):310–320.

Ha R, Chang P, Karcich J, Mutasa S, Van Sant EP, Connolly E, et al. Predicting post neoadjuvant axillary response using a novel convolutional neural network algorithm. *Ann Surg Oncol.* 2018 October;25(10):3037–3043.

Hamidinekoo A, Denton E, Rampun A, Honnor K, Zwiggelaar R. Deep learning in mammography and breast histology, an overview and future trends. *Med Image Anal.* 2018 July;47:45–67.

Harvey H, Karpati E, Khara G, Korkinof D, Ng A, Austin C, et al. The role of deep learning in breast screening [Internet]. *Curr Breast Cancer Rep.* 2019;11:17–22. doi: 10.1007/s12609-019-0301-7.

Hofvind S, Geller BM, Skelly J, Vacek PM. Sensitivity and specificity of mammographic screening as practised in Vermont and Norway. *Br J Radiol.* 2012 Dec; 85(1020):e1226–e1232.

Houssami N, Kirkpatrick-Jones G, Noguchi N, Lee CI. Artificial Intelligence (AI) for the early detection of breast cancer: A scoping review to assess AI's potential in breast screening practice [Internet]. *Expert Rev Med Devices.* 2019;16:351–362. doi: 10.1080/17434440.2019.1610387.

Jalalian A, Mashohor SBT, Mahmud HR, Saripan MIB, Ramli ARB, Karasfi B. Computer-aided detection/diagnosis of breast cancer in mammography and ultrasound: A review. *Clin Imaging.* 2013 May;37(3):420–426.

Kavanagh AM, Giles GG, Mitchell H, Cawson JN. The sensitivity, specificity, and positive predictive value of screening mammography and symptomatic status. *J Med Screen*. 2000;7(2):105–110.

Keating NL, Pace LE. New federal requirements to inform patients about breast density: Will they help patients? *JAMA*. 2019 June 18;321(23):2275–2276.

Kerlikowske K, Vachon CM. Breast density: More than meets the eye [Internet]. *J Natl Cancer Inst*. 2016 October;108(10). doi: 10.1093/jnci/djw128.

Kim E-K, Kim H-E, Han K, Kang BJ, Sohn Y-M, Woo OH, et al. Applying data-driven imaging biomarker in mammography for breast cancer screening: Preliminary study. *Sci Rep*. 2018 February 9;8(1):2762.

Kohli A, Jha S. Why CAD failed in mammography. *J Am Coll Radiol*. 2018;15(3):535–537.

Kyono T, Gilbert FJ, van der Schaar M. MAMMO: A deep learning solution for facilitating radiologist-machine collaboration in breast cancer diagnosis [Internet]. 2018 [cited 2019 September 29]. Available from: http://arxiv.org/abs/1811.02661.

LeCun Y, Bengio Y, Hinton G. Deep learning. *Nature*. 2015 May 28;521(7553): 436–444.

Lee RS, Gimenez F, Hoogi A, Miyake KK, Gorovoy M, Rubin DL. A curated mammography data set for use in computer-aided detection and diagnosis research. *Sci Data*. 2017 December 19;4:170177.

Lehman CD, Arao RF, Sprague BL, Lee JM, Buist DSM, Kerlikowske K, et al. National performance benchmarks for modern screening digital mammography: Update from the breast cancer surveillance consortium. *Radiology*. 2017 April;283(1):49–58.

Lubner MG. Reflections on radiogenomics and oncologic radiomics. *Abdom Radiol (NY)*. 2019 June;44(6):1959.

Mann GB, Bruce Mann G, Fahey VD, Feleppa F, Buchanan MR. Reliance on hormone receptor assays of surgical specimens may compromise outcome in patients with breast cancer [Internet]. *J Clin Oncol*. 2005;23:5148–5154. doi: 10.1200/jco.2005.02.076.

Møller MH, Lousdal ML, Kristiansen IS, Støvring H. Effect of organized mammography screening on breast cancer mortality: A population-based cohort study in Norway. *Int J Cancer*. 2019 February 15;144(4):697–706.

Moreira IC, Amaral I, Domingues I, Cardoso A, Cardoso MJ, Cardoso JS. INbreast: Toward a full-field digital mammographic database. *Acad Radiol*. 2012 Feb;19(2):236–248.

Moss SM, Wale C, Smith R, Evans A, Cuckle H, Duffy SW. Effect of mammographic screening from age 40 years on breast cancer mortality in the UK Age trial at 17 years' follow-up: A randomised controlled trial [Internet]. *Lancet Oncol*. 2015 September;16(9):1123–1132. doi: 10.1016/s1470-2045(15)00128-x.

Mutasa S, Chang P, Van Sant EP, Nemer J, Liu M, Karcich J, et al. Potential role of convolutional neural network based algorithm in patient selection for DCIS observation trials using a mammogram dataset [Internet]. *Acad Radiol*. 2019. doi.: 10.1016/j.acra.2019.08.012.

Nyström L, Andersson I, Bjurstam N, Frisell J, Nordenskjöld B, Rutqvist LE. Long-term effects of mammography screening: Updated overview of the Swedish randomised trials [Internet]. *Lancet*. 2002;359:909–919. doi: 10.1016/s0140-6736(02)08020-0.

Nyukat. nyukat/breast_cancer_classifier [Internet]. GitHub. [cited 2019 September 30]. Available from: https://github.com/nyukat/breast_cancer_classifier.

Paraskevi T. Quality of life outcomes in patients with breast cancer [Internet]. *Oncol Rev*. 2012;6:2. doi: 10.4081/oncol.2012.e2.

Pareja F, Murray MP, Des Jean R, Konno F, Friedlander M, Lin O, et al. Cytologic assessment of estrogen receptor, progesterone receptor, and HER2 status in metastatic breast carcinoma. *J Am Soc Cytopathol*. 2017;6(1):33.

Ribeiro M, Singh S, Guestrin C. "Why Should I Trust You?": Explaining the predictions of any classifier [Internet]. *Proceedings of the 2016 Conference of the North American Chapter of the Association for Computational Linguistics: Demonstrations*. 2016. Available from: http://dx.doi.org/10.18653/v1/n16-3020.

Ribli D, Horváth A, Unger Z, Pollner P, Csabai I. Detecting and classifying lesions in mammograms with deep learning. *Sci Rep*. 2018 March 15;8(1):4165.

Rodriguez-Ruiz A, Lång K, Gubern-Merida A, Broeders M, Gennaro G, Clauser P, et al. Stand-alone artificial intelligence for breast cancer detection in mammography: Comparison with 101 radiologists [Internet]. *J Natl Cancer Inst*. 2019a March 5. doi: 10.1093/jnci/djy222.

Rodriguez-Ruiz A, Lång K, Gubern-Merida A, Teuwen J, Broeders M, Gennaro G, et al. Can we reduce the workload of mammographic screening by automatic identification of normal exams with artificial intelligence? A feasibility study. *Eur Radiol*. 2019b September;29(9):4825–4832.

Rossi S, Cinini C, Di Pietro C, Lombardi CP, Crucitti A, Bellantone R, et al. Diagnostic delay in breast cancer: Correlation with disease stage and prognosis. *Tumori*. 1990 December 31;76(6):559–562.

Saadatmand S, Bretveld R, Siesling S, Tilanus-Linthorst MMA. Influence of tumour stage at breast cancer detection on survival in modern times: population based study in 173 797 patients [Internet]. *BMJ*. 2015:h4901. doi: 10.1136/bmj.h4901.

Shapiro S, Venet W, Strax P, Venet L, Roeser R. Selection, follow-up, and analysis in the health insurance plan study: A randomized trial with breast cancer screening. *Natl Cancer Inst Monogr*. 1985 May;67:65–74.

Shen L, Margolies LR, Rothstein JH, Fluder E, McBride RB, Sieh W. Deep learning to improve breast cancer early detection on screening mammography [Internet]. 2017 [cited 2019 August 19]. Available from: http://arxiv.org/abs/1708.09427.

Sinha VC, Piwnica-Worms H. Intratumoral heterogeneity in ductal carcinoma in situ: Chaos and consequence. *J Mammary Gland Biol Neoplasia*. 2018 December;23(4):191–205.

Stomper PC, D'Souza DJ, DiNitto PA, Arredondo MA. Analysis of parenchymal density on mammograms in 1353 women 25-79 years old. *AJR Am J Roentgenol*. 1996 November;167(5):1261–1265.

Strax P, Venet L, Shapiro S. Value of mammography in reduction of mortality from breast cancer in mass screening. *Am J Roentgenol Radium Ther Nucl Med.* 1973 March;117(3):686–689.

SysAdmin. Risk factors | Breast cancer risk factors: Cancer Australia [Internet]. [cited 2019 September 29]. Available from: https://breastcancerriskfactors.gov.au/risk-factors.

Tabár L, Gad A, Holmberg LH, Ljungquist U, Fagerberg CJG, Baldetorp L, et al. Reduction in mortality from breast cancer after mass screening with mammography [Internet]. *Lancet.* 1985;325:829–832. doi: 10.1016/s0140-6736(85)92204-4.

Tabár L, Vitak B, Chen TH-H, Yen AM-F, Cohen A, Tot T, et al. Swedish two-county trial: Impact of mammographic screening on breast cancer mortality during 3 decades [Internet]. *Radiology.* 2011;260:658–663. doi: 10.1148/radiol.11110469.

Teare P, Fishman M, Benzaquen O, Toledano E, Elnekave E. Malignancy detection on mammography using dual deep convolutional neural networks and genetically discovered false color input enhancement. *J Digit Imaging.* 2017 August;30(4):499–505.

Toss MS, Pinder SE, Green AR, Thomas J, Morgan DAL, Robertson JFR, et al. Breast conservation in ductal carcinomain situ(DCIS): what defines optimal margins? [Internet]. *Histopathology.* 2017;70:681–692. doi: 10.1111/his.13116.

Turing AM. I.—Computing machinery and intelligence [Internet]. *Mind.* 1950;LIX:433–460. doi: 10.1093/mind/lix.236.433.

UpToDate [Internet]. [cited 2019 September 28]. Available from: https://www.uptodate.com/contents/prognostic-and-predictive-factors-in-early-non-metastatic-breast-cancer.

van Ravesteyn NT, van Lier L, Schechter CB, Ekwueme DU, Royalty J, Miller JW, et al. Transition from film to digital mammography: Impact for breast cancer screening through the national breast and cervical cancer early detection program. *Am J Prev Med.* 2015 May;48(5):535–542.

Welch HG, Prorok PC, O'Malley AJ, Kramer BS. Breast-cancer tumor size, overdiagnosis, and mammography screening effectiveness. *N Engl J Med.* 2016 October 13;375(15):1438–1447.

WHO |WHO position paper on mammography screening. 2014 November 24 [cited 2019 June 30]. Available from: https://www.who.int/cancer/publications/mammography_screening/en/.

Winsberg F, Elkin M, Macy J, Bordaz V, Weymouth W. Detection of radiographic abnormalities in mammograms by means of optical scanning and computer analysis [Internet]. *Radiology.* 1967;89:211–215. doi: 10.1148/89.2.211.

Wood B, Junckerstorff R, Sterrett G, Frost F, Harvey J, Robbins P. A comparison of immunohistochemical staining for oestrogen receptor, progesterone receptor and HER-2 in breast core biopsies and subsequent excisions [Internet]. *Pathology.* 2007;39:391–395. doi: 10.1080/00313020701444465.

Wu J-L, Tseng H-S, Yang L-H, Wu H-K, Kuo S-J, Chen S-T, et al. Prediction of axillary lymph node metastases in breast cancer patients based on pathologic information of the primary tumor. *Med Sci Monit.* 2014 April 8;20:577–581.

Wu N, Phang J, Park J, Shen Y, Huang Z, Zorin M, et al. Deep neural networks improve radiologists' performance in breast cancer screening [Internet]. 2019 [cited 2019 April 5]. Available from: http://arxiv.org/abs/1903.08297.

Wu Y, Giger ML, Doi K, Vyborny CJ, Schmidt RA, Metz CE. Artificial neural networks in mammography: Application to decision making in the diagnosis of breast cancer. *Radiology.* 1993 April;187(1):81–87.

Yala A, Lehman C, Schuster T, Portnoi T, Barzilay R. A deep learning mammography-based model for improved breast cancer risk prediction. *Radiology.* 2019a July;292(1):60–66.

Yala A, Schuster T, Miles R, Barzilay R, Lehman C. A deep learning model to triage screening mammograms: A simulation study. *Radiology.* 2019b August 6;293:38–46.

Youngwirth LM, Boughey JC, Hwang ES. Surgery versus monitoring and endocrine therapy for low-risk DCIS: The COMET trial. *Bull Am Coll Surg.* 2017 January;102(1):62–63.

*Chapter 5*

# Mammographic Screening and Breast Cancer Management – Part 2

Mark R. Traill
*University of Michigan*

## Contents

## 5.1  Introduction

The anatomy of the breast is relatively simple compared to other anatomic areas. Parenchyma and fat make up most of the image on a mammogram. Additional common findings are various types of calcifications, skin and lymph nodes. This relative simplicity makes the breast a great starting point for the emergence of artificial intelligence (AI) algorithms as a first-line diagnostic tool that can potentially completely answer the clinical question being asked by the physician ordering the screening mammogram. Other emerging clinical algorithms can also identify a significant finding such as the presence of blood on a CT scan of the brain (Halon, 2015), but detecting that finding alone does not come close to a complete report for the CT brain scan. There are many other pathologies in the brain such as a stroke that would need to be commented upon for the study report to be complete. A breast cancer detection algorithm has the potential of producing essentially a complete report for the screening mammographic study, remembering, however, that the decision to proceed with a biopsy to prove cancer is made by a radiologist after additional diagnostic mammogram views and/or ultrasound are completed.

The question being asked by the clinician who orders a screening mammogram is relatively straight forward: Is there cancer? While other processes may be present, such as a breast cyst, the point of doing the screening mammogram is to answer "MAYBE" or "NO" to the question of cancer presence on the images. Indeed, every screening mammogram dictation finishes with a very brief summary that is a BI-RADS code. For a screening exam, the final report summary is either a BI-RADS 0,1 or 2. A "MAYBE" answer results in a BI-RADS 0 summary score which means the evaluation of the breast is incomplete as there may be a malignancy present. This score leads to the patient being called back for additional diagnostic mammogram views and/or targeted ultrasound to determine if a biopsy is indicated. A BI-RADS 1 (negative findings) or 2 (benign findings) summary score means the patient needs no further workup as no areas suspicious for cancer are detected. If the design of the algorithm can be focused and limited to detecting the morphologic changes that it has been taught are associated with malignancy, then it can potentially satisfy the clinical mission of the screening mammogram study.

Humans do their best at trying to answer this "MAYBE" or "NO" question when reading mammograms. Unfortunately, human performance is at times unacceptable. Recent retrospective studies have shown that up to 35% of interval cancers (cancers that were newly discovered on a screening mammogram) were present on the prior screening mammograms but were missed by the prior human reader (Hofvind et al., 2005; Hoff et al., 2012). This is a very high and unacceptable percentage. The radiologist who is looking at large volumes of mammograms every day needs to rely on their powers of recognition to see these cancers. This is an intuitive process that is also described as fast, type I thinking. They literally have seconds for this noncognitive function to happen or not happen. Being distracted or fatigued can contribute to human errors. These human errors can have fatal consequences. While the adoption of digital breast tomography (DBT) has improved the cancer detection rate and reduced the recall rate, the extra time needed to view 300 images versus the 4 images from a 2D digital mammogram has added additional pressures on the busy radiologist working under time constraints.

Interestingly, radiologists in the USA have been looking at computers to help them find breast cancer on screening mammograms for some time. It has been estimated that over 83% of the mammograms read in the USA have had some form of non-AI computer-assisted diagnosis (CAD) program retrospectively checking the images for cancer (Lehman et al., 2015). At these levels of usage, the practice is basically the standard of care. This adoption occurred even though the benefit of non-AI CAD was far from clear with some studies actually showing the sensitivity for detecting cancer with non-AI CAD was significantly lower than the sensitivity for cancer detection without non-AI CAD (Fenton, 2015). So clearly the need for computer assistance has been understood and sought for some time, even when the actual CAD performance was not functionally helpful.

## 5.2 AI-Enabled CAD

This brings us now to the current disruptive force of the new AI-based CAD algorithms being rapidly developed by multiple research teams. Companies such as Enlitic, Zebra Medical and Qure ai are releasing very focused algorithms to detect multiple different pathologies. New breast cancer AI algorithms are rapidly being developed for detecting breast cancer on screening mammography by companies such as *iCAD* and *CureMetrix*. These developing algorithms appear to be able to perform at a level equal to or above their human counterparts. One recent study showed the AI system for breast cancer detection had an AUC higher than 61.4% of the radiologists (Rodriquez-Ruiz et al., 2019). Another study showed improved radiologist performance for detecting breast cancer on mammograms when using an AI computer system for support (Rodriquez-Ruiz et al., 1918). In a recent literature review of 60 studies that compared the diagnostic performance of deep learning models to their human counterparts for detecting a wide range of pathologies, Liu et al. found little difference in the overall performance in the sensitivity and specificity between AI platforms and physicians (Liu et al., 2019). The authors did note, however, that less than half of the studies had undergone out-of-sample external validation to see how performance would transfer to other patient populations or working environments.

Again, these algorithms typically look for only one finding, such as a pulmonary nodule or intracranial hemorrhage. For a chest CT therefore, current algorithm performance does not come close to providing a complete clinical interpretation of the CT scan as it is looking for only one finding when many findings need to be excluded. In the case of screening mammography, however, identifying the single finding of cancer is essentially all that is needed to answer the key clinical question being asked by the clinician ordering the imaging study. This dramatic potential has resulted in the release of several first-line clinical AI tools that now have FDA approval for screening mammography. These breast cancer algorithms have performance metrics similar or superior to comparison human metrics.

## 5.3 ProFound AI

To illustrate the current status of what a radiologist can expect from commercially available AI systems, we will look in detail at a recent FDA-approved AI CAD called *ProFound* from iCAD. Interestingly, *Forbes* magazine called the release of *ProFound* one of the most significant AI events of 2018 (Tom, 2018). At the end of 2018, *ProFound* was granted FDA approval as the first commercially available AI CAD system for breast cancer detection and localization on screening DBT. This algorithm was approved for screening mammography use only. For clinical use by a radiologist, *ProFound* functions by placing a "mark" on any area that it recognizes as having features similar to the cancer cases that the algorithm was trained on (Figure 5.1). The identified area also receives a "confidence" score of between 0 and 100 that reflects the percentage of cancers in the training cases that had similar features to the identified and now marked finding on the screening mammogram.

A confidence score of over 60 is typically considered to be a significantly suspicious finding (Figure 5.2). However, cancer can still be present with a confidence score below that cut-off number. It is still up to the interpreting radiologist to review the marked findings and make the final call as to whether or not the patient will need further study with diagnostic mammograms. An overall case score is also generated by *ProFound* that reflects the likelihood that there is cancer included on the images as a whole. *ProFound* was also approved for "concurrent viewing" which means that unlike prior CAD systems, the marks are placed on the study when it is first opened. Prior CAD systems could only be used after the initial human review of the

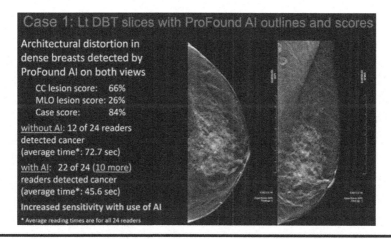

**Figure 5.1 Architectural distortion in breast detected by AI. (iCAD.)**

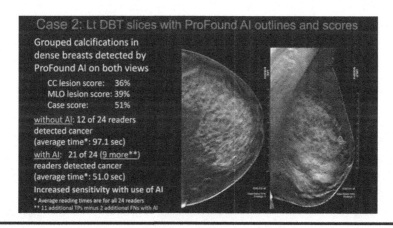

**Figure 5.2 Grouped calcification in breast detected by AI. (iCAD.)**

images was completed. This adds a new dimension to the radiologist's overall workflow that can potentially influence how a radiologist approaches the interpretation process.

*ProFound* was trained on over 12,000 DBT cases that equaled over 3.5 million individual images. The training cohort was enriched with a total of 4,000 cancer cases. The validation reader study used for FDA approval was published in September 2019 (Conant et al., 2019). The reader study was a multi-reader, multi-case, cross-over design. Twenty-four experienced radiologists reviewed 260 cases with and without AI during two separate reading sessions that were separated by at least 4 weeks. The case dataset was cancer enriched and included 66 biopsy-proven malignancies and 65 biopsy-proven benign lesions. Endpoints included an overall performance for detecting cancers (AUC), sensitivity, specificity, recall rates in non-cancer cases and reading times.

Radiologist performance for the detection of malignant lesions, measured by mean AUC, increased from 0.795 without AI to 0.852 with AI. Sensitivity increased from 77% without AI to 85% with AI. Specificity increased from 62.7% to 69.6%. And reading time decreased by a whopping 52%. And the recall rate for non-cancers decreased from 38% without to 30.9% with *ProFound* AI. The authors concluded, "this study suggests that both improved efficiency and accuracy could be achieved in clinical practice using an effective AI system". Performance plots (Figures 5.3 and 5.4) graphically show the changes in the radiologist's performance when interpreting mammograms with and without *ProFound*. Note the more uniform performances with improved metrics causing a collective shift to the upper left corner of

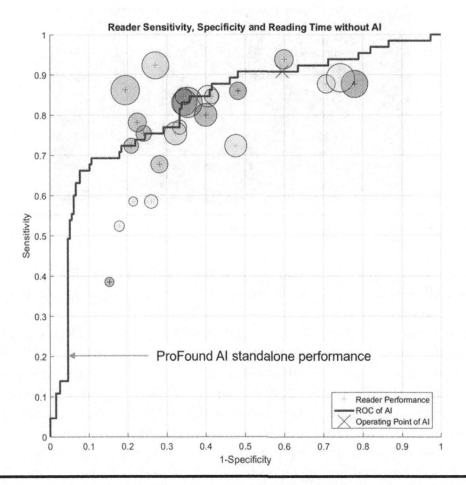

**Figure 5.3   Performance of radiologists interpreting mammograms without AI. (RSNA.)**

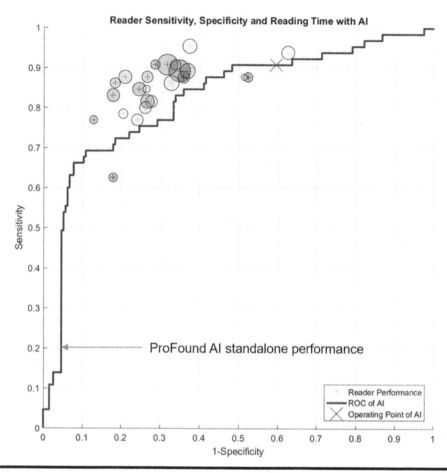

**Figure 5.4    Performance of radiologists interpreting mammograms with AI. (RSNA.)**

the plot when using AI. Another very interesting observation was that the *ProFound* standalone performance had a sensitivity higher than 22 of the 24 readers reading without AI. However, the standalone performance had a specificity lower than 20 of the 24 readers reading without AI.

Based on these findings, one would be hard-pressed to argue strongly against the rapid adoption of this new clinical tool in the interpretation of screening mammograms. Fundamentally, finding just one cancer that would have been missed without AI would justify the additional expense and workflow adjustment involved with adopting. The reading time savings alone are a dramatic benefit. Given that a missed breast cancer on mammography is one of the most common reasons for a malpractice suit against a radiologist in the USA (Wang et al., 2013), one would also expect this algorithm to be further embraced.

## 5.4 Other AI Applications

Another possible workflow integration of AI going forward is to use it in the context of an automated, retrospective quality assurance tool that is used to check a prior human reading. Double reading is required for facility certification in both the USA and the EU. Double reading, in general, has been shown to increase mammogram report accuracy (Lauren Sen, 2018; Taylor-Phillips, 2018). From the radiologist's point of view, while helpful, the double reading task itself is an unpopular activity. At our institution, we are currently testing the effectiveness of an AI-based QA review process that could not only catch cancer that was missed on prior reading but also potentially provide performance metrics for a specific radiologist. These metrics could then be used as feedback to improve the human reader's performance going forward.

Another clinical application for AI that is now currently available with FDA approval is the triage product from *CureMetrix* called *cmTriage*. Released in 2019, this algorithm conducts an automated review of 2D mammograms that are pending interpretation (Figure 5.5). The algorithm then prioritizes those cases that have a potential cancer finding so they can be seen first and with more attention than other negative studies (Figure 5.6). This will be very useful in expediting the care of a patient with a true abnormal finding.

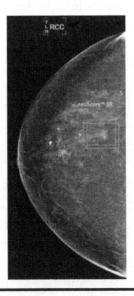

**Figure 5.5    Automated review of the 2D mammogram by AI. (CureMetrix.)**

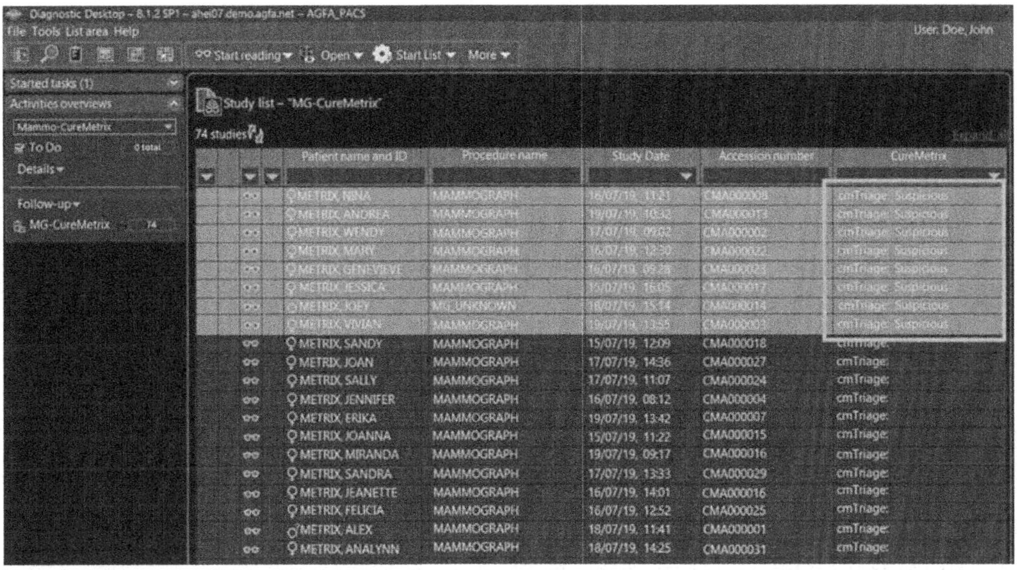

**Figure 5.6   Prioritization of suspicious cases by AI. (CureMetrix.)**

In addition, *CureMetrix* offers solutions as a pay-per-use-software that is accessible through the cloud. This approach would offer the advantage of the flexibility of use and cost. However, many health systems in the USA are still reluctant to share patient health information outside of their closed systems.

## 5.5 Conclusion

Going forward, another very exciting use of AI in mammography will be focusing on risk assessment for the development of future breast cancers. One recent study has shown the potential of deep learning linked health records and screening mammograms as an effective future cancer risk predictor (Akselrod-Ballin et al., 2019). This will help focus screening resources on the patients who are most at risk. The next few years will see many new FDA-approved algorithms in medical imaging and specifically for breast cancer detection. Future functionality that includes AI comparison with findings on prior studies will be very helpful by adding the rate of change to the cancer detection equation. Improved lesion morphology pattern recognition will improve lesion characterization and specificity. It should also become increasingly apparent that the improved precision of the reports obtained with AI results in more lives saved and greatly reduced overall treatment costs. AI interpretation assistance in mammography will be a very disruptive force going forward.

# References

Akselrod-Ballin A, Chorev M, Shoshan Y, Spiro A, Hazan A, Melamed R, et al. (2019) Predicting breast cancer by applying deep learning linked health records and mammograms. *Radiology*, Online: June 18, 2019. doi: 10.1148/radiol.2019182622.

Conant EF, Toledano AY, Periaswamy S, Fotin SV, Go J, Boatsman JE, et al. (2019) Improving accuracy and efficiency with concurrent use of artificial intelligence for digital breast tomosynthesis. *Radiology: Artificial Intelligence.* 1(4):e180096.

Fenton JJ. (2015 September 28) Is it time to stop paying for computer-aided mammography? *AMA Internal Medicine.* 175:1837–1838.

Halon E. (2019) Zebra Medical wins FDA clearance for AI intracranial hemorrhage Detection. June 17.

Hoff SR, Abrahamsen AL, Samset JH, Vigeland E, Klepp O, Hofvind S. (2012) Breast cancer: missed interval and screening-detected cancer at full-field digital mammography and screen-film mammography – results from a retrospective review. *Radiology.* 246:378–386.

Hofvind S, Skaane P, Vitak B, Wang H, Thoresen S, Eriksen L, et al. (2005) Influence of review design on percentages of missed interval breast cancers: a retrospect study of interval cancers in a population-based screening program. *Radiology.* 237:437–443.

Lauren Sen MD. (2018 July) Impact of second-opinion interpretation of breast imaging in patients not currently diagnosed with breast cancer. *Journal of the American College of Radiology.* 15(7):980–987.

Lehman CD, Wellman RD, Buist DS, Kerlikowske K, Tosteson AN, Miglioretti DL. (2015 September 28) Diagnostic accuracy of digital screening mammography with and without computer-aided detection. *AMA Internal Medicine.* 175:1828–1837.

Liu X, Faes L, Kale AU, Wagner SK, Fu DJ, Bruynseels A, et al. (2019 October 1) A comparison of deep learning performance against health-care professionals in detecting diseases from medical imaging: a systematic review and meta-analysis. *The Lancet Digital Health.* 1(6):PE271–E297.

Rodriquez-Ruiz A, Elizabeth K, Jan-Jurre M, Kathy S, Sylvia HH, Ioannis S, et al. (1918 November 20; 2019) Detection of breast cancer with mammography: effect of an artificial intelligence support system. *Radiology, Radiology.* 290(2):305–314. doi:10.1148/radiol.2018181371.

Rodriquez-Ruiz A, Lång K, Gubern-Merida A, Broeders M, Gennaro G, Clauser P, et al. (2019 September) Stand-alone artificial intelligence for breast cancer detection in mammography: comparison with 101 radiologists. *Journal of the National Cancer Institute.* 111(9):916–922.

Taylor-Phillips, S, Jenkinson, D, Stinton, C, Wallis, MG, Dunn, J, Clarke, A. (2018 April) Double reading in breast cancer screening: cohort evaluation in the CO-OPS trial. *Radiology.* 287(3):749–757.

Tom T. (2018 December 22) 2018's Biggest moments in AI. Forbes.

Wang JS, Baker SR, Patel R, Luk L, Castro III A. (2013 February 1) The causes of medical malpractice suits against radiologists in the United States. *Radiology,* Online.

*Chapter 6*

# Deep Learning for Drawing Insights from Patient Data for Diagnosis and Treatment

Dinesh Kumar and Dharmendra Sharma
*University of Canberra*

## Contents

## 6.1 Introduction

The world is experiencing a *technological revolution* where people have begun to use digital technology in most facets of their life to make their work easier, for entertainment and education, to monitor their health conditions and for assistive driving using self-driving cars, to name a few. Not only using such technologies make our work easier, but they also capable of collecting data on our activities, actions and conditions. This has led to the enormous growth of both structured and unstructured data in formats such as text, images and video for many domains of our life. This data explosion has challenged the research community into finding appropriate methods and algorithms to extract patterns and insights from this abundance of data.

In response, several traditional machine learning (ML) algorithms such as support vector machines (SVM), Bayesian models, decision trees and Artificial Neural Networks have been used to extract relevant knowledge and patterns from datasets (Agarwal et al., 2012; Li & Ma, 2010; Xie et al., 2016). However, researchers using these traditional ML methods often faced hurdles in processing large datasets leading to model overfitting issues and the inability to process data in its original form (LeCun et al., 2015). Thus, in several instances pre-processing the data was essential prior to model training. These included transforming the data into suitable formats for the ML algorithm to operate on or manual extraction of features. In order to manually extract features required researchers to have considerable domain knowledge and spend considerable time to extract relevant features. With increasing volumes and dimensions of data has propelled the need for new approaches and algorithms to effectively mine such datasets preferable in its raw form. Thus, this has spawned the birth of new sets of artificial intelligent (AI) models and algorithms referred to as deep learning (DL) algorithms or models (Kumar & Sharma, 2019) such as deep feed-forward networks (FFNs), convolutional neural networks (CNNs) and recurrent neural networks (RNNs). Research in DL has provided breakthroughs in finding solutions for which traditional ML algorithms were not quite able to solve or provide optimal solutions, thus overcoming their limitations. Large datasets act as fuel to DL algorithms and hence enable the extraction of meaningful patterns and inferences.

More recently, DL models have been successfully applied in various fields such as image and video processing, text processing for sentiment analysis, object recognition, speech recognition and time series analysis. CNN is a popular DL algorithm that has achieved great success in various computer vision tasks such as image classification, object detection, visual concept discovery, semantic segmentation and boundary detection. Algorithms purely based on CNNs or used as a basis of other complicated algorithms are applied in various practical domains such as in self-driving cars, defense and security, mobile devices, medical image processing and quality assurance in manufacturing industries. In this chapter, we focus on these CNN classes of algorithms applied on skin lesion datasets.

Although research is still ongoing in the development of new AI algorithms, the focus has shifted in the application of AI into real-life problem domains for the betterment of people's health and improvement in their lifestyle. Several AI-based systems have been designed as an early warning or diagnostic tool for chronic illnesses, for example, diagnosing depression and diabetics (Sourla et al., 2012). The advancements in digital imaging technology in medicine and through conventional devices such as smartphones are enabling medical practitioners and researchers alike to collect images and video data of various medical conditions. Such data includes, for example, retinal scan images, MRI images, CAT scans, X-ray and skin lesion images alongside natural images and videos such as facial expression recordings. These image- and video-based datasets are now a source of valuable information for research into areas including skin lesion classification, depression analysis and MRI segmentation.

This chapter investigates DL and the application of CNN algorithms on image-based medical datasets particularly for the classification of skin lesion images. The aim of CNN is to classify skin lesion images as benign (non-cancerous) or malignant (cancerous). Arguably skin cancer is one of the deadliest forms of cancer with millions of reported cases around the world of which many cases become fatal (American Cancer Society, 2019; Esteva et al., 2017; Vesal et al., 2018). This problem is further escalated by a lack of access or availability of qualified dermatologists and equipment in developing countries or in remote regions to diagnose skin cancer early. Furthermore, there is a lack of knowledge on understanding signs of skin cancer leading to delayed proactive action by patients. Hence, there is a great need to use technology for educating people on understanding skin lesions as well as to develop AI systems that can be used as early warning diagnosis tools, prognosis and monitoring cancer treatment and detecting any resistance to therapeutic drugs. The aim of AI systems is not any replaced dermatologists but to focus on developing AI to assist in early detection of skin cancer and to alert patients to take immediate proactive actions.

The early detection and monitoring of skin cancer have attracted the attention of ML researchers in investigating possible AI methods that can be utilized as an early warning diagnosis tool for detecting melanoma using skin lesion images. Previous studies show promising and competitive results of using CNN-based algorithms that classify skin lesion images that are comparable to dermatologist-level diagnosis (Esteva et al., 2017). A key ingredient and driver for such research to be conducted is the publicly available skin lesion datasets such as International Skin Imaging Collaboration (ISIC) (Tschandl et al., 2018) dataset. CNN-based models can then be trained on these datasets and resultant models deployed as diagnosis apps on smart devices such as mobile phones. Using built-in camera hardware in smartphones, such apps can be used to focus on suspected lesion regions on the patient's skin and determine if the lesion is possible benign or malignant. Immediate actions can be taken which can ultimately save people's life. Such systems would prove extremely beneficial for the general public particularly in regions where availability of dermatologist services is limited. The contributions of this chapter are therefore as follows:

1. We investigate the application of DL algorithms on image-based medical datasets particularly on skin cancer images. Here, we discuss innovative CNN-based networks that have been applied on skin lesion datasets.
2. We introduce the skin cancer classification problem and describe the skin lesion datasets available to the research community and their characteristics.
3. We demonstrate how the CNN-based VGG network (Simonyan & Zisserman, 2014) can be applied on ISIC 2018 skin lesion dataset using transfer learning.
4. We highlight ongoing research and efforts in the development of mobile applications using deep AI engines available to the community that can be used as an early warning system for the detection of skin cancer.
5. We identify major research challenges and future directions.

Since this chapter focuses on applying DL on image-based skin lesion datasets using CNNs, we describe the basic architecture of CNNs and its physiological basis in Section 6.2. Section 6.3 describes the skin cancer classification problem, introduces a common skin lesion dataset used by researchers, and provides a review of some of the current research conducted on using innovative CNN-based networks on skin lesion images. Section 6.4 describes an experiment applying transfer learning on the ISIC dataset. The results are discussed in Section 6.5. Section 6.6 describes the deployment of trained CNN-based models on skin lesion datasets on smartphones followed by a conclusion and future research directions in Section 6.7.

## 6.2 Convolutional Neural Networks

Pioneering studies such as Adelson et al. (1984), Hubel and Wiesel (1959, 1968), and Riesenhuber and Poggio (1999) have attempted to describe how the visual system of primates performs the function of sight. They revealed that object detection and recognition in the brain are made based on low-level features extracted in the lower or early part of the visual pathway. The low-level features are then assimilated into global features before being sent to the visual cortex for processing. Here, low-level features are classified as lines and curves, whereas shapes and color are labeled as global features. The visual cortex then performs the appropriate task of detection, recognition or classification. Zheng et al. (2018) defined computational models that use this above technique of feature extraction as *local-to-global* models. Figure 6.1 describes the conical structure of the cells in the visual pathway of cats in the studies of Hubel and Wiesel (1959, 1968). Simple cells in the earlier part of the visual pathway are fine-tuned to extract low-level features. Complex cells deeper in the visual pathway reconstruct object shapes from these low-level features. These high-level features are then processed in the cortex to perform the task of object detection or recognition. Hence, the basis of efficient object detection and recognition in the biological system is its ability to extract low-level features from visual scenes fed from receptors in the retina of eyes.

LeCun et al. (1998) formalized the modern framework of CNNs using Hubel's descriptions of how the visual system recognizes objects based on low-level features. A generic CNN structure contains two major parts in order to mimic the functions of the visual system: (i) the feature extraction part and (ii) the fully connected neural network part. Feature extraction is enabled by several key sub-parts also called layers in a CNN, namely, the convolution, activation and pooling layers. Figure 6.2 illustrates the

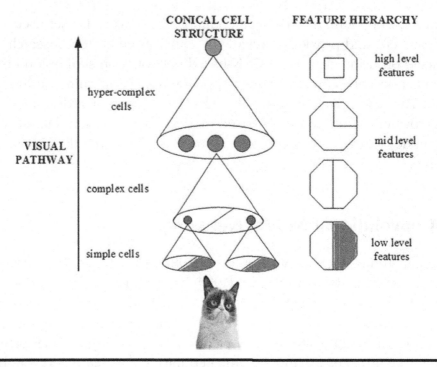

**Figure 6.1** **The hierarchical structure of cells in the visual pathways of cats as described in the studies of (Hubel & Wiesel, 1959).**

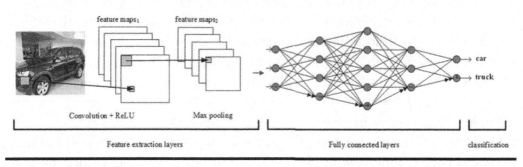

**Figure 6.2** **The architecture of a CNN. (Taken from Kumar and Sharma (2019).)**

lateral view of a CNN architecture. They are described in the following sub-sections.

**Convolutional layer**: The key component of a convolution layer is the filers organized as a two-dimensional array of size ($m \times n$). These filters (also called weights or kernels) are convolved across the input image (also a 2D array) performing a sum of the dot products of the filter and the input values within the receptive field of the filter. The receptive field of the filter is the patch on the image where the filter is applied. In this fashion, the input image is *scanned* with the filter starting from the top left to the bottom right of the image. Every time the filter slides, it scans a small portion of the input image. In this fashion, a 2D feature map is formed as the filter convolves the input image. Hence for each filter, a corresponding feature map is output. Within the convolution layer, several filters can be used, resulting in several feature maps as output. Since CNN is a special kind of ANN, several iterations via forwarding and back-propagation fine-tune the filters of the convolution layer to detect a particular feature from the input space. For example, filter $f^1$ is fine-tuned to detect a horizontal line, $f^2$ detects a vertical line while $f^3$ a top-left to the bottom-right oblique line. To extract higher-level features, further convolution layers are added to the CNN. Extracted features from previous convolution layers become an input to new convolution layers. Figure 6.3 describes the convolution process visually.

**Activation layer**: The purpose of the activation layer is to introduce non-linearity in the model and to squash the feature map outputs within given thresholds. It also helps to detect non-linear features and is a mechanism to avoid model overfitting on training data. A popular activation function used with CNNs is the rectifier linear units (ReLUs) (Glorot et al., 2011).

**Pooling layer**: On a CNN, there can be several convolution layers, and each layer can have several filters in it. As a result, several 2D feature maps from each convolution layer are output. This increases computational time to process all the feature maps in subsequent layers. Pooling in CNN is a technique applied to downsample the feature map so that there

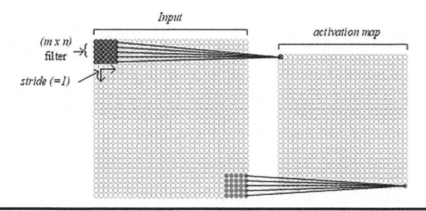

**Figure 6.3    The convolution process is shown with an input image of size 32 × 32, 5 × 5 filter and stride of one (Taken from Kumar and Sharma (2019)). The value of stride controls the convolution step of the filter. Using these parameters, a feature map of size 27 × 27 is generated as output.**

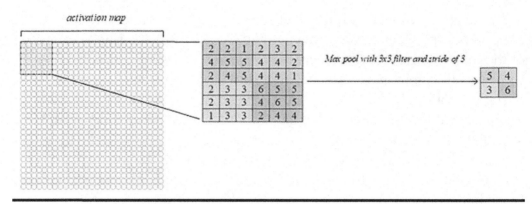

**Figure 6.4 Max pooling a feature map with a 3 × 3 pool window and stride of one. (Taken from Kumar and Sharma (2019).)**

is less convolution operation required to be performed in the successive convolution layer. This reduces computation time. Further pooling also avoids overfitting and introduces some translation invariance in the model (Xu et al., 2014). A popular pooling method is *max pooling* which takes the feature map as input and returns the max value of a local patch of units. The size of the local patch is governed by the *pool size* which defines the receptive field of the pool window. How the pool window is convolved across the feature map is controlled by the value of *stride*. Figure 6.4 shows an example of max pool operation on a feature map.

Since CNNs approximate the functioning of the visual system, they are best suited for data that are in the two-dimensional form (Kumar & Sharma, 2019) such as images in grayscale (one-channel) or in color (three-channel) and audio spectrograms (LeCun et al., 2015). CNNs have been successful in practical applications such as self-driving cars, facial recognition authentication systems such as mobile phones, medical image processing and quality assurance in manufacturing industries. In addition, CNNs have also proven useful in processing video datasets where frames can be treated as 2D images. In the following section, we describe recent research where CNNs are applied to the diagnosis of skin cancer based on skin lesion image datasets.

## 6.3 Skin Lesion Classification Problem

Skin cancer is one of the deadliest forms of diseases affecting millions of people around the world (American Cancer Society, 2019; Hosny et al., 2019). It is mostly triggered by extended and unprotected exposure to harmful ultraviolet (UV) rays of the sun that damage the DNA of the skin and genes that control cell growth (Refianti et al., 2019). Increasing world industrialization contributing to global warming and depleting the ozone layer has heightened the threat of more people being exposed to UV rays and developing cancerous skin cells. Several kinds of literature report melanoma cancer as one of the most dangerous types of skin cancer (Brinker et al., 2018; Hosny et al., 2019; Li & Shen, 2018; Mirunalini et al., 2017; Qi et al., 2017; Refianti et al., 2019). If untreated, melanoma can spread on the skin on other parts of the body. A common first step to diagnosing melanoma is through physical examination of the suspected area by a dermatologist usually by using dermoscopy images. Based on experience and using results from dermoscopy examinations that are matched with prior confirmed melanoma cases, dermatologists produce conclusions on a case-by-case basis. They also utilize various methods such as the ABCDE (asymmetry, border irregularity, color patterns, diameter and evolving size) (Nachbar et al., 1994) and the seven-point rule (Argenziano et al., 1998) for this task. The problem with such approaches to diagnosing melanoma is that it is influenced by human subjectivity (Refianti et al., 2019) and thus susceptible to inconsistent diagnosis at times. Furthermore, access to qualified dermatologists is limited by their shortage and availability particularly in remote areas and developing countries. This usually leads to delayed diagnosis and follow-up treatment, thus making situations life-threatening.

### 6.3.1 The HAM10000 Image-Based Skin Cancer Dataset and Its Characteristics

The ISIC archive is a popular source of skin lesion dataset used by researchers studying the application of DL on skin lesion classification and segmentation tasks. ISIC provides various images of skin lesions for early diagnosis. The archive contains multiple databases and currently contains over 13,000 dermatoscopic images collected from leading clinical centers and from a variety of devices. The database, however, contains many nevi or melanoma images (12,893 out of 13,786), making it biased towards melanocytic lesions (Tschandl et al., 2018). One of the contributing datasets to the ISIC archive is the HAM10000 (Human Against Machine with 10,000 training images) dataset by (Codella et al., 2015; Tschandl et al., 2018). The principle goal of this dataset was to boost the automated diagnosis of dermatoscopic images. Ten thousand and fifteen dermatoscopic images were

**Table 6.1   Composition of Images in HAM10000 Train and Test Dataset**

| Lesion Class | Diagnosis Name | Total Images | Test Images Reserved |
|---|---|---|---|
| akiec | Actinic keratose and intraepithelial carcinoma | 327 | 33 |
| bcc | Basal cell carcinoma | 514 | 51 |
| bkl | Benign keratosis | 1,099 | 110 |
| df | Dermatofibroma | 115 | 12 |
| nv | Melanocytic nevi | 6,705 | 671 |
| mel | Melanoma | 1,113 | 111 |
| vasc | Vascular skin lesions | 142 | 14 |

collected over a period of 20 years from the Medical University of Vienna, Austria, and Cliff Rosendahl's skin cancer practice in Queensland, Australia. The images are categorized into seven diagnostic classes: *apiece* (actinic keratose and intraepithelial carcinoma), *bcc* (Basal cell carcinoma), *bkl* (benign keratosis), *df* (dermatofibroma), *nv* (melanocytic nevi), *mel* (Melanoma) and *vasc* (Vascular skin lesions). The ground truth of 50% of the lesion images is validated by histopathology, while the rest are validated by follow-up, expert consensus or confirmation by in-vivo confocal microscopy (Tschandl et al., 2018). Table 6.1 shows the number of images in each class in the HAM10000 dataset. Metadata for each sample lesion image contains the person's age, sex, localization of the image and the validation method of the case. The HAM10000 train dataset is also biased towards melanoma. In order to obtain a balanced dataset, one technique to use is data augmentation as explained in Section 6.4.1.2. Some sample class images from the HAM10000 dataset are given in Table 6.2. Other notable skin lesion datasets used by the ML research community are given in Table 6.3.

## 6.3.2  CNN Approaches to Skin Cancer Classification

The need to develop assistive technology for early skin cancer diagnosis coupled with access to publicly available skin lesion datasets such as the ISIC 2018 has propelled many researchers to develop state-of-the-art classifiers based on CNN for skin lesion classification (Brinker et al., 2018). In addition to skin lesion classification, another area that is attracting the attention of computer vision scientists is on skin lesion segmentation. However, for

**Table 6.2  Samples Class Images from HAM10000 Dataset**

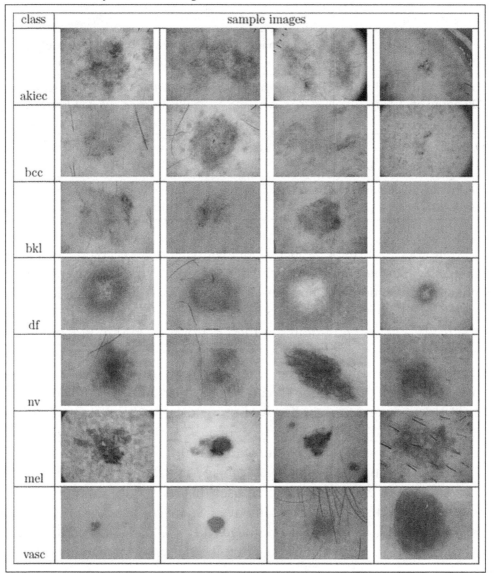

| class | sample images | | | |
|-------|---------------|---|---|---|
| akiec | | | | |
| bcc | | | | |
| bkl | | | | |
| df | | | | |
| nv | | | | |
| mel | | | | |
| vasc | | | | |

the purpose of this chapter, we concentrate on the skin lesion classification problem. Current approaches in skin lesion classification can be categorized in two ways as described in sub-sections 6.3.2.1 and 6.3.2.2.

## 6.3.2.1  Using Pre-Trained Model and Freezing Its Weights

In this approach, pre-trained weights of the feature extractor part of the CNN trained on another large dataset such as ImageNet 2014 Challenge are used.

**Table 6.3   Other Notable Skin Lesion Data Repositories**

| Dataset Name | Source Type | URL |
|---|---|---|
| MED-NODE (Giotis et al., 2015) | Digital image | http://www.cs.rug.nl/ imaging/ databases/melanoma naevi/ |
| Dermofit Image Library (Ballerini et al., 2013) | Biopsy-proven | https://licensing.edinburgh-innovations.ed.ac.uk/i/software/ dermo_t-image-library.html |
| Dermatology IS (Amelard et al., 2012) | Standard cameras | http://www.dermis.net |
| DermQuest (Amelard et al., 2012) | Standard cameras | https://www.derm101.com/ dermquest/ |

Classification is performed by incorporating an alternate classifier such as the K-nearest, support vector machines (SVMs) or ANNs. During training, weights of convolution layers in feature extractor part of the CNN are frozen. This means during training no updates to weights of convolution layers are made. End-to-end training is then performed on skin lesion images where the CNN relies on the feature extractor trained on natural images to identify useful features. The network learns features in the classification layer through back-propagation. It can be argued whether features from non-medical image datasets generalize well on medical image datasets. However, Menegola et al. (2017) justify models trained on non-medical image data that can be used on lesion images as the learnt features have sufficient quality for lesion classification. An obvious advantage of this approach is it takes less training time. One such work that uses this procedure is reported in Qi et al. (2017). They used a VGG16 (Simonyan & Zisserman, 2014) network for dense segmentation tasks on lesion images. Prior to using the pre-trained network trained on the ImageNet dataset, the network was modified by discarding the last two classification layers and replacing the remaining classification layers with randomly initialized convolution layers. The rest of the network layers remained unchanged.

Using pre-trained AlexNet on lesion images taken from a standard camera is investigated in the work of Pomponiu et al. (2016) where the researchers combined a k-nearest neighbor classifier using cosine distance metrics with AlexNet and trained on 399 images. Though not tested on an independent dataset, their algorithm obtained an accuracy of 93.64%. A similar approach using AlexNet is studied in the work of Codella et al. (2015) where they used an SVM as the classifier, incorporated low-level handcrafted features and features from sparse coding and a convolutional U-network (Ronneberger et al., 2015). A pre-trained AlexNet is also used in the work of Kawahara et al. (2016). They investigate whether the networks trained on natural images generalized well to multi-class *non-dermoscopy* skin lesion images. In addition to findings that the features learnt by AlexNet on natural images generalized well, their experiments on Dermofit Image Library (Ballerini et al., 2013) skin lesion images achieved an accuracy of 81.8%, outperforming previous results on the same dataset.

## 6.3.2.2 *End-to-End Training Using Pre-Trained Model Weights*

In this approach, CNN is trained end-to-end from scratch on the skin lesion dataset. This approach can be further adopted in two different ways.

First, a CNN network is trained from scratch for several iterations on the dermoscopy dataset. Li and Shen (2018) use this approach to propose two DL frameworks towards melanoma detection – Lesion Indexing Network (LIN) and Lesion Feature Network (LFN). Their experiments conducted on ISIC 2017 dataset show promising accuracies on melanoma, seborrheic keratosis and nevus detection tasks. Other works but not limited to the use this approach are reported in Refianti et al. (2019) where they use a LeNet5 CNN architecture (LeCun et al., 1998), in Vesal et al. (2018) who use a U-network for lesion segmentation tasks and in Nasr-Esfahani et al. (2016) who use a CNN trained from scratch on non-dermoscopy images taken by digital camera (Giotis et al., 2015).

Second, pre-trained weights of the feature extractor part of the CNN trained on another large dataset are used. However, instead of keeping the weights frozen (such as the weights of convolution layers in the feature extractor), the weights are fine-tuned during the training process to fit the new lesion image data. This technique is referred to as *transfer learning* and is useful in cases where datasets are small. Despite the availability of skin lesion datasets for research purposes, these datasets still suffer from limited samples. Hence, transfer learning is a common approach to mitigate this issue for lesion classification and segmentation tasks. In recent times, several works using transfer learning on skin lesion image datasets are reported. For example, Esteva et al. (2017) used Google's Inception V3 CNN architecture pre-trained on the 2014 ImageNet Challenge dataset to train on ISIC and Stanford Hospital dermoscopic images. They stripped the final classification layer of the Inception V3 network to match the number of classes in their dataset and performed end-to-end training. Overall, their dataset contained

129,450 clinical images consisting of 2,032 different diseases. They compared the classification results from their CNN model on two specific binary classification use cases, namely, keratinocyte carcinomas versus benign seborrheic keratoses; and malignant melanomas versus benign nevi with 21 board-certified dermatologists' assessments on the same use cases. Their results show CNN-based classification performed on par with all certified dermatologists, demonstrating competitive comparability. Recent research by Hosny et al. (2019) for classification of skin lesions applied transfer learning using AlexNet CNN in different ways. These included data augmentation with fixed and random rotation angles and replacing the classification layer with softmax to output probabilities for two or three classes of skin lesions.

Other popular CNN-based models used on skin lesion classification such as those used in the ISIC 2019 challenge include variants of EfficientNet (Tan & Le, 2019), DenseNet, GoogleNet, MobileNet and ResNet (ISIC-2019-LeaderBoard, 2019; Pacheco, 2019).

## 6.4 Transfer Learning on HAM10000 Dataset

In this section, we describe transfer learning using VGG16 CNN pre-trained on ImageNet 2014 dataset using the HAM10000 dataset from the ISIC archive. We use the approach described in Section 6.3.2.1 where we freeze the feature extraction part of the VGG16 network and replace the last classification layer with a softmax layer. Instead of training in a few classes, we train on all seven classes in the HAM10000 dataset. Hence, the new softmax layer predicts the probabilities of seven classes. Since the HAM10000 dataset is imbalanced, we use data augmentation to make samples in all classes equal. We describe the data augmentation method used to balance the samples across all classes. Algorithms and sample codes are provided for reproducibility and for readers to easily get started with research in this scope.

### 6.4.1 Pre-Processing HAM10000 Dataset

#### 6.4.1.1 Establishing Train and Test Sets

There are no test images present in the HAM10000 dataset. Since in ML (and in DL) it is important to evaluate the performance of models on unseen data (images in our case), we reserve 10% of images from every class for testing. This equates to a total of 1,002 images for testing. Table 6.1 shows the number of images reserved from each class for testing.

## 6.4.1.2 Data Augmentation

DL algorithms are data hungry, and CNNs are no exception. To learn discriminative features, a large dataset of training samples is needed. In addition, to avoid the model overfitting to any specific class, a balanced dataset is generally desired. Table 6.1 identifies the HAM10000 dataset to be grossly imbalanced. For example, class *NV* has 6,705 samples, whereas class *df* only has 115 samples. This imbalance will cause the model to be biased towards predicting test cases as *nv* more than *df*.

In order to balance the dataset, we use the *ImageDataGenerator* class in Python to applying augmentation. We used transformation techniques such as rotation, horizontal and vertical flips, translation, and zoom. The parameter values for the *ImageDataGenerator* class are described in Yu (2018). For the purpose of our study, we capped the number of images in each class to 6,000. The number of images in each class was boosted in this fashion except for class *nv* where we randomly removed 34 images to balance with other classes. All train images were saved in their respective class directories under a parent *train_dir* folder. No augmentation was applied on the test dataset. However, a similar folder structure was used where all test images were placed in their respective class directories. The algorithm to pre-process the HAM10000 dataset is given in Algorithm 1, most of which are translated in Python code (Yu, 2018).

## 6.4.2 VGG16 Model for HAM10000 Dataset

Proposed by Simonyan and Zisserman (2014), VGG16 is a popular CNN model used by researchers in the computer vision field for image classification and segmentation tasks. It was originally trained on the ImageNet dataset containing over 14 million images categorized into 1,000 classes. It achieved top-five test accuracy of 92.7% becoming the first runner-up in the ImageNet 2014 challenge classification task behind GoogLeNet. Several configurations of the VGG CNN exist, ranging from 11, 13, 16 and 19 weight layers. These configurations are labeled A-E and differ only in the depth. In our work, we use configuration D that contains 16 weight layers comprising of 13 convolutions and three hidden layers in the fully connected part of the network. All convolution layers are configured with $3 \times 3$ filter sizes. The network also uses max-pooling layers (Table 6.4).

**Table 6.4   VGG16 – Configuration D – CNN Architecture**

| VGG16 – Configuration D – 16 Weight Layers | | | |
|---|---|---|---|
| Input Image Size: 224 × 224 RGB Image | | | |
| *Layer* | *Layer Type* | *No. of Filters/Neurons* | *Filter/Pool Size* |
| 1 | Convolution | 64 | $3 \times 3$ |
| 2 | Convolution | 64 | $3 \times 3$ |
| | Max pool | | $2 \times 2$ |
| 3 | Convolution | 128 | $3 \times 3$ |
| 4 | Convolution | 128 | $3 \times 3$ |
| | Max pool | | $2 \times 2$ |
| 5 | Convolution | 256 | $3 \times 3$ |
| 6 | Convolution | 256 | $3 \times 3$ |
| 7 | Convolution | 256 | $3 \times 3$ |
| | Max pool | | $2 \times 2$ |
| 8 | Convolution | 512 | $3 \times 3$ |
| 9 | Convolution | 512 | $3 \times 3$ |
| 10 | Convolution | 512 | $3 \times 3$ |
| | Max pool | | $2 \times 2$ |
| 11 | Convolution | 512 | $3 \times 3$ |
| 12 | Convolution | 512 | $3 \times 3$ |
| 13 | Convolution | 512 | $3 \times 3$ |
| | Max pool | | $2 \times 2$ |
| 14 | Fully connected | 4,096 | |
| 15 | Fully connected | 4,096 | |
| 16 | Fully connected | 1,000 | |
| | softmax | | |

## Algorithm 1 Data Augmentation Algorithm.
## Translated to Python Code (Yu, 2018)

**Data**: HAM10000 images (jpg format), HAM10000_metadata.csv

**Result**:

train_dataset: 42000 images (6000 images in 7 classes) after augmentation, test_dataset: 10002 with no augmentation

Make train_dir folder and in it make directories for each class

Make val_dir folder and in it make directories for each class

Load HAM10000\_metadata.csv file

Set 'dx' column as class label - y

Split the metadata into training and test lists

Find the number of values in the train set (train-list) and test set (test-list)

**For** {each image name in train-list}

{

Transfer the actual train images into class directories in train_dir

}

**For** {each image name in test-list}

{

Transfer the actual test images into class directories in val_dir

}

Establish class-list = ['akiec', 'bcc', 'bkl', 'df', 'mel', 'vasc']

Set maximum number of images per class = 6000

**For** {each class in train_dir directory}

{

Define the ImageDataGenerator object

Determine the number of images already in class

Generate the remaining images using ImageDataGenerator object so that max images = 6000

}

## 6.4.3 Model Training

We perform end-to-end training of the VGG16 network on the HAM10000 dataset. As described in Section 6.3.2.1, weights of the feature extraction part of VGG16 are frozen from updates via the back-propagation operation, while the classifier layer weights would be updatable. The last layer in the classier is replaced with a new layer containing seven neurons to match the number of classes in the HAM10000 dataset. The model is trained for 20 epochs with a fixed learning rate of $10^{-4}$. Stochastic gradient descent and cross-entropy are used as learning and loss function, respectively. We use a weight decay of $10^{-4}$ and a momentum of 0.9. For training, we use a batch size of four and one for testing. We implement our models using PyTorch version 1.2.0 on a Dell Optiplex i5 48GB RAM computer with Cuda support using NVIDIA GeForce GTX 1050 Ti 4GB graphics card.

The HAM10000 dataset contains images of different sizes. Hence during training, all images are resized on-the-fly using PyTorch's *transforms* function. The images are resized to 224 × 224 using a center-crop technique which is the same as the sizes of the ImageNet dataset images. This enables us to use the VGG16 feature extractor part without any modifications. The RGB pixel values are also normalized to be in the range [0–255]. The images are read using helper functions *Imagefolder* from library *torchvision.dataset* and *Dataloader* from *torch.utils.data.datas*. Listing 1 describes a complete *Dataloader* function that loads the HAM10000 train and test dataset.

### Listing 1 PyTorch *DataLoader* Function

```
def LoadISIC_HAM10000():
# Python data loading code
traindir = 'data'+os.sep+'HAM10000'+os.sep+'base_dir'+os.sep+'train_dir'
valdir = 'data'+os.sep+'HAM10000'+os.sep+'base_dir'+os.sep+'val_dir'
train_transform = tv.transforms.Compose([
tv.transforms.Resize(225),
tv.transforms.CenterCrop(224),
tv.transforms.ToTensor()])
test_transform = tv.transforms.Compose([
tv.transforms.Resize(225),
tv.transforms.CenterCrop(224),
tv.transforms.ToTensor()])
trainset = torchvision.datasets.ImageFolder(root=traindir,
transform=train_transform)
trainloader = datas.DataLoader(trainset, batch_size=4, shuffle=True,
num_workers=4)
testset = torchvision.datasets.ImageFolder(root=valdir,
transform=test_transform)
testloader = data.DataLoader(testset, batch_size=1, shuffle=True,
num_workers=4)
return trainset, train loader, testset, test loader
```

## 6.5 Preliminary Results

Table 6.5 shows the train and test results of the VGG16 network on the HAM10000 dataset. The network uses the learnt features from natural images of the ImageNet dataset to extract features from skin lesion images. Only the weights of the classifier are updated during training. Also, we trial our experiments on all classes of the HAM10000 database. Since we have an imbalanced class distribution in our test dataset, we use micro-average precision, recall and f1 to analyze our results. The model achieves a high train accuracy of 97.9% and a loss of 0.068. The results indicate features from natural images are beneficial in extracting features from lesion images. These results are reinforced by the test accuracy of 78.2 on unseen lesion images. Given the analysis of the accuracy metric, we conclude features from natural images are worthwhile to investigate to extract features from lesion images. Although the effectiveness of the model can be measured by other metrics, we do note the precision, recall and F1-score are below 50%. In the case of precision, this indicates a high false-positive rate meaning fewer images were classified as their true class. In the case of a recall, the results indicate a high false-negative rate. F1-score is the harmonic mean of precision and recall, and is generally used for imbalanced classes such as in our case, hence obtaining the same results as precision and recall. The learning curves (for accuracy and loss) in Figure 6.5 also indicate smoother adaptability of natural image features on lesion images.

The confusion matrices for our experiment shown in Figure 6.6 further explain the reasons for the low F1-score. Considering the values in the leading diagonal (top left to bottom right), low accuracy is recorded on all classes except for class *nv* where accuracy is 66.0%. This is because class *nv* had the highest number of test images compared to the rest of the classes. Hence, accuracy on class *nv* is boosting the overall test accuracy. However,

**Table 6.5  Train and Test Statistics**

| *Metric* | *Train_statistics* | *Test_statistics* |
|---|---|---|
| Accuracy | 97.9% | 78.2% |
| Loss | 0.068 | |
| Precision | | 0.467 |
| Recall | | 0.467 |
| F1-score | | 0.467 |

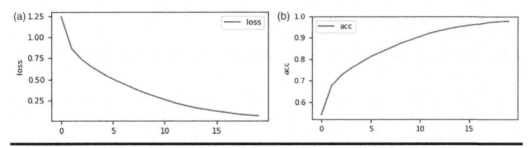

**Figure 6.5    Loss curve (a) and accuracy curve (b) generated during training (*epochs* = 20).**

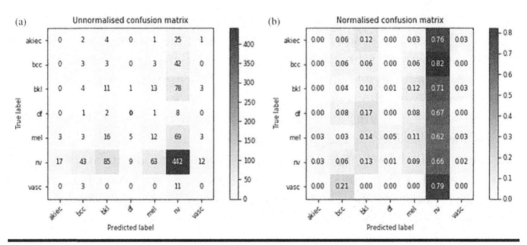

**Figure 6.6    Un-normalized (a) and normalized (b) confusion matrices generated on test data.**

the confusion matrix accurately shows the prediction on other classes needs improvement. One-way prediction accuracy of other classes can be improved by obtaining more real images of lesion classes where the sample size is low in order to obtain a balanced dataset. However, the challenge is finding patients who have those specific conditions. Data augmentation is an alternate method to boost the number of samples. Since the augmented images are copies of the same original images, the variability in the samples remains small. Hence, the model is not able to get enough different images of a class to be able to learn to distinguish it from other classes. Instead of applying standard transformation on the available images to generate augmented images, techniques such as image overlaying, blending and masking can be used as alternate data augmentation methods. This, however, requires further investigation and to be validated through experiments.

## 6.6 Deployment on Smart Phones

Technologies to train DL models have improved tremendously over the last decade such as high-end GPU cards with thousands of floating-point processing cores and DL libraries such as TensorFlow, PyTorch and Keras. There are also several types of devices that make use of DL models in the form of AI models. Examples, where AI models are embedded in hardware, include self-driving cars, AI-based autopilot systems in flight simulators, Apple's iPhone X Face ID, and fault detection AI systems on assembly lines in factories using cameras such as in-car and food manufacturing. Uber's ridesharing app, Google Maps route planning and traffic jam plots, Google Translate and Apple's Animoji, and personal digital assistants such as Cortana, Siri and Google Assistant are few examples of software-based AI applications.

Deploying AI-based systems to improve people's health and well-being is attracting a lot of attention in the research community. For example, a system developed by scientists in CSIRO Lab, Australia, helps patients with diabetic retinopathy receive treatment faster. It works by taking high-resolution images of their eyes and analyzing them by the technology for signs of diabetic retinopathy. Similarly in the area of automatic skin lesion analysis, commercial applications such as *SpotMole* (Munteanu & Cooclea, 2009), *MelApp* (Corporation, 2011), *SkinScan* (SkinVision, 2019), *VisualDX* and *SPF* have emerged, some of which are studied in the work of (Brewer et al., 2013).

Making health- and well-being-specific DL models accessible to the public in the form of applications is a challenge. This is usually due to a huge number of parameters in the DL model causing the trained model size to be extremely large to be deployed on devices with less storage and memory capacity. There are two common ways that are currently being deployed. First, the trained models are hosted on the Cloud such as on Google, Amazon or Microsoft. Using web apps images can then be uploaded to the cloud to get predictions. Alternatively, a light version of the web app can be hosted on mobile phones. Using in-built cameras, images can be taken and uploaded to the Cloud to get predictions (Figure 6.7). A problem with this approach is the latency associated with sending information back and forth from the mobile phone and the Cloud. Second, advancements in internal storage capability, processor speed and memory in modern mobile devices provide a motivation to host DL models on the device itself. In this way, model predictions can be done locally to obtain quicker results. In order to provide a platform to support pre-trained DL models on mobile phones,

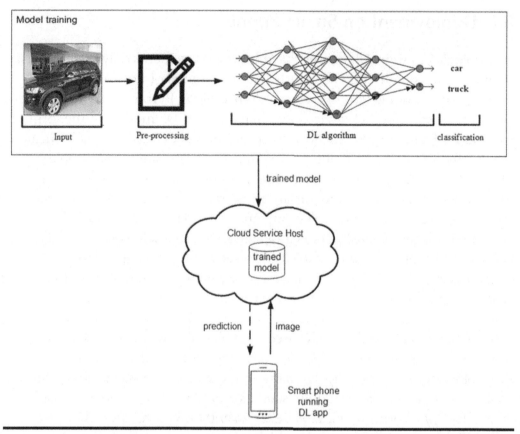

**Figure 6.7   The model architecture of deploying DL trained models on the cloud and access via mobile phones.**

special mobile ML APIs have been developed such as *CoreML, TensorFlow Lite* and *Caffe2* for iOS and Android.

## 6.7  Conclusion and Future Directions

This chapter presents an insight into applications of AI algorithms from DL in the classification of skin lesion images. DL is a large neural network that uses multiple layers in its architecture to automatically extract features from raw data. The major advantage of DL is the ability to process large datasets and extract features automatically, hence eliminating the need to manually extract features for learning. For example, a class of DL called CNN uses lower layers to extract features such as lines and curves, whereas higher-level features may identify shapes relevant to the dataset such as actual digits, faces or natural objects. As such CNNs are widely used in image and video processing.

In recent times, several medical imaging datasets are now publicly available such as the HAM10000 skin lesion images studied in this chapter. These datasets provide unique opportunities to researchers to apply DL algorithms to extract patterns and insights and deploy them as applications for early detection or diagnosis of certain conditions.

In this chapter, we investigate the application of DL algorithms on image-based medical datasets particularly on skin cancer images. We describe publicly available ISIC HAM10000 dataset that is widely used to train DL models. The dataset contains a rich collection of 10,015 dermato-scopic images divided into seven cancer classes. We further demonstrate how CNN-based VGG16 network can be applied to this dataset using transfer learning. In our approach, we first describe a simple data augmentation method to overcome the limitation of an imbalanced number of samples in each class in the HAM10000 dataset. Then, we train the VGG16 network using weights pre-trained on the ImageNet dataset. The last layer of the VGG16 network is replaced to match the number of classes in the HAM10000 dataset. We freeze the weights of the feature extraction part of the VGG16 network but fine-tune the classifier weights during training.

Our results show transfer learning is an effective way to train DL models on skin lesion images and that features from natural images can be used to identify features from skin lesion images. Using this method, we obtain a training accuracy of 97.9% and a test accuracy of 78.2%. Here, our main goal was to demonstrate the promise of DL in the classification of lesion images. In order to make DL models useful to patients, we describe a method where models trained on skin lesion images (such as on the HAM10000 dataset) can be effectively deployed as apps on smartphones. Using built-in cameras patients can use the app to take images of skin lesions or moles to get predictions and take proactive steps. Such systems will prove beneficial particularly in situations where there is a limited access to qualified dermatologists such as in remote areas.

Several challenges remain to be investigated. First, the HAM10000 dataset contains drastically imbalanced samples in each class. Using data augmentation, we can boost the number of samples. However, the variability in the samples remains small as most of the images are copies of the same original images. This perhaps causes the model to overfit the class. It is evident in the confusion matrix results where poor classification performances are shown in classes where augmented samples are large. Therefore, how much data augmentation to apply remains an interesting research question. Second, different data augmentation techniques may also play an important role in improving the classification accuracies of the DL models. This requires investigation into finding optimal parameters for the transformations in the data augmentation function. Third, unlike in natural images where we usually find less variation in the orientation of the objects, skin lesion images, on the other hand, have no defined orientation, hence leading to the problem of spatial invariance that must be learnt by the DL model on skin lesion images. Finally, there is still research that needs to be done in order to explain how DL address ABCDE characteristics that are used to assess lesion images in order to diagnose them as benign or malignant.

# References

Adelson, E. H., Anderson, C. H., Bergen, J. R., Burt, P. J., & Ogden, J. M. (1984). Pyramid methods in image processing. *RCA Engineer, 29*(6), 33–41.

Agarwal, S., Pandey, G. N., & Tiwari, M. D. (2012). Data mining in education: data classification and decision tree approach. *International Journal of e-Education, e-Business, e-Management and e-Learning, 2*(2), 140–140.

Amelard, R., Wong, A., & Clausi, D. A. (2012). *Extracting morphological high-level intuitive features (HLIF) for enhancing skin lesion classification.* Paper presented at the 2012 Annual International Conference of the IEEE Engineering in Medicine and Biology Society.

American Cancer Society. (2019). Cancer facts and figures 2019. Retrieved from https://www.cancer.org/research/cancer-facts-statistics/all-cancer-facts-figures/cancer-facts-figures-2019.html.

Argenziano, G., Fabbrocini, G., Carli, P., De Giorgi, V., Sammarco, E., & Delfino, M. (1998). Epiluminescence microscopy for the diagnosis of doubtful melanocytic skin lesions: comparison of the ABCD rule of dermatoscopy and a new 7-point checklist based on pattern analysis. *Archives of Dermatology, 134*(12), 1563–1570.

Ballerini, L., Fisher, R. B., Aldridge, B., & Rees, J. (2013). A color and texture based hierarchical K-NN approach to the classification of non-melanoma skin lesions. In Celebi, M. E., & Schaefer, G. (eds.), *Color Medical Image Analysis* (pp. 63–86): Springer, Dordrecht.

Brewer, A. C., Endly, D. C., Henley, J., Amir, M., Sampson, B. P., Moreau, J. F., & Dellavalle, R. P. (2013). Mobile applications in dermatology. *JAMA Dermatology, 149*(11), 1300–1304.

Brinker, T. J., Hekler, A., Utikal, J. S., Grabe, N., Schadendorf, D., Klode, J., … von Kalle, C. (2018). Skin cancer classification using convolutional neural networks: systematic review. *Journal of Medical Internet Research, 20*(10), e11936–e11936.

Codella, N., Cai, J., Abedini, M., Garnavi, R., Halpern, A., & Smith, J. R. (2015). *Deep learning, sparse coding, and SVM for melanoma recognition in dermoscopy images*. Paper presented at the International Workshop on Machine Learning in Medical Imaging.

Corporation, H. D. (2011). MelApp. Retrieved from https://www.healthdiscovery-corp.com/.

Esteva, A., Kuprel, B., Novoa, R. A., Ko, J., Swetter, S. M., Blau, H. M., & Thrun, S. (2017). Dermatologist-level classification of skin cancer with deep neural networks. *Nature, 542*(7639), 115–115.

Giotis, I., Molders, N., Land, S., Biehl, M., Jonkman, M. F., & Petkov, N. (2015). MED-NODE: a computer-assisted melanoma diagnosis system using non-dermoscopic images. *Expert Systems with Applications, 42*(19), 6578–6585.

Glorot, X., Bordes, A., & Bengio, Y. (2011). *Deep sparse rectifier neural networks*. Paper presented at the Proceedings of the Fourteenth International Conference on Artificial Intelligence and Statistics.

Hosny, K. M., Kassem, M. A., & Foaud, M. M. (2019). Classification of skin lesions using transfer learning and augmentation with Alex-net. *PLoS One, 14*(5), e0217293–e0217293.

Hubel, D. H., & Wiesel, T. N. (1959). Receptive fields of single neurons in the cat's striate cortex. *The Journal of Physiology, 148*, 574–591.

Hubel, D. H., & Wiesel, T. N. (1968). Receptive fields and functional architecture of monkey striate cortex. *The Journal of Physiology, 195*, 215–243.

ISIC-2019-LeaderBoard. (2019). ISIC 2019 Leaderboard. Retrieved from https://challenge2019.isic-archive.com/leaderboard.html.

Kawahara, J., BenTaieb, A., & Hamarneh, G. (2016). *Deep features to classify skin lesions*. Paper presented at the 2016 IEEE 13th International Symposium on Biomedical Imaging (ISBI).

Kumar, D., & Sharma, D. (2019). Deep learning in gene expression modeling. In Balas, V., Roy, S., Sharma, D., Samui, P. (eds.), *Handbook of Deep Learning Applications* (pp. 363–383): Springer, Cham.

LeCun, Y., Bengio, Y., & Hinton, G. (2015). Deep learning. *Nature, 521*(7553), 436–444.

LeCun, Y., Bottou, L., Bengio, Y., & Haffner, P. (1998). Gradient-based learning applied to document recognition. *Proceedings of the IEEE, 86*(11), 2278–2324.

Li, Y., & Ma, W. (2010). *Applications of artificial neural networks in financial economics: a survey*. Paper presented at the 2010 International Symposium on Computational Intelligence and Design.

Li, Y., & Shen, L. (2018). Skin lesion analysis towards melanoma detection using deep learning network. *Sensors, 18*(2), 556–556.

Menegola, A., Fornaciali, M., Pires, R., Bittencourt, F. V., Avila, S., & Valle, E. (2017). *Knowledge transfer for melanoma screening with deep learning*. Paper presented at the 2017 IEEE 14th International Symposium on Biomedical Imaging (ISBI 2017).

Mirunalini, P., Chandrabose, A., Gokul, V., & Jaisakthi, S. M. (2017). Deep learning for skin lesion classification. *arXiv preprint arXiv:1703.04364*.

Munteanu, C., & Cooclea, S. (2009). Spotmole – melanoma control system. Retrieved from https://play.google.com/store/apps/details?id=com. spotmole&hl=en_AU.

Nachbar, F., Stolz, W., Merkle, T., Cognetta, A. B., Vogt, T., Landthaler, M., … Plewig, G. (1994). The ABCD rule of dermatoscopy: high prospective value in the diagnosis of doubtful melanocytic skin lesions. *Journal of the American Academy of Dermatology, 30*(4), 551–559.

Nasr-Esfahani, E., Samavi, S., Karimi, N., Soroushmehr, S. M. R., Jafari, M. H., Ward, K., & Najarian, K. (2016). *Melanoma detection by analysis of clinical images using convolutional neural network.* Paper presented at the 2016 38th Annual International Conference of the IEEE Engineering in Medicine and Biology Society (EMBC).

Pacheco, A. G., Ali, A.-R., & Trappenberg, T. (2019). Skin cancer detection based on deep learning and entropy to detect outlier samples. *arXiv preprint arXiv:1909.04525.*

Pomponiu, V., Nejati, H., & Cheung, N. M. (2016, 2016). *Deepmole: deep neural networks for skin mole lesion classification.* Paper presented at the 2016 IEEE International Conference on Image Processing (ICIP).

Qi, J., Le, M., Li, C., & Zhou, P. (2017). Global and local information based deep network for skin lesion segmentation. *arXiv preprint arXiv:1703.05467.*

Refianti, R., Mutiara, A. B., & Priyandini, R. P. (2019). Classification of melanoma skin cancer using convolutional neural network. *IJACSA, 10*(3), 409–417.

Riesenhuber, M., & Poggio, T. (1999). Hierarchical models of object recognition in cortex. *Nature Neuroscience, 2,* 1019–1025.

Ronneberger, O., Fischer, P., & Brox, T. (2015). *U-net: convolutional networks for biomedical image segmentation.* Paper presented at the International Conference on Medical image computing and computer-assisted intervention.

Simonyan, K., & Zisserman, A. (2014). Very deep convolutional networks for large-scale image recognition. *arXiv preprint arXiv:1409.1556.*

SkinVision. (2019). Skin scan. Retrieved from https://www.skinvision. com/?locale=en.

Sourla, E., Sioutas, S., Syrimpeis, V., Tsakalidis, A., & Tzimas, G. (2012). CardioSmart365: artificial intelligence in the service of cardiologic patients. *Advances in Artificial Intelligence, 2012,* 2–2.

Tan, M., & Le, Q. V. (2019). EfficientNet: rethinking model scaling for convolutional neural networks. *arXiv preprint arXiv:1905.11946.*

Tschandl, P., Rosendahl, C., & Kittler, H. (2018). The HAM10000 dataset, a large collection of multi-source dermatoscopic images of common pigmented skin lesions. *Scientific Data, 5,* 180161–180161.

Vesal, S., Ravikumar, N., & Maier, A. (2018). SkinNet: a deep learning framework for skin lesion segmentation. *arXiv preprint arXiv:1806.09522.*

Xie, H., Shi, J., Lu, W., & Cui, W. (2016). *Dynamic Bayesian networks in electronic equipment health diagnosis.* Paper presented at the 2016 Prognostics and System Health Management Conference (PHM-Chengdu).

Xu, Y., Xiao, T., Zhang, J., Yang, K., & Zhang, Z. (2014). Scale-invariant convolutional neural networks. *CoRR, abs/1411.6369*. Retrieved from http://arxiv.org/abs/1411.6369.

Yu, A. (2018). Skin-lesion-classifier. Retrieved from https://github.com/uyxela/Skin-Lesion-Classifier.

Zheng, Y., Huang, J., Chen, T., Ou, Y., & Zhou, W. (2018). *Processing global and local features in convolutional neural network (CNN) and primate visual systems*. Paper presented at the Mobile Multimedia/Image Processing, Security, and Applications 2018.

*Chapter 7*

# A Simple and Replicable Framework for the Implementation of Clinical Data Science

## Juan Luis Cruz
*Puerta de Hierro University Hospital*
*Universidad Politécnica de Madrid*

## Mariano Provencio
*Puerta de Hierro University Hospital*
*Universidad Autónoma de Madrid*

## Ernestina Menasalvas
*Universidad Politécnica de Madrid*

## Contents

# 7.1 Background/Introduction

A large amount of clinical data generated in the hospital environment allows us to imagine the possibilities that their analysis would offer. Different technologies such as Big Data, Data Science (DS), machine learning (ML) or artificial intelligence (AI) can be applied in order to improve prevention and early detection, diagnosis, treatment and monitoring, research and management in multiple pathologies of high incidence and high human and economic cost. Although these technologies promise to revolutionize medicine as we know it, the reality that we can currently observe in the hospitals of the Spanish National Health System (SNS) shows us that we are not yet able to implement these technologies in an effective and broad way. There are different reasons why their real implementation in the hospital environment is still scarce, among which are organizational reasons and availability of resources, the highly fragmented map of information systems at hospitals and therefore of clinical data, problems of governance and related to the very nature of clinical data and the need to guarantee the protection of personal data. However, despite the importance of all these issues, we consider that the key problem is the lack of a framework, understood as a set of concepts, procedures and tools, which facilitates the availability of adequate data and the multidisciplinary analysis of clinically relevant problems. Without having this framework implemented in the hospital, the different techniques and algorithms (from linear regressions to deep learning) lack practical utility.

On the other hand, cancer continues to be a major health and economic problem. Specifically, lung cancer causes the most deaths and causes the greatest economic impact. Patients undergo acute and chronic care phases in many cases, participating in a complex care process that necessarily involves the intervention of different professionals in different care settings, which causes communication and coordination issues among the different professionals involved, and a high fragmentation of the data generated in each of the health interventions performed on the patient. The possibility of predicting, for an individual patient, aspects such as the efficacy of the treatment and the probability of response or progression, the toxicity experienced by the patient, the possibility of a relapse in the disease, progression-free and overall survival, or consumption of healthcare resources is key to the management of cancer patients. In this context, new healthcare paradigms such as Personalized and Precision Medicine or Value-Based Healthcare (VBHC) offer the hope of better results for patients and greater efficiency for the healthcare system. However, they rely heavily on the data and their analysis.

Thus, in this chapter, we consider answering the following question: how could we effectively apply these data analysis technologies to obtain new knowledge of clinical and managerial interest, and to enable paradigms such as Personalized and Precision Medicine and Value-Based Medicine, with the ultimate goal of improving health outcomes in oncology? A full discussion on this topic can be found in the doctoral thesis work of the main author (Cruz-Bermúdez, 2019) and in its associated publications (Cruz-Bermúdez et al., 2019a, 2019b).

## 7.1.1 What Is the Problem with Clinical Data Analysis in Oncology?

First, it is necessary to establish an operational definition of the concept of clinical data analysis (CDA). Thus, we define it as the detailed study of data related to the physical condition and health of people in order to acquire or improve their knowledge.

Among the different possible applications of CDA in oncology, we will focus on these two:

■ Prediction and planning of healthcare resources needed through the analysis of previously collected data on healthcare activity (USAID, 2019).
■ Description of healthcare provided to patients based on their clinical characteristics, and characterization of its cost, to inform clinical and management decisions (Skinner et al., 2018; Reeve et al., 2018; Knust et al., 2017).

## 7.1.1.1 Lack of a Framework in the Hospital Setting

CDA is a habitual activity in the hospitals of the SNS, consubstantial with their triple assistance, research and teaching mission. However, the analysis of clinical data lacks a framework that facilitates its implementation and reproducibility in the hospital setting, establishing a set of concepts, and architecture of functions and data, and a method for performing CDA in a systematic way. On the contrary, we identify the following characteristics of CDA performed in our hospitals today:

■ **Local scope**: An analysis is typically limited to a departmental environment (medical, surgical or central service) and even to a specific pathology, which usually causes clinical professionals to deal with the problem individually, or at least not benefits from learning in the subject that has been obtained in other departments. Additionally, this generally prevents shared analysis between different departments involved in patient care that could provide a broader view centred on the patient, as well as the performance of multicentre analysis that increases the volume of data analysed.

■ **Low level of methodology documentation**: Although the results are usually published in scientific journals or in conference communications, the methodological and technical aspects, especially with regard to obtaining and processing the data, are usually simplified for the benefit of the description of the results obtained and their implications (which is logical, since they have a greater clinical interest, at least in the short term). This again causes that the knowledge generated in the process is not fully available to other professionals who consider performing CDA in their respective fields.

■ **Avoidable efforts**: The realization of data analysis projects implies an important effort, especially in the initial phases of obtaining and preparing data, which is typically approached as a complementary activity to the clinical activity of hospital professionals. The lack of a framework implies a sub-optimal project development that increases the efforts to be made every time, thus leading to a waste of valuable clinician time.

■ **Difficulty in applying data-based innovation in the clinical environment**: Beyond conducting observational clinical studies or clinical trials, whose performance is well dominated by clinical professionals, other innovative applications of CDA that require multidisciplinary teams tend not to contemplate the problem as a whole, facing additional difficulties that may end in failure. Thus, it is typical to find initiatives aimed at supporting decision-making (e.g., detection of patients at risk of sepsis) that do not focus the necessary efforts on having quality structured clinical data or on the appropriate integration with the clinical workstation.

■ **Lack of participation of other professional profiles**: The dynamics established in CDA usually involve the participation of the physician generating the hypothesis and manually obtaining the data and the statistician doing all the data analysis alone, with a low level of interaction between the two, in a client–provider model. The massive integration of data and the application of DS, ML or AI techniques will require the incorporation of other profiles (such as computer engineers). Again, having a framework such as the one indicated could facilitate their incorporation into these projects.

## 7.1.1.2 Nature and Governance of Oncological Clinical Data

The different phases in the cancer care process generate clinical data that can be analysed. Regardless of the time of its generation, clinical oncological data share a number of characteristics, which we list here based on international references in this area such as ICHOM (International Consortium for Health Outcomes Measurement, 2017) or the recent report prepared for EPFIA (European Federation of Pharmaceutical Industries and Associations) (Montouchet et al., 2018). Thus, the following are common characteristics of oncological clinical data:

■ They are associated with different clinical entities:
 – Patient: demographic data (including date of birth, sex or race), habits (especially smoking and alcohol consumption), clinical data associated with the patient (weight, comorbidities, personal and family history, data collected on physical examination, results of complementary tests, including analytical and imaging tests, health status of the patient and functional capacity), data related to the care activity carried out with the patient (external consultations, administered outpatient treatments, complementary tests, emergency care, hospital admissions, surgical interventions), genetic sequencing data and data related to patient's death.

- Tumour: diagnosis date, histology, stage, evaluation of the response to treatment, genetic mutations (driver mutations) and genetic sequencing of the tumour (both from tissue and liquid biopsy).
- Treatment: types of treatment applied, dates of treatments, complications and adverse effects of treatments, and cost of treatments.

■ They present temporary variations, and it is usual that their registration happens at different moments of clinical interest that are not always pre-specified by a protocol:
- At the initial moment, at diagnosis (baseline).
- In each of the care contacts (clinical events or episodes) of the patient.
- In the beginning, end or during events of interest of each applied treatment (treatment lines). For example, in the face of adverse effects.
- During patient follow-up (survival phase).
- In the last days of the patient's life (end-of-life) and after his or her death.

■ They are recorded both in a structured way (categorical or continuous data) and unstructured, that is, as text written in natural language (free text):
- As a free text, in the clinical notes and reports written by the doctors and nurses in the different care contacts (outpatient consultations and treatments, emergencies, inpatient admissions).
- As structured data, in automated records (appointments, inpatient admissions, analytical tests, genetic sequencing data) or in manual records through forms containing the variables to be recorded and their possible values.

■ They are registered by different professionals (doctors of different specialties, nurses, pharmacists, geneticists, etc.) in different services, units and care settings (hospital, primary care) which generates data dispersion in multiple information systems, often not integrated.

■ They present different problems related to the lack of adequate data governance, such as the following:
- Lack of standardization and the absence of shared standards. The same variables, even when registered in a categorical way, contain different values depending on the centre, service or unit and even the person making the registration. This lack of normalization has its origin in the absence of commonly used cancer data standards and in the lack of coordination between countries and regions in this

area (Montouchet et al., 2018) and generates significant problems for the integration of data from different centres for joint analysis and for effective interoperability, which would allow the implementation of work processes between centres.

– The disparity of criteria (definitions). Even beyond the lack of normalization, the absence of common data dictionaries implies the appearance of different interpretations about the content of variables, according to the different interpretations of the concept that they intend to represent (e.g., is the date of diagnosis the date on which the first visit in oncology is carried out after the availability of the pathology report? Is it the date of completion of the pathology report? Is it the date of obtaining the sample that allows the report to be made?).

– Difficulty in establishing responsibilities regarding the registration and updating of data. Although the data recorded in the electronic medical record (EMR) have clear authorship (that of the user authenticated in the EMR system) and a protocolized collection dynamics (typically coinciding with clinical acts, such as first visits or follow-up visits), the basis of clinical and research data that typically complement EMR information and that are often implemented through office tools, lack proper regulation in both aspects. Clinical and research databases (RDBs) constitute up to 75% of existing cancer data records (Montouchet et al., 2018), being usually filled in by different professionals at different time points. Their fulfilment depends in many cases on the workloads and individual will of each professional when registering clinical data of interest for the future, non-care uses, often not specified a priori by the protocol of a specific study.

– Low data quality. The above aspects have a significant impact on the quality of the recorded data, from both semantic and formal points of view. This materializes in an incorrect organization of the data (variables in columns, observations in rows and tables that represent a single concept, or, in other words, databases that do not meet the third normal form of Codd (1990)) as in variables with lost data, with equivalent values recorded differently or with extreme values derived from collection errors (Wickham, 2014). These quality problems have a substantial impact on the development of projects based on the analysis of the data since it has been estimated that 80% of the effort required in them is devoted to data cleaning (Dasu & Johnson, 2003).

In addition to these key problems, there are other circumstances that greatly complicate the analysis of oncological clinical data in hospitals, in particular, the lack of an organizational structure dedicated to these issues, the highly fragmented map of information systems at hospitals and therefore of clinical data, and the growing threats to cybersecurity and personal data protection, while a new regulatory framework (GDPR) is still being implemented in the EU.

## 7.2 Methods

We propose a five-phase methodology designed ad hoc to achieve our objectives, which is described next (Figure 7.1).

### 7.2.1 Selection of a Concrete and Relevant Clinical Problem

One of the first decisions to be taken is to propose the development of the framework in a specific clinical setting, with the intention that the results be subsequently generalized to other clinical problems. This would allow us to deepen enough to demonstrate a clinical and managerial utility of the results that validate the framework, without sacrificing in return the generalization capacity of the framework. For this, it is necessary to select a specific pathology with the following criteria:

- High-complexity and multidisciplinary treatment, so that it can benefit especially from the intensive application of CDA and new healthcare paradigms such as Precision Medicine and VBHC.
- High social impact, from both health and economic points of view.
- Availability of structured clinical data.
- Clinical leadership and availability to participate in the development, implementation and application of the framework.

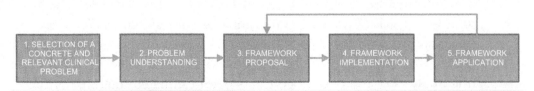

**Figure 7.1    Phases of the methodology applied for the definition, implementation and application of the framework for the analysis of oncological clinical data.**

## 7.2.2 Problem Understanding

Although it may seem obvious, a proper detailed understanding of the local problem is an essential step towards achieving the objective. And yet, one of the main causes of the lack of adoption of innovative solutions in the healthcare field is the lack of connection between the different actors involved in the development of digital solutions, especially between users (healthcare professionals) and developers (Rudin et al., 2016). One of the main barriers in this regard is the lack of organizational structures that enable this approach. Having the real situation of the data, their processes of governance and the technology that supports them is key to developing a framework with real possibilities of implementation, which maximizes the probability of offering results of clinical utility.

## 7.2.3 Framework Proposal

As we stated at the beginning, we consider that it is necessary to have a framework, defined as a set of concepts, procedures and tools, which facilitates the availability of adequate data and the multidisciplinary analysis of relevant clinical problems.

Among the desired characteristics for the framework, we identify the following:

- **Feasible**: The framework should be implemented with reasonable effort, taking into account the lack of IT resources usually found in the SNS.
- **Useful**: The application of the framework must serve to obtain results that also provide added value for clinical professionals and for decision-making in the healthcare field. The measure of utility will be obtained through the following mechanisms:
  - The opinion of the clinical professionals themselves, both those involved in the work and those to whom different dissemination actions are directed during the development of the work.
  - Publication of the concrete results obtained that validate the approach made, both through specialized conferences and in peer-reviewed scientific journals.
- **Replicable**: The framework should be general enough so that it can be applied to other pathologies and medical specialties in other centres with minimal modifications that do not distort the global approach.

- **Open**: The framework must allow different technologies to be accommodated, regardless of their manufacturer, thus facilitating its application in different centres.
- **Inclusive**: In order to achieve the objectives set out, it is essential to address multiple tasks in different fields, which necessarily requires multidisciplinary collaboration between IT staff and clinical staff.

## 7.2.4 Framework Implementation

Since the framework we propose would require actions in our hospital (Puerta de Hierro University Hospital, HUPHM), it is essential to have the authorization and resources of the hospital management. Thus, for the implementation, we will need not only the IT department for the technical implementation but also the support from the successive Managing Directors of the HUPHM and from the Head of the Medical Oncology Department. For the development of some functions, such as those related to the EMR, it is also necessary to involve the Clinical Records and Clinical Documentation Commission in the HUPHM.

## 7.2.5 Framework Application

The application of the framework to a pathology, and to a specific clinical problem within this pathology, allows us to obtain and evaluate its results, both internally and especially externally. This application, in addition to specific results, would allow us to validate the framework as long as the results obtained are novel and have a clinical and management interest.

To carry out the application of the framework, it is necessary to have the approval of the Ethical Committee for Research on Medicines of the HUPHM for the secondary use of data from healthcare. The framework's ability to generalize to other problems and pathologies and, in other national and international hospitals, should be demonstrated in the future. However, the validity in the HUPHM may be a valid indicator of its possible validity in other centres, given that the HUPHM has a relatively modern system map (implemented for its opening in 2008, which implies that it is relatively young in the hospital standard) and was recognized in 2013 with the stage 6 in the EMRAM EMR maturity model, defined by the Healthcare Information and Management Systems Society (HIMSS). Thus, since the HUPHM had the EMRAM stage 6 during the development of this work, it can be considered that it had a high level of computerization that is homogeneous with the rest of hospitals worldwide that follow this maturity model (in 2015, a 17.9% of the 5,467 hospitals that had been evaluated worldwide with the EMRAM standard had a stage 6, that is, 979 hospitals) (Hoyt, 2015).

## 7.3 Results

In accordance with the established criteria, we chose lung cancer as the pathology to study for the development of our framework. We did a detailed study of the local problem existing in the HUPHM with regard to CDA in lung cancer, and thus, it provided us with the following findings:

1. The registration process of healthcare data in the EMR is separated from the process of data registration for the research and care improving purpose, thus duplicating the registration work, inducing differences in interpretation and errors.
2. Beyond the EMR, there is no structured, unique and updated registry that contains a unique reference for each patient belonging to the oncology service for purposes of care improvement or research. There is a database of new patients (first consultations) of manual completion, fragmented into different databases over time, and not always updated in a timely manner. Nor is there a structured longitudinal register with the clinical follow-up information of the patients.
3. Activity data are available in those healthcare areas that are organized by the EMR (appointments in external consultations, inpatient admissions, day hospital, emergency department attendances, tests and interconsultations requested). In the areas in which the activity is coded (as in hospitalization through the mandatory minimum data set defined by the Spanish Ministry of Health, called CMBD), there are also clinical data associated with that activity. In the rest of the areas, only clinical data are available in the EMR (usually in free text), and in many cases, it is difficult to get activity data (e.g., cancer patients seen in the emergency department can be counted only through the interconsultations from ED to the Medical Oncology Department that are registered in the EMR).
4. The unstructured records of the EMR (in free text) require very intensive manual work to obtain the variables of interest and thus feed the RDBs.
5. There is no standard coding of structured values, nor a clear, written and shared definition by all users who enter data into the databases.

This affects the quality of the data and the possibilities to interoperate (integrate) with other records.

6. RDBs are created with specific objectives and therefore with specific data models for their purposes. However, they contain general patient data and specific variables that may be duplicated (and thus being inconsistent) between different RDBs. These RDBs do not have a unified reference that brings together a minimum set of oncological data (demographic and clinical).

7. We identify two main types of RDBs:
   - RDBs created ad hoc for a specific research project. They are typically created after the definition of the project (hypothesis definition leads to necessary variables). They should contain a specific set of variables that were not available in other databases, but this is not always the case.
   - RDBs contain care records that group patients with specific criteria for selection (patient cohorts), but without a closed definition a priori of the information that will be required for further research. They are created by the impossibility of locating these patients in the EMR by other means other than registering all the cases that meet criteria in a specific database. Sometimes, they are made with a core purpose, but can be used for further research (secondary use of information), serving as a list of patients to study (subsequently obtaining informed consent for this and also new variables once the research project has been fully determined).
   - In both cases, the absence of common definitions of data and standardized values, of clear responsibilities regarding the creation and maintenance of subsequent data, together with a non-technical design, makes the data quality low in most cases. This requires additional efforts preparing data when it is decided to finally conduct an investigation.

8. In most cases, having a sufficiently structured patient database (a case register) would avoid the need to prepare different care records by pathology. When an investigation had to be conducted, a case registry query would be done and those patients that met criteria would be selected. From there, new specific information fields could be added for the desired investigation.

9. Although the function of the case registry could be assumed by the hospital's EMR system, the reality is that the existing system (in the HUPHM and in many other Spanish hospitals, being also very similar

to other national and international solutions) does not have the facilities for the autonomous management of the variables to be collected and for the exploitation of data that this unified case register would require. Although it can be proposed as a future possibility, it is necessary to propose a short-term alternative that allows progress in this area.

10. Although there are a large number of form templates in our EMR (846), up to 60% of them have been completed less than ten times. It is significant how variations are observed in different historical periods (with different management teams governing the hospital). Analysing the volume of records made perform template, it was observed how only four forms accumulated 73% of the total structured records of the EMR. These data suggest the low effective volume of clinical data that are structured in the EMR by the users themselves, beyond the data that is generated in a structured way in an automatic or semi-automatic way and of those that are captured as an essential part of a process of established work. In order to obtain better results in the structuring of the data by the users in the EMR, it is necessary that the users are willing to do so, either because they obtain a return of the additional effort that it entails against an unstructured registry, or because the structuring of data is an essential part of a work process established and enforced by the management team. In any case, the first option will always be the desirable one, since the second one can lead to situations of discontent and even burnout (Friedberg et al., 2013).

11. Regarding the volume of data, we observe that the number of patients of a specific pathology such as lung cancer, in a single centre, may not have sufficient volume to perform CDA using ML techniques, especially in case of selecting specific subpopulations. However, the large number of related entities (consultations, treatments, admissions, emergencies, etc.) and of variables that describe each of them over time (date of realization, performer, active principle, dose, discharge date, diagnosis date, etc.) does allow to have a high dimensionality and therefore a high volume of data for the application of advanced analysis techniques. In any case, the integration of information from different centres is essential for these technologies to offer their full potential.

12. Regarding the variety of data, another characteristic usually evaluated in the field of Big Data and DS, we observe that we mainly deal with clinical data collected as text or image. However, we can integrate other sources of information. Recently, the development of personalized medicine in oncology has promoted the incorporation of molecular

(genetic) information, with the near perspective of exponential growth, by having mechanisms of massive sequencing and analysis of proteins or microbiome that could be of interest to establish a unique profile of the patient at each time. At the same time, the integration in the future of other data of the individual, derived from its location in a population context, such as cultural, socioeconomic and demographic, epidemiological and public health data, habits and behaviours or values and preferences (the so-called social determinants of health or SDOH) is foreseeable.

13. Finally, in relation to the speed of data generation or the generation of a response to them (whether generated knowledge, a prediction or an action), we observe a growing need. However, the bulk of the data identified in our work does not have special processing speed requirements.

## 7.3.1 Proposed Framework

We proposed a conceptual model and an associated functional architecture (which includes functions and data) in order to facilitate the analysis of clinical data in oncology and specifically in the field of lung cancer. It is important to highlight that, although the architecture proposed contains functional blocks, data and their flows, it does not necessarily define which information systems must support those functional blocks. This definition of systems may be adapted to the characteristics of each hospital and the information systems available to it, thus making the proposed framework more flexible.

The proposed architecture is shown in Figure 7.2.

In the proposed architecture, we identify the following functional blocks (refer to Figure 7.2):

■ Electronic medical record (EMR).
■ Oncological data model (ODM).
■ Clinical data analysis (CDA).
■ Clinical decision support (CDS).

Functional blocks are grouped into two main types according to their main function: data repository (EMR and ODM) or data analysis (CDA, CDS). The blocks also have sub-functions (indicated as boxes of more intense colour within the boxes corresponding to the block).

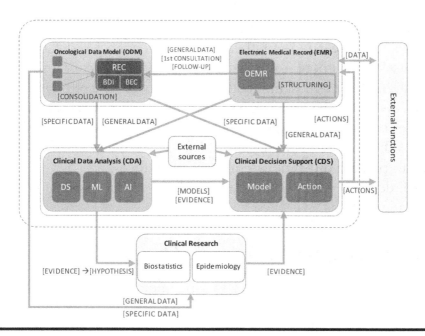

**Figure 7.2   Proposed architecture for the analysis of clinical data in oncology.**

Additionally, other functional blocks are identified that not being part of the architecture and interact with it (white boxes in the figure).

Finally, data exchange or data processing actions are identified between the different functional blocks (Figure 7.2). We distinguish between the exchange or processing of general clinical data (variables available to all patients) and specific clinical data (corresponding to specific cancer pathology, such as lung cancer). Although we defined our own data model for simplicity and speed to obtain results, we recommend validating the use of reference models in this area, such as dual models based on the CEN/ISO EN13606 standard (International Organization for Standardization (ISO), 2008) or the OpenEHR open standard (https://www.openehr.org/) that make a distinction between clinical information (immutable) and associated clinical knowledge (set of concepts of a particular clinical domain and therefore may evolve over time) (Serrano et al., 2009). These models represent clinical knowledge through archetypes (metadata structures) linked to previously established terminologies (such as SNOMED-CT, (http://www.snomed.org/)), thus facilitating semantic interoperability between systems and the homogeneous representation of the data, regardless of the institution that generates them.

According to the analysis performed, we found that there was no structured, unique and updated record that contained a unique reference for each of the patients belonging to the oncology service for purposes of care improvement or research, but rather multiple unconnected databases and the EMR itself, all without a standard coding for the structured values, nor a clear, written and shared definition by all users who entered data in those databases. As we have seen, this impacted the quality of the data and the possibilities of interoperating (integrating) with other records. Therefore, having a sufficiently structured patient database (a case registry) would avoid the need to prepare different care records by pathology.

We will describe some of the main blocks of the proposed architecture in the following sections.

## 7.3.2 Oncological Electronic Medical Record (OEMR)

The EMR provides, regardless of its specific implementation, and among many other advantages, a set of structured data related to both the patient (demographic data) and the healthcare activity carried out. However, there is no definition of the minimum content of the EMR depending on the specialty of pathology. Thus, and based on the analysis of other reference models in this area (International Consortium for Health Outcomes Measurement (ICHOM), 2017) (Provencio et al., 2019), we propose an Oncological Electronic Medical Record (OEMR) integrated into the hospital's general EMR system as a subset of it, which contains in a structured way a minimum number of key variables for subsequent analysis. Having a minimum number of structured variables would allow completing the OEMR in the time available in a typical consultation, without entailing a significant workload for the physician. Pretending a higher number of structured variables in the OEMR, although a priori would be very useful in the architecture proposed from a technical point of view, might not be a goal attainable as stated previously.

The OEMR should allow the registration of the most relevant variables for any cancer patient, corresponding to both the first consultation and the rest of the follow-up consultations. These variables should be previously defined in a data dictionary available to all users who would perform the registration of data in the OEMR, in order to unify criteria for their registration.

## 7.3.3 Oncological Data Model (ODM)

Since the EMR available in the HUPHM does not have the necessary facilities for the autonomous management of the variables to be collected, nor for the exploitation of data that this unified case register would require,

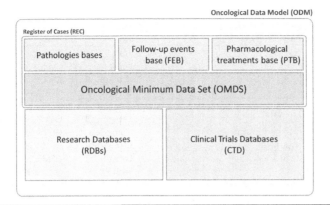

**Figure 7.3    Components of the proposed ODM.**

we proposed a specific functional block to solve this problem, called the Oncological Data Model (ODM). We identified the following components of the ODM (Figure 7.3):

1. **Register of Cases (REC)**: The REC compiles the longitudinal set of structured and non-anonymized care data that are considered of interest for patient care follow-up and for the location of cases that meet certain criteria. Likewise, it will have a secondary use to carry out activities for improving care, researching and teaching that is not specified a priori. In this case, its data will be the basis for the elaboration of RDBs, prior approval by the Ethical Committee, and has to be anonymized or pseudonymized. The REC is subdivided into the following components:

   – **Oncological Minimum Data Set (OMDS)**: Static data, created in the first healthcare contact of the patient in the outpatient setting (first medical oncology consultation) of the first oncological process diagnosed. These data are available in the EMR (demographic) and in the OEMR (through a form of first Medical Oncology consultation), which are common for all cancer patients and will be automatically integrated into the OMDS. In this way, it is guaranteed that every patient followed in the Medical Oncology Department, regardless of their specific pathology, has at least these data in the REC (Figure 7.4):

   – **Pathologies Bases**: Each of the pathologies (organs or types of cancer, such as lung cancer, colon cancer and lymphoma) may have its own data model that is of specific interest for the disease, and that is not contemplated therefore in the OMDS. In any case,

| Variable | Type | Origin |
|---|---|---|
| Hospital unique patient ID (NHC) | Numerical | EMR |
| Spanish National citizen ID (NIF) | Text | EMR |
| Patient name | Text | EMR |
| Birth date | Fecha | EMR |
| Sex | Categorical | EMR |
| Race | Categorical | OEMR 1st consultation |
| History of cancer in first grade relatives | Categorical | OEMR 1st consultation |
| Smoking habits | Categorical | OEMR 1st consultation |
| Smoking habits (quantification) | Numerical | OEMR 1st consultation |
| Organ (cancer type) | Categorical | OEMR 1st consultation |
| Initial cancer stage | Categorical | OEMR 1st consultation |
| Date of diagnosis | Fecha | OEMR 1st consultation |
| Date of first visit in Medical Oncology | Fecha | EMR |
| ECOG-PS at diagnosis | Categorical | OEMR 1st consultation |
| Histology | Categorical | OEMR 1st consultation |
| Histologic subtype | Categorical | OEMR 1st consultation |
| Histologic grade | Categorical | OEMR 1st consultation |
| Molecular biomarkers analyzed | Categorical | OEMR 1st consultation |
| Previous history of personal cancer | Categorical | OEMR 1st consultation |

**Figure 7.4   Variables proposed for the OMDS.**

referential integrity will be maintained with the patient's medical history number contained in the OMDS (data from patients in a specific pathology that are not previously in OMDS should not be included) so that each patient in the OMDS may have one or several registered pathologies, with their respective variables.

– **Follow-Up Events Base (FEB)**: A data model will be available to contain the evolutionary follow-up of patients that contains all the events of interest recorded for a patient in their care course: care contacts, procedures and complementary tests, response or progression, toxicities, etc. Since keeping this base up-to-date implies a high workload, integration with the data recorded in the EMR, such as care activity data, will be sought as much as possible. These follow-up data are currently registered in an unstructured manner in the EMR, although the gradual introduction of a form in the EMR with the same content as the FEB for its integration is proposed, depending on the maturity of the organization for the structuring of the information in the EMR.

– **Pharmacological Treatment Base (PTB)**: It will contain the temporal record of all the cancer treatments administered to the patient that has been prescribed by the Medical Oncology Department. It excludes treatments administered inside the hospital (emergency, hospitalization), those prescribed for hospital pickup (outpatients) or

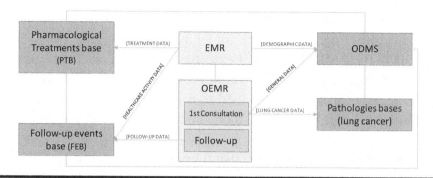

**Figure 7.5    Relationship between the components of the case registry and the EMR.**

those OTC meds prescribed in the hospital or in primary care. This information will be obtained from the hospital's prescription and medication administration system.

The relationships between the different components of the REC and the EMR and OEMR functional block introduced in the previous chapter are shown in Figure 7.5.

2. **Research Databases (RDBs)**: They will be created exclusively for specific projects, once the study variables that are needed are known and verified that they are not already included in the REC. The variables they contain should be standardized and added to a single dictionary, and will necessarily have referential integrity with the OMDS during its preparation. Once prepared, anonymization or pseudonymization will be carried out to carry out the analysis corresponding to the approved research.

3. **Clinical Trial Databases (CTDs)**: It will contain updated data of the clinical trials in the centre, in its different stages of development, as well as of the recruited patients, having referential integrity to the OMDS.

## 7.3.4 Clinical Data Analysis (CDA)

The functional block of CDA facilitates the detailed study of data related to the physical condition and health of people in order to acquire or improve their knowledge. To this end, existing technologies and analysis techniques will be applied (DS, ML and AI, according to their definition and state of the art), with the following means:

- **Data**: The clinical data will be obtained through downloads, ETL processes or other mechanisms of integration with the analysis tools, from the ODM, the EMR-OEMR and external data sources. These data will be pseudonymized in the process of obtaining so that the confidentiality of the information is protected to a greater extent and the possibility of participation of researchers not directly involved in patient care is enabled.

- **Methodology**: Although the usual approach from the point of view of clinical research is to propose a hypothesis and then obtain the data to validate it, we observed how in our approach we had assistance data in the first place, and we considered how to obtain an additional value of them. Therefore, we started from the need to perform an analysis of clinical oncological data without specifying a previous hypothesis or a series of specific objectives, but multiple areas of interest to explore through a methodology that allowed us to perform this process in an optimal and systematic way. Therefore, to carry out the data analyses necessary to achieve the proposed objective, CRISP-DM has been used as a methodological framework (Chapman et al., 2000). We have applied this methodology adapting it to the needs of the healthcare environment and the problem of analysis, taking as reference previous studies that apply this methodology to the analysis of clinical and healthcare data (Rivo et al., 2012) (Pérez et al., 2015). Thus, we propose the adoption of CRISP-DM with phases adapted and developed in an iterative life cycle until the desired results are obtained. We propose an inhomogeneous distribution of the data analysis project efforts in the different iterations of the CRISP-DM cycle. Thus, the first iterations will be more focused on obtaining clear analysis objectives and understanding them properly to obtain the necessary data from the available sources. The following iterations will focus more on the preparation of the data and the development of initial models for evaluation by clinical staff. Finally, the last iterations will try to focus their efforts on refining the models and evaluating them in detail, as well as obtaining results that can be exploited in the clinical setting (Figure 7.6).

- **Tools**: Our proposal allows complete freedom when selecting the most appropriate technological tools to achieve the proposed objectives.

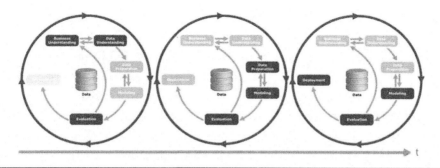

**Figure 7.6 Succession of CRISP-DM cycles over time with an inhomogeneous distribution of efforts in their different phases. (Adapted from https://es.wikipedia.org/wiki/Cross_Industry_Standard_Process_for_Data_Mining.)**

Thus, the final product of CDA will be the following:

- **Knowledge**: Regarding the analysed data (a piece of evidence) that in many cases could be the starting point for new research hypotheses or for supporting clinical decision-making.
- **Mathematical models**: Trained on the available data that could be deployed, after a proper validation, in the clinical environment (production) to support clinical decision-making.

## 7.4 Outcomes/Impact on Healthcare Delivery

The proper management of the lung cancer patient during the continuum of care determines to a large extent the clinical results and the quality of life, and allows to generate economic savings for the health system. Based on the conviction that the management of patients with lung cancer can be improved through the analysis of data on healthcare use, available in the EMR, we implemented and applied our proposed framework to this issue.

To this end, we obtained from the OMD, built using REDCap (Research Electronic Data Capture) (Harris et al., 2009), a cohort of 522 patients diagnosed from January 1, 2009 to December 31, 2016, and therefore, we had all healthcare attendances registered in our EMR, which went life in September 2008. Healthcare activity data from the EMR were obtained through Oracle Business Intelligence Discoverer 10g version 2 (10.1.2.1). For data preparation, crossing and depuration, Microsoft Excel 2016 was used as it is a simple tool that is widely available in the hospital environment.

The analysis was performed using a classical statistical approach, through univariate and Poisson multivariate regression or binomial multivariate regression analyses, using common tools widely available in any hospital such as Stata 12.0, Joinpoint 4.5.0.1 for the analysis of tendencies (Kim et al., 2000) and the R language. The initial exploratory visual analyses were mainly performed through Tableau 10.3, a visual analysis tool that allows rapid identification of relations and tendencies between data.

Under these conditions, we obtained the following conclusions of clinical and managerial interest in improving healthcare for these patients:

1. The total average cost per patient per year, excluding outpatient medication and radiotherapy, amounted to 16,406 euro, 10% attributable to outpatient care, 3% to emergency care and 87% to inpatient admissions.
2. We observe an increasing trend in the incidence of lung cancer in women since 2003, of approximately 1.5% annually, so maintaining the trend it is estimated that in 2020, 35% of lung cancer cases will occur in women.
3. The patients in our study have a median of 36 outpatient attendances per year of follow-up, being the attendances in the Medical Oncology Department and the day hospital a 50% of them.
4. We observe an increasing trend in the number of successive consultations for stage 4 patients, with an increase of 0.72 attendances per patient per year, which should serve to inform decisions regarding the sizing of the staff for the Medical Oncology Department.
5. The consumption of outpatient care per year of patient follow-up is directly related to the patient's stage at diagnosis, with the consumption of emergency attendances of the patient, with the comorbidity of the patient, with the existence of a history of cancer in relatives of first grade and inversely with age at diagnosis.
6. Seventy-four per cent of patients went to the emergency department (ED) at least once, with a median of 1.2 hospital emergencies per year of follow-up; 76.6% of the ED attendances had an urgent or very urgent triage (levels 1 to 3 of the Manchester scale), 22.6% had a less urgent triage (level 4) and only 0.8% had a non-urgent triage (level 5). We observed a relationship between the level of triage and the existence of subsequent inpatient admission. However, 30% of cases with less urgent triage ended up being admitted to hospitalization.
7. The consumption of ED attendances per year of patient follow-up is directly related to the patient's stage of diagnosis, the number of inpatient

admissions per follow-up period, the patient's comorbidity, the value of the ECOG-PS at diagnosis, the age at diagnosis, the number of emergencies in the 180 days prior to diagnosis and the number of prior outpatient care. These results are suggestive that the older population could be more targeted for proactive actions that would allow ED attendances to be avoided (with home follow-up, for example) and that frequent attendance in emergencies after diagnosis may depend to some extent on the previous history of the patient in his consumption of healthcare.

8. Fifty-five per cent of the patients had some inpatient admission after their diagnosis of lung cancer in the period analysed, with a median of 1.35 admissions per year of follow-up. The median days that pass from diagnosis to admission is 80 days, and 180 between discharge and death.

9. Fifty-seven per cent of inpatient admissions are ordered from the ED, resulting in death in 8% of cases. For stage 4, the figures rise to 79% ordered from the ED and to 16% resulting in death.

10. The number of inpatient admissions per year of patient follow-up is directly related to the patient's comorbidity and the number of emergencies in the 180 days prior to diagnosis. We also noted that patients who never smoked had 40% fewer inpatient admissions than ex-smokers.

# References

Chapman, P., Clinton, J., Kerber, R., Khabaza, T., Reinartz, T., Shearer, C., & Wirth, R. (2000). CRISP-DM 1.0 Step-by-step data mining guide (SPSS). ftp://ftp.software.ibm.com/software/analytics/spss/support/Modeler/Documentation/14/UserManual/CRISP-DM.pdf

Codd, E.F. (1990). *The Relational Model for Database Management : Version 2.* Boston, MA: Addison-Wesley.

Cruz-Bermúdez, J. (2019). Desarrollo e implantación de herramientas para el registro y análisis de datos y el soporte a la decisión como base para la medicina de precisión en Oncología. Universidad Politécnica de Madrid.

Cruz-Bermúdez, J.L., Parejo, C., Martínez-ruíz, F., Cristóbal, J., Gómez-bravo, R., Martín-vegue, A.R., & Royuela, A. (2019a). Aplicación de métodos y herramientas de la ciencia de datos para el análisis del coste de la asistencia sanitaria de los pacientes con cáncer de pulmón en un hospital universitario de tercer nivel en España. *Rev. Española Econ. La Salud 14*, 2–17.

Cruz-Bermúdez, J.L., Parejo, C., Martínez-Ruíz, F., Sánchez-González, J.C., Ramos Martín-Vegue, A., Royuela, A., Rodríguez-González, A., Menasalvas-Ruiz, E., & Provencio, M. (2019b). Applying data science methods and tools to unveil healthcare use of lung cancer patients in a teaching hospital in Spain. *Clin. Transl. Oncol. 21*, 1472–1481.

Dasu, T., & Johnson, T. (2003). *Exploratory Data Mining and Data Cleaning*. Haboken, NJ: Wiley-Interscience.

Friedberg, M.W., Chen, P.G., Van Busum, K.R., Aunon, F., Pham, C., Caloyeras, J., Mattke, S., Pitchfork, E., Quigley, D.D., Brook, R.H., et al. (2013). Factors affecting physician professional satisfaction and their implications for patient care, health systems, and health policy. *Rand. Health Q. 3*, 1.

Harris, P.A., Ph, D., Taylor, R., Thielke, R., Payne, J., Gonzalez, N., & Conde, J.G. (2009). Research Electronic Data Capture (REDCap) – a metadata-driven methodology and workflow process for providing translational research informatics support. *J. Biomed. Inform. 42*, 377–381.

Hoyt, J.P. (2015). European Hospitals EMRAM Maturity Overview. CIO Summit 2015. https://na.eventscloud.com/file_uploads/0cf548ab2f4eaeafd0a6b4ce6 15f0399_Hoyt_Session_1_European_Hospitals_EMRAM_Maturity_Overview_ CIOSummit.pdf

International Consortium for Health Outcomes Measurement (ICHOM). (2017). Lung cancer data collection. Measuring results that matter social functioning. https://ichom.org/files/medical-conditions/lung-cancer/lung-cancer-reference-guide.pdf

International Organization for Standardization (ISO). (2008). ISO 13606-1:2008 health informatics – electronic health record communication – Part 1: Reference model. https://www.iso.org/standard/40784.html

Kim, H.-J., Fay, M.P., Feuer, E.J., & Midthune, D.N. (2000). Permutation tests for joipoint regression with applications to cancer rates. *Stat. Med. 19*, 335–351.

Knust, R.E., Portela, M.C., Pereira, C.C.D.A., & Fortes, G.B. (2017). Estimated costs of advanced lung cancer care in a public reference hospital. *Rev. Saude Publica 51*, 53.

Montouchet, C., Thomas, M., Anderson, J., & Foster, S. (2018). The oncology data landscape in Europe: report. https://efpia.eu/media/412192/efpia-onco-data-landscape-1-report.pdf

Pérez, J., Iturbide, E., Olivares, V., Hidalgo, M., Martínez, A., & Almanza, N. (2015). A data preparation methodology in data mining applied to mortality population databases. *J. Med. Syst. 39*, 152.

Provencio, M., Carcereny, E., Rodríguez-abreu, D., López-castro, R., & Guirado, M. (2019). Lung cancer in Spain : information from the Thoracic Tumors Registry (TTR study). *Trans. Lung Cancer Res. 8*, 461–475.

Reeve, R., Srasuebkul, P., Langton, J.M., Haas, M., Viney, R., Pearson, S.-A., & EOL-CC study authors. (2018). Health care use and costs at the end of life: a comparison of elderly Australian decedents with and without a cancer history. *BMC Palliat. Care 17*, 1.

Rivo, E., de la Fuente, J., Rivo, Á., García-Fontán, E., Cañizares, M.-Á., & Gil, P. (2012). Cross-Industry Standard Process for data mining is applicable to the lung cancer surgery domain, improving decision making as well as knowledge and quality management. *Clin. Transl. Oncol. 14*, 73–79.

Rudin, R.S., Bates, D.W., & MacRae, C. (2016). Accelerating innovation in health IT. *N. Engl. J. Med. 375*, 815–817.

Serrano, P., Moner, D., Sebastian, T., Maldonado, J.A., Navalón, R., Robles, M., & Gómez-Delgado, A. (2009). Utilidad de los arquetipos ISO 13606 para representar modelos clínicos detallados. *RevistaeSalud.Com 5*, 100–110.

Skinner, K.E., Fernandes, A.W., Walker, M.S., Pavilack, M., & VanderWalde, A. (2018). Healthcare costs in patients with advanced non-small cell lung cancer and disease progression during targeted therapy: a real-world observational study. *J. Med. Econ. 21*, 192–200.

USAID. (2019). Artificial intelligence in global health: defining a collective path forward. https://rmportal.net/library/content/ai-in-global-health-defining-a-collective-path-forward/at_download/file

Wickham, H. (2014). Tidy Data. *Journal of Statistical Software, Articles, 59*(10), 1–23. https://doi.org/10.18637/jss.v059.i10

*Chapter 8*

# Clinical Artificial Intelligence – Technology Application or Change Management?

Christopher Pearce, Adam McLeod,
Anna Fragkoudi, and Natalie Rinehart

*Outcome Health*

## Contents

## 8.1 Introduction

The practice of medical care is changing and changing rapidly (Coiera, 2018, 2019a; Topol, 2019). Health is not immune to the wide societal changes brought on by our increasingly digital existence (*The Economist*, 2017). It has, however, been late to realize these transformative changes, unlike banking and other industries (Brynjolfsson & McAfee, 2011). This is because health has always been heavily reliant on human interaction, which has delayed many aspects of adoption. Artificial intelligence (AI), in its various guises, is increasingly having an impact on the clinical world (Coiera, 2019b; Topol, 2019). With an initial emphasis on pattern recognition (radiology, dermatology), the usefulness of AI is broadening to other areas. Facing this clinical medicine is having to adjust how it creates and conceptualizes care. Indeed, as we will argue later, the changes wrought by digital health care are as fundamental to changing care delivery as the advent of the scientific method was in the 18th century.

To frame the conversation, we will examine our initial experiences with the development of an AI tool designed to inform decision-making at the consultation level in a primary care context, at this time best placed to have an impact on patient care. Essentially, we used machine learning to design a means of informing general practitioners (GPs – also known as family practitioners) and patients of the risk of attending an emergency department within the next 30 days. As part of that study, we researched practitioner attitudes to the tool and, in doing so, developed some insights into the future needs of AI-enhanced health care.

A well-recognized area of concern in modern western medicine is reducing hospital emergency department visits. Whilst often these patients require the attention of a specialist facility (for myocardial infarction or serious trauma, for instance), there remain several categories that may be managed in primary care, to prevent and/or reduce costly emergency attendances. These include (but are not limited to) chronic diseases such as cardiac failure and diabetes, as well as low acuity problems such as infection. We chose to approach this problem using the availability of digital health, using big data approaches, by extracting and linking records of all those who attended local emergency departments with their general practice data, and using machine learning to develop a prediction model.

The resultant tool, when tested on trial data, was able to accurately predict the risk of ED attendance within 30 days, based on the primary care data alone. In other words, at the time of the GP consultation, a screen popup will inform the GP (and the patient) of the risk (Pearce, McLeod, Rinehart, Patrick, et al., 2019). It is therefore designed to deliver the information at the time best able to have actions taken to correct the problem. Because of this success, the tool is currently being deployed across 2,000 practices in the east of Australia.

However, the deployment of the tool raised several issues in its delivery (Pearce, McLeod, Rinehart, Whyte, et al., 2019). Ranging from governance to clinical safety, we had to develop approaches to many new problems along the way. Whilst the tool is accurate 75% of the time, deployment of the program represents a new way of informing the clinical interaction, one that we believe requires a new clinical method, a new way of clinician to think about what it is to deliver care (Pearce, McLeod, Rinehart, Whyte, et al., 2019).

During the tool development, we tried to examine this in more detail. As part of the study, we engaged in a small qualitative assessment of the GP reactions, to further understand the impact on clinical thinking. The aim of this aspect of the project was to collect GP's perceptions of the risk algorithm scores, the patient attributes and their potential treatment changes based on their own active patients. Implementing the risk scores in a live general practice environment and consequently acquiring feedback on the accuracy and utility of the report was considered an essential step to validate the future use of the alert tool.

## 8.2 Methods

The tool was trialed in ten general practices in eastern Melbourne. We used historical data from within the practice. One hundred patients were identified at each practice, and a selection had the risk rating presented to their usual GP. Participants then rated the tool performance. Seven of the GPs participated in follow-up interviews. Participants were required to review 60 patient records each (equaling to a total 420) with a spread of scores (high, medium and low risk) to ensure adequate evaluation across all score spectrums. Patient information shown for review, when available, included

- Patient name
- Demographics: Age, gender, pensioner, DVA, Aboriginal or Torres Strait Islander status
- Risk Factors: Smoking
- Diagnoses.
  - Current Diagnoses: Marked as active in GP software or identified in the last visit
  - Historical Diagnoses: Up to ten years.
- Medications
  - Current medications: Marked as current in GP software or used in the past eight months
  - Historical medications: used in the last 9–24 months.
- Pathology Tests and Results
  - Current pathology: Tests and results reviewed in the last visit
  - Historical pathology: Tests and results reviewed in the last 12 months.
- GP Measurements (i.e. BMI, BP, Temperature, weight, etc.)
  - Current Measurements: Tests and results reviewed in the last visit
  - Historical Measurements: Tests and results reviewed in the last five years.
- Patient risk scores for the 0–30 day and 31–365 day

GP participants answered a range of questions concerning the

- Accuracy of the risk score
- Accuracy of the attributes presented for each patient
- Any changes they would make in patient treatment given the score.

## 8.3 Recruitment and Consent

GPs who participated in the study were employed by practices that had pre-existing contract agreements, in both urban and rural settings in Eastern Victoria. All practitioners were required to work a minimum of three sessions per week (0.3 FTE), in order to ensure that participants had sufficient active patient counts in the last 12 months to evaluate the risk scores. Due to a technical issue with one practice and two GPs not completing the process, the final sample consists of seven participants that completed both the patient record evaluation, final survey and the one-on-one semi-structured telephone interview.

## 8.4 Data Collection Tools

The patient record evaluation application was developed for study purposes and was hosted on pre-existing software utilized by the practice's data extraction and analytical system – POLAR GP (Pearce, Mcleod, Rinehart, Ferrigi, & Shearer, 2019). The survey presented demographic and clinical attributes of patients' medical history and allowed GPs to evaluate the efficacy of the risk scores based on the attributes included in each patient record.

The patient's evaluation tool comprises 15 items containing clinical information for each patient and nine questions, which allowed GPs to evaluate the accuracy of the risk score, the attributes presented and any treatment changes identified for the patients based on their clinical judgment, as shown in Figure 8.1.

A final survey was developed as an adjunct to the patient's evaluation form. This form used Likert scales over 11 questions, allowing GPs to evaluate the accuracy of the report overall, the usefulness and the intention of usage. The purpose was to acquire additional feedback, which would allow us to investigate whether the results from different approaches well class.

An interview guide was developed to support the one-on-one semi-structured telephone interviews that occurred during the week after the completion of the patient evaluation records. The topics discussed during the interviews concerned the experience of GPs using the tool.

## 8.5 Data Collection Process

Data extracted from the participating practices included patients that have visited the GPs during the past year of the extraction commencement. Approximately 1,000 patient records were extracted from each practice. The records were run through the algorithm in order to identify patients at risk of an emergency presentation at the hospital. A list of patients' de-identified IDs was created to perform a randomized application, which ensured a spread of scores (high, medium and low risk) across the two time periods (0–30 days and 31–365 days). The randomly selected patients met the pre-determined alert criteria that have historically identified patients who are at risk of hospital presentation and provided to GPs for evaluation. The included attributes were specified in the report.

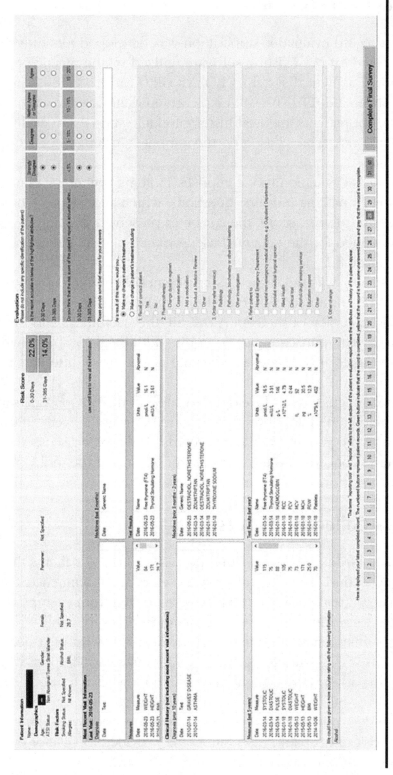

**Figure 8.1   Patient risk score sample.**

After reading the explanatory statement and signing the consent form, the participating GPs were asked to log in to POLAR GP, already installed in the practice's computing system. Each GP completed 60 patient reports totaling 420 unique patient records. Following the evaluation of the 60 patient records, practitioners completed a semi-structured survey with some free-response items. GPs began reviewing patient records May–July 2017 and were given incentives for their time. The final data collection took place during the telephone interview during the week following the completion of the patient evaluations. The interview was held at a day and time that suited participants, with an expectation that most GPs would want to be interviewed over the phone in between consultations.

## 8.6 Results

GPs were generally accepting of the technology as a support to their practice. They were more likely to agree with the tool when it predicted a low risk but less likely to agree when it predicted a high risk. This was particularly evident in the pediatric age group. Comments revolved around the concepts of usability and accuracy, and the GPs made many comments on ways to improve the tool deployment (Table 8.1).

As shown above, GPs generally found the format of the report easy to use and would likely use a report to provide additional support to higher-risk patients. However, there was less agreement concerning the accuracy

**Table 8.1   Final GP Survey Responses**

| Question | Likert M (SD) |
|---|---|
| The format of the report is easy to use. | 3.00 (0.58) |
| In general, the report is accurate in targeting patients at risk of ED admission. | 2.29 (0.49) |
| The report is a useful addition to clinical support strategies. | 2.57 (0.79) |
| If the report was offered in real-time to my desktop, it would be useful. | 2.71 (1.11) |
| I would likely use a real-time report as part of my practice. | 2.86 (1.22) |
| I would be likely to use the report for high-risk patients to provide or access additional support (i.e., care coordinators, practice nurses etc.). | 3.14 (1.22) |

and if they would use it if it was delivered as a real-time report within their practice. GPs identified within their comments that some of these concerns related to those in the higher-risk categories, which was also suggested within the individual patient record evaluations.

## 8.6.1 GPs Evaluation of Risk Algorithm: Qualitative

All interviews were audio-recorded and transcribed and reviewed by two researchers. The interviews were coded using the NVivo 11.0 software. A qualitative phenomenological approach was applied in conducting the semi-structured interviews and thematic analysis to analyze the transcripts.

The experience of using the tool was perceived as positive from most of the participants. The accuracy of the tool was an overarching theme in GP's stories. Reflecting on their participation in the study and whilst evaluating the patient records, GPs said that a predictive tool constitutes an innovative idea that is useful and helpful to guide their thinking and decisions towards a patient's care. However, although the idea of using a predictive tool as part of their practice is beneficial, there were some suggestions that the tool needs further refinement in order to ensure better accuracy.

During the thematic analysis of the interview transcripts, three themes emerged.

## 8.6.2 Accuracy

Responses appeared to be mixed when GPs evaluated the tool's accuracy and whether the scores were realistic or not. Opinions seemed to be divided, expanding on the reasons that led them to form this decision.

> Yes, generally, I would say they did [align with my clinical experience]. I think generally it's a fairly good predictor
> ...The reports were reasonably realistic, but they are only as good as the data that the GP has put them into the program
> I thought that the accuracy of the report was quite a long way off, of what my assessment of the preference is...I think it overestimated the risk in the 30 months {meaning days] significantly and I think it underestimated the risk in the 12 months period

Certain groups seemed to be more accurate than others, especially elderly people and low-risk patients.

...the predictions ...particularly I think for the lowest-risk patients were really accurate...

...Probably the older ones were more accurate when they had multiple risk factors...

Some participants stressed the need of having knowledge around the type of algorithm that was used, which calculated the risk score. Participants mentioned that this might have helped them to have a complete image and provide answers that are more accurate.

...if I knew the algorithm, I could then have suggested that the long-term risk score for this patient would be higher than the short-term risk...

Well, since I don't know how you do them [calculations], it is very difficult to kind of make a meaningful comment about...

Keeping this in mind, it might be that GP's lack of knowledge concerning how the algorithm was calculating risk scores was frustrating for them and their evaluation of the tool. This concept of AI tools being a 'black box' is well recognized.

## 8.6.3 Usability

All of the GPs were in an agreement that a predictive tool consists of an innovative idea that is very useful and helpful for GPs' daily practice. Having a predictive tool offers the opportunity to predict and potentially prevent a number of people presenting to emergency departments. Although some participants reported the tool needs further revising and improvement, most of them said that it constitutes a useful alerting tool. Reviewing a patient's record in a single scan and the time efficiency this represented was also highlighted as valuable.

It might provide an early warning to people who I might not be considering as potential risk to go into hospital.

...that was easy to absorb and to read, it was quite well presented. It was a good summary.

It got quicker as you went along because I knew most of the patients, that was pretty quick, the ones that I didn't know or hadn't see for a long time, it took a bit longer.

### 8.6.4 Suggestions for Improvement

The third theme identified participants' suggestions for inclusion of further items, which might have provided better estimation around a patient's health. The views of the participants were mostly personal preferences, all underpinned by the same needs, and the reason that a patient is flagged as high risk in the system. Suggestions offered by the GPs when applied to the tool might provide better accuracy and understanding and, as a result, create a more constructive tool.

> Well, it would be helpful if the program flagged why it thought, that this risk was so high in that particular person…why was that person flagged as being as high risk…

## 8.7 Discussion

The findings from this limited study are not sufficient to be truly considered significant in its own right. However, in the context of the overall study, and the activities of our organization in implementing extensive tools in practice, the findings highlight the conditions that need to be dealt with for the use of AI in the primary care context. In deciding to develop and then deploy the tool, we sought to make decisions about several areas of ambiguity. In researching the options, we realized that in many areas, we were making decisions on issues about which, to date, there had been only theoretical discussions. We found limited literature in this regard. We found adopting a traditional, randomized controlled trial path non-pragmatic and not necessarily suited for this model of care (Greenhalgh & Abimbola, 2019). The rest of this chapter summarizes some of these issues and frames them with the pragmatic decisions we made at the time. We hope this will inform future research in this area.

In many ways, we were surprised at the degree of acceptance of the tool by the GPs. However, on reflection, the tool represents not a wildly new concept, but an extension of an existing trend. Clinicians have always been information managers. And computers are par excellence, information managers. As the amount of available information increases exponentially, computers have long been an aid to manage this. In Australia, computers arrived as basically electronic prescription pads (Western, Dwan, Makkai, Del Mar, & Western, 2001). Australia has a complex system of drug prescribing and subsidies, and computerization removed the need for GPs to memorize the many variables of drug strength, pack size, repeats and subsidies for specific conditions (Pearce, 2013). Each jurisdiction had its own drivers for computer adoption. In the USA, billing needs has overwhelmingly driven computerization, to the detriment of human relationships (Toll, 2012). However, whilst the drivers are unique, the overall effect is that computers in developed – and increasingly in developing (Pearce, 2018) – environments are moving from common to ubiquitous.

This change is not just about computerization, but about the fundamental changes in society due to the digital world, and the concomitant changes that are occurring in health.

We have first listed elsewhere some of the challenges to the future of medicine (Pearce, McLeod, Rinehart, Whyte, et al., 2019), and this article is an opportunity to expand on these. An important framing discussion is about computers/big data/AI sitting at an intersection that is arguably somewhere between human and true machine, with concepts such as 'convergence' (Gill, 2019), or even 'singularity' (Kurzweil, 2005) blurring the lines where biological humanity ends and technologically enhanced humanity begins. Either way, there are many traditionally 'human' things that now can be done as well, if not better, by computers (Kuflik, 2007).

Seemingly, these concepts seem far-fetched, but indeed we need (as this discussion will show) to confront some of them sooner rather than later. Clearly, the GPs in our study viewed the decision support as a tool, similar to the stethoscope or the textbook. And, in keeping with the principles of technology adoption, which in part means at first humans relate the familiar to the unfamiliar (Latour, 1987), we have deliberately framed our program as such a tool. So, at the beginning of the 20th century, humans called cars 'horseless carriages' because humans understood horses and carriages, even though these transport devices were much more. Even today, we still call some devices 'phones', although an old school telephone call is the least used function of these increasingly smart computers in our pockets. In the same light, AI-driven aids that are being developed are far more than a tool and will change the interactions we have in medicine. The discussion that follows uses our thoughts on several areas that arose during the development of the risk prediction tool.

## 8.7.1 Decision Support

Decision support is generally described as providing clinicians, staff, patients or other individuals with knowledge and person-specific information, intelligently filtered or presented at appropriate times, to enhance health and health care (Osheroff et al., 2007), but is entering a new, AI-driven realm (Pollard & Whetton, 2005). In the past, decision support could be as simple as offering information about drug interactions, through to decision trees to support clinical decision-making (Neame, Chacko, Surace, Sinha, & Hawcutt, 2019). However, the next generation of tools is going to significantly alter the interaction and the power balance between clinicians and consumers. Examples of this exist today with the potential to change the traditional roles of doctor, patient and computer: Propeller Health, a company that will track (and adjust) medication use on your smartphone (Merchant et al., 2018), or an Australian solution that can predict FEV1 (a measure of breathing capacity) and/or the presence of pneumonia, based on cough analysis on your smartphone (Moschovis et al., 2019), as examples. Patients themselves will have access not just to information, but diagnostic tools that change the power and information dynamic. No longer will it be 'doctor I have a cough', but 'doctor, I have pneumonia'.

We believe it is important that these new tools provide decision support, not decision replacement. Whilst some areas might be more prone to human replacement (radiology is a commonly raised area), Decision Support Tools (DSTs) should, where appropriate, support clinicians at the time of interaction and acknowledge the role of the existing human dyad (Pearce, Arnold, Phillips, Trumble, & Dwan, 2011). What these changes to clinical processes might entail should be the subject of the post-implementation study. Individual social circumstance, or subtler medical circumstance, cannot be known by 'the machine', and the relationship should always remain the authority, with the DST assisting the doctor–patient dyad to make a decision. We no longer talk of the algorithm but of the DST, with support being the operative word. Human interaction will be, and must always be, part of the healthcare experience.

In dealing with this issue in our context, we deliberately have designed the tool to provide general information rather than a recommendation – it is still up to the doctor–patient dyad to decide what to do. In other words, we aim for the computer to be part of the interaction, not a replacement. In the example used, whilst the doctor no longer needs to make the diagnosis, there is still a large scope for understanding the context of the illness to inform choices about care. Management of pneumonia in a homeless person in the inner city is vastly different from a middle-class grazier in a rural area.

## 8.7.2 Regulation

Regulation for tools such as ours is currently absent in most jurisdictions (Coiera & Westbrook, 2006). In deciding to deploy our DST, there was no regulation or guideline to assist us, unlike if we were recommending a new treatment or procedure. In the absence of any other direction, we used our internal processes. Our own governance and clinical risk assessment framed any risk as low, as the recommendation is to the clinician, who must then decide using their usual skills on what to do (or not do). However, we acknowledge that this is not adequate for the future.

The question that then challenges us is how these tools should be regulated? In health, largely there are three types of regulation: the profession themselves have the ability to self-regulate – indeed, this is one of the categorical features of a profession (Starr, 1982). In turn, the state offers an extra layer by regulating the registration of individual practitioners. The second type is accreditation, whereby individuals, institutions or programs must periodically comply with a set of standards. This model has been applied to electronic medical records, but not AI tools (De Clercq, 2007). The third model is the approval process for individual interventions, most commonly used for drugs (Whitstock, Eckermann, Marjoribanks, & Pearce, 2008) and surgical devices. In this model, manufacturers or providers must provide evidence of benefits and cost-effectiveness, often through the previously mentioned randomized controlled trials.

The issue then becomes the method by which AI tools should be regulated. Each method has pros and cons. These AI-driven supports are not pure tools, so they are not amenable to the latter category of trial effectiveness and even cost-effectiveness analyses. Accreditation would work, but developing the criteria represents a difficult area in a new field. Training and standards-setting by the profession seem illogical, but understanding the training parameters and ensuring they are fit for purpose is important in ensuring safety and generalizability. The next sections cover areas beyond simply the effectiveness of such interventions.

## 8.7.3 Ethics

Ethics has long been a significant part of medical practice (Beauchamp & Childress, 2013) and underpins the very nature of the profession. Medical ethics are famously associated with the Hippocratic oath dating from ancient Greece – a statement that was designed to guide doctors in their relationships with patients and colleagues. Modern ethics were first codified in 1803 (Armstrong, 2006) a document that described a set of principles for doctors dealing with each other. Now, most medical societies have some form of ethical code that is used to guide their inter-professional and professional conduct. However, as medicine is more than just an individual doctor's relationship with an individual patient, ethical codes need to take into account the conflicting issues that can occur in fields such as public health, for instance (Miettinen, 2005). Ethical thinking has been slowly moving to the concepts of the impacts of decisions, not just actions (Goodman, 2005). Then, there are the ethical frameworks that may apply to institutions (McCrickerd, 2000). All of these have an impact on the clinical space.

And similarly, there has been considerable consideration of AI agents as moral and ethical actors (Sandvig, Karahalios, & Langbort, 2016). Mostly, this has been in the context of either ethical decisions regarding autonomous vehicles (Fleetwood, 2017) or robots (van der Plas, Smits, & Wehrmann, 2010). Yet, these two concepts are only now beginning to be brought together. (Arnold & Pearce, 2008; Hand, 2018; Spriggs, Arnold, Pearce, & Fry, 2012). Our solution was to frame it according to a human dyad. By providing advice to the clinician, we fell back on existing ethical frameworks and rely on doctor–patient relationships. However, this will not last without due consideration of a new ethical framework. Ethics now needs to be seen as an end-to-end process, not segmented into the profession, the institution and research. Ethics is now about how we deal with patients, and the patient includes their data; these are not separate nor indivisible.

### 8.7.4 Legal

A brief word about legal issues is provided here, as they will be at the forefront of practitioner minds, especially in jurisdictions such as the USA. Again, as is a theme across most of this discussion, the use of intelligent supports to clinical practice blurs the boundary between humans and computers (Cath, 2018; O'Sullivan et al., 2019). Most of the current work, and indeed our own project, assumes human oversight – but what that means in the context of a rapidly moving vehicle, or decision made on the basis of an algorithm in which the practitioner does not know how or why the DST came to a decision is unclear. From a medico-legal viewpoint, we need to consider who will be responsible for what. What are the implications of a clinician ignoring a DST recommendation, or when following the recommendation and the patient experiencing a bad outcome? And if the DST is wrong, is it the program or the programmer or the data that is held responsible? And is it now a medico-legal requirement to provide good data for an advanced DST to do its work?

It would be better for these to be considered before a court has to make a call. These issues are starting to be considered, with the release of a recent EU report (Expert Group on Liability and New Technology, 2019). This report acknowledges the limitations of current liability law and makes several recommendations, many of which impose ultimate responsibility on the humans – which may or may not be appropriate as we move to more sophisticated approaches. Again, by providing only information to the consultation, especially without recommendations, we side-stepped this issue. The ultimate responsibility fell to the GP along existing lines. This approach, however, also hobbles the DST from making significant recommendations to the clinicians.

## 8.7.5 Quality of Data

The existence of good quality data is vital to DST success. But good quality data cannot be mandated – they must be driven by providing clinical utility. Once it was enough for a 'good' doctor not to be held accountable to any standard or measure. This became inadequate in the last century, and moves to set standards, even for basic elements such as the keeping of records, became mandatory (Collings, 1950). Records have moved from a memory aid for an individual doctor to one that enhances communication and patient care within a practice (Murtagh, 2002) or any other institution. Our view is that this must now be extended to state that good quality data is now an essential part of good medical practice (Bainbridge, 2019), and clinicians who do not create good quality data are not providing good quality care, for a range of reasons such as denying patient access to tools such as DSTs. It is not enough to record blood pressure or smoking, and it must be recorded in such a way as to be useable for both the clinician, the patient and the computer.

This integrated governance approach (Liaw, Pearce, Liyanage, Liaw, & de Lusignan, 2014) underpins the POLAR program allowing the data be used for a variety of purposes, all of which benefit patient care – from individual consultation through population health initiative and AI applications (Pearce, Mcleod, Rinehart, Ferrigi, et al., 2019). A sideline of this is that clinicians must be careful about identifiable data – much of the cleaning work we had to do to make the data applicable for our purposes was to strip out identifiable data (patient names, etc.) from unlikely fields such as diagnosis, or even referral headings. A clinician who would shrink from mentioning a patient name in a public space is happy to write identifiable information throughout the record, in areas that are not germane to their use. Data in the clinical record should be considered as potentially public and always shareable.

This data should also come from multiple sources not just that generated in the EMR. Data should not be confined to a single institution but be brought from multiple sources to meet the need of the patient at the time. Thus, a 'patient-centered' view of data is required, rather than an 'institutional' view.

## 8.7.6 New Clinical Methods

Ultimately, clinicians need to change their viewpoint of the clinical process. The clinical method is 'the means by which physicians discover facts about the sick or well patient and enter them into the diagnostic and therapeutic process in equal partnership with information about disease, pathophysiology, and technology' (Cassell, 1997). The dominant paradigm at the moment is that of the 'person-centered' clinical method (Stewart, 2003) – which creates a patient-centered view of the clinical problem for the clinician to work with. However, this method assumes a dyad, when increasingly the future is a triadic relationship.

Using DSTs is creating a new clinical method. Some DSTs will be better than humans at what they do. This does not mean that doctors are missing vital information, and it simply means that computing power can now process data and make connections in ways that humans cannot. In some ways, it is analogous to other elements of the clinical interaction. The stethoscope provides information that cannot be obtained without it. However, AI will transform this process into something unrecognizable to today's clinicians. This is not about new information, but about new ways of thinking. By the same token, computers lack intuition and the capacity for emotional connections (Dreyfus, Dreyfus, & Athanasiou, 1986). The clinical interaction of the future will acknowledge the strengths of each party (computer, clinician and patient). It will be the same process of negotiation, but with different players. And the patient will face new challenges. The process of doctors becoming guides rather than sources of knowledge will accelerate (Szasz & Hollander, 1956).

## 8.8 Conclusion

The current state of AI is not if, but when, AI will have a significant impact on clinical practice. Our tool (now called POLAR DIVERSION) is being retooled with a larger set of data (including hospital data) and being deployed across 2,000 practices (20% of the Australian total) in the east of Australia. And we are but one of many AI projects in play. AI is breaching the walls of the traditional doctor–patient relationship. Whilst the AI programs in radiology and dermatology raise the issues of the ongoing roles of specific specialty groups, so to do new ideas that change the role of the 'patient' in health care. If a patient can diagnose their own pneumonia by coughing in the presence of their smartphone (Moschovis et al., 2019), or monitor and modify their medication use similarly (Merchant et al., 2018) with the same reliability and validity as being advised by a human clinician, it is time to rethink the role of the clinician in this new world. For just as the coming of autonomous vehicles is inevitable, so too will AI change the way we do medicine – we need to be ready for the largest change to healthcare delivery since the introduction of the scientific method.

## Acknowledgment

This research was undertaken with the generous assistance from the HCF Research Foundation. The foundation exerted no influence over the design or the progress of the study.

We acknowledge the Primary Health Networks who assisted us with the implementation of this work.

## References

Armstrong, D. (2006). Embodiment and ethics: constructing medicine's two bodies. *Social Health Illn*, 28(6), 866–881.

Arnold, M., & Pearce, C. M. (2008). Is technology innocent? Holding technologies to moral account. Technology and Society Magazine.

Bainbridge, M. (2019). Big data challenges for clinical and Precision medicine. In M. Househ, A. Kushniruk, & E. Borycki (Eds.), *Big Data, Big Challenges: A Healthcare Perspective* (pp. 17–32). Cham: Springer.

Beauchamp, T. L., & Childress, J. F. (2013). *Principles of Biomedical Ethics* (7th ed.). New York: Oxford University Press.

Brynjolfsson, E., & McAfee, A. (2011). *Race against the Machine: How the Digital Revolution is Accelerating Innovation, Driving Productivity, and Irreversibly Transforming Employment and the Economy*. Lexington, MA: Digital Frontier Press.

Cassell, E. J. (1997). *Doctoring: The Nature of Primary Care Medicine*. New York: Oxford University Press.

Cath, C. (2018). Governing artificial intelligence: ethical, legal and technical opportunities and challenges. *Philos Trans A Math Phys Eng Sci*, 376(2133). doi: 10.1098/rsta.2018.0080.

Coiera, E. (2018). The fate of medicine in the time of AI. *Lancet*, 392(10162), 2331–2332. doi: 10.1016/S0140-6736(18)31925-1.

Coiera, E. (2019a). On algorithms, machines, and medicine. *Lancet Oncol*, 20(2), 166–167. doi: 10.1016/S1470-2045(18)30835-0.

Coiera, E. (2019b). The price of artificial intelligence. *Yearb Med Inform*, 28(1), 14–15. doi: 10.1055/s-0039-1677892.

Coiera, E. W., & Westbrook, J. I. (2006). Should clinical software be regulated? *Med J Aust*, 184(12), 601–602.

Collings, J. (1950). General practice in England, a reconnaisance. *Lancet*, 255(6604), 555.

De Clercq, E. (2007). From a conceptual problem-oriented electronic patient record model to running systems: a nationwide assessment. *Int J Med Inform*. doi: 10.1016/j.ijmedinf.2007.07.002.

Dreyfus, H. L., Dreyfus, S. E., & Athanasiou, T. (1986). *Mind Over Machine: The Power of Human Intuition and Expertise in the Era of the Computer*. New York: Free Press.

Expert Group on Liability and New Technology. (2019). Liability for artificial intelligence and other emerging technologies. Retrieved from https://ec.europa.eu/transparency/regexpert/index.cfm?do=groupDetail. groupMeetingDoc&docid=36608.

Fleetwood, J. (2017). Public health, ethics, and autonomous vehicles. *Am J Public Health*, 107(4), 532–537. doi: 10.2105/AJPH.2016.303628.

Gill, K. (2019). Artificial intelligence: looking though the Pygmalion lens. *AI SOC*, 34(6), 391. doi: 10.1007/s00146-018-0873-1.

Goodman, K. W. (2005). Ethics, evidence, and public policy. *Perspect Biol Med*, 48(4), 548–556.

Greenhalgh, T., & Abimbola, S. (2019). The NASSS framework – a synthesis of multiple theories of technology implementation. *Stud Health Technol Inform*, 263, 193–204. doi: 10.3233/SHTI190123.

Hand, D. J. (2018). Aspects of data ethics in a changing world: where are we now? *Big Data*, 6(3), 176–190. doi: 10.1089/big.2018.0083.

Kuflik, A. (2007). *Computers in Control: Rational Transfer of Authority or Irresponsible Abdication of Autonomy?* London: Routledge.

Kurzweil, R. (2005). *The Singularity is Near: When Humans Transcend Biology*. New York: Penguin Group (USA) Viking.

Latour, B. (1987). *Science in Action: How to Follow Scientists and Engineers Through Society*. Cambridge, MA: Harvard University Press.

Liaw, S. T., Pearce, C., Liyanage, H., Liaw, G. S., & de Lusignan, S. (2014). An integrated organisation-wide data quality management and information governance framework: theoretical underpinnings. *Inform Prim Care*, 21(4), 199–206. doi: 10.14236/jhi.v21i4.87.

McCrickerd, J. (2000). Metaphors, models and organisational ethics in health care. *J Med Ethics*, 26(5), 340–345.

Merchant, R., Szefler, S. J., Bender, B. G., Tuffli, M., Barrett, M. A., Gondalia, R., … Stempel, D. A. (2018). Impact of a digital health intervention on asthma resource utilization. *World Allergy Organ J*, 11(1), 28. doi: 10.1186/s40413-018-0209-0.

Miettinen, O. S. (2005). Idealism and ethics of public-health practitioners. *Eur J Epidemiol*, 20(10), 805–807.

Moschovis, P. P., Sampayo, E. M., Porter, P., Abeyratne, U., Doros, G., Swarnkar, V., … Carl, J. C. (2019). A cough analysis smartphone application for diagnosis of acute respiratory illnesses in children. *Am J Resp Critic Care Med*, 199. Retrieved from <Go to ISI>://WOS:000466771100183.

Murtagh, J. (2002). *General Practice* (3rd ed.). Sydney: McGraw-Hill.

Neame, M. T., Chacko, J., Surace, A. E., Sinha, I. P., & Hawcutt, D. B. (2019). A systematic review of the effects of implementing clinical pathways supported by health information technologies. *J Am Med Inform Assoc*, 26(4), 356–363. doi: 10.1093/jamia/ocy176.

O'Sullivan, S., Nevejans, N., Allen, C., Blyth, A., Leonard, S., Pagallo, U., … Ashrafian, H. (2019). Legal, regulatory, and ethical frameworks for development of standards in artificial intelligence (AI) and autonomous robotic surgery. *Int J Med Robot*, 15(1), e1968. doi: 10.1002/rcs.1968.

Osheroff, J. A., Teich, J. M., Middleton, B., Steen, E. B., Wright, A., & Detmer, D. E. (2007). A roadmap for national action on clinical decision support. *J Am Med Inform Assoc*, 14(2), 141–145.

Pearce, C. (2013). The adoption of computers by Australian general practice – a complex adaptive systems approach. *OMICS J Gen Pract*, 1(3), 1–3. doi: 10.4172/2329-9126.1000121.

Pearce, C. (2018). Chronic disease in a digital health environment. *Fam Med Commun Health*, 6(1), 20–25. doi: 10.15212/FMCH.2017.0144.

Pearce, C., Arnold, M., Phillips, C., Trumble, S., & Dwan, K. (2011). The patient and the computer in the primary care consultation. *J Am Med Inform Assoc JAMIA*, 18(2), 138–142. doi: 10.1136/jamia.2010.006486.

Pearce, C., Mcleod, A., Rinehart, N., Ferrigi, J., & Shearer, M. (2019). What does a comprehensive, integrated data strategy look like: the population level analysis and reporting (POLAR) program. *Stud Health Technol Inform*, 264, 303–307. doi: 10.3233/SHTI190232.

Pearce, C., McLeod, A., Rinehart, N., Patrick, J., Fragkoudi, A., Ferrigi, J., … Shearer, M. (2019). POLAR diversion: using general practice data to calculate risk of emergency department presentation at the time of consultation. *Appl Clin Inform*, 10(1), 151–157. doi: 10.1055/s-0039-1678608.

Pearce, C., McLeod, A., Rinehart, N., Whyte, R., Deveny, E., & Shearer, M. (2019). Artificial intelligence and the clinical world: a view from the front line. *Med J Aust*, 210(Suppl 6), S38–S40. doi: 10.5694/mja2.50025.

Pollard, C., & Whetton, S. (2005). Decision support systems. In S. Whetton (Ed.), *Health Informatics: A Socio-Technical Perspective*. South Melbourne: Oxford University Press.

Sandvig, C., Hamilton, K., Karahalios, K., & Langbort, C. (2016). When the algorithm itself is a racist: diagnosing ethical harm in the basic components of software. *Int J Commun*, 10. doi: 1932-8036/20160005.

Spriggs, M., Arnold, M. V., Pearce, C. M., & Fry, C. (2012). Ethical questions must be considered for electronic health records. *J Med Ethics*, 38(9), 535–539. doi: 10.1136/medethics-2011-100413.

Starr, P. (1982). *The Social Transformation of American Medicine*. New York: Basic Books.

Stewart, M., Brown, J., Weston, W., McWhinney, L., McWilliam, C., & Freeman, T. (2003). *Patient-Centred Medicine: Transforming the Clinical Method* (2nd ed.). Oxford: Radcliffe Medical Press.

Szasz, T., & Hollander, M. (1956). A contribution to the philosophy of medicine: the basic models of the doctor-patient relationship. *Arch Int Med*, 97(5), 585–592.

The Economist. (2017, May 7). The world's most valuable resource is no longer oil, but data. The Economist.

Toll, E. (2012). A piece of my mind. The cost of technology. *JAMA*, 307(23), 2497–2498. doi: 10.1001/jama.2012.4946.

Topol, E. J. (2019). High-performance medicine: the convergence of human and artificial intelligence. *Nat Med*, 25(1), 44–56. doi: 10.1038/s41591-018-0300-7.

van der Plas, A., Smits, M., & Wehrmann, C. (2010). Beyond speculative robot ethics: a vision assessment study on the future of the robotic caretaker. *Account Res*, 17(6), 299–315. doi: 10.1080/08989621.2010.524078.

Western, M., Dwan, K., Makkai, T., Del Mar, C., & Western, J. (2003). Computerisation in Australian general practice. *Aust Fam Physician*, 32(3), 180.

Whitstock, M. T., Eckermann, E. J., Marjoribanks, T. K., & Pearce, C. M. (2008). Pharmaceutical economics and politics vs. patient safety: Lumiracoxib in Australia. *Int J Risk Safety Med*, 20(3), 161–167.

*Chapter 9*

# Impacting Perioperative Quality and Patient Safety Using Artificial Intelligence

Piyush Mathur
*Cleveland Clinic*

Jacek B. Cywinski and Francis A. Papay
*Cleveland Clinic*
*Case Western Reserve University*

## Contents

## 9.1  Introduction

Since adoption of value-based care in the USA and many other countries, there has been an increasing emphasis on measuring quality and performance. At the same time, there has been rapid increase in adoption of electronic health records (EHRs), leading to ever-increasing availability of digitized data (big data). Harnessing this ever-expanding data coupled with the need for analysis and reporting has led to proliferation of machine learning (ML) applications in health care. Key focus of these applications has been in areas of generation of appropriate diagnosis, image analysis, predictive analytics, clinical decision support and therapeutic guidance. Various perioperative patient cohorts (such as plastic surgery, neurosurgery, critical care patients) have been a focus of ML research and development over the last few years (Kanevsky et al., 2016; Mathur & Burns, 2019; Senders et al., 2018). Applications of ML for surgical patients have been helping with patient selection, measuring appropriateness of care and assessment of clinical performance (Kwong & Asrani, 2018).

Various techniques of ML including supervised learning, unsupervised learning and lately reinforcement learning are being investigated for different applications across the world with great deal of success. Neural networks have been developed and are increasingly being implemented for image analysis and waveform interpretation (Hatib et al., 2018; Liew, 2018). These algorithms are not just for clinical decision support but also to help analyze data related to workflows and achieve operational efficiencies during surgeries (Padoy, 2019). With FDA increasingly evaluating and approving ML algorithms, there is likely to be increasing adoption of these in clinical areas leading to improvements in quality and patient safety (Karnik, 2014).

## 9.2 Quality Measurement-Cohort and Performance Analysis

At an organizational level, with increasing application of quality improvement metrics and measurement of performance for continuous improvement, there has been an increasing need for rapid-cycle data analysis. In order to make a meaningful change, the availability of real-time, actionable data analysis is needed, and the standard methods have been found to be lacking. Also, with increasing emphasis on population health, the size of the data generated from large cohorts and plethora of variables required to be measured are both increasing exponentially. To replace manual chart abstractions and increase efficiencies in data analysis, various ML solutions are being applied. These include data abstraction using natural language processing (NLP), protocol adherence measurement and cohort comparisons using supervised and/or unsupervised ML methods (Vranas et al., 2017). Maheshwari et al. (2018) in their study of more than 1,700 patients undergoing colorectal surgery demonstrated application of unsupervised ML and topographical data analysis to rapidly discover characteristics of nine different groups based on their risk and outcome profile. Individual events including medication administration and laboratory results amongst other interventions were analyzed to understand clinical variations which otherwise take many man-hours and is difficult to scale up onto larger cohorts. These abilities are critical for following surgical patient populations, rapidly discovering any non-adherence to pre-defined protocols and generating actionable reports valuable to quality management groups.

Risk prediction models and expected outcomes from surgeries are being derived leveraging ML solutions such as artificial neural networks and Bayesian algorithms which are likely to change current methods using standard registries (Aminsharifi et al., 2017; Ehlers et al., 2017). Ehlers et al. (2017) demonstrated significant superiority of Bayesian algorithm against Charleston comorbidity risk index used to predict risk of surgery for over 400,000 patients. Charleston comorbidity index predicted 57% of adverse events and 59% of deaths, whereas the Naive Bayes algorithm predicted 79% of adverse events and 78% of deaths.

## 9.3 Predictive Analytics

The amount of health care data has been increasing exponentially in the past decade, and this trend will continue. Constant stream of information into EHRs, ever-increasing computational power and advances in ML all make possible to develop not only more precise but also more dynamic prediction models. Conventional approach in developing prediction models relies on regression analysis to identify important factors and weight their contribution to the overall prediction of different outcomes. These models however are rather static and usually work well for the same cohort they were developed on, which very often limits generalizability.

Systemic analyses comparing logistic regression models with ML (supervised and unsupervised) showed that ML has improved accuracy and diagnostic performance compared to logistic regression models. ML and AI on the other hand allow dynamic and real-time generation of prediction, based and adjusted as new data are fed into the model (Arvind, Kim, Oermann, Kaji, & Cho, 2018; Asadi, Dowling, Yan, & Mitchell, 2014; Chen et al., 2018; Jeon, Kim, Oh, Kim, & Kim, 2018; Kendale, Kulkarni, Rosenberg, & Wang, 2018; Lee, Yoon, Nam, et al., 2018; Lee, Yoon, Yang, et al., 2018; Meyer et al., 2018).

ML can easily analyze large amount of patient data across different domains (medical history, test results, monitors data, clinician notes, etc.) and recognize patterns, which are refined as more data becomes available. Big data analysis using ML techniques provides the means to move beyond group-level statistics into individual subject outcomes based on accuracy, sensitivity, specificity and area under the receiver operating characteristic (ROC) curve (AUC) with area under curve receiver operating characteristic (AUROC). Also, ML includes more features in the model development which may improve accuracy and taking into account heterogeneity of the population. Unsupervised ML can recognize complex patterns that can identify relationships between large amounts of diverse data; incorporation of feature selection in the process can automatically select subgroups of predictors that are most relevant for a model, providing simpler and more clinically useful results. These techniques have been already implemented into many aspects of clinical practice, most commonly to predict probability of the outcomes of interest (Parthipan et al., 2019; Stonko et al., 2018; Yoon et al., 2018).

## 9.4 Diagnosis and Image Analysis

Various techniques, especially artificial neural networks and specifically convolutional neural networks, have been developed to analyze imaging data and provide diagnostic interpretations to the clinicians (Chudzik, Majumdar, Caliva, Al-Diri, & Hunter, 2018). These are not just restricted to radiology or pathology images but are also being applied for real-time guidance during procedures such as colonoscopy (Hirasawa et al., 2018). Surgical decision to treat, evaluation of therapy and prognosis are all being guided by these enhanced radiomic techniques, which discover patterns in not only the affected tissues but also those surrounding the lesion. (Peeken et al., 2018; Wang et al., 2018) Hepatic steatosis assessment was demonstrated by Moccia et al., using pictures of liver graft obtained by smartphone cameras in the operating room. Prediction of the liver graft function achieved sensitivity, specificity and accuracy of 95%, 81% and 88% respectively, using the ML model (Moccia et al., 2018). Use of semi-supervised models, such as these in the operating room, will make decision-making not only more accurate but also more efficient.

Support vector machine derived classification model, such as one developed by Sengupta et al. (2018), has demonstrated ability to differentiate between infiltrative tumor and surrounding vasogenic edema with significant accuracy amongst high-grade glioma patients. Algorithms like these are likely to supplement traditional evaluation methods dependent on expert opinions from radiologist in both pre-operative, intraoperative and postoperative patient management.

## 9.5 Decision Support

ML algorithms are not a substitute for clinician decision-making. These are being developed in most instances to provide a thorough analysis of data, provide pattern recognition in an efficient and detailed manner using multimodal data and thus support and enhance clinician's decision-making capacity (Shortliffe & Sepulveda, 2018). Taggart et al. demonstrated ability to identify populations at risk of bleeding amongst critically ill patients by analyzing clinical notes using NLP (Taggart et al., 2018). It is conceivable that postoperative patients in the future will be triaged to intensive care units by using similar techniques in addition to the current scoring methods or based on clinical expertise alone.

Many examples of clinical decision support in perioperative areas including critical care, ranging from diagnosis to prognosis, are being developed using various ML techniques (Belard et al., 2017; Celtikci, 2018; Mendez et al., 2018). Prediction of hypotension using arterial waveform analysis has demonstrated effectiveness in both the operating room and critical care units (Davies, Vistisen, Jian, Hatib, & Scheeren, 2019). Techniques such as feature engineering to develop such predictions map out features in millions which can then be refined to a few 1000 meaningful ones' with map out millions of features (Hatib et al., 2018). These are replacing traditional basic assessments such as heart rate, heart rate variability and stroke volume variability, amongst others. Complex analysis like these are predicting warning events in advance with interpretable guidance of the cause, preparing clinicians in advance to prevent these harmful events and suggesting most effective treatment strategy.

Decision tree algorithm has been used by Parecco et al., to predict prolonged mechanical ventilation and need for early tracheostomy with a mean AUC of greater than 0.80 in critically ill patients, majority of which were admitted in surgical ICU. Prognostic classifications such as these are very valuable to patients and families in quality of life decision-making and application of advanced directives.

## 9.6 Therapeutics

From guiding medication delivery to assisting with procedures, ML is increasingly being researched and used in operating rooms and procedural areas. Applications focused on assessment and delivery of intravenous fluid status have been developed and are being evaluated by many. These applications are likely to help with prevention of hypotension in the operating room and ICU which has been associated with significant morbidity and mortality (Maheshwari et al., 2019). Reljin et al. proposed a support vector ML model using photoplethysmography recordings to discriminate between patients with hypovolemia and euvolemia with 88% accuracy amongst trauma patients with suspected hemorrhage (Reljin et al., 2018). Similarly, Celi et al. developed a Bayesian network to predict a range of fluid therapy amongst critically ill patients with an accuracy of 77.8% (Celi, Hinske, Alterovitz, & Szolovits, 2008). Decision to prescribe fluids for patients with acute kidney injury and oliguria in a critical care unit is even more complex. Zhang et al. developed a XGBoost model which accurately makes distinction between patients who would benefit from and respond to fluid therapy. This model outperformed the traditional logistic regression-based model, with an AUC of 0.86 vs. an AUC of 0.72, respectively (Zhang, Ho, & Hong, 2019).

Closed-loop therapies such as those used for glycemic control using artificial pancreas is another example of automated ML-based delivery of care (DeJournett & DeJournett, 2016; Piemonte, 2018). Based on evidence that perioperative glycemic control, especially in critically ill patients, impacts outcomes, applications like artificial pancreas are likely to positively impact outcomes.

Similar to blood glucose management, titration of medications with narrow therapeutic index is better guided by ML algorithms. Accurate Tacrolimus dosing is critical to graft survival and prevention of complications after kidney transplant. O'Neil and P. Bastard developed an artificial neural network which estimates tacrolimus in these patients with an AUC of 93% (Niel & Bastard, 2018). Such methods are also likely to decrease the need for expensive blood testing for tacrolimus measurement and improve patient satisfaction.

Tighe et al. demonstrated ability of ML algorithms using various methods including Least Absolute Shrinkage and Selection Operator (LASSO), decision tree, support vector machine, neural network and k-nearest neighbor (k-NN) to predict postoperative pain. Using 796 variables collected from EHR, these ML models outperformed traditional logistic regression in accuracy of prediction of postoperative pain (Tighe et al., 2015). Better prediction of postoperative pain using ML can also help target resources and use of multimodal analgesia in a more targeted manner, preventing overuse of opioids and their associated side effects.

## 9.7 Future Prospects

To make a significant change in quality and delivery of care with ever-expanding patient populations and availability of data, we need to adopt ML for automation of data abstraction, analysis and reporting. Change in patient management also requires processing of real-time data and availability of actionable guidance. ML techniques ranging from simple classification models, artificial neural networks to deep reinforcement learning will likely see applications in all areas of perioperative care of surgical patients. Techniques such as radiomics are likely to see routine application to robotic surgeries, stereotactic guidance for surgeries, evaluation of disease progression and response to therapy. Objective analysis of multimodal data including unstructured data using NLP will help identify risk such as limb ischemia and populations at risk in an enhanced manner (Afzal et al., 2018; Luo et al., 2018). Surgeons and perioperative clinicians will adopt the use of artificial intelligence selecting validated methods providing more accurate measurement and therapeutic guidance (Mirnezami & Ahmed, 2018; Wang & Majewicz Fey, 2018).

## References

Afzal, N., Mallipeddi, V. P., Sohn, S., Liu, H., Chaudhry, R., Scott, C. G., … Arruda-Olson, A. M. (2018). Natural language processing of clinical notes for identification of critical limb ischemia. *Int J Med Inform, 111*, 83–89. doi: 10.1016/j.ijmedinf.2017.12.024.

Aminsharifi, A., Irani, D., Pooyesh, S., Parvin, H., Dehghani, S., Yousofi, K., … Zibaie, F. (2017). Artificial neural network system to predict the postoperative outcome of percutaneous nephrolithotomy. *J Endourol, 31*(5), 461–467. doi: 10.1089/end.2016.0791.

Arvind, V., Kim, J. S., Oermann, E. K., Kaji, D., & Cho, S. K. (2018). Predicting surgical complications in adult patients undergoing anterior cervical discectomy and fusion using machine learning. *Neurospine, 15*(4), 329–337. doi: 10.14245/ns.1836248.124.

Asadi, H., Dowling, R., Yan, B., & Mitchell, P. (2014). Machine learning for outcome prediction of acute ischemic stroke post intra-arterial therapy. *PLoS One, 9*(2), e88225. doi: 10.1371/journal.pone.0088225.

Belard, A., Buchman, T., Forsberg, J., Potter, B. K., Dente, C. J., Kirk, A., & Elster, E. (2017). Precision diagnosis: a view of the clinical decision support systems (CDSS) landscape through the lens of critical care. *J Clin Monit Comput, 31*(2), 261–271. doi: 10.1007/s10877-016-9849-1.

Celi, L. A., Hinske, L. C., Alterovitz, G., & Szolovits, P. (2008). An artificial intelligence tool to predict fluid requirement in the intensive care unit: a proof-of-concept study. *Crit Care, 12*(6), R151. doi: 10.1186/cc7140.

Celtikci, E. (2018). A systematic review on machine learning in neurosurgery: the future of decision-making in patient care. *Turk Neurosurg, 28*(2), 167–173. doi: 10.5137/1019–5149.Jtn.20059-17.1.

Chen, H. L., Yu, S. J., Xu, Y., Yu, S. Q., Zhang, J. Q., Zhao, J. Y., … Zhu, B. (2018). Artificial neural network: a method for prediction of surgery-related pressure injury in cardiovascular surgical patients. *J Wound Ostomy Continence Nurs, 45*(1), 26–30. doi: 10.1097/won.0000000000000388.

Chudzik, P., Majumdar, S., Caliva, F., Al-Diri, B., & Hunter, A. (2018). Microaneurysm detection using fully convolutional neural networks. *Comput Methods Programs Biomed, 158*, 185–192. doi: 10.1016/j.cmpb.2018.02.016.

Davies, S. J., Vistisen, S. T., Jian, Z., Hatib, F., & Scheeren, T. W. L. (2019). Ability of an arterial waveform analysis-derived hypotension prediction index to predict future hypotensive events in surgical patients. *Anesth Analg.* doi: 10.1213/ANE.0000000000004121.

DeJournett, L., & DeJournett, J. (2016). In silico testing of an artificial-intelligence-based artificial pancreas designed for use in the intensive care unit setting. *J Diabetes Sci Technol, 10*(6), 1360–1371. doi: 10.1177/1932296816653967.

Ehlers, A. P., Roy, S. B., Khor, S., Mandagani, P., Maria, M., Alfonso-Cristancho, R., & Flum, D. R. (2017). Improved risk prediction following surgery using machine learning algorithms. *EGEMS (Wash DC), 5*(2), 3. doi: 10.13063/2327-9214.1278.

Hatib, F., Jian, Z., Buddi, S., Lee, C., Settels, J., Sibert, K., … Cannesson, M. (2018). Machine-learning algorithm to predict hypotension based on high-fidelity arterial pressure waveform analysis. *Anesthesiology.* doi: 10.1097/ALN.0000000000002300.

Hirasawa, T., Aoyama, K., Tanimoto, T., Ishihara, S., Shichijo, S., Ozawa, T., … Tada, T. (2018). Application of artificial intelligence using a convolutional neural network for detecting gastric cancer in endoscopic images. *Gastric Cancer, 21*(4), 653–660. doi: 10.1007/s10120-018-0793-2.

Jeon, J. P., Kim, C., Oh, B. D., Kim, S. J., & Kim, Y. S. (2018). Prediction of persistent hemodynamic depression after carotid angioplasty and stenting using artificial neural network model. *Clin Neurol Neurosurg, 164*, 127–131. doi: 10.1016/j.clineuro.2017.12.005.

Kanevsky, J., Corban, J., Gaster, R., Kanevsky, A., Lin, S., & Gilardino, M. (2016). Big data and machine learning in plastic surgery: a new frontier in surgical innovation. *Plast Reconstr Surg, 137*(5), 890e–897e. doi: 10.1097/PRS.0000000000002088.

Karnik, K. (2014). FDA regulation of clinical decision support software. *J Law Biosci, 1*(2), 202–208. doi: 10.1093/jlb/lsu004.

Kendale, S., Kulkarni, P., Rosenberg, A. D., & Wang, J. (2018). Supervised machine-learning predictive analytics for prediction of postinduction hypotension. *Anesthesiology, 129*(4), 675–688. doi: 10.1097/ALN.0000000000002374.

Kwong, A. J., & Asrani, S. K. (2018). Artificial neural networks and liver transplantation: are we ready for self-driving cars? *Liver Transpl, 24*(2), 161–163. doi: 10.1002/lt.24993.

Lee, H. C., Yoon, H. K., Nam, K., Cho, Y. J., Kim, T. K., Kim, W. H., & Bahk, J. H. (2018). Derivation and validation of machine learning approaches to predict acute kidney injury after cardiac surgery. *J Clin Med, 7*(10). doi: 10.3390/jcm7100322.

Lee, H. C., Yoon, S. B., Yang, S. M., Kim, W. H., Ryu, H. G., Jung, C. W., … Lee, K. H. (2018). Prediction of acute kidney injury after liver transplantation: machine learning approaches vs. logistic regression model. *J Clin Med, 7*(11). doi: 10.3390/jcm7110428.

Liew, C. (2018). The future of radiology augmented with artificial intelligence: a strategy for success. *Eur J Radiol, 102*, 152–156. doi: 10.1016/j.ejrad.2018.03.019.

Luo, L., Zhang, F., Yao, Y., Gong, R., Fu, M., & Xiao, J. (2018). Machine learning for identification of surgeries with high risks of cancellation. *Health Informatics J.* doi: 10.1177/1460458218813602.

Maheshwari, K., Cywinski, J., Mathur, P., Cummings, K. C., 3rd, Avitsian, R., Crone, T., … Kurz, A. (2018). Identify and monitor clinical variation using machine intelligence: a pilot in colorectal surgery. *J Clin Monit Comput.* doi: 10.1007/s10877-018-0200-x.

Maheshwari, K., Shimada, T., Fang, J., Ince, I., Mascha, E. J., Turan, A., … Sessler, D. I. (2019). Hypotension prediction index software for management of hypotension during moderate- to high-risk noncardiac surgery: protocol for a randomized trial. *Trials, 20*(1), 255. doi: 10.1186/s13063-019-3329-0.

Mathur, P., & Burns, M. L. (2019). Artificial intelligence in critical care. *Int Anesthesiol Clin, 57*(2), 89–102. doi: 10.1097/AIA.0000000000000221.

Mendez, J. A., Leon, A., Marrero, A., Gonzalez-Cava, J. M., Reboso, J. A., Estevez, J. I., & Gomez-Gonzalez, J. F. (2018). Improving the anesthetic process by a fuzzy rule based medical decision system. *Artif Intell Med, 84*, 159–170. doi: 10.1016/j.artmed.2017.12.005.

Meyer, A., Zverinski, D., Pfahringer, B., Kempfert, J., Kuehne, T., Sundermann, S. H., … Eickhoff, C. (2018). Machine learning for real-time prediction of complications in critical care: a retrospective study. *Lancet Respir Med, 6*(12), 905–914. doi: 10.1016/S2213-2600(18)30300-X.

Mirnezami, R., & Ahmed, A. (2018). Surgery 3.0, artificial intelligence and the next-generation surgeon. *Br J Surg, 105*(5), 463–465. doi: 10.1002/bjs.10860.

Moccia, S., Mattos, L. S., Patrini, I., Ruperti, M., Pote, N., Dondero, F., … Cesaretti, M. (2018). Computer-assisted liver graft steatosis assessment via learning-based texture analysis. *Int J Comput Assist Radiol Surg, 13*(9), 1357–1367. doi: 10.1007/s11548-018-1787-6.

Niel, O., & Bastard, P. (2018). Artificial intelligence improves estimation of tacrolimus area under the concentration over time curve in renal transplant recipients. *Transpl Int, 31*(8), 940–941. doi: 10.1111/tri.13271.

Padoy, N. (2019). Machine and deep learning for workflow recognition during surgery. *Minim Invasive Ther Allied Technol, 28*(2), 82–90. doi: 10.1080/136457 06.2019.1584116.

Parthipan, A., Banerjee, I., Humphreys, K., Asch, S. M., Curtin, C., Carroll, I., & Hernandez-Boussard, T. (2019). Predicting inadequate postoperative pain management in depressed patients: a machine learning approach. *PLoS One, 14*(2), e0210575. doi: 10.1371/journal.pone.0210575.

Peeken, J. C., Goldberg, T., Knie, C., Komboz, B., Bernhofer, M., Pasa, F., … Combs, S. E. (2018). Treatment-related features improve machine learning prediction of prognosis in soft tissue sarcoma patients. *Strahlenther Onkol, 194*(9), 824–834. doi: 10.1007/s00066-018-1294-2.

Piemonte, V. (2018). Predictive models control of the artificial pancreas: compartmental or neural networks models? *Artif Organs, 42*(3), 251–253. doi: 10.1111/aor.13104.

Reljin, N., Zimmer, G., Malyuta, Y., Shelley, K., Mendelson, Y., Blehar, D. J., … Chon, K. H. (2018). Using support vector machines on photoplethysmographic signals to discriminate between hypovolemia and euvolemia. *PLoS One, 13*(3), e0195087. doi: 10.1371/journal.pone.0195087.

Senders, J. T., Zaki, M. M., Karhade, A. V., Chang, B., Gormley, W. B., Broekman, M. L., … Arnaout, O. (2018). An introduction and overview of machine learning in neurosurgical care. *Acta Neurochir (Wien), 160*(1), 29–38. doi: 10.1007/s00701-017-3385-8.

Sengupta, A., Agarwal, S., Gupta, P. K., Ahlawat, S., Patir, R., Gupta, R. K., & Singh, A. (2018). On differentiation between vasogenic edema and non-enhancing tumor in high-grade glioma patients using a support vector machine classifier based upon pre and post-surgery MRI images. *Eur J Radiol, 106*, 199–208. doi: 10.1016/j.ejrad.2018.07.018.

Shortliffe, E. H., & Sepulveda, M. J. (2018). Clinical decision support in the era of artificial intelligence. *JAMA, 320*(21), 2199–2200. doi: 10.1001/jama.2018.17163.

Stonko, D. P., Dennis, B. M., Betzold, R. D., Peetz, A. B., Gunter, O. L., & Guillamondegui, O. D. (2018). Artificial intelligence can predict daily trauma volume and average acuity. *J Trauma Acute Care Surg, 85*(2), 393–397. doi: 10.1097/TA.0000000000001947.

Taggart, M., Chapman, W. W., Steinberg, B. A., Ruckel, S., Pregenzer-Wenzler, A., Du, Y., ... Shah, R. U. (2018). Comparison of 2 natural language processing methods for identification of bleeding among critically ill patients. *JAMA Netw Open, 1*(6), e183451. doi: 10.1001/jamanetworkopen.2018.3451.

Tighe, P. J., Harle, C. A., Hurley, R. W., Aytug, H., Boezaart, A. P., & Fillingim, R. B. (2015). Teaching a machine to feel postoperative pain: combining high-dimensional clinical data with machine learning algorithms to forecast acute postoperative pain. *Pain Med, 16*(7), 1386–1401. doi: 10.1111/pme.12713.

Vranas, K. C., Jopling, J. K., Sweeney, T. E., Ramsey, M. C., Milstein, A. S., Slatore, C. G., ... Liu, V. X. (2017). Identifying distinct subgroups of ICU patients: a machine learning approach. *Crit Care Med, 45*(10), 1607–1615. doi: 10.1097/CCM.0000000000002548.

Wang, Z., & Majewicz Fey, A. (2018). Deep learning with convolutional neural network for objective skill evaluation in robot-assisted surgery. *Int J Comput Assist Radiol Surg, 13*(12), 1959–1970. doi: 10.1007/s11548-018-1860-1.

Wang, Z., Xin, J., Sun, P., Lin, Z., Yao, Y., & Gao, X. (2018). Improved lung nodule diagnosis accuracy using lung CT images with uncertain class. *Comput Methods Programs Biomed, 162*, 197–209. doi: 10.1016/j.cmpb.2018.05.028.

Yoon, J., Zame, W. R., Banerjee, A., Cadeiras, M., Alaa, A. M., & van der Schaar, M. (2018). Personalized survival predictions via trees of predictors: an application to cardiac transplantation. *PLoS One, 13*(3), e0194985. doi: 10.1371/journal.pone.0194985.

Zhang, Z., Ho, K. M., & Hong, Y. (2019). Machine learning for the prediction of volume responsiveness in patients with oliguric acute kidney injury in critical care. *Crit Care, 23*(1), 112. doi: 10.1186/s13054-019-2411-z.

*Chapter 10*

# Application of an Intelligent Stochastic Optimization Nonlinear Model

Gonzalo Hernández[*]

*Centro Científico y Tecnológico de Valparaíso*

Fernando A. Crespo

*Universidad Mayor*

## Contents

[*] Gonzalo J. Hernandez, PhD. He passed away on February 28, 2020. A colleague committed to transparency, work, ethical standards and scientific development. You will live in the memory of those who knew and appreciated you, and that you rest in peace.

## 10.1 Introduction

In Chile, the methods and techniques called "intelligent", i.e., that come from Computational Intelligence, have been developed and implemented mainly to solve some operational problems (demand forecast per example), and sales and risk assessment in the finance and retail sectors. Up to date, there is a large deficit of this type of technological solution to date in the health and education sectors. In the Chilean Public and Private Health System, until now there are no intelligent solutions that can be applied to improve the service of transfer of critical patients due to chronic diseases, emergencies or accidents that occurred in the home or on public spaces. Currently, emergency vehicles (ambulances) are located in the hospitals, with the consequence of significantly longer travel times from and to the corresponding medical center, which causes worsening in the condition of the patient and in some cases his death for lack of timely initial para-medical treatment. For example, the SAMU – Sistema de Atención Médica Móvil de Urgencia (Urgent Mobile Health Care System) has an availability of 53 ambulances in all the metropolitan region that serve 24 hours a day to patients mainly of types P1, P2 and P3 (P1: the person needs immediate attention; P2: the person needs attention very urgently; P3: the person needs urgent attention) (see reference Ministerio (2019)). Although it is a significant number of ambulances, the geographical region they serve is extensive in area and densely populated, which causes delays in the arrival of ambulances to the place of events due to the high demand for emergencies and travel times.

In the Santiago Metropolitan Region (Chile), there are 18 public hospitals up to date. The public hospitals attended during 2017 and 2018 between a number of 58,370 and 85,434 weekly emergencies, according to "Ministerio de Salud de Chile" (MINSAL) report data (see reference Ahmadi-Javid et al. (2017)). This trend has been maintained during the course of 2019 with small variations. It should be noted that only the Central Urgency Hospital (called "Poster Central") attended during 2017 and 2019 between 672 and 1,525 weekly emergencies. It is worth mentioning that up to date, there is no intelligent system of location and assignment, neither in the public nor in the private system, and currently ambulances. The existence of a stochastic optimization model for locating and assigning of ambulances in a decentralized way will improve the service of transfer of chronic or emergency patients, decreasing the arrival times of the ambulances to the place of the event, that is, decreasing the waiting time of the patient; decreasing the travel times of ambulances to the attention centers;

decreasing the fixed and variable costs of the patient transfer system; and therefore increasing the availability of emergency vehicles for the attention of new events. All of the above will generate a significant improvement in the quality of service to both public and private emergency patients.

For this reason, this chapter proposed a stochastic optimization model for the location and assignment that determines the location and an optimum number of ambulances needed to improve the arrival times to medical emergencies, based on the prediction of the probable occurrence of this type of events in a city. That is, it is proposed to decentralize the location of ambulances, taking them out of hospitals and assigning them to "hot spots" in order to attend to the occurrence of medical emergencies. This chapter is organized as follows. Section 10.2 presents the stochastic optimization model, the methodology that was used to solve this problem and the results obtained. Finally, in Section 10.3 are presented our main conclusions.

## 10.2 Stochastic Optimization Models for Locating Ambulances

As we mentioned before, the models, methods and techniques called intelligence, i.e., based on Computational Intelligence Methods, in Chile, have been developed and implemented mainly to solve different problems and improve the operation, sales and risk assessment in the finance and retail sectors. There is a large deficit of this type of technological solutions to date in the health and education sectors (Engelbrecht, 2007; Kruse, 2013; Bishop, 1996, 2006; Theodoridis and Koutroumbas, 2008; Ripley, 2008). Currently, associated with the problem that is proposed to solve, there are only some tools for monitoring and routing of ambulances, which do not allow addressing the total solution of the problem of transfer of emergency patients to public and private hospitals (Ahmadi-Javid et al., 2017; Altan Ardogan, 2017; Dae et al., 2017; Fancello et al., 2017; Karaoglan et al., 2018; Leknes et al., 2017; Khayal et al., 2015). It is worth mentioning that there is no intelligent technological solution up to date like the one that is studied in this chapter.

There are three main benefits for the users and clients of the proposed system, which are given in the following:

(B1) Reduction of the arrival times of the ambulances to the place of the event, that is, the waiting time of the patient and decrease of the travel times of the ambulances to care centers.

(B2) Increase the availability of emergency vehicles for the attention of new emergency events.

(B3) Reduction of fixed and variable costs of the patient transfer system will imply a significant improvement in the quality of service to both public and private patients, as well as an increase in the effectiveness and efficiency of the transfer of emergency or chronic patients.

The main assumptions of the model studied are the following:

(Assumption 1) In order to reduce the data complexity, the geographical region under consideration will be modeled as a collection of 20 circular sectors for the data considered.

(Assumption 2) The emergency vehicles will be located at the center of each sector in order to decrease the dimensionality of the stochastic data.

(Assumption 3) The emergency calls in the sector $I$ of some medium-size city (less than 1.000.000 habitants) occur randomly according to a Poisson distribution with an average call rate per hour equal to $\lambda_i$.

(Assumption 4) The travel time from the location of the ambulances (center of each sector) to the location of the emergency (event) follows a uniform distribution.

(Assumption 5) The travel time from the location of the emergency to the Medical Center follows a uniform distribution.

(Assumption 6) The service time in the location of the emergency follows an exponential distribution.

The definition of the model is the following (Figure 10.1):

Data:

$\lambda_i$ [call/hour]: Number of average emergency calls generated per hour in sector $i$.

$\mu_i$ [call/hour]: Number of average emergency calls answered per hour in sector $i$.

$\rho_i$ [call/hour]: Utilization/Service factor in sector $i$.

$at$ [hour/call]: Average total attention time observed for emergency vehicles within sector $i$.

$attv_i$ [hour/call]: Average travel time per call observed for emergency vehicles within sector $i$.

$mintt_i$ [hour/call]: Minimum travel time per observed call of emergency vehicles within sector $i$.

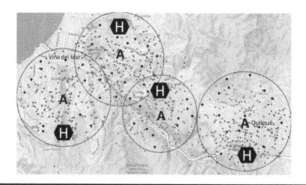

**Figure 10.1 Example of emergency events in a region (black- patients P1 and P2, grey- patient P3).**

max$tt_i$ [hour/call]: Maximum travel time per observed call of emergency vehicles in sector $i$.

$aost_i$ [hour/call]: Average on-site service time per call in sector $i$.

$tst_i$ [hour/call]: Total attention time per call in the sector $I$, including travel and service times.

$qos_i$ [hour]: Quality of service defined in sector $i$.

$N_a$: Number of total available ambulances considering all sectors $fc_i$ [m\$/(month×vehicle)]: Monthly fixed costs per emergency vehicle assigned to sector $i$.

$vc_i$ [m\$/call]: Variable costs per emergency call in sector $i$.

$x_i$: Number of emergency vehicles assigned to sector $i$

## 10.2.1 Stochastic Optimization Model

$$\min_{x_i,\, i=1,\ldots,20} OF = \sum_{i=1}^{20} fc_i x_i + (30)(24) \sum_{i=1}^{20} vc_i \lambda_i x_i$$

$$att_i = attv_i + tst_i + \lambda_i \frac{1}{attv_i + tst_i}$$

$$\sum_{i=1}^{20} fc_i x_i \le N_a$$

$$\lambda_i \frac{\lambda_i}{\lambda_i x_i} \le 0.85$$

$$IP(W_i \le qos_i) = \lambda_i e^{-(aost_i^{-1} - \lambda_i)qos_i}$$

This stochastic optimization model was implemented in @Risk© for 20 sectors, its objective function corresponds to the total monthly operating cost and it has only three constraints:

■ A total number of available ambulances for the 20 sectors.
■ Upper bound for the utilization rate.
■ Quality of service, QoS = 0.15, 0.05

In order to simplify the stochastic model, we considered only one kind of patient (not three as usual), and as we mentioned before a Poisson distribution for the emergency calls, a continuous uniform distribution for the travel times and an exponential distribution for the QoS. Despite the simplification made to the model, it corresponds to a nonlinear, stochastic optimization model with respect to the constraint of QoS (Hernández and Crespo, 2019).

Figure 10.2 shows the final solution found after 5,000 trial solutions and 1,000 samples of the random numbers: $\lambda_i$ ("lambda_i_alea"), travel times ("tt_i_alea") and quality of service equals to 0.15.

Figure 10.3 shows the objective function of empirical and theoretical distributions for the different samples corresponding to the best solution found (shown in Figure 10.2) for QoS = 0.15.

If the QoS is significantly increased to 0.05, the number of ambulances also increased, as it is shown in Figure 10.4.

Figure 10.5 shows the objective function of empirical and theoretical distributions for the different samples corresponding to the best solution found (shown in Figure 10.4) for QoS = 0.05.

In Figure 10.6, we show the evolution of the @Risk iterations for the best QoS model.

It is observed from Figure 10.6 that only 1,500 trial solutions in the @Risk setting are sufficient to produce excellent results. This can be explained by the fact that the samples of the random variables were enough to reflect the difficulty of the model.

From these results, we can affirm that the model increasing the QoS in the sense service quality was improved and the availability of "idle" ambulances that can handle new emergencies was increased. Additionally, the efficiency and effectiveness of the transfer system were increased. Moreover, Figures 10.3 and 10.5 can be affirmed that this model is consistent because the theoretical and empirical distributions are very similar.

The studied model produces interesting and validated solutions since the number of ambulances needed to meet the QoS constraint increases as the

| Sector | lambda_i | lambda_i_alea | att_i | mintt_i | maxtt_i | tt_i_alea | aost_i | qos_i_alea | tst_i | mu_i | qos_i | fc_i | vc_i | xi |
|---|---|---|---|---|---|---|---|---|---|---|---|---|---|---|
| 1 | 0.837 | 0.000 | 0.34 | 0.28 | 0.43 | 0.29 | 0.50 | 0.03 | 0.33 | 3.07 | 0.50 | 2000 | 25 | 5 |
| 2 | 0.756 | 0.000 | 0.41 | 0.34 | 0.54 | 0.46 | 0.50 | 0.07 | 0.53 | 1.90 | 0.50 | 2000 | 25 | 1 |
| 3 | 0.729 | 0.000 | 0.34 | 0.23 | 0.53 | 0.37 | 0.50 | 1.00 | 1.37 | 0.73 | 0.50 | 2000 | 25 | 3 |
| 4 | 0.702 | 0.000 | 0.28 | 0.21 | 0.47 | 0.26 | 0.50 | 0.08 | 0.34 | 2.93 | 0.50 | 2000 | 25 | 1 |
| 5 | 0.810 | 2.000 | 0.30 | 0.26 | 0.45 | 0.31 | 0.50 | 0.08 | 0.39 | 2.59 | 0.50 | 2000 | 25 | 1 |
| 6 | 0.756 | 0.000 | 0.38 | 0.23 | 0.54 | 0.41 | 0.50 | 0.11 | 0.51 | 1.96 | 0.50 | 2000 | 25 | 5 |
| 7 | 0.756 | 0.000 | 0.39 | 0.30 | 0.51 | 0.50 | 0.50 | 0.04 | 0.54 | 1.86 | 0.50 | 2000 | 25 | 2 |
| 8 | 0.702 | 1.000 | 0.43 | 0.30 | 0.53 | 0.38 | 0.50 | 3.35 | 3.73 | 0.27 | 0.50 | 2000 | 25 | 17 |
| 9 | 0.702 | 2.000 | 0.41 | 0.34 | 0.60 | 0.57 | 0.50 | 1.22 | 1.79 | 0.56 | 0.50 | 2000 | 25 | 1 |
| 10 | 0.702 | 2.000 | 0.32 | 0.24 | 0.56 | 0.35 | 0.50 | 1.43 | 1.79 | 0.56 | 0.50 | 2000 | 25 | 1 |
| 11 | 0.729 | 1.000 | 0.34 | 0.19 | 0.58 | 0.32 | 0.50 | 0.39 | 0.70 | 1.42 | 0.50 | 2000 | 25 | 2 |
| 12 | 0.702 | 1.000 | 0.39 | 0.30 | 0.62 | 0.56 | 0.50 | 0.21 | 0.77 | 1.30 | 0.50 | 2000 | 25 | 1 |
| 13 | 0.702 | 0.000 | 0.45 | 0.34 | 0.60 | 0.49 | 0.50 | 0.06 | 0.55 | 1.82 | 0.50 | 2000 | 25 | 6 |
| 14 | 0.702 | 1.000 | 0.47 | 0.28 | 0.62 | 0.50 | 0.50 | 0.08 | 0.58 | 1.73 | 0.50 | 2000 | 25 | 1 |
| 15 | 0.702 | 0.000 | 0.51 | 0.41 | 0.75 | 0.47 | 0.50 | 0.07 | 0.54 | 1.86 | 0.50 | 2000 | 25 | 1 |
| 16 | 0.259 | 1.000 | 0.68 | 0.60 | 0.94 | 0.71 | 0.50 | 0.02 | 0.73 | 1.37 | 0.50 | 2000 | 25 | 7 |
| 17 | 0.238 | 0.000 | 0.71 | 0.54 | 1.04 | 0.63 | 0.50 | 0.71 | 1.34 | 0.75 | 0.50 | 2000 | 25 | 1 |
| 18 | 0.238 | 0.000 | 0.79 | 0.68 | 0.98 | 0.97 | 0.50 | 0.10 | 1.07 | 0.93 | 0.50 | 2000 | 25 | 5 |
| 19 | 0.194 | 0.000 | 0.75 | 0.64 | 1.16 | 1.05 | 0.50 | 0.13 | 1.19 | 0.84 | 0.50 | 2000 | 25 | 1 |
| 20 | 0.194 | 0.000 | 0.84 | 0.71 | 1.03 | 0.73 | 0.50 | 0.37 | 1.11 | 0.90 | 0.50 | 2000 | 25 | 1 |

| OF | | C1 | | C2 | | C3 | |
|---|---|---|---|---|---|---|---|
| FC | 126000 | 63 | 600 | 4.3 | 0.0000 | 0.0000 | 0.15 |
| VC | 1433379 | | | 0.9 | 0.0000 | 0.0000 | 0.15 |
| TC | 1559379 | | | 2.6 | 0.0000 | 0.0000 | 0.15 |
| | | | | 0.9 | 0.0000 | 0.0000 | 0.15 |
| | | | | 0.9 | 0.7708 | 0.5725 | 0.15 |
| Stats | | | | 4.3 | 0.0000 | 0.0000 | 0.15 |
| Mean | 1555355 | | | 1.7 | 0.0000 | 0.0000 | 0.15 |
| Std Dev | 221301 | | | 14 | 3.7277 | 0.1975 | 0.15 |
| Min | 977471 | | | 0.9 | 3.5802 | 7.3604 | 0.15 |
| Max | 2282055 | | | 0.9 | 3.5791 | 7.3575 | 0.15 |
| Simetria | 0 | | | 1.7 | 0.7040 | 0.2221 | 0.15 |
| Kurtosis | 3 | | | 0.9 | 0.7709 | 0.6645 | 0.15 |
| 25%P | 1382058 | | | 5.1 | 0.0000 | 0.0000 | 0.15 |
| 50%P | 1560084 | | | 0.9 | 0.5791 | 0.4026 | 0.15 |
| 75%P | 1712907 | | | 0.9 | 0.0000 | 0.0000 | 0.15 |
| 80%P | 1744382 | | | 6 | 0.7280 | 0.0562 | 0.15 |
| 85%P | 1790686 | | | 0.9 | 0.0000 | 0.0000 | 0.15 |
| 90%P | 1838215 | | | 4.3 | 0.0000 | 0.0000 | 0.15 |
| 95%P | 1921467 | | | 0.9 | 0.0000 | 0.0000 | 0.15 |
| | | | | 0.9 | 0.0000 | 0.0000 | 0.15 |

**Figure 10.2** Model (Equation 10.1) final solution found after 5,000 trial solutions and 1,000 samples of the random numbers for a quality of service of 0.15.

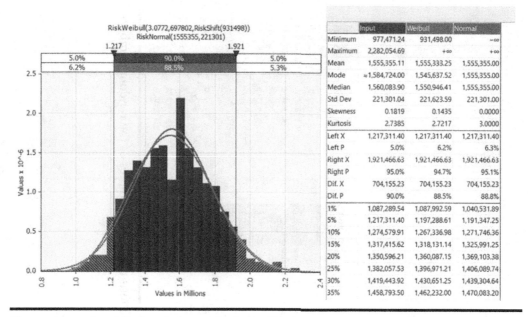

**Figure 10.3 Empirical and theoretical distributions of the objective function for QoS of 0.15.**

| Sector | lambda_i | lambda_i_alea | att_i | mintt_i | maxtt_i | tt_i_alea | aost_i | aos_i_alea | tst_i | mu_i | qos_i | fc_i | vc_i | xi |
|---|---|---|---|---|---|---|---|---|---|---|---|---|---|---|
| 1 | 0.837 | 0.837 | 0.34 | 0.28 | 0.43 | 0.34 | 0.50 | 0.50 | 0.84 | 1.19 | 0.50 | 2000 | 25 | 12 |
| 2 | 0.756 | 0.756 | 0.41 | 0.34 | 0.54 | 0.41 | 0.50 | 0.50 | 0.91 | 1.10 | 0.50 | 2000 | 25 | 1 |
| 3 | 0.729 | 0.729 | 0.34 | 0.23 | 0.53 | 0.34 | 0.50 | 0.50 | 0.84 | 1.19 | 0.50 | 2000 | 25 | 8 |
| 4 | 0.702 | 0.702 | 0.28 | 0.21 | 0.47 | 0.28 | 0.50 | 0.50 | 0.78 | 1.28 | 0.50 | 2000 | 25 | 1 |
| 5 | 0.810 | 0.810 | 0.30 | 0.26 | 0.45 | 0.30 | 0.50 | 0.50 | 0.80 | 1.25 | 0.50 | 2000 | 25 | 1 |
| 6 | 0.756 | 0.756 | 0.38 | 0.23 | 0.54 | 0.38 | 0.50 | 0.50 | 0.88 | 1.14 | 0.50 | 2000 | 25 | 13 |
| 7 | 0.756 | 0.756 | 0.39 | 0.30 | 0.51 | 0.39 | 0.50 | 0.50 | 0.89 | 1.12 | 0.50 | 2000 | 25 | 5 |
| 8 | 0.702 | 0.702 | 0.43 | 0.30 | 0.53 | 0.43 | 0.50 | 0.50 | 0.93 | 1.07 | 0.50 | 2000 | 25 | 48 |
| 9 | 0.702 | 0.702 | 0.41 | 0.34 | 0.60 | 0.41 | 0.50 | 0.50 | 0.91 | 1.10 | 0.50 | 2000 | 25 | 1 |
| 10 | 0.702 | 0.702 | 0.32 | 0.24 | 0.56 | 0.32 | 0.50 | 0.50 | 0.82 | 1.22 | 0.50 | 2000 | 25 | 1 |
| 11 | 0.729 | 0.729 | 0.34 | 0.19 | 0.58 | 0.34 | 0.50 | 0.50 | 0.84 | 1.19 | 0.50 | 2000 | 25 | 5 |
| 12 | 0.702 | 0.702 | 0.39 | 0.30 | 0.62 | 0.39 | 0.50 | 0.50 | 0.89 | 1.12 | 0.50 | 2000 | 25 | 1 |
| 13 | 0.702 | 0.702 | 0.45 | 0.34 | 0.60 | 0.45 | 0.50 | 0.50 | 0.95 | 1.05 | 0.50 | 2000 | 25 | 15 |
| 14 | 0.702 | 0.702 | 0.47 | 0.28 | 0.62 | 0.47 | 0.50 | 0.50 | 0.97 | 1.03 | 0.50 | 2000 | 25 | 1 |
| 15 | 0.702 | 0.702 | 0.51 | 0.41 | 0.75 | 0.51 | 0.50 | 0.50 | 1.01 | 0.99 | 0.50 | 2000 | 25 | 1 |
| 16 | 0.259 | 0.259 | 0.68 | 0.60 | 0.94 | 0.68 | 0.50 | 0.50 | 1.18 | 0.85 | 0.50 | 2000 | 25 | 20 |
| 17 | 0.238 | 0.238 | 0.71 | 0.54 | 1.04 | 0.71 | 0.50 | 0.50 | 1.21 | 0.82 | 0.50 | 2000 | 25 | 1 |
| 18 | 0.238 | 0.238 | 0.79 | 0.68 | 0.98 | 0.79 | 0.50 | 0.50 | 1.29 | 0.78 | 0.50 | 2000 | 25 | 14 |
| 19 | 0.194 | 0.194 | 0.75 | 0.64 | 1.16 | 0.75 | 0.50 | 0.50 | 1.25 | 0.80 | 0.50 | 2000 | 25 | 1 |
| 20 | 0.194 | 0.194 | 0.84 | 0.71 | 1.03 | 0.84 | 0.50 | 0.50 | 1.34 | 0.74 | 0.50 | 2000 | 25 | 1 |

| OF | | | C1 | | C2 | | C3 | |
|---|---|---|---|---|---|---|---|---|
| FC | 302000 | | 151 | 600 | 10 | 0.7010 | 0.0333 | 0.05 |
| VC | 2825774 | | | | 0.9 | 0.6899 | 0.5820 | 0.05 |
| TC | 3127774 | | | | 6.8 | 0.6105 | 0.0440 | 0.05 |
| | | | | | 0.9 | 0.5484 | 0.4108 | 0.05 |
| Stats | | | | | 0.9 | 0.6480 | 0.5200 | 0.05 |
| Mean | 3127774 | | | | 11 | 0.6615 | 0.0296 | 0.05 |
| Std Dev | 0 | | | | 4.3 | 0.6757 | 0.0833 | 0.05 |
| Min | 3127774 | | | | 41 | 0.6537 | 0.0080 | 0.05 |
| Max | 3127774 | | | | 0.9 | 0.6406 | 0.5261 | 0.05 |
| Simetria | 0 | | | | 0.9 | 0.5748 | 0.4433 | 0.05 |
| Kurtosis | 0 | | | | 4.3 | 0.6105 | 0.0723 | 0.05 |
| 25%P | 3127774 | | | | 0.9 | 0.6274 | 0.5094 | 0.05 |
| 50%P | 3127774 | | | | 13 | 0.6669 | 0.0269 | 0.05 |
| 75%P | 3127774 | | | | 0.9 | 0.6801 | 0.5765 | 0.05 |
| 80%P | 3127774 | | | | 0.9 | 0.7064 | 0.6105 | 0.05 |
| 85%P | 3127774 | | | | 17 | 0.3046 | 0.0100 | 0.05 |
| 90%P | 3127774 | | | | 0.9 | 0.2881 | 0.2148 | 0.05 |
| 95%P | 3127774 | | | | 12 | 0.3059 | 0.0149 | 0.05 |
| | | | | | 0.9 | 0.2430 | 0.1795 | 0.05 |
| | | | | | 0.9 | 0.2612 | 0.1984 | 0.05 |

**Figure 10.4 Model (Equation 10.1) final solution found after 5,000 trial solutions and 1,000 samples of the random numbers with better QoS of 0.15.**

quality of service increases. Therefore, the model contributes to improving the QoS which has a significant impact on the efficiency of the system. Moreover, we believe that this simple model can be improved considering two different kinds of patients P1 and P2 together with a constraint for each kind of patient, and also a budget constraint.

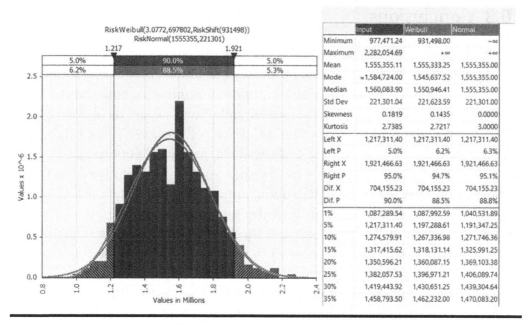

| | Input | Weibull | Normal |
|---|---|---|---|
| Minimum | 977,471.24 | 931,498.00 | −∞ |
| Maximum | 2,282,054.69 | +∞ | +∞ |
| Mean | 1,555,355.11 | 1,555,333.25 | 1,555,355.00 |
| Mode | ≈1,584,724.00 | 1,545,637.52 | 1,555,355.00 |
| Median | 1,560,083.90 | 1,550,946.41 | 1,555,355.00 |
| Std Dev | 221,301.04 | 221,623.59 | 221,301.00 |
| Skewness | 0.1819 | 0.1435 | 0.0000 |
| Kurtosis | 2.7385 | 2.7217 | 3.0000 |
| Left X | 1,217,311.40 | 1,217,311.40 | 1,217,311.40 |
| Left P | 5.0% | 6.2% | 6.3% |
| Right X | 1,921,466.63 | 1,921,466.63 | 1,921,466.63 |
| Right P | 95.0% | 94.7% | 95.1% |
| Dif. X | 704,155.23 | 704,155.23 | 704,155.23 |
| Dif. P | 90.0% | 88.5% | 88.8% |
| 1% | 1,087,289.54 | 1,087,992.59 | 1,040,531.89 |
| 5% | 1,217,311.40 | 1,197,288.61 | 1,191,347.25 |
| 10% | 1,274,579.91 | 1,267,336.98 | 1,271,746.36 |
| 15% | 1,317,415.62 | 1,318,131.14 | 1,325,991.25 |
| 20% | 1,350,596.21 | 1,360,087.15 | 1,369,103.38 |
| 25% | 1,382,057.53 | 1,396,971.21 | 1,406,089.74 |
| 30% | 1,419,443.92 | 1,430,651.25 | 1,439,304.64 |
| 35% | 1,458,793.50 | 1,462,232.00 | 1,470,083.20 |

**Figure 10.5** **Empirical and theoretical distributions of the objective function for a QoS of 0.05.**

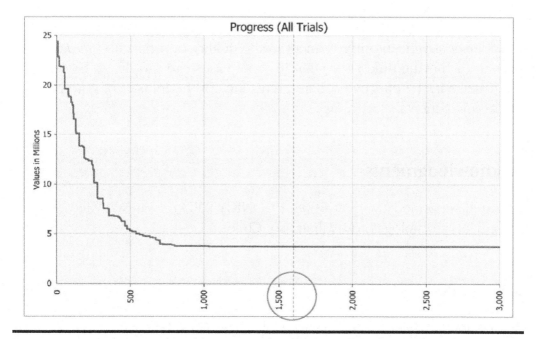

**Figure 10.6** **Evolution of the @Risk iterations for the best optimal solution for a QoS = 0.05.**

## 10.3 Conclusions

In this work, an intelligent stochastic nonlinear optimization model for the decentralized location and assignment of ambulances was studied in order to determine the location and an optimal number of ambulances necessary to improve the arrival times of ambulances to medical emergencies. The model was used two different quality of services. The model was implemented and solve in Excel©+@Risk© for up to 5,000 initial trial solutions and 1,000 samples of the random data for each initial trial solution. Only the feasible final solution, computed with a standard Genetic Algorithm, from an initial trial and all the samples are considered as a probable solution of this problem, and the best of them is chosen as the best solution of the stochastic nonlinear optimization problem studied, under the validity of assumptions formulated for this model.

The results summarized in the last section allow us to affirm that this model can be applied to improve the service of transfer of chronic or emergency patients, reducing the arrival times of ambulances to the place of the event, that is, the waiting time of the patient; decreasing the travel times of ambulances to the centers of attention; reducing the fixed and variable costs of the patient transfer system; and therefore increasing the availability of emergency vehicles for the attention of new events. All of the above considers a significant improvement in the quality of service to emergency patients, achieving timely care that in some cases can save lives, as well as an increase in the effectiveness and efficiency of the transfer of emergency or chronic patients.

## Acknowledgments

Research supported by grant FB0821 CONICYT PIA/Basal CCTVal: Centro Científico y Tecnológico de Valparaíso, Chile.

## References

Ahmadi-Javid, A., et al., (2017). A survey of healthcare facility location, *Computers & Operations Research* 79, 223–263.

Altan Ardogan, M., (2017) Location analysis of emergency vehicles using an approximate queueing model, *Transportation Research Procedia* 22, 430–439.

Bishop, C.M., (1996) *Neural Networks for Pattern Recognition*, Oxford University Press, Oxford, UK.

Bishop, C.M., (2006) *Pattern Recognition and Machine Learning*, Springer, New York.

Dae, Y., et al., (2016) Location, capacity and capability design of emergency medical centers with multiple emergency diseases, *Computers & Industrial Engineering* 101, 10–20.

Engelbrecht, A.P., (2007) *Computational Intelligence: An Introduction*, 2nd Edition, John Wiley & Sons, Chichester.

Fancello, G., et al., (2017) An emergency vehicles allocation model for major industrial disasters, *Transportation Research Procedia* 25, 1164–1179.

Hernandez, G., F. Crespo, (2019) An intelligent stochastic optimization model for localization and assignment of ambulances.

Karaoglan, I., et al., (2018) The multi-vehicle probabilistic covering tour problem, *European Journal of Operational Research* 271, 278–287.

Khayal, D., et al., (2015) A model for planning locations of temporary distribution facilities for emergency response, *Socio-Economic Planning Sciences* 52, 22–30.

Kruse, R., et al., (2013) *Computational Intelligence: A Methodological Introduction*, Springer, London.

Leknes, H., et al., (2017) Strategic ambulance location for heterogeneous regions, *European Journal of Operational Research* 260, 122–133.

Ripley, B. (1996). *Pattern Recognition and Neural Networks*. Cambridge: Cambridge University Press. doi:10.1017/CBO9780511812651.

Theodoridis, S., K. Koutroumbas, (2008) *Pattern Recognition*, 4th Edition, Academic Press, Orlando, FL..

*Chapter 11*

# Audit of Artificial Intelligence Algorithms and Its Impact in Relieving Shortage of Specialist Doctors

Vidur Mahajan and Vasanth Venugopal

*Mahajan Imaging*

## Contents

## 11.1 Introduction

The shortage of specialist doctors is one of the major challenges in healthcare delivery in developing countries. Radiologists are one such specialist cohort who play a crucial role in the diagnosis of diseases and the monitoring of disease progression. There is an emerging consensus among global leaders in public health to leverage the potential of artificial intelligence in radiology. Audit of algorithms with the view of deploying them unsupervised by a specialist or under supervision of a non-specialist is a major area of research interest for academic groups, technological companies and public health organizations alike. In this chapter, we try to present an overview of the potential impact of AI algorithms in rural settings using India as a case study and a brief technical outline for performing audits of algorithms.

## 11.2 Radiology in India

In India, while no official data exists, conversations with health experts reveal that approximately 100–200 million radiology examinations are possibly conducted every year. Out of these, the vast majority would comprise of X-rays and ultrasounds, and only about 300,000–500,000 would be CT or MRI. With the announcement of the Prime Minister's Jan Arogya Yojna (PMJAY) (NHA, 2019), the world's largest insurance scheme through which 500 million individuals would come under Government-sponsored insurance, these radiology investigations are bound to increase exponentially. Estimates state that 2,500 more hospitals of 100 beds each are needed to cater to this scheme of the Government.

Unfortunately, approximately 50%–60% of scans done in India, the majority of these being X-rays, go unreported by radiologists. This is attributed to the shortage of radiologists – there are total 15,667 radiologists (Indian Radiology & Imaging Association Membership as of April 2019 – 13,120 life members, 2,557 members-in-training) in India yielding a radiologist to population ratio of an abysmal 1 in 100,000, compared to 1 in 10,000 in the

United States (Fischer, 2017). The radiologist to population ratio may improve in future as there is an active intervention by the Government to increase the number of specialists in the country (Nagarajan, 2019). Another potential reason for unreported scans is the low reimbursement rates associated with performing and reporting these examinations.

Of these unreported examinations, the majority are performed in rural India. In fact, PMJAY is designed primarily to cater to patients residing in rural areas. Rural India is defined by the Reserve Bank of India, as any township having a population of less than 49,000 (tier 3–tier 6 cities), and constitutes about 70% of the population of the country (2016). It is also important to determine whether there are any adverse effects associated with these scans not being reported. In general, as is true in any part of the world, chest X-rays and musculoskeletal X-rays are the most frequently ordered scans across India usually by general physicians, pulmonologists or orthopedic surgeons, all of whom are trained to read X-rays (Guidelines, 2019). That said, it is important to know that apart from physicians who are trained in allopathic medicine, a lot of care in rural India is provided by physicians whose exposure to allopathic medicine is limited (e.g., Bachelor of Ayurvedic Medicine & Surgery, traditional Indian medicine). Faster, cheaper and accurate radiology services in rural parts of the country can assist in improving the clinical outcomes and reduce overall healthcare costs.

## 11.3 Technological Advances in Radiology

Technology is playing a vital role in improving radiology services across the country. With 4G telecommunications penetrating rural India, teleradiology has gained traction in such parts of the country as a cost-effective replacement for an on-site radiologist. Based on the expert assessment, there are at least 50 structured teleradiology companies in India, with about 1,000 radiologists involved in teleradiology in one way or another. It has also attracted venture capital funding in the recent past with investors betting heavily on the growing radiology sector in India (Healthtech startup, 2019). Unfortunately, in cost-constrained environments, teleradiology reporting is either limited or delayed, both of which mean that the treating clinician might never actually get to use the radiologist's report to treat.

Following teleradiology, the next technological advancement is touted to be artificial intelligence (AI). With globally about $448 million invested into start-ups as of June 2018 (Funding analysis, 2018), there is no denying that

AI will come into the medical imaging domain and transform it. Through this chapter, we take a deep dive into commercially available AI-based technologies, those under research and those that, as far as published literature goes, are not currently being developed. We examine the potential impact each can have in addressing the problem of radiologists' shortage in rural India.

Typically, while examining the role that AI can play in radiology, it is wise to view the applications from a point of view of radiology workflow, that is,

- Pre-scanning – includes patient scheduling, preparation and other administrative activities
- Scanning – includes patient positioning, image acquisition and reconstruction
- Post-scanning – includes post-processing, segmentation, visualization and measurements
- Diagnosis – radiologists' role – making a diagnosis by looking at images.

For the purposes of this chapter, we will focus on the diagnosis part of the radiology workflow, since the shortage of radiologists is addressed by the ability of AI to assist in diagnosis. Further, we divide this chapter into two parts – first, we examine some use-cases which are either published in literature or presented in conferences, and subsequently present a 'Wishlist' of applications which once developed could address the shortage of radiologists in rural India.

## 11.4 Use-Cases

### 11.4.1 Automated Chest X-Ray Reporting Using AI

Automation of chest X-ray reporting is one of the most popular applications that engineers and deep learning scientists are working on primarily due to the easy availability of publicly available datasets ChestXRay14 by NIH (ChestX-ray8, 2019), CheXpert by Stanford University (Irvin et al., 2019) and MIMIC-CXR by Massachusetts Institute of Technology (Johnson et al., 2019). Additionally, since X-ray images are two-dimensional, they are easier to run through convolutional neural networks. Recently, there have been three peer-reviewed publications, by Singh et al. (2018), Rajpurkar et al. (2018) and Hwang et al. (2019) demonstrating technical feasibility and the potential of AI in the field of chest X-ray. We discuss three published use-cases of automated chest X-ray reporting which can reduce the workload of overburdened radiologists catering to rural India.

## 11.4.2 Normal vs. Abnormal Chest X-Ray Classification

At the European Congress of Radiology in 2019, we presented our work on retrospective validation of a high-sensitivity deep learning algorithm for normal/abnormal delineation of chest X-rays (Venugopal et al., 2019a). We evaluated the algorithm, trained on more than a million chest X-ray images, originally described by Singh et al., on a spectrum-biased dataset comprising of 430 chest X-rays with 285 abnormal and 145 normal scans. The algorithm delivered a sensitivity of >97%, with only five clinically significant false negatives (three pneumothorax, two rib fractures cases) which the algorithm was not trained to detect anyway. Since it is common knowledge that more than 50% of chest X-rays done in an outpatient setting are usually normal, such an algorithm can serve as a powerful tool not only by freeing up radiologists' time by automatically reading normal scans but also by empowering physicians in rural India to read their own X-rays possibly through a smartphone camera. It can also be powerful in a setting of teleradiology (since the volume in such a set-up is much higher than a routine outpatient practice) enabling radiologists to focus on the abnormal cases, thereby speeding up reporting and improving quality.

## 11.4.3 Automated Diagnosis of Tuberculosis on Chest X-Ray

Putha et al., from Qure.ai, presented their work on automated tuberculosis detection using deep learning at the European Congress of Radiology in 2018 (Putha et al., 2018). Their algorithm at the time, trained on 400,000+ chest X-rays and their corresponding reports, gave an area under the curve of 0.91, 0.87 and 0.83 for the detection of tuberculosis on three external datasets. The ground truth for such data is the report and opinion of the radiologist. Given that tuberculosis is endemic in India, especially in crowded rural areas, such algorithms can go a long way in ensuring that patients' chest X-rays are reported and can hence be acted upon in a more informed way. There are several organizations such as FIND Diagnostics, PATH and Tata Trusts which are actively working towards the complete eradication of tuberculosis – an effort which is only made possible if everyone who has tuberculosis is treated. In fact, today, there are unpublished efforts underway which aim to predict the GeneXpert status of sputum of patients, which is the gold standard for diagnosis of active pulmonary tuberculosis, from chest X-ray images using deep learning.

### 11.4.4 AI as a Quality Assessment Tool

In a presentation made at the Radiological Society of North America (RSNA) annual conference in November 2018, Sahu et al. (2018) demonstrated a use-case where a deep learning algorithm was used to parse through 3,945 randomly selected chest X-rays of adult patients scanned on an out-patient basis as part of a wellness check-up. Seven hundred and eighty-nine (20%) scans were discordant; that is, the AI-generated findings and clinical reports did not match. Subsequently, 405 of these discordant scans were re-read by three radiologists, and it turned out that in 263 (64.9%) scans, the initial clinical report was wrong. In rural India, where a primary clinical report itself is rare, such reviews performed by AI can not only help relieve the shortage of radiologists but also improve the overall quality of diagnostics and care delivery.

### 11.4.5 Automated Head CT Reporting in Emergencies

In a paper published in the Lancet, Chilamkurthy et al. describe their deep learning algorithm trained on more than 300,000 non-contrast CT scans and validated on an independent dataset from six imaging centers from across New Delhi, India (Chilamkurthy, 2018). The algorithm had an area under the curve of 0.94 for the detection of intracranial bleeds, 0.96 for the detection of skull fractures and 0.96 for the midline shift. Given that in rural India, the instantaneous availability of radiologists, and hence radiology reports, is limited, such an algorithm can play a very important role in guiding treatment by providing a provisional report with a high degree of confidence.

### 11.4.6 Chest CT Screening Using AI

In India, lung cancer constitutes 6.9% of all new cancer cases and 9.3% of all cancer-related deaths in both sexes (Malik and Raina, 2015). Also, it is the commonest cancer and cause of cancer-related mortality in men. In rural India, smoking of indigenous cigarettes (bidi) and water-pipes

(Hookah), combined with a lack of education about its harmful effects, leads to increased risk of developing tobacco lung cancer. Another reason for the high prevalence of respiratory diseases, not necessarily cancer, is the use of wood or coal for cooking inside small homes in the villages. This makes the case for using low-dose CT for lung cancer screening in high-risk populations. Unfortunately, while multi-detector CT scanners with the capability to perform low-dose CT are generally available in rural India, radiologists with experience of picking up small nodules (<30 mm in size) are generally lacking. Aberle et al., in the National Lung Cancer Screening Trial, have demonstrated low-dose CT's capability to reduce relative risk by 20%, but with a false positivity of up to 95% (The National Lung Screening Trial Research Team, 2011). Algorithms can help significantly reduce this false positivity. In a poster at the European Congress of Radiology in 2019, we presented a validation study of a deep learning algorithm developed by Predible Health which automatically detects and characterizes lung nodules between the size of 3and 30 mm (Venugopal et al., 2019b). The algorithm proved superior to four radiologists with 2, 5, 8 and 15 years' experience of reading chest CT on a validation dataset of 100 CT scans with their corresponding biopsy results taken as ground truth. This work demonstrates the ability of deep learning algorithms to undertake the detection of abnormalities in a screening setting, thereby reducing the workload on radiologists working in a rural setting and improving accuracy and hence outcomes for patients.

## 11.5 Audit

While the use-cases described above have the capability to affect the rural population to a certain degree, to truly address the problem of radiologists' shortage in rural India specific solutions that reduce the workload of radiologists practicing in such settings need to be developed. It is safe to assume that radiologists in rural India spend much of their time doing ultrasound scans – a scanner that automatically performs obstetric and/or abdominal ultrasound and gives a 'normal' vs. 'abnormal' reading could help scale up radiology practice in rural India by many folds. Of course, one must be cognizant of the Pre-Natal Diagnostic & Testing Act (PNDT Act) in India which governs ultrasound and other imaging modalities from point of view of being used for gender determination and hence selection while performing obstetric ultrasound (Bhaktwani, 2012). Additionally, as radiologists in rural India generally perform and read scans across multiple modalities, automation of normal vs. abnormal delineation of all possible scans should be the primary target for all developers of AI systems. As we envision a future where all 'normal' scans are 'read' by AI, it is mandatory to develop algorithms with a very high negative predictive value – initially, radiologists will be open to accepting false positives, but a false negative can be potentially catastrophic.

## 11.5.1 Algorithmic Audit

An 'algorithmic audit' methodology can be used by radiologists to evaluate the performance of an AI algorithm, and share relevant feedback with vendors in order to help them improve the performance of the algorithms. The method includes preparing datasets especially focused on validation of algorithms, examining failed cases post-testing of AI on these validation images and a series of other steps that are described further in more detail.

## 11.5.2 Independent Validation

Lack of generalizability of AI algorithms is a major hindrance to the adoption of such tools in clinical practice. Kim et al. found that as of late August 2018, only 6% of the 516 studies published on radiology AI did external or truly independent validation (Kim et al., 2019), an essential component of the algorithmic audit. To understand the nuances of true independent validation, one must understand how a deep learning algorithm is developed and validated. We take the example of MRNet, an algorithm to automatically detect anterior cruciate ligament tears on knee MRIs, developed by Rajpurkar et al. (Bien et al., 2018). The authors first obtained a dataset of 1,370 knee MRIs along with their corresponding reports. These 1,370 MRIs were broken into three separate datasets – one training set of 1,130 MRIs, one tuning set of 120 MRIs and one validation set of another 120 MRIs. Note that all three sets are subsets of the larger dataset of 1,370 MRIs all of which have been obtained from the same hospital – Stanford University Hospital. The training set was used to create the deep learning algorithm, the tuning set used to fine-tune the parameters of the deep learning algorithm and finally the validation set used to determine the performance of the algorithm. The algorithm was also tested on an external validation dataset from Stajduhar et al. (Dhanlaxmi Bank, 2019) of 917 MRIs, from a different country altogether. MRNet gave an impressive area under curve (AUC) of 0.96 on the Stanford Hospital validation dataset, which dropped to 0.82 on the Stajduhar et al. dataset – the truly independent dataset, thereby demonstrating the problem of generalizability of AI algorithms across datasets. The problem of generalizability is well documented in research, but as such no concrete metric exists to measure both generalizability and the lack of it.

Another example of true independent validation comes from Chilamkurthy et al. (2018) where a deep learning algorithm that automatically detects critical findings in head CT scans was validated on an external dataset from multiple hospitals. This was one of the first peer-reviewed studies of an AI algorithm giving AUC of more than 0.90 for all its findings on an external test set, comprising of data obtained from clinical sites where the algorithm was not trained on. Such results make the case for true independent external validation of AI algorithms before putting them to use in clinical environments. Since the performance of AI algorithms is typically much better on data it was trained on, as a radiologist or a radiology manager wanting to work with vendors to develop or validate AI algorithms, it is important to think through whether one would like to contribute data for the development of algorithms, or would one like to use their data exclusively for validation. Developing and validating an algorithm on data from the same clinical site may not provide the true picture of the performance of algorithms.

## 11.5.3 *Stratification of Data for Audit*

Once a test dataset with corresponding ground truth has been assembled, it is important to determine the mix of cases required to aptly validate the AI algorithm. Generally, there are two types of algorithmic errors one is looking for – false positives and false negatives. False positives are cases that the AI calls out to be positive, but they in fact are negative (for the finding under question). To check for algorithms false-positive rate, it is important to have a dataset that comprises heavily of cases without many positives – this gives the validator a chance to see how frequently the AI calls a truly negative case as positive and is only possible when there are a high number of negatives. The same is true for false negatives, which are cases where in fact there is a finding, but the algorithm misses it. For this, a dataset comprising mainly of positive cases is required to determine whether (and to what extent) AI misses' positive cases. This is especially important in today's scenario when AI is being pegged as a tool for either triaging (Johnson et al., 2019) or for automatically identifying normal cases (Irvin et al., 2019; Singh et al., 2018) with a high degree of confidence.

### 11.5.4 The Far North and Far South Cases

As a clinical group conducting an audit of AI algorithms, another concept we describe is that of the far north and far south cases. Most often, the output of an AI algorithm is a probability or abnormality score using which the decision of whether an abnormality is present or not is taken. Such a score is a measure of the 'certainty' with which an AI algorithm is giving an output. Typically, developers of algorithms determine a 'threshold' beyond which a finding is taken to be present, and below which a finding is determined to be not present.

These concepts are best understood using an example – let us take the hypothetical case of a deep learning algorithm for the detection of fractures in an X-ray. Assume that the algorithm gives a probability estimate of whether a fracture is present in an X-ray on a scale of 0%–100%, with a threshold of 50% – a probability of >50% implies the presence of a fracture, and less than 50% means no fracture. Let us further assume we have six test images (1–6) out of which images 1–3 are normal (no fracture), and images 4–6 have fractures. The AI algorithm gives a probability estimate of 25% for image 1, 60% for image 2, 90% for image 3, 75% for image 4, 40% for image 5 and 10% for image 6, implying that the algorithm is most 'certain' about the presence of a fracture in image 3, then image 4 and then image 2. Note that image 1 is hence a true negative and image 4 is a true positive, and the rest of the images are situations where the algorithm was wrong based on the threshold of 50% for positivity.

Now, while one would not be wrong in clubbing images 2 and 3 into false positives, and images 5 and 6 into false negatives, it would be wrong to equate the 'extent of falseness'. The algorithm was 90% certain that image 3 has a fracture and 60% certain that image 2 has a fracture, whereas both do not have fractures. It is important to understand that the error made by the algorithm in image 3 was much 'worse' than image 2 since it is an error that cannot be fixed by simply adjusting the threshold of the probability. Similarly, the algorithm was very certain that image 6 does not have a fracture (10% estimate) and fairly certain that image 5 does not have a fracture (40%), whereas both in reality had fractures, but again the mistake made by the algorithm in image 6 is much worse than image 5. Such cases are dubbed as far north (high-probability false positives) and far south (low-probability false negatives) by our group.

It is essential to monitor and test algorithms from point of view of identifying far north and far south cases because they demonstrate fundamental issues in algorithms' ability to understand an image and make a prediction. A radiologist, in contrast, is able to state their uncertainty and hence seek appropriate guidance in cases where help is needed. For AI to be a reliable companion to radiologists, the probability estimates given by AI need to be less divergent in terms of correlating with the ground truth.

## 11.5.5 *Real-World Deployment and Testing*

The litmus test for any medical imaging AI algorithm is whether radiologists use it or not, how frequently radiologists need to change the findings of the algorithm and how long they take to 'trust' it. Unfortunately, there is hardly any published literature around real-world deployments and testing of algorithms. From our experience of deploying AI algorithms that automatically classify chest X-rays into normal or abnormal and that automatically detect and characterize lung nodules on chest CT scans, we understood that it is important to present the findings of the AI algorithm in the most radiologist-friendly way possible. This insight comes from two main reasons – first, most radiologists use workstations which are 'locked'; that is, additional software cannot be loaded on them, limiting the ways in which AI results can be displayed at them. Second, and possibly, more importantly, it is very difficult to toggle between viewers for specific cases, and such toggling negatively impacts the adoption of new software and solutions. To counter this, we suggest either HL7 integration with the radiology reporting software or, in situations where the AI generates an image/segmentation, simply 'writing' no raw DICOM (Digital Imaging and Communications in Medicine) images like a 'screensaver' image.

One successful implementation strategy for AI that automatically classifies chest X-rays into normal or abnormal, in the workflow, is the following – first, chest X-rays are automatically extracted from PACS using DCM4CHEE16-based tools every 2 minutes to process them in real time; next, the AI algorithm is run on the chest X-ray, and if the AI is unable to find any abnormality in the image, a 'normal' report template is automatically sent to the reporting software using an HL7 message such that the radiologist simply has to approve the report after looking at the chest X-ray. The radiologist has full freedom to change the report, and such changes are measured in real time to determine the accuracy of the algorithm, displayed through a real-time dashboard. Such prospective validation studies, akin to phase 4 clinical trials for drugs, will help in improving algorithms in the long term and are the only way to realistically measure the impact of such algorithms in real clinical practice.

Another real-world deployment strategy for AI algorithms is an AI-enabled retrospective quality audit. In this quality audit, several hundred or thousands of chest X-rays that are deemed 'normal' based on their previous radiology reports are read by an AI algorithm at once. Subsequently, abnormality scores (probability of each X-ray having an abnormality) are determined, and images having high abnormalities are re-read by a second arbitration radiologist. It is highly likely that the AI finds 'missed' findings which the radiologists either did not pick up on or did not feel the need to comment on – either way, the AI algorithm gives a low-risk method to pick mistakes and improve the quality of radiology reporting in general.

## 11.5.6 Improving the Algorithm

The outcome of an algorithmic audit should ideally be solutions or suggestions using which vendors can improve the functioning of the algorithm. There are two possible solutions, in our experience. The first possible solution may be to retrain the model using false positives and false negatives found during the audit, especially the far north and far south cases. Such retraining can also be done locally, i.e., at the deployment site using a technique called federated learning (Chilamkurthy et al., 2018) where data does not need to leave the premises of the hospital/healthcare provider. The second possible solution is to use 'dynamic thresholds'. A dynamic threshold refers to a threshold value (for determining the presence or absence of an abnormality, as discussed earlier) that changes based on the given clinical context. Although not published in the literature, preliminary work done by our group demonstrates the ability of dynamic thresholds to significantly reduce the error rate of algorithms by adding a layer of 'clinical sense' into the output of AI algorithms. It is intuitive and can be explained using an example – a patient who has come for a screening chest X-ray for a routine health check should have a very high threshold for detecting pneumothorax, as opposed to one who is in the intensive care unit with falling oxygen saturation. Adding a simple checkbox to determine the patient's clinical context (screening, trauma, fever, cough, intensive care, etc.) can aid in improving AI's accuracy and making it more accessible.

## 11.6 More Power to Clinicians

The easiest, fastest and possibly most impactful way to address the shortage of radiologists in rural India is by giving clinicians and surgeons the ability to read scans on their own using assistance provided by AI. General physicians and pulmonologists in rural India often order chest X-rays for their patients but seldom get reports for them – an app on their smartphone linked to a cloud-based AI system can help them read these scans faster and more accurately. Abdominal surgeons in India are already reading CT scans – imagine a situation where AI directs them to the abnormality and confirms the provisional diagnosis made by them. Clinicians often complain that they find it hard to read MRI scans because of the different 'contrasts' that MRI presents – AI can potentially combine all MRI sequences to make a 'CT-like' image which is easily readable by them. In such a scenario, one can assume that most routine, mundane, day-to-day reporting tasks would be handled by clinicians in conjunction with AI, and radiologists could instead focus on the more difficult rare cases, thereby optimally utilizing their time. That said, just as how chess amateurs team up with computers to beat experts (Centaur chess, 2019), could one envision a day when primary care clinicians team up with AI to become better than radiologists?

In summary, AI will surely address the shortage of radiologists in rural India in the short term but the extent to which it would affect impact on-ground would depend on use-cases chosen by developers, the accuracy of the algorithms and economics involved in development and deployment of such solutions. But for the successful deployment of algorithms, we need a systematic methodology to validate and audit these algorithms.

# References

Bhaktwani, A. (2012) The PC-PNDT act in a nutshell. *Indian Journal of Radiology Imaging.* 22(2), 133–134. doi: 10.4103/0971-3026.101114.

Bien, N., Rajpurkar, P., Ball, R. L., et al. (2018) Deep-learning-assisted diagnosis for knee magnetic resonance imaging: development and retrospective validation of MRNet. *PLoS Medicine.* 15, e1002699.

Centaur chess shows power of teaming human and machine. Retrieved from https://www.huffpost.com/entry/centaur-chess-shows-power_b_6383606 (accessed on April 2, 2019).

ChestX-ray8: hospital-scale chest X-ray database and benchmarks on weakly-supervised classification and localization of common thorax diseases. (n.d.). Retrieved from https://arxiv.org/abs/1705.02315 (accessed on November 4, 2019).

Chilamkurthy, S., Ghosh, R., Tanamala, S., et al. (2018). Deep learning algorithms for detection of critical findings in head CT scans: a retrospective study. *The Lancet.* 392, 2388–2396.

Dhanlaxmi Bank. (2019). In-focus: rural India – where is it? Retrieved from https://www.dhanbank.com/pdf/reports/InFocus-December%201,%202010.pdf (accessed on April 2, 2019).

Fischer, D. (2017). Need a CT scan in India? You might have to look around. *Global HealthCare Insights Magazine.* Retrieved from https://globalhealthi.com/2017/04/20/medical-imaging-india/ (accessed on November 4, 2019).

Funding analysis of companies developing machine learning solutions for medical imaging; Simon Harris, Signify Research, June 2018.

Guidelines for competency based postgraduate training programme for MS in Orthopedics. Retrieved from https://old.mciindia.org/PG-Curricula/MS-Orthopedics.pdf (accessed on April 2, 2019).

Healthtech startup 5C network raises funding from Unitus Ventures, Axilor and CIIE-IIMA (2019). Retrieved from https://yourstory.com/2019/01/healthtech-startup-5c-network-funding.

Hwang, E. J., Park, S., Jin, K. N., et al. (2019). Development and validation of a deep learning–based automated detection algorithm for major thoracic diseases on chest radiographs. *JAMA Network Open.* 2, e191095.

Irvin, J., Rajpurkar, P., Ko, M., et al. (2019). CheXpert: a large chest radiograph dataset with uncertainty labels and expert comparison. arXiv:1901.07031 [cs, eess]. Retrieved from http://arxiv.org/abs/1901.07031.

IvanŠtajduhar, Mihaela Mamula, Damir Miletić, and GözdeÜnal. Semi-automated detection of anterior cruciate ligament injury from MRI. *Computer Methods and Programs in Biomedicine*, 140:151–164, Mar 2017. doi: 10.1016/j.cmpb.2016.12.006.

Johnson, A. E. W., Pollard, T. J., Greenbaum, N. R., et al. (2019). MIMIC-CXR: a large publicly available database of labeled chest radiographs. arXiv:1901.07042 [cs, eess]. Retrieved from http://arxiv.org/abs/1901.07042.

Kim, D. W., Jang, H. Y., Kim, K. W., Shin, Y. & Park, S. H. (2019). Design characteristics of studies reporting the performance of artificial intelligence algorithms for diagnostic analysis of medical images: results from recently published papers. *Korean Jornal of Radiology.* 20, 405.

Malik, P. S., & Raina, V. (2015). Lung cancer: prevalent trends & emerging concepts. *Indian Journal of Medical Research.* 141(1), 5–7.

Nagarajan, R. (2019). Services, PSU hospitals can churn out 1,100 more specialists. *Times News Network.* Retrieved from https://timesofindia.indiatimes.com/india/services-psu-hospitals-can-churn-out-1100-more-specialist-docs-niti-aayog/articleshow/68441374.cms (accessed on April 2, 2019).

NHA. (2019). About Pradhan Mantri Jan Arogya Yojana (PM-JAY) | Ayushman Bharat. Retrieved from https://pmjay.gov.in/about-pmjay (accessed on November 4, 2019).

Putha, P., Tadepalli, M., Jain, S., et al. (2018). Efficacy of deep learning for screening pulmonary tuberculosis. *European Congress of Radiology 2018*, February 28–March 4, 2018, Vienna. SS 1805 – Deep Learning.

Rajpurkar, P., Irvin, J., Ball, R. L., et al. (2018). Deep learning for chest radiograph diagnosis: a retrospective comparison of the CheXNeXt algorithm to practicing radiologists. *PLoS Medicine.* 15, e1002686.

Sahu, A. K., Aggarwal, B., Dhar, A., Kapoor, G., & Rao, P. (2018). Evaluating the use of a deep learning algorithm for radiology quality assurance in out-patient chest X-ray reporting. *Radiological Society of North America 2018 Scientific Assembly and Annual Meeting*, November 25–November 30, 2018, Chicago IL. Retrieved from http://archive.rsna.org/2018/18015032.html.

Singh, R., Kalra, M. K., Nitiwarangkul, C., et al. (2018). Deep learning in chest radiography: detection of findings and presence of change. *PLoS One.* 13, e0204155.

The National Lung Screening Trial Research Team. (2011). Reduced lung-cancer mortality with low-dose computed tomographic screening. *New England Journal of Medicine.* 365, 395–409.

Venugopal, V., Manoj, T. D. L., Bhargava, R., et al. (2019a). Automated classification of chest X-rays as normal/abnormal using a high sensitivity deep learning algorithm. *European Congress of Radiology 2019*, February 27–March 3, 2019, Vienna. SS1905a – Machine Learning in chest radiology.

Venugopal, V., Vaidya, A., Ahuja, A., et al. (2019b). Towards radiologist-level malignancy detection on chest CT scans: a comparative study of the performance of convolutional neural networks and four thoracic radiologists. *European Congress of Radiology 2019*, February 27–March 3, 2019, Vienna. Scientific Exhibit. doi: 10.26044/ecr2019/C-2065.

*Chapter 12*

# Knowledge Management in a Learning Health System

Uli K. Chettipally

*InnovatorMD*

## Contents

## 12.1 Introduction

Over the past few centuries, medical science has been growing steadily. The pace has accelerated in the last few decades. This new knowledge is slow to change the practice of medicine, although we have been using information technology tools for data collection, manipulation and analysis. Sample sizes have grown bigger over the years for clinical trials. Today, with the implementation of electronic health record (EHR), availability of clinical data has increased. It is now possible to study the whole population instead of a sample using machine learning and artificial intelligence tools. The speed and capacity to manipulate and analyze data have increased tremendously with the availability of larger capacity of hardware, faster software and better algorithms. We are about to see a flurry of new discoveries and new knowledge. This chapter will discuss the role of (i) knowledge curation, (ii) knowledge translation and (iii) new knowledge generation in medicine using machine learning and artificial intelligence in a learning health system.

## 12.2  History

Medical knowledge includes an understanding of all established and evolving biomedical, clinical, epidemiological and social-behavioral sciences (NEJM, 2016). The process of creating medical knowledge started with the observation of humans many centuries ago. One would observe the normal state and the diseased state. This exploration leads to the examination of the human body both outside and inside, through dissection of cadavers and sometimes operating on living humans. The modern science of observation and measurement did not start until the early 1600s. The observation of hygiene and its effect on the mortality of wounded soldiers, the incidence of cholera in a certain geographic area in London and the incidence of lung cancer in cigarette smokers are all great examples of how observational science started making its way into medical practice. The traditional use of clinical trials in medical treatment became popular with the birth of the pharmaceutical industry in the late 1800s. The study of populations and statistics became popular as tools in science and medicine in the late 19th century.

## 12.3  Current Practice

According to a paper by Peter Densen, there are several challenges facing medical education and medical knowledge today (Densen, 2011):

1. The majority of medical education is focused on biology, but most of the disease is caused by non-biological factors, like behavioral choices and the environment.

2. The majority of medical education happens in a hospital setting, while the majority of the practice of medicine happens in the outpatient clinic setting.
3. Major emphasis on basic science research, but a lot of it is not very applicable to the medical practice at the bedside.

There is a gap between what medical science has discovered as new knowledge and the access and usability of that knowledge to benefit patients. This is also called the bench-to-bedside gap (Mohyuddin, 2015). There are several barriers to this process of transfer of knowledge. Factors that are contributing to this gap between evidence and practice of medicine are

1. The exponential growth of knowledge and the number of studies, with the number of studies doubling every few months (Corish, 2018).
2. An increasing population that is also having a growing number of older individuals with heart disease and cancer, which are still the leading causes of death (AHRQ, 2017).
3. Increasing amounts of healthcare data from EHRs, imaging studies and genomic information (IDC, 2014).
4. Physicians are unable to keep up with evidence-based care, resulting in less than half of the patients receiving it with resulting increased mortality and morbidity (Holmes et al., 2004).

The importance of clinical trials and the scrutiny they get have been enhanced by the modern drug development practices and the rigorous regulatory framework that has been established to protect the people from ineffective or dangerous drugs, devices or treatments getting into the practice of medicine. The invention of new compounds, molecules and biologics has accelerated this process. Some of the challenges faced by the industry like the increasing cost of bringing treatment into the market, the enormous failure rate of these treatments in the clinical trials and sometimes the lacklustre performance of these treatments when they have been disseminated into a population have all been documented. Once studies have confirmed that a treatment works, it is picked up by the professional organizations that will include this evidence into clinical practice guidelines. These guidelines are disseminated widely to the practicing physicians through publications. Physicians and healthcare institutions have to voluntarily include this guideline-based knowledge into their practices. This cost, time and quality inefficiency has been plaguing the medical world for quite some time and more so recently.

## 12.4 Cost of Generating New Knowledge

Clinical trials, the current gold standard of research, are expensive. The average cost to bring a new drug or treatment to market is estimated to cost 1 billion dollars. This does not take into consideration the large amounts of basic science research that the government and research institutions spend in order to support these treatment explorations. This process of spending large amounts of money has some unintended consequences for certain conditions. Public money is mostly spent on what is trending as an important problem in public discourse, which is a very subjective way of allocating resources. It also has many political and social implications. Research covering rare diseases or unpopular conditions has difficulty in getting funded. Conditions, where the life span is cut short by the disease itself, are also difficult to study as there is not enough time to do it. Disease areas that affect the affluent get more funding than the ones affecting the poor. Even after successful regulatory approval of drugs and treatments, they may fail in the post-market evaluations. There have been several examples of such failures. This capital inefficiency affects the number of successful treatments reaching the population in need of them.

## 12.5 Time Inefficiency of Generating New Knowledge

It takes an average of ten years for a particular treatment to start its journey from the bench and make its way to the patient. The rigorous testing, screening of compounds and recruiting for clinical trials is a long arduous process. Most of the work has to be done manually. Although this process is designed to decrease the risk of untoward problems caused by the new treatment, it adds to the length of time it takes to do it. The involvement of multiple stakeholders including researchers, patients, academic institutions, clinical research organizations, institutional review boards and company staff is huge. A lot of times these studies have to be discontinued due to several difficulties such as non-availability of resources, inability to recruit enough patients and failure of the agent being evaluated to show a positive response. All these costs add into the cost of the next treatment for the disease. Since the investors and shareholders of these private entities expect a return on investment or the value of their shares to grow, there is tremendous pressure on the companies to show positive results of their research on the products they are developing.

## 12.6 A Learning Healthcare System

A Learning Healthcare System was defined by the Institute of Medicine (IoM), as a system in which "science, informatics, incentives, and culture are aligned for continuous improvement and innovation, with best practices seamlessly embedded in the delivery process and new knowledge captured as an integral by-product of the delivery experience." (Olsen et al., 2007)

1. The Learning Healthcare System was a product of the work done starting in 2006 at IoM, at a workshop that started this movement. The three dimensions of the challenge were (Figure 12.1).
2. "Fostering progress toward the long-term vision of a learning healthcare system, in which evidence is both applied and developed as a natural product of the care process.
3. Advancing the discussion and activities necessary to meet the near-term need for expanded capacity to generate the evidence to support medical care that is maximally effective and produces the greatest value.

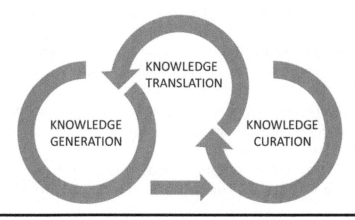

**Figure 12.1   AI- and machine learning-based Clinical Knowledge Management.**

4. Improving public understanding of the nature of evidence-based medicine, the dynamic nature of the evidence development process, and the importance of supporting progress toward medical care that reflects the best evidence." (Olsen et al., 2007)

## 12.7 Clinical Knowledge Management

The current process of knowledge moving from bench to bedside has several hurdles. Machine learning technology can be a solution to many of these problems. Here are areas where machine learning can be most useful:

1. **Knowledge curation**: With the vast amounts of new knowledge that is being generated, it is humanly not possible to track and curate this knowledge for practical purposes. Companies are creating machine learning tools to be able to go through the vast number of papers and curate detailed summaries, validating existing hypotheses, revealing hidden connections and creating new hypotheses. The use of these tools can help speed up the process of analyzing and assimilating current knowledge on a topic and help researchers summarize the findings into a current knowledge base. Although such tools are not widely in use right now, the path to that possibility is clear. This knowledge can then be used to create clinical practice guidelines, where the current process of creating guidelines takes years to gather and analyze such data. In the meantime, the knowledge has grown or changed, and by the time the clinical practice guidelines are published and disseminated, some of it has already become obsolete (Extance, 2018).

2. **Knowledge translation**: Once we have access to new knowledge and the guidelines that are created from this knowledge, the next step is to make it available to the clinician at the point of care in real time where the decisions are being made. This process being able to access a patient's current clinical information through various systems including EHRs and other streams of data is crucial. Machine learning tools can extract data about the patient from the patient's records and can be used for analysis. This analysis, in turn, can power clinical

decision support systems that can prompt and suggest treatments to the physician or provider based on the patient's risk profile or treatment category. Intelligent systems have been developed to be able to do this in real time and at the point of care (Menzies et al., 2015).

3. **Knowledge generation**: With the advent of EHRs, large amounts of longitudinal clinical data are available on patients, which never existed before. There are structured and unstructured data like clinician notes in the EHRs. The availability of such data and the accessibility of machine learning and artificial intelligence tools make it possible to generate new knowledge. This knowledge is created from the observational study of this data. When clinical interventions are involved, this data can be used to create a synthetic control group and compare outcomes. Such real-world data is valuable in generating real-world evidence and new knowledge which was not possible in the past. This methodology can guide treatments in identifying responders to certain treatments and in the selection of patients for clinical trials. In certain complex conditions, machine learning can create a customized clinical pathway for individual patients where the condition is complex and the patient's status is ever-changing. A good example of this is in the treatment of sepsis (Komorowski et al., 2018).

## 12.8 Business Model of Healthcare

Most of the USA and some other parts of the world have established fee-for-service as their healthcare business model. In this model, the healthcare provider generates revenue or income, based on the number of patients seen, the number of procedures performed or the number of hospitalizations. This business model depends on the patients getting sick and availing of the services provided. Introduction of machine learning models which can predict outcomes and help in preventing a lot of downstream care and expense can be a detriment to the fee-for-service business model. It helps the value-based care model which is the opposite of the fee-for-service model. In value-based care, the idea is to prevent patients from getting sick and requiring costly treatments. This caveat may help in selecting the institution or organization, where these models are most aligned with the incentives to healthcare providers.

## 12.9 Conclusion

Healthcare has gone through a major transformation over the past few centuries. The pace of change has increased with growth in new knowledge. Current systems are not in a position to handle this tsunami of new knowledge in order to benefit patients. New tools like machine learning have the potential to speed up the process of knowledge curation, knowledge translation and knowledge creation. This will have a positive impact on the work of scientists, the practice of medicine and ultimately the health of millions of people in the near future.

## References

AHRQ. (2017). *2016 National Healthcare Qualities and Disparity Report.* Agency for Healthcare Research and Quality, Rockville, MD. Retrieved from: https://www.ahrq.gov/sites/default/files/wysiwyg/research/findings/nhqrdr/nhqdr16/final2016qdr-cx.pdf.

Corish, B. (2018). Medical knowledge doubles every few months; how can clinicians keep up? Elsevier Connect. Retrieved from: https://www.elsevier.com/connect/medical-knowledge-doubles-every-few-months-how-can-clinicians-keep-up.

Densen, P. (2011). Challenges and opportunities facing medical education. *Trans Am Clin Climatol Assoc*; 122:48–58.

Extance, A. (2018). How AI technology can tame the scientific literature. *Nature*; 561:273–274. Retrieved from: https://www.nature.com/articles/d41586-018-06617-5.

Holmes, JS, Shevrin, M, Goldman, B & Share, D. (2004 December). Translating research into practice: Are physicians following evidence-based guidelines in the treatment of hypertension? *Med Care Res Rev*; 61(4):453–473. PubMed PMID: 15536209.

IDC. (2014). *The Digital Universe-Driving Data Growth in Healthcare.* IDC, Framingham, MA. Retrieved from: https://www.cycloneinteractive.com/cyclone/assets/File/digital-universe-healthcare-vertical-report-ar.pdf.

Komorowski, M, Celi, LA, Badawi, O, Gordon, AC & Faisal, AA. (2018). The artificial intelligence clinician learns optimal treatment strategies for sepsis in intensive care. *Nature Med*; 24:1716–1720.

Menzies, S, Duz, J & Kinch, R. (2015). Knowledge transfer at point of care: investigating new strategies for implementing guideline recommendations. *J Contin Educ Health Prof*; 35:S22–S23.

Mohyuddin. (2015). Bridging the gap from bench to bedside-an informatics Infrastructure for Integrating Clinical, Genomics and Environmental Data (ICGED). Chapter in MEDINFO 2015: eHealth enabled Health. Retrieved from: http://ebooks.iospress.nl/publication/40511.

NEJM. (2016). *Exploring the ACGME Core Competencies: Medical Knowledge.* NEJM Knowledge Plus. Retrieved from: https://knowledgeplus.nejm.org/blog/acgme-core-competencies-medical-knowledge/.

Olsen, L, Aisner, D & McGinnis, M. (2007). *The Learning Healthcare System*. The National Academies Press, Washington, DC. Retrieved from: http://www.nationalacademies.org/hmd/reports/2007/the-learning-healthcare-system-workshop-summary.aspx.

## Chapter 13

# Transfer Learning to Enhance Amenorrhea Status Prediction in Cancer and Fertility Data with Missing Values

Xuetong Wu, Hadi Akbarzadeh Khorshidi,
Uwe Aickelin, Zobaida Edib, and Michelle Peate
*University of Melbourne*

## Contents

## 13.1 Introduction

Collecting sufficient labelled training data for health and medical problems is difficult (Antropova et al., 2018). Also, missing values are unavoidable in health and medical datasets, and tackling the problem arising from the inadequate instances and missingness is not straightforward (Snell et al. 2017; Sterne et al. 2009). However, machine learning algorithms have achieved significant success in many real-world healthcare problems, such as regression and classification, and these techniques could possibly be a way to resolve the issues.

Amenorrhoea status (i.e. a marker for infertility) prediction post-cancer treatment is crucial for women who wish to conceive in the future as this can guide fertility preservation decisions before they receive infertility-causing cancer treatment and post-treatment contraceptive choices (Peate et al. 2011). However, collecting substantial labelled data for amenorrhoea prediction after cancer is challenging and very often the relevant data will present vast amount of missing values (Peate & Edib, 2019).

Traditional machine learning algorithms start with the hypothesis that the training dataset and testing dataset have the same input space and distribution, which may not be practical in the real world. To address this issue, constructing a general learning model which can adapt to several similar domains quickly is necessary. Such a framework will reduce the cost of re-building and re-calibrating the learning models due to changes of distribution and input space features, which is known as 'transfer learning'. Transfer learning is useful in many real-world applications, such as natural language processing (NLP) (Han & Eisenstein, 2019; Kim, Gao & Ney, 2019), medical and clinical analysis (Christodoulidis et al. 2016; Uran et al. 2019), E-commerce (Zhao, Li, Shuai, & Yang, 2018) and acoustic recognition (Gharib, Drossos, Çakir, Serdyuk, & Virtanen, 2018). In our study, we aim to address the distribution divergence in the large dataset consisting of several subsets by transfer learning. We first define the objective subset as *target domain* and impute missing values to align the feature spaces with another auxiliary subset, namely, the *source domain*. Second, we try to improve classification accuracy by leveraging the information across two subsets where a single target dataset may not be sufficiently expressed.

The prepared dataset describes the relationship between the health status and amenorrhoea status at 12 months from the start of the chemotherapy, for breast cancer patients internationally. The dataset includes six sub-datasets (the names of these datasets are masked due to confidentiality issues), and these sub-datasets were collected from different institutions/hospitals. Consequently, the data is not likely to be sampled from exactly the same distribution but shares some similarity; for example, there are many common features between two subsets. To better predict the amenorrhea status across different subsets, we need to first align features using cross-imputation, then map the source and target to a common latent space to maximize correlation.

The flowchart of our method is shown in Figure 13.1, where the learning process is divided into training and testing phases. As transfer learning aims to maximize the correlation between the source and target, our imputation and classification methods are both distance-based. In the training phase, we use zero or $k$–nearest neighbour imputation ($kNNI$) to align the features, and we assume the source dataset will be more abundant, while target instances are more limited. Then, we perform the closest pairing considering

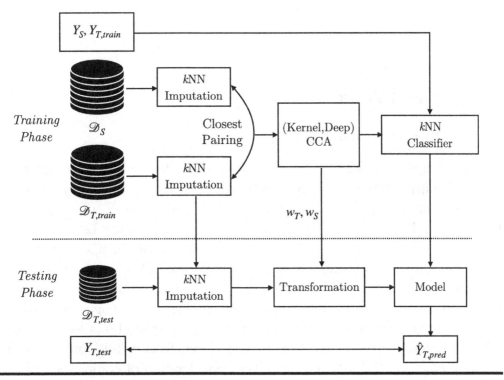

**Figure 13.1   Supervised pairing CCA method.**

the label before canonical correlation analysis (CCA), mapping vectors $w_T$ and $w_S$ are then learned to transform paired source and target to a common latent space, eventually distance-based classifier such as $k$-nearest neighbour ($kNN$) is learned in this common space. The contributions of this chapter are summarized as follows:

1. The work explores the impact of imputation techniques on clinical datasets and provides an efficient way to deal with missing values for transfer learning.
2. As a single dataset is insufficiently expressed, we leverage another similar dataset and further improve the performance using linear CCA, kernel CCA and deep CCA regarding the classification tasks on prediction of amenorrhoea 12 months after breast cancer diagnosis and treatment. The results show that the transfer with kernel CCA and deep CCA can boost the classification accuracy and yield promising improvements.

This chapter is structured as follows: Section 13.2 introduces related studies on amenorrhoea prediction to cancer status, missing values with imputation techniques and CCA-based transfer learning methods. Section 13.3 proposes our methods in detail. The experiments are conducted, and the results are portrayed and discussed in Section 13.4. Section 13.5 concludes the chapter.

## 13.2 Related Work

### 13.2.1 Amenorrhoea Status Prediction

Chemotherapy-related amenorrhoea (CRA) is usually caused by gonadotoxic chemotherapy; younger (pre-menopausal) patients should be informed of the possibility of amenorrhoea or recovery of menstruation and contraceptive choices (Peate et al. 2011) to plan for further pregnancy. Lee et al. (2009) pointed out that the occurrence of CRA is predicted by the age at diagnosis. For those who are older than 40 years, CRA is more likely to occur and be permanent. Also Liem et al. (2015) reported that the age at diagnosis is the main factor correlated to post-cancer infertility. Apart from age, CRA also hinges on personal factors (REF). Peate et al. (2011) found that low knowledge can reduce the quality of decision-making. To conclude, prediction of chemotherapy-related infertility involves consideration of complex factors such as age, lifestyle factors, fertility history, ovulation, history of previous medical and gynaecological diseases, cancer-related factors and type of treatment. (Johnson et al. 2006). Decision support is critical in ensuring patients can make informed choices about fertility preservation in a timely manner, but in practice, women are making this decision without knowing their infertility risk, which has the potential for adverse effects. The key challenge with fertility prediction is that the data we use usually contains substantial missing elements which adversely impact the prediction results. Imputation methods can help to accommodate this issue.

## 13.2.2 *Missing Value Imputation*

Missing values are unavoidable in clinical datasets, and this lack of information has serious drawback for data analysis. The reasons for missing data may differ, relevant knowledge cannot be acquired promptly, data will be absent due to unpredictable factors or the cost for accessing the data is unaffordably high. Types of missing data are defined by Little and Rubin (2019), who categorizes missing data into three types, which are *missing completely at random* (MCAR), *missing at random* (MAR) and *missing not at random* (MNAR).

MCAR cases happen when the missingness is independent of the variable itself or any other related factors; for example, chemical data may be lost accidentally, some occasional collection is omitted for questionnaires, or a few medical records will present manual documenting errors. MAR is the case when the missing representation is independent of the variable itself but can be predicted from the observed entries. A typical case is that young breast cancer patients have more missingness in fertility, compared with older patients, which can be shown by leveraging the observed age information. MNAR situations occur when the missingness is related to the variable itself, and this type of missing data cannot be predicted only from the present data. For example, breast cancer patients will be more inclined to conceal private information unrelated to the cancer such as education and salary levels, which are unlikely to be predictable. Handing this category of missing data is problematic, and there are no general methods that can resolve this issue properly.

In our case, as the MNAR type is rare in the mixture of different missing data types (Goeij et al., 2013), we may consider that the missing values are only under MCAR or MAR assumptions if a feature is not totally missing. When missing data are MCAR or MAR, they are termed 'ignorable' or 'learnable', which implies that researchers can impute data with certain procedures, e.g., by statistical analysis or machine learning approaches.

Machine learning has achieved great success in many fields, and the flexibility allows us to capture high-order interactions in the data (Jerez et al., 2010) and thus impute missing values.

Let us quickly revisit the *kNNI* routines-related machine learning concepts. *kNNI* is a type of hot deck supervised learning method, providing a path to find the most similar cases for given instances, in which the nearest neighbour is a useful algorithm that matches a case with its closest *k* neighbours in the multi-dimensional space. For missing data imputation, *kNNI* aims to find the nearest neighbours to minimize the heterogeneous Euclidean-overlap metric distance (Wilson & Martinez, 1997) between two samples, and missing items are further substituted with the values from *k* complete cases. The advantage of *kNNI* is that it is a simple and comprehensive method and it is suitable for large amount of missing data, but the disadvantage is that it has high computational complexity as it will compare all datasets and find the most similar cases.

### 13.2.3 *Transfer Learning*

Transfer learning resolves the issues that the training source and testing target are drawn from different distribution where a common classifier usually does not perform well. Formally, transfer learning is defined as follows (Pan & Yang, 2009).

**Definition 1**

(Transfer Learning) Two different domains, namely, source domain and target domain, are given. Given a source domain $\mathcal{D}_S$ and the source task $\mathcal{T}_S$, a target domain $\mathcal{D}_T$ and the target task $\mathcal{T}_T$, transfer learning aims to help improve the learning of the target task $\mathcal{T}_T$ using the knowledge in both source and target domains, where $\mathcal{D}_S \neq \mathcal{D}_T$, or $\mathcal{T}_S \neq \mathcal{T}_T$.

In the definition above, the domains are not equal that $\mathcal{D}_S \neq \mathcal{D}_T$ implies that either $\mathcal{X}_S \neq \mathcal{X}_T$ or $P_S(X) \neq P_T(X)$. Similarly, $\mathcal{T}_S \neq \mathcal{T}_T$ implies that $\mathcal{Y}_S \neq \mathcal{Y}_T$ or $P_S(y \mid X) \neq P_T(y \mid X)$. In traditional machine learning methods, $\mathcal{D}_S = \mathcal{D}_T$ and $\mathcal{T}_S = \mathcal{T}_T$. Weiss, Khoshgoftaar and Wang (2016) categorize the transfer learning into homogeneous and heterogeneous types. Homogeneous transfer learning (HomoTL) assumes that the input instances are drawn from the same input space and distribution in both source and target, but the tasks are different. In heterogeneous transfer learning (HeteTL), features from source and target do not share the same feature space $(\mathcal{X}_S \neq \mathcal{X}_T)$, a typical case is transferring the info from image to text (Zhao, Sun, Hong, Yao, & Wang, 2019) and it does not require that the inputs should have an identical space and distribution. Formally, homogeneous transfer learning and heterogeneous transfer learning are defined as follows.

## Definition 2

(Homogeneous Transfer Learning) Given a source domain $\mathcal{D}_S$ and the source task $\mathcal{T}_S$, a target domain $\mathcal{D}_T$ and the target task $\mathcal{T}_T$, Homogeneous transfer learning is a type of transfer learning, where $\mathcal{D}_S = \mathcal{D}_T$, but $\mathcal{T}_S \neq \mathcal{T}_T$.

## Definition 3

(Heterogeneous Transfer Learning) Given a source domain $\mathcal{D}_S$ and the source task $\mathcal{T}_S$, a target domain $\mathcal{D}_T$ and the target task $\mathcal{T}_T$, heterogeneous transfer learning is a type of transfer learning, where $\mathcal{D}_S \neq \mathcal{D}_T$, but $\mathcal{T}_S$ can be either equal or not equal to the target task $\mathcal{T}_T$.

More specifically, the transfer learning hierarchy (Long, 2014) is illustrated in Figure 13.2. In our study, the prepared data consists of different sub-datasets, which have different distributions and input spaces, implying that $\mathcal{D}_S \neq \mathcal{D}_T$. To tackle this problem, we will first appropriately transform the heterogeneous transfer learning problem into homogeneous learning problem and then utilize existing homogeneous learning methods (in the domain adaptation category) for better classification.

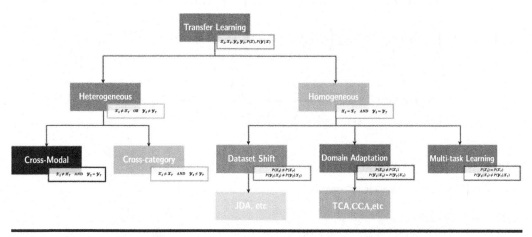

**Figure 13.2   Types of transfer learning based on the feature space, label space, feature marginal distribution and conditional distribution.**

## 13.2.3.1 CCA-Based Transfer Learning

CCA is a correlation-based multivariate data analysis tool that finds the maximum correlation between two sets of features in a specific subspace. In other words, CCA aims to learn a transformation that projects two datasets into a common subspace where transformed features are maximally correlated. CCA has been widely used in many fields such as software defect prediction (Jing, Wu, Dong, Qi, & Xu, 2015), computer vision and NLP (Hardoon, Szedmak and Shawe-Taylor, 2004), medical (Parkhomenko, Tritchler and Beyene, 2009) and acoustic processing (Sargin, Yemez, Erzin, & Tekalp, 2007). CCA is used for dimensionality reduction, feature mapping and learning and fusing multiple modalities for prediction. CCA methods require that both datasets are paired; that is, the number of instances should be identical. As the optimization problem is nonlinear, we can map the datasets to the reproducing kernel Hilbert space (RKHS), leading to the kernel version of CCA (KCCA) (Fukumizu, Bach, & Gretton, 2007). To accurately model complex datasets with mixed types, deep neural networks are introduced to learn the corresponding representations, referring to deep CCA (DCCA) (Andrew, Arora, Bilmes, & Livescu, 2013). In this section, we will briefly revisit these three types of CCA.

### 13.2.3.1.1 Standard Linear CCA with Regularization

Given paired source and target datasets $\hat{X}_S \in \mathbb{R}^{\mathcal{F}_U \times N}$, $\hat{X}_T \in \mathbb{R}^{\mathcal{F}_U \times N}$, CCA finds pairs of linear projections $w_S \in \mathbb{R}^{\mathcal{F}_U \times r}$, $w_T \in \mathbb{R}^{\mathcal{F}_U \times r}$ of the two views $\left( w_S^T \hat{X}_S \in \mathbb{R}^{r \times N}, \ w_T^T \hat{X}_T \in \mathbb{R}^{r \times N} \right)$ that are maximally correlated, where $(\cdot)^T$ denotes the transpose. The optimization problem can be described as follows:

$$\left( w_S^*, \ w_T^* \right) = \arg \max_{w_S, \, w_T} \mathrm{corr} \left( w_S^T \hat{X}_S, \ w_T^T \hat{X}_T \right)$$

$$= \arg \max_{w_S, \, w_T} \frac{w_S^T \mathrm{cov} \left( \hat{X}_S \hat{X}_T^T \right) w_T}{\sqrt{w_S^T \mathrm{var} \left( \hat{X}_S, \ \hat{X}_S^T \right) w_S w_T^T \mathrm{var} \left( \hat{X}_T, \ \hat{X}_T^T \right) w_T}} \tag{13.1}$$

where the cross-covariance $\mathrm{cov} \left( w_S^T \hat{X}_S, \ w_T^T \hat{X}_T \right)$ and variance $\mathrm{var} \left( \hat{X}_S, \ \hat{X}_S^T \right)$ and $\mathrm{var} \left( \hat{X}_T, \ \hat{X}_T^T \right)$ are defined as

$$\mathrm{var} \left( \hat{X}_S, \ \hat{X}_S^T \right) := \frac{1}{N} \sum_{i=1}^{N} \left( \hat{X}_S^i - \mu_S \right) \left( \hat{X}_S^i - \mu_S \right)^T \in \mathbb{R}^{\mathcal{F}_U \times \mathcal{F}_U}$$

$$\text{var}\left(\hat{X}_T, \hat{X}_T^T\right) := \frac{1}{N}\sum_{i=1}^{N}\left(\hat{X}_T^i - \mu_T\right)\left(\hat{X}_T^i - \mu_T\right)^T \in \mathbb{R}^{\mathcal{F}_U \times \mathcal{F}_U}$$

$$\text{cov}\left(\hat{X}_S, \hat{X}_T\right) := \frac{1}{N}\sum_{j=1}^{N}\left(\hat{X}_S^i - \mu_S\right)\left(\hat{X}_T^i - \mu_T\right)^T \in \mathbb{R}^{\mathcal{F}_U \times \mathcal{F}_U}$$

where $\hat{X}_S^i \in R_U^{\mathcal{F}}$, for $i = 1, 2, \ldots, N$ and $\hat{X}_T^i \in R^{\mathcal{F}_U}$, for $i = 1, 2, \ldots, M$ are the instances from the unified source and target dataset. And $\mu_S \in R^{\mathcal{F}_U}$, $\mu_T \in R^{\mathcal{F}_U}$ denote the mean vector for unified source and target datasets as

$$\mu_S := \frac{1}{N}\sum_{i=1}^{N}\hat{X}_S^i$$

$$\mu_T := \frac{1}{N}\sum_{i=1}^{N}\hat{X}_T^i$$

By normalization, CCA finds the maximum canonical correlation as:

$$\text{Maximise } w_S^T \Sigma_{ST} w_T$$

$$\text{Subjectto } w_S^T \Sigma_S w_S = 1, w_T^T \Sigma_T w_T = 1 \tag{13.2}$$

The solution to this optimization problem is given by

$$\Sigma_{ST} \Sigma_T^{-1} \Sigma_{TS} \mathbf{w}_s = \lambda^2 \Sigma_S \mathbf{w}_s$$

$$\Sigma_S^{-1} \Sigma_{ST} \Sigma_T^{-1} \Sigma_{TS} \mathbf{w}_s = \lambda^2 \mathbf{w}_s$$

which can also be written as

$$\begin{pmatrix} 0 & \Sigma_{ST} \\ \Sigma_{TS} & 0 \end{pmatrix}\begin{pmatrix} w_S \\ w_T \end{pmatrix} = \lambda^2 \begin{pmatrix} \Sigma_S & 0 \\ 0 & \Sigma_T \end{pmatrix}\begin{pmatrix} w_S \\ w_T \end{pmatrix} \tag{13.3}$$

Equation (13.3) leaves an eigenvalue problem. Regularized CCA is introduced to address the problem that if $\Sigma_S$ and $\Sigma_T$ are singular, then CCA is ill-posed and the generalized eigenvalue problem cannot be solved properly. Imposing the L2 penalty maintains the convexity of the problem and the generalized formulation. The optimization object function is expressed by

$$\left(w_S^*,\ w_T^*\right) = \arg\max_{w_S,\ w_T}\ \mathrm{corr}\left(w_S^T\hat{X}_S,\ w_T^T\hat{X}_T\right)$$

$$= \arg\max_{w_S,\ w_T} \frac{w_S^T\,\mathrm{cov}\left(\hat{X}_S\hat{X}_T^T\right)w_T}{\sqrt{\left(w_S^T\mathrm{var}\left(\hat{X}_S,\ \hat{X}_S^T\right)w_S + \rho\|w_S\|^2\right)\left(w_T^T\mathrm{var}\left(\hat{X}_T,\ \hat{X}_T^T\right)w_T + \rho\|w_T\|^2\right)}}$$

(13.4)

The eigenvalue problem is formulated by

$$\begin{pmatrix} 0 & \boldsymbol{\Sigma}_{ST} \\ \boldsymbol{\Sigma}_{TS} & 0 \end{pmatrix}\begin{pmatrix} w_S \\ w_T \end{pmatrix} = \lambda^2\begin{pmatrix} \boldsymbol{\Sigma}_S + \rho I & 0 \\ 0 & \boldsymbol{\Sigma}_T + \rho I \end{pmatrix}\begin{pmatrix} w_S \\ w_T \end{pmatrix}$$

and the solution to the problem above is to find the largest $r$ eigenvalues for the matrix:

$$\begin{pmatrix} \boldsymbol{\Sigma}_S + \rho I & 0 \\ 0 & \boldsymbol{\Sigma}_T + \rho I \end{pmatrix}^{-1}\begin{pmatrix} 0 & \boldsymbol{\Sigma}_{ST} \\ \boldsymbol{\Sigma}_{TS} & 0 \end{pmatrix}$$

### 13.2.3.1.2 Kernel CCA

KCCA finds a pair of nonlinear projection of the two views. The functions in RKHS are denoted as $\mathcal{H}_S$, $\mathcal{H}_T$, and the associated positive definite kernels are denoted as $\boldsymbol{\Phi}_S$, $\boldsymbol{\Phi}_T$. The optimal projections from low dimension $\mathcal{F}_U$ to high dimension $\mathcal{F}_U^H$ are any functions $b_S \in \mathcal{H}_S$, $b_T \in \mathcal{H}_T$ to maximize the correlation as

$$\left(b_S^*,\ b_T^*\right) = \arg\max_{f_S \in \mathcal{H}_S,\, f_T \in \mathcal{H}_T}\ \mathrm{corr}\left(b_S\left(\hat{X}_S\right),\ b_T\left(\hat{X}_T\right)\right)$$

$$= \arg\max_{b_S \in \mathcal{H}_S,\, b_T \in \mathcal{H}_T} \frac{\mathrm{cov}\left(b_S\left(\hat{X}_S\right),\ b_T\left(\hat{X}_T\right)\right)}{\sqrt{\mathrm{var}\left(b_S\left(\hat{X}_S\right)\right)\mathrm{var}\left(b_T\left(\hat{X}_T\right)\right)}}$$

$$= \frac{w_S K_S K_T w_T}{\sqrt{w_S^T K_S^2 w_S}\,\sqrt{w_T^T K_T^2 w_T}}$$

(13.5)

where $w_S$, $w_T \in \mathbb{R}^{\mathcal{F}_U^H}$, and we define the centralized kernel matrix $K_S$, $K_T \in \mathbb{R}^{\mathcal{F}_U^H \times \mathcal{F}_U^H}$ as

$$K_S := \frac{1}{N} \sum_{j=1}^{N} \left( \Phi\left(\hat{x}_S^j\right) - \hat{u}_S \right) \left( \Phi\left(\hat{x}_S^j\right) - \hat{u}_S \right)^T$$

$$K_T := \frac{1}{N} \sum_{j=1}^{N} \left( \Phi\left(\hat{x}_T^j\right) - \hat{u}_T \right) \left( \Phi\left(\hat{x}_T^j\right) - \hat{u}_T \right)^T$$

where $\Phi\left(\hat{x}_S^j\right) \in \mathbb{R}^{\mathcal{F}_U^H}$, for $j = 1, 2, \cdots, N$, and $\Phi\left(\hat{x}_T^j\right) \in \mathbb{R}^{\mathcal{F}_U^H}$, for $j = 1, 2, \cdots, N$, $\hat{u}_S$ and $\hat{u}_T$ are the mean values for transformed data matrix regarding each feature. By normalization, KCCA finds the maximum canonical correlation with

$$\text{Maximise } w_S^T K_S K_T w_T$$

$$\text{Subject to } w_S^T K_S^2 w_S = 1, w_T^T K_T^2 w_T = 1 \tag{13.6}$$

which can be modified to the following generalized eigenvalue problems:

$$\begin{bmatrix} 0 & K_S K_T \\ K_T K_S & 0 \end{bmatrix} \begin{bmatrix} w_S \\ w_T \end{bmatrix} = \lambda \begin{bmatrix} K_S^2 & 0 \\ 0 & K_T^2 \end{bmatrix} \begin{bmatrix} w_S \\ w_T \end{bmatrix}$$

### 13.2.3.1.3 Deep CCA

Instead of constructing standard CCA, deep CCA using two neural networks is illustrated as follows:

The deep neural network is used to learn a common latent space where the correlation between two views is as high as possible. The neural network shown in Figure 13.3 is defined as $w_S$ and $w_T$ in both views. We denote the neural network models of source and target views as $f_S(\cdot)$ and $f_T(\cdot)$, and then, we aim to find the optimal $w_S^*$ and $w_T^*$, where

$$\left(w_S^*, \ w_T^*\right) = \underset{(w_S, \ w_T)}{\arg\max} \text{corr}\left( f_S\left(\hat{X}_S; w_S\right), f_T\left(\hat{X}_T; w_T\right) \right) \tag{13.7}$$

Let $H_S \in \mathbb{R}^{r \times N}$ and $H_T \in \mathbb{R}^{r \times N}$ be the learned representations produced by the deep models on the two views. To make the matrices centred, we define $\bar{H}_S = H_S - \frac{1}{N} H_S \mathbf{I}_N$, and the sample covariance is defined as $\hat{\Sigma}_{ST} = \frac{1}{N} \bar{H}_S \bar{H}_T^T$, and the variance for source domain is given by $\hat{\Sigma}_S = \frac{1}{N} \bar{H}_S \bar{H}_S^T + \lambda_S I$

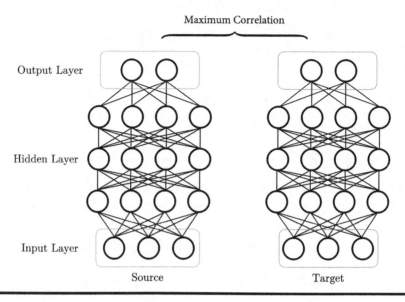

**Figure 13.3   Deep CCA network structure, left network corresponds to the source training, and right network is utilized for the target samples, and the correlation coefficient of output layers of source and target are maximized.**

with regularization constant $\lambda_S$. The centred matrix and variance for target domain is defined similarly. The total correlation of the top $r$ components of $H_S$ and $H_T$ is the sum of the top $r$ singular values of the matrix $\hat{\Sigma}_r = \hat{\Sigma}_S^{-1/2}\hat{\Sigma}_{ST}\hat{\Sigma}_T^{-1/2}$. Using the singular value decomposition of $\hat{\Sigma}_r = UDV^T$, then the gradient for the source data is computed by

$$\frac{\partial \mathrm{corr}\left(H_S,\ H_T\right)}{\partial H_S} = \frac{1}{N}\left(2\nabla_S \bar{H}_S + \nabla_{ST} \bar{H}_T\right)$$

where

$$\nabla_{ST} = \hat{\Sigma}_S^{-1/2} UV^T \hat{\Sigma}_T^{-1/2}$$

$$\nabla_S = -\frac{1}{2}\hat{\Sigma}_S^{-1/2} UDU^T \hat{\Sigma}_S^{-1/2}$$

The gradient for the target domain is symmetric

$$\frac{\partial \mathrm{corr}\left(H_S,\ H_T\right)}{\partial H_T} = \frac{1}{N}\left(2\nabla_T \bar{H}_T + \nabla_{ST} \bar{H}_S\right)$$

where

$$\nabla_{ST} = \hat{\Sigma}_S^{-1/2} UV^T \hat{\Sigma}_T^{-1/2}$$

$$\nabla_T = -\frac{1}{2} \hat{\Sigma}_T^{-1/2} UDU^T \hat{\Sigma}_T^{-1/2}$$

These gradients are back-propagated for training the neural network model.

## 13.3 Method

### 13.3.1 Unified Feature Representation with Imputation

In this section, we present our method with subspace embedding diagram as shown in Figure 13.4, where source and target datasets are projected in a common latent space and a generic classifier is learned to distinguish the labels. Given source and target datasets $\mathcal{D}_S$ and $\mathcal{D}_T$ with $N$ and $M$ ($N \neq M$) samples, to apply CCA in both datasets, the number of instances should be identical, which is not likely for real-world scenarios. We propose a method for pairing, which is finding the nearest pair for the dataset with the smaller number of instances (target) in another one (source) by aligning the feature space first.

Assume we have two datasets with common binary label $\mathcal{Y}$, namely, domain source and target source, which are denoted as $\mathcal{D}_S$ and $\mathcal{D}_T$, respectively. As the two databases are not fully aligned, we split the feature space

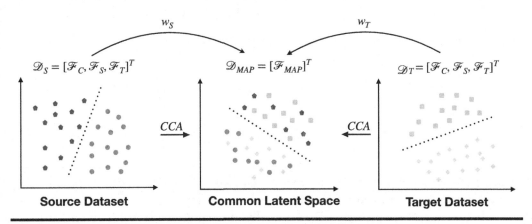

**Figure 13.4　Subspace embedding learning representation.**

into three components according to the missing rate, e.g. *common features* $F_C$, *target-specific features* $F_T$ and *source-specific features* $F_S$ as shown in the Figure 13.5, where $F_C$ are the features that both $\mathcal{D}_S$ and $\mathcal{D}_T$ observe, and here, the term 'observe' entails that the observed instances are substantial enough for each feature (at least one observation). $F_T$ contains features that are only observed in the target and is totally missing in the source, and similarly, $F_S$ consists of features observed in the source and is totally missing in the target.

More formally, given two datasets, namely, source domain $\mathcal{D}_S$ and target domain $\mathcal{D}_T$ regarding the same binary label $\mathcal{Y} \in \{0,1\}$. Input feature spaces for each domain are denoted as $\mathcal{X}_S$ and $\mathcal{X}_T$, and then, we define common feature space $F_C = \mathcal{X}_S \cap \mathcal{X}_T$, target-specific feature space $F_T = \mathcal{X}_T \backslash Fsu$ and source-specific feature space $F_S = \mathcal{X}_S \backslash F_C$.

The imputation involves two procedures, which are *cross-transfer imputation* and *feature creation imputation*. Cross-transfer imputation aims to fill the missing values in $F_C$ using existing imputation techniques, while feature creation imputation can be achieved in two ways: the first is to complete $F_T$ for the source set and $F_S$ for the target set by utilizing the data from target and source, respectively, and the second is to simply pad zeros for missing values in $F_T$ and $F_S$.

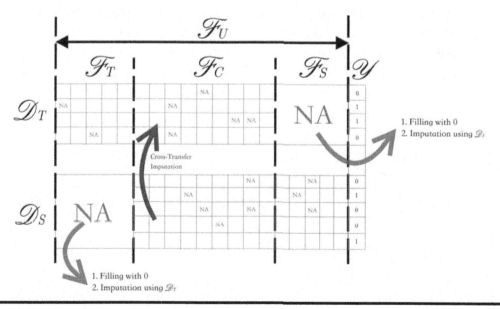

**Figure 13.5   Unified feature representation for two datasets $\mathcal{D}_T$ and $\mathcal{D}_S$. NAs in grid suggest data are missing, observed feature entries are left blank and two large NA indicate that $F_T$ and $F_S$ in $\mathcal{D}_S$ and $\mathcal{D}_S$ are totally missing. Cross-transfer and feature creation imputation are performed on source- and target-specific features.**

## 13.3.2  Nearest Pairing Methods

For each sample in the target dataset, we desire to identify the most similar one from the source dataset. We propose a heuristic pairing algorithm in this section. First, the distance matrix ($N \times M$) is created using Euclidean metrics. Each column represents source indices between all source instances and one specific target instance sorted by distance in ascending order. That is, the first row represents the target index where target instance and source instance have minimal distance and vice versa. Then, in the first row of the distance matrix, we find the largest number of non-replicated instances from the source and then delete these paired instances from source and target until all pairings are finished. The algorithm is shown below.

**Algorithm 1: Nearest Pairing**

  **Input:** Source with $N$ instances, target $M$ instances, assume $M \leq N$.
  **Output:** Paired source and target datasets.
  **Step-1:** Data normalization and pre-processing;
  **Step-2: while** *Instance*($\mathcal{D}\_S$ ) $> 0$ **do**
      {
          $Dist\_Mtx \leftarrow Euclidean\_Distance(\mathcal{D}_S, \mathcal{D}_T)$;
      Find largest non-replicated pairs in the first row, which are denoted
  as $\mathcal{D}_{S,P}, \mathcal{D}_{T,P}$;
        $\mathcal{D}_S \leftarrow \mathcal{D}_S \setminus \mathcal{D}_{S,P}$;
        $\mathcal{D}_T \leftarrow \mathcal{D}_T \setminus \mathcal{D}_{T,P}$;
      }
  **Step-3:** Return $\mathcal{D}_S, \mathcal{D}_T$.

## 13.3.3  CCA Transformation

**Algorithm 2: Classification with Nearest Pairing**

  **Input:** Source: $\mathcal{D}_S \in R^{n_S \times d_S}$, target: $\mathcal{D}_T \in R^{n_T \times d_T}$, assume $n_S \leq n_T$.
  **Output:** Predict amenorrhea status after cancer treatments.
  **Step-1:** $\mathcal{F}_S \leftarrow$ observed_features($\mathcal{D}_S$);
  **Step-2:** $\mathcal{F}_T \leftarrow$ observed_features($\mathcal{D}_S$);
  **Step-3:** $\mathcal{F}_C \leftarrow \mathcal{F}_T \cap \mathcal{F}_S$;
  **Step-4:** Data normalization and pre-processing;
  **Step-5:** Cross-transfer imputation with *kNNI*;

Once we obtain the paired source and target datasets, we can apply the linear CCA with regularization (Equation 13.4), the kernel CCA (Equation 13.6) or the deep CCA (Equation 13.7) for finding a common latent space. A classifier is then employed in the common latent space. Details are shown in Algorithm 2.

## 13.4 Experiments and Result

### 13.4.1 Data Description

The full dataset is authorized by the Fertility after Cancer Predictor (FoRECAsT) Study, University of Melbourne (Peate & Edib, 2019). The dataset summary and five samples are described in Tables 13.1 and 13.2. The data contains 1,565 samples in total with six sub-datasets. From the view of features, most are categorical, and there are a few numerical ones. Each sub-dataset suffers from missingness more or less, from 8.6% to 23.6%. As the features are highly misaligned, the total missingness reaches an excessive rate, at 72.5%. In this section, we will conduct the nearest paring algorithms for the FoRECAsT datasets and compare the performance with some benchmarks in terms of classification accuracy.

### 13.4.2 Result

To investigate the effectiveness of the CCA-based methods for the infertility classification task, three approaches are adopted, which include CCA, kernel CCA and deep CCA, where the benchmark is the accuracy based on a classifier using the original sub-dataset only. All modules are implemented in Python 3.7 (Van Rossum & Drake Jr, 1995) in the operating system Mac OS 10.14.3. For hyper-parameter tuning, cross-imputation uses 5 NN, the latent space dimensionality is set to be fixed half of the rank $r = \frac{1}{2}\min\left(\text{rank}\left(\mathcal{D}_S\right); \text{rank}\left(\mathcal{D}_T\right)\right)$ and the classifier is set to be 1 NN as suggested by many existing papers (Jing et al. 2015; Wang et al. 2017). The neural network model parameters for both source and target views are summarized in Table 13.3.

**Table 13.1  Data Description for FoRECAsT Dataset; the Dataset is Split into Six Subsets Regarding the Sources**

| Data Track | Instances | Observed Features | Categorical | Numerical | Missingness | Label |
|---|---|---|---|---|---|---|
| Track 0 | 725 | 19 | 19 | 0 | 8.6% | |
| Track 1 | 280 | 36 | 36 | 0 | 9.1% | |
| Track 2 | 209 | 34 | 29 | 5 | 10.5% | 'Amen_ST12' |
| Track 3 | 154 | 20 | 19 | 1 | 22.2% | |
| Track 4 | 101 | 42 | 40 | 2 | 23.6% | |
| Track 5 | 96 | 47 | 43 | 4 | 18.3% | |
| Overall | 1,565 | 87 | 76 | 11 | 72.5% | |

Observed feature here implies that the feature has at least one observation within the dataset, and missingness relates to the observed features.

**Table 13.2 Five Instances Sampled from the FoRECAsT Datasets**

| ID | Age | Age_category | Smoking | LiveBirth | Menarche age | ER | TT | n. … | Amen_ST12 |
|----|-----|--------------|---------|-----------|--------------|-----|-----|------|-----------|
| 5249 | 47.3949 | 0 | 0 | 1 | 13 | 1 | 1 | … | 1 |
| 5250 | 33.4565 | 1 | 0 | 1 | 15 | 1 | NA | … | 1 |
| 5258 | 52.2081 | 0 | 1 | 1 | 1 | 1 | NA | … | 1 |
| 5259 | 52.3559 | 0 | 0 | 1 | 15 | 0 | NA | … | 1 |
| 5263 | 50.4038 | 0 | 1 | 1 | NA | 1 | NA | … | 1 |

The entry 'NA' implies that the corresponding data is missing.

**Table 13.3   The Neural Network Model Parameters for Both Source and Target Views**

| p. Layers | Dimension for Target | q. Dimension for Source | r. Activation Function |
|---|---|---|---|
| 1 | 512 | 512 | Sigmoid |
| 2 | 512 | 512 | Sigmoid |
| 3 | 512 | 512 | Sigmoid |
| 4 | r | r | Sigmoid |

## 13.4.2.1 Distance Metrics Evaluation

### 13.4.2.1.1 Proxy-A-Distance

Ben-David et al. (2010) propose a distance metric to evaluate the distribution divergence, which is known as '$\mathcal{A}$-distance'. Computing the $\mathcal{A}$-distance can be approximated by learning a classifier; suppose we have two datasets $\mathcal{D}_S$ and $\mathcal{D}_T$, then a classifier $h$ is learned which achieves minimum error on the binary classification problem of discriminating between points generated by the two distributions.

To see this, suppose we have two samples $U_S$ and $U_T$ sampled from the source and target datasets with the same length $m$, define the error of a classifier $h$ on the task of discriminating between points sampled from different distributions as

$$\text{err}(h) = \frac{1}{2m} \sum_{i=1}^{2m} \left| h(\mathbf{x}_i) - I_{\mathbf{x}_i \in U_S} \right|$$

where $I_{\mathbf{x}_i \in U_S}$ is the binary indicator that where the sample $\mathbf{x}_i$ lies in $U_S$ or not, and the proxy-mathcal$\mathcal{A}$ distance is defined as

$$d_A(U_S,\ U_T) = 2\left(1 - 2\min_h \text{err}(h)\right)$$

It is important to note that it does not provide us with a valid upper bound on the target error, but gives some intuition on how different the source and target datasets are and also gives us some useful insights about the representations for domain adaptation.

### 13.4.2.1.2 Maximum Mean Discrepancy

Maximum mean discrepancy is a kernel evaluation metric proposed by Borgwardt et al. (2006), which is a relevant criterion for comparing distributions based on $\mathbb{R}$. Let $X = x_1, x_2, \cdots, x_n$ and $Y = y_1, y_2, \cdots, y_m$ be random variables with distribution $\mathcal{P}$ and $\mathcal{Q}$. Then, the empirical estimate of distance between $\mathcal{P}$ and $\mathcal{Q}$ is defined as

$$\text{Dist}(X, Y) = \left\| \frac{1}{n} \sum_{i=1}^{n} \phi(x_i) - \frac{1}{m} \sum_{i=1}^{m} \phi(y_i) \right\|_{\mathcal{H}}$$

where $\mathcal{H}$ is a universal RKHS and $\phi(\cdot)$ is a mapping function: $\mathcal{X} \rightarrow \mathcal{H}$.

### 13.4.2.1.3 Coral Loss Function

The coral loss function is defined in the study by Sun & Saenko (2016). This metric evaluates the distance between the second-order statistics (covariances) of the source and target features:

$$l_{\text{CORAL}} = \frac{1}{4d^2} \| C_S - C_T \|_F^2$$

where $\|\cdot\|_F^2$ denotes the squared matrix Frobenius norm. And the covariance matrices of the source and target data are given by

$$C_S = \frac{1}{n_S - 1} \left( D_S^T D_S - \frac{1}{n_S} \left( 1^T D_S \right)^T \left( 1^T D_S \right) \right)$$

$$C_T = \frac{1}{n_T - 1} \left( D_T^T D_T - \frac{1}{n_S} \left( 1^T D_T \right)^T \left( 1^T D_T \right) \right)$$

where 1 is a column vector with all elements equal to 1. And $d$ is the number of features.

## 13.4.2.2 Prediction Accuracy

Transfer learning aims to extract the similarity between the source and target datasets and, and many studies use the divergence metrics to evaluate how different two datasets are and try to learn a common latent space to minimize the according loss function. We will evaluate these metrics on FoRECAsT datasets, and the losses will give us a useful insight on how well CCA transfer learning works. We transfer the knowledge from the dataset that contains more samples to that with fewer; for example, track 5 transferring to track 1 is abbreviated as $T5 \rightarrow T1$, leading to 15 sets of experiments. The distance metrics results and prediction accuracy are shown in Tables 13.4 and 13.5; each column is represented as a different baseline, given as follows:

- ■ S → T: Source dataset transfers to the target dataset.
- ■ Original: Using the target only.
- ■ ZPC: Closest pairing with zero padding for feature creation imputation.
- ■ IMC: Closest pairing with *kNNI* for feature creation imputation.
- ■ ZPCCA: Linear CCA based on the ZPC.
- ■ IMCCA: Linear CCA based on the IMC.
- ■ ZPKCCA: Kernel CCA based on the ZPC using linear kernel.
- ■ IMKCCA: Kernel CCA based on the IMC using linear kernel.
- ■ ZPDCCA: Deep CCA based on the ZPC.
- ■ IMDCCA: Deep CCA based on the IMC.

In Table 13.5, the negative transfers are highlighted in dark grey cells, while positive cases are highlighted in grey cells. The highest accuracy is highlighted in bold for each row. We set the result from the original data as our benchmark. Zero padding and *kNNI* for feature creation imputation are both conducted and compared with and without CCA procedures.

## 13.4.3 Discussion

From the divergence results, we can observe that after CCA, both three distance metrics drop close to zero and this implies that CCA reduces the distribution differences as $P\left(D_{S,\ \mathrm{CCA}}\right) \approx P\left(D_{T,\ \mathrm{CCA}}\right)$. Comparing the zero padding approach with *kNNI* for $F_T$ and $F_S$ in the source and target datasets, the latter method reduces the domain divergence due to the introduction of interference from the source domain, while the former maintains the structure of the data and increases the domain divergence by importing large number of zeros. However, as the algorithm does not take the conditional distribution $P\left(Y_S \mid D_{S,\ \mathrm{CCA}}\right)$ into account, negative transfer will happen if

**Table 13.4  Distance Metrics from Different Baselines**

| Methods | MMD | | | | A-distance | | | | Coral Loss | | | |
|---|---|---|---|---|---|---|---|---|---|---|---|---|
| S→T | ZPC | IMC | ZPCCA | IMCCA | ZPC | IMC | ZPCCA | IMCCA | ZPC | IMC | ZPCCA | IMCCA |
| T4→T5 | 5.18 | 0.25 | 0.00 | 0.00 | 1.96 | 1.08 | 0.00 | 0.00 | 4.7e7 | 2.1e7 | 0.00 | 0.00 |
| T3→T5 | 4.80 | 0.02 | 0.00 | 0.00 | 1.96 | 0.17 | 0.00 | 0.00 | 77.58 | 1.164 | 0.00 | 0.00 |
| T2→T5 | 1.18 | 0.09 | 0.00 | 0.00 | 2.00 | 0.68 | 0.04 | 0.00 | 2.7e9 | 7.4e7 | 0.00 | 0.00 |
| T1→T5 | 5.10 | 4.81 | 0.00 | 0.01 | 2.00 | 1.96 | 0.08 | 0.00 | 90.78 | 90.80 | 0.00 | 0.00 |
| T0→T5 | 4.80 | 0.12 | 0.03 | 0.00 | 1.96 | 0.68 | 0.17 | 0.08 | 122.4 | 4.82 | 0.00 | 0.00 |
| T3→T4 | 5.23 | 0.17 | 0.01 | 0.00 | 1.88 | 1.13 | 0.20 | 0.04 | 1.3e8 | 4.6e7 | 0.00 | 0.00 |
| T2→T4 | 3.04 | 0.11 | 0.00 | 0.00 | 1.88 | 0.78 | 0.00 | 0.00 | 2.1e9 | 1.1e8 | 0.00 | 0.00 |
| T1→T4 | 5.23 | 0.26 | 0.01 | 0.00 | 1.88 | 1.13 | 0.20 | 0.04 | 1.1e8 | 2.8e7 | 0.00 | 0.00 |
| T0→T4 | 5.23 | 0.04 | 0.14 | 0.01 | 1.88 | 0.55 | 0.20 | 0.04 | 1.8e8 | 2.2e7 | 0.03 | 0.00 |
| T2→T3 | 1.20 | 0.04 | 0.01 | 0.01 | 2.00 | 0.73 | 0.13 | 0.10 | 3.1e9 | 2.9e8 | 0.00 | 0.00 |
| T1→T3 | 6.82 | 0.22 | 0.02 | 0.02 | 2.00 | 1.40 | 0.21 | 0.05 | 0.185 | 0.009 | 0.00 | 0.00 |
| T0→T3 | 0.86 | 0.03 | 0.05 | 0.01 | 2.00 | 0.57 | 0.83 | 0.08 | 0.003 | 0.003 | 0.00 | 0.00 |
| T1→T2 | 1.31 | 0.30 | 0.01 | 0.01 | 2.00 | 1.28 | 0.04 | 0.00 | 3e10 | 3.4e9 | 0.00 | 0.00 |
| T0→T2 | 1.31 | 0.00 | 0.06 | 0.01 | 2.00 | 0.93 | 0.44 | 0.21 | 4.5e9 | 2.6e7 | 0.01 | 0.00 |
| T0→T1 | 6.87 | 0.22 | 0.12 | 0.03 | 2.00 | 1.63 | 1.13 | 0.87 | 0.97 | 0.02 | 0.00 | 0.00 |

**Table 13.5    The Classification Results with acc ± dev with 5-Fold Cross-Validation**

| S→T | Original | ZPC | IMC | ZPCCA | IMCCA | ZPKCCA | IMKCCA | ZPDCCA | IMDCCA |
|---|---|---|---|---|---|---|---|---|---|
| T4→T5 | 0.834 ± 0.060 | 0.834 ± 0.060 | 0.844 ± 0.093 | 0.750 ± 0.070 | 0.771 ± 0.023 | 0.875 ± 0.041 | 0.844 ± 0.058 | 0.865 ± 0.053 | **0.896 ± 0.065** |
| T3→T5 | 0.834 ± 0.060 | 0.834 ± 0.060 | 0.834 ± 0.060 | 0.876 ± 0.050 | 0.845 ± 0.071 | 0.875 ± 0.041 | 0.875 ± 0.041 | **0.917 ± 0.025** | 0.906 ± 0.052 |
| T2→T5 | 0.834 ± 0.060 | 0.834 ± 0.060 | 0.740 ± 0.044 | 0.761 ± 0.024 | 0.771 ± 0.040 | **0.875 ± 0.041** | 0.751 ± 0.035 | 0.854 ± 0.039 | 0.823 ± 0.027 |
| T1→T5 | 0.834 ± 0.060 | 0.834 ± 0.060 | 0.834 ± 0.060 | 0.751 ± 0.086 | 0.761 ± 0.078 | **0.875 ± 0.041** | **0.875 ± 0.041** | 0.854 ± 0.051 | 0.792 ± 0.044 |
| T0→T5 | 0.834 ± 0.060 | 0.834 ± 0.060 | 0.834 ± 0.060 | 0.824 ± 0.050 | 0.782 ± 0.060 | 0.875 ± 0.041 | 0.875 ± 0.041 | **0.948 ± 0.001** | 0.907 ± 0.037 |
| T3→T4 | 0.644 ± 0.085 | 0.644 ± 0.085 | 0.605 ± 0.078 | 0.642 ± 0.110 | 0.575 ± 0.059 | 0.663 ± 0.068 | 0.634 ± 0.021 | **0.672 ± 0.055** | 0.662 ± 0.126 |
| T2→T4 | 0.644 ± 0.085 | 0.644 ± 0.085 | 0.584 ± 0.102 | 0.603 ± 0.066 | 0.526 ± 0.124 | 0.653 ± 0.084 | 0.554 ± 0.049 | **0.673 ± 0.069** | 0.663 ± 0.068 |
| T1→T4 | 0.644 ± 0.085 | 0.644 ± 0.085 | 0.605 ± 0.103 | 0.603 ± 0.092 | 0.634 ± 0.100 | 0.693 ± 0.087 | **0.703 ± 0.052** | 0.623 ± 0.043 | 0.594 ± 0.050 |
| T0→T4 | 0.644 ± 0.085 | 0.644 ± 0.085 | 0.605 ± 0.101 | 0.574 ± 0.043 | 0.584 ± 0.076 | 0.663 ± 0.068 | **0.693 ± 0.087** | 0.613 ± 0.041 | 0.644 ± 0.083 |

*(Continued)*

**Table 13.5 (Continued)    The Classification Results with acc ± dev with 5-Fold Cross-Validation**

| S→T | Original | ZPC | IMC | ZPCCA | IMCCA | ZPKCCA | IMKCCA | ZPDCCA | IMDCCA |
|---|---|---|---|---|---|---|---|---|---|
| T2→T3 | 0.590 ± 0.050 | 0.584 ± 0.062 | 0.578 ± 0.087 | 0.689 ± 0.079 | 0.571 ± 0.090 | 0.676 ± 0.077 | 0.519 ± 0.086 | 0.662 ± 0.015 | **0.714 ± 0.048** |
| T1→T3 | 0.590 ± 0.050 | 0.597 ± 0.050 | 0.629 ± 0.073 | 0.540 ± 0.051 | 0.585 ± 0.092 | 0.656 ± 0.081 | **0.702 ± 0.078** | 0.702 ± 0.101 | 0.598 ± 0.080 |
| T0→T3 | 0.590 ± 0.050 | 0.590 ± 0.050 | 0.662 ± 0.051 | **0.727 ± 0.060** | 0.539 ± 0.063 | 0.715 ± 0.078 | 0.715 ± 0.032 | 0.643 ± 0.074 | 0.702 ± 0.046 |
| T1→T2 | 0.766 ± 0.027 | 0.761 ± 0.029 | 0.761 ± 0.039 | **0.785 ± 0.015** | 0.741 ± 0.031 | 0.770 ± 0.055 | 0.780 ± 0.050 | 0.650 ± 0.065 | 0.690 ± 0.077 |
| T0→T2 | 0.766 ± 0.027 | 0.761 ± 0.029 | 0.770 ± 0.041 | 0.761 ± 0.036 | 0.727 ± 0.068 | 0.767 ± 0.040 | **0.770 ± 0.038** | 0.672 ± 0.063 | 0.683 ± 0.068 |
| T0→T1 | 0.518 ± 0.054 | 0.500 ± 0.054 | 0.625 ± 0.040 | 0.629 ± 0.056 | 0.636 ± 0.063 | 0.661 ± 0.049 | 0.656 ± 0.048 | 0.770 ± 0.035 | **0.780 ± 0.020** |
| Average | 0.704 | 0.703 | 0.701 | 0.700 | 0.670 | **0.753** | 0.730 | 0.741 | 0.737 |

Negative transfers are highlighted in dark grey boxes, positive transfers are highlighted in light grey boxes  and the largest accuracy is highlighted in bold for each row.

$P\left(Y_S \mid D_{S, \text{CCA}}\right) \neq P\left(Y_T \mid D_{T, \text{CCA}}\right)$; that is, the accuracy drops after transferring, compared to the original results. For example, if the classification accuracy happens to be relatively low in the source domain, it may not be helpful in distinguishing the label in the target domain. To address this, we apply kernel CCA to provide stronger discriminant power, and this method gives promising accuracy improvements.

From the results of classification accuracy, *kNNI* for feature creation imputation can help the target domain improve classification accuracy, except for subset *T*4. For linear CCA cases, negative transfer occurs regardless of the imputation techniques; despite the domain divergence being reduced, the conditional probability may still differ, which indicates that the elementary linear dimensionality reduction transformation cannot achieve promising results. When using kernel CCA, the classification becomes linearly separable in high dimensional space. Both zero-padding and *kNNI* yield good results. As for deep CCA, zero and cross-imputation can help classify the labels, although negative transfer happens for dataset *T*2. In conclusion, zero padding can achieve better results overall, while *kNNI* is more likely to produce the best results.

In general, whilst the standard CCA minimizes the distribution difference between the source and target datasets, it still cannot generalize the knowledge efficiently from the source domain using linear transformation, except *T*1 → *T*2 and *T*0 → *T*3 with zero padding, while the kernel CCA with zero padding performs strongly with no negative transfers. Regarding the highest accuracy, cross-imputation with kernel CCA and zero padding with deep CCA show remarkably positive transfers. By observing the average accuracy, compared with the benchmark using the original datasets, transfer learning with kernel and deep methods achieves promising prediction results for amenorrhoea prediction accuracy improvements, while standard CCA cannot tackle the problem properly.

However, the algorithm requires that source instances should be larger than target, which is a limitation because the knowledge from the source dataset is not fully utilized and reverse transferring is not possible in our algorithm. In addition, finding appropriate mapping dimension is fixed to be $\frac{1}{2}\min\left(\text{rank}\left(\mathcal{D}_S\right); \text{rank}\left(\mathcal{D}_T\right)\right)$ in our case. We will investigate these issues in future work.

## 13.5 Conclusion

This chapter proposes a CCA-based transfer learning classification for the amenorrhoea status prediction of breast cancer patients using the nearest pairing algorithm and missing values imputation methods. To address the domain divergence issues, CCA minimizes the domain difference by maximizing the correlation between the source and the target. Utilizing kernel or deep CCA achieves ideal results and boosts the classification performance. However, the pairing algorithm introduces limitations and may cause information loss of the source. Developing efficient learning to take advantages of all source information is left to future work. In addition, the results show that the reduction in distribution divergence (measured by distance metrics) cannot guarantee increase in accuracy. There are other factors such as conditional probabilities may cause the reduction in accuracy. More investigations on these factors and correlation between distance metrics and accuracy improvement are suggestions for the further research. This study provides a new roadmap for health researchers dealing with medical data with large amounts of missing values using the transfer learning framework.

## Acknowledgement

This work is fully funded by Melbourne Research Scholarships (MRS), Granted 19/03 and partially supported by Fertility After Cancer Predictor (FoRECAsT) Study. Michelle Peate is currently supported by an MDHS Fellowship, University of Melbourne. The FoRECAsT study is supported by the FoRECAsT Consortium and Victorian Government through a Victorian Cancer Agency (Early Career Seed Grant) awarded to Michelle Peate.

## References

Andrew, G., Arora, R., Bilmes, J., & Livescu, K. (2013). Deep canonical correlation analysis. *International Conference on Machine Learning*, (pp. 1247–1255).

Antropova, N., Bream, A., Beaulieu-Jones, B. K., Chen, I., Chivers, C., Dalca, A., … Hughes, M. (2018). Machine Learning for Health (ML4H) workshop at NeurIPS 2018. *arXiv preprint arXiv:1811.07216*.

Ben-David, S., Blitzer, J., Crammer, K., Kulesza, A., Pereira, F., & Vaughan, J. W. (2010). A theory of learning from different domains. *Machine Learning, 79*, 151–175.

Borgwardt, K. M., Gretton, A., Rasch, M. J., Kriegel, H.-P., Schölkopf, B., & Smola, A. J. (2006). Integrating structured biological data by kernel maximum mean discrepancy. *Bioinformatics, 22*, e49–e57.

Christodoulidis, S., Anthimopoulos, M., Ebner, L., Christe, A., & Mougiakakou, S. (2016). Multisource transfer learning with convolutional neural networks for lung pattern analysis. *IEEE Journal of Biomedical and Health Informatics, 21*, 76–84.

Fukumizu, K., Bach, F. R., & Gretton, A. (2007). Statistical consistency of kernel canonical correlation analysis. *Journal of Machine Learning Research, 8*, 361–383.

Gharib, S., Drossos, K., Çakir, E., Serdyuk, D., & Virtanen, T. (2018). Unsupervised adversarial domain adaptation for acoustic scene classification. *arXiv preprint arXiv:1808.05777*.

Goeij, M. C., Diepen, M., Jager, K. J., Tripepi, G., Zoccali, C., & Dekker, F. W. (2013). Multiple imputation: Dealing with missing data. *Nephrology Dialysis Transplantation, 28*, 2415–2420.

Han, X., & Eisenstein, J. (2019). Unsupervised domain adaptation of contextualized embeddings: A case study in early modern English. *arXiv preprint arXiv:1904.02817*.

Hardoon, D. R., Szedmak, S., & Shawe-Taylor, J. (2004). Canonical correlation analysis: An overview with application to learning methods. *Neural Computation, 16*, 2639–2664.

Jerez, J. M., Molina, I., García-Laencina, P. J., Alba, E., Ribelles, N., Martín, M., & Franco, L. (2010). Missing data imputation using statistical and machine learning methods in a real breast cancer problem. *Artificial Intelligence in Medicine, 50*, 105–115.

Jing, X., Wu, F., Dong, X., Qi, F., & Xu, B. (2015). Heterogeneous cross-company defect prediction by unified metric representation and CCA-based transfer learning. *Proceedings of the 2015 10th Joint Meeting on Foundations of Software Engineering*, (pp. 496–507).

Johnson, N. P., Bagrie, E. M., Coomarasamy, A., Bhattacharya, S., Shelling, A. N., Jessop, S., … Khan, K. S. (2006). Ovarian reserve tests for predicting fertility outcomes for assisted reproductive technology: The International Systematic Collaboration of Ovarian Reserve Evaluation protocol for a systematic review of ovarian reserve test accuracy. *BJOG: An International Journal of Obstetrics & Gynaecology, 113*, 1472–1480.

Kim, Y., Gao, Y., & Ney, H. (2019). Effective cross-lingual transfer of neural machine translation models without shared vocabularies. *arXiv preprint arXiv:1905.05475*.

Lee, S., Kil, W. J., Chun, M., Jung, Y.-S., Kang, S. Y., Kang, S.-H., & Oh, Y.-T. (2009). Chemotherapy-related amenorrhea in premenopausalwomen with breast cancer. *Menopause, 16*, 98–103.

Liem, G. S., Mo, F. K., Pang, E., Suen, J. J., Tang, N. L., Lee, K. M., … Yip, C. C. (2015). Chemotherapy-related amenorrhea and menopause in young Chinese breast cancer patients: Analysis on incidence, risk factors and serum hormone profiles. *PLoS One, 10*, e0140842.

Little, R. J., & Rubin, D. B. (2019). *Statistical Analysis with Missing Data* (Vol. 793). Wiley, Hoboken, NJ.

Long, M. (2014). *Transfer Learning: Problems and Methods.* Ph.D. dissertation, Tsinghua University.

Pan, S. J., & Yang, Q. (2009). A survey on transfer learning. *IEEE Transactions on Knowledge and Data Engineering, 22,* 1345–1359.

Parkhomenko, E., Tritchler, D., & Beyene, J. (2009). Sparse canonical correlation analysis with application to genomic data integration. *Statistical Applications in Genetics and Molecular Biology, 8,* 1–34.

Peate, M., & Edib, Z. (2019, March). Fertility after cancer predictor (FoRECAsT) study. https://medicine.unimelb.edu.au/research-groups/obstetrics-and-gynaecology-research/psychosocial-health-wellbeing-research/fertility-after-cancer-predictor-forecast-study.

Peate, M., Meiser, B., Friedlander, M., Zorbas, H., Rovelli, S., Sansom-Daly, U., … Hickey, M. (2011). It's now or never: Fertility-related knowledge, decision-making preferences, and treatment intentions in young women with breast cancer—an Australian fertility decision aid collaborative group study. *Journal of Clinical Oncology, 29,* 1670–1677.

Sargin, M. E., Yemez, Y., Erzin, E., & Tekalp, A. M. (2007). Audiovisual synchronization and fusion using canonical correlation analysis. *IEEE Transactions on Multimedia, 9,* 1396–1403.

Snell, J., Swersky, K., & Zemel, R. (2017). Prototypical networks for few-shot learning. In I. Guyon, U. V. Luxburg, S. Bengio, H. Wallach, R. Fergus, S. Vishwanathan, & R. Garnett (Eds.), *Advances in Neural Information Processing Systems 30* (pp. 4077–4087). Curran Associates, Inc. Retrieved from http://papers.nips.cc/paper/6996-prototypical-networks-for-few-shot-learning.pdf.

Sterne, J. A., White, I. R., Carlin, J. B., Spratt, M., Royston, P., Kenward, M. G., … Carpenter, J. R. (2009). Multiple imputation for missing data in epidemiological and clinical research: Potential and pitfalls. *BMJ, 338,* b2393.

Sun, B., & Saenko, K. (2016). Deep coral: Correlation alignment for deep domain adaptation. *European Conference on Computer Vision,* (pp. 443–450).

Uran, A., Gemeren, C., Diepen, R., Chavarriaga, R., & Millán, J. d. (2019). Applying transfer learning to deep learned models for EEG analysis. *arXiv preprint arXiv:1907.01332.*

Van Rossum, G., & Drake Jr, F. L. (1995). *Python Tutorial.* Centrum voor Wiskunde en Informatica, Amsterdam.

Wang, J., Chen, Y., Hao, S., Feng, W., & Shen, Z. (2017). Balanced distribution adaptation for transfer learning. *2017 IEEE International Conference on Data Mining (ICDM),* (pp. 1129–1134).

Weiss, K., Khoshgoftaar, T. M., & Wang, D. D. (2016). A survey of transfer learning. *Journal of Big Data, 3.* doi: 10.1186/s40537-016-0043-6.

Wilson, D. R., & Martinez, T. R. (1997). Improved heterogeneous distance functions. *Journal of Artificial Intelligence Research, 6,* 1–34.

Zhao, B., Sun, X., Hong, X., Yao, Y., & Wang, Y. (2019). Zero-shot learning via recurrent knowledge transfer. *2019 IEEE Winter Conference on Applications of Computer Vision (WACV),* (pp. 1308–1317).

Zhao, K., Li, Y., Shuai, Z., & Yang, C. (2018). Learning and transferring IDs representation in e-commerce. *Proceedings of the 24th ACM SIGKDD International Conference on Knowledge Discovery & Data Mining,* (pp. 1031–1039).

*Chapter 14*

# AMD Severity Prediction and Explainability Using Image Registration and Deep Embedded Clustering

Dwarikanath Mahapatra

*Inception Institute of Artificial Intelligence*

## Contents

## 14.1 Introduction

Most approaches to deep learning (DL)-based medical image classification output a binary decision about the presence or absence of a disease without explicitly justifying decisions. Moreover, disease severity prediction in an unsupervised approach is not clearly defined since the absence of disease labels prevents validation of decisions, as in diabetic retinopathy (Son et al., 2020). Diseases such as age-related macular degeneration (AMD) do not have a standard clinical severity scale, and it is left to the observer's expertise to assess severity. While class activation maps (CAMs) (Zhou et al., 2016) highlight image regions that have high response to the trained classifier, they do not provide measurable parameters to explain the decision. Explainability of classifier decisions is an essential requirement of modern diagnosis systems.

In this chapter, we propose a convolutional neural network (CNN)-based optical coherence tomography (OCT) image registration method that (i) predicts the disease class of a given image (e.g., normal, diabetic macular edema (DME) or dry AMD), (ii) uses registration output to grade disease severity on a normalized scale of [1, 10] where 1 indicates normal and 10 indicates confirmed disease and (iii) provides explainability by outputting measurable parameters.

Previous approaches to DL-based image registration include regressors (de Vos et al., 2017; Sokooti et al., 2017) and generative adversarial networks (GANs) (Mahapatra et al., 2018). Balakrishnan et al. (2018) learn a parameterized registration function from training data without the need for simulated deformations in Sokooti et al. (2017). Although there is considerable research in the field of interpretable machine learning, their application to medical image analysis problems is limited (Pereira et al., 2018; Graziani et al., 2018). The CAMs of (Zhou et al., 2016) serve as visualization aids rather than showing quantitative parameters. We propose a novel approach to overcome the limitations of CAM, by providing quantitative measures and their visualization for disease diagnosis based on image registration. Image registration makes the approach fast and enables projection of registration parameters to a linear scale for comparison against normal and diseased cases. It also provides localized and accurate quantitative output compared to CAMs. Our chapter makes the following contributions: (i) a novel approach for AMD severity estimation using registration parameters and clustering, and (ii) mapping registration output to a classification decision and output quantitative values explaining classification decision.

# 14.2 Method

Our proposed method consists of (i) atlas construction for different classes; (ii) end-to-end training of a neural network to estimate registration parameters and assign severity labels; (iii) assign a test volume to a disease severity scale, output its registration parameters and provide quantitatively interpretable information.

## 14.2.1 Atlas Construction Using Groupwise Registration

All normal volumes are coarsely aligned using their point cloud cluster and the iterated closest point (ICP) algorithm. Groupwise registration using ITK (the insight segmentation and registration toolkit) on all volumes gives the atlas image $A_N$. Each normal image is registered to $A_N$ using B-splines. The registration parameters are displacements of grid nodes. They are easier to store and predict than a dense 3D deformation field and can be used to generate the 3D deformation field. The above steps are used to obtain atlases for AMD ($A_{AMD}$) and DME ($A_{DME}$).

## 14.2.2 Deep Embedded Clustering Network

Deep embedded clustering (DEC) (Xie et al., 2016) is an unsupervised clustering approach and gives superior results than traditional clustering algorithms. To cluster n points $x_i \in X_{i=1}^n$ into $k$ clusters, each represented by a centroid $\mu_j, j = 1,\ldots, k$, DEC first transforms the data with a nonlinear mapping $f_\theta: X \to Z$, where $\theta$ are learnable parameters and $Z$ is the latent feature space with lower dimensionality than $X$.

Similarity between embedded point $z_i$ and cluster centroid $\mu_j$ is given by Student's t-distribution as

$$q_{ij} = \frac{\left(1+\left\|z_j - \mu_j\right\|^2/\alpha\right)^{-\frac{a+1}{2}}}{\sum_{j'}\left(1+\left\|z_i - \mu_{j'}\right\|^2/\alpha\right)^{-\frac{a+1}{2}}} \tag{14.1}$$

where $\alpha = 1$ for all experiments. DEC simultaneously learns $k$ cluster centers in feature space $Z$ and the parameters $\theta$. It involves: (i) parameter initialization with a deep autoencoder (Simonyan et al., 2014) and (ii) iterative parameter optimization by computing an auxiliary target distribution and minimizing the Kullback–Leibler (KL) divergence. For further details, we refer the reader to Xie et al., 2016.

## 14.2.3 Estimation of Registration Parameters

Conventional registration methods output a deformation field from an input image pair, while we jointly estimate the grid displacements and severity label using end-to-end training. Figure 14.1 depicts our workflow. An input volume of dimension $512 \times 1024 \times N$, $N$ is number of slices, is converted to a stack of $N$ convolution feature maps by downsampling to $256 \times 512 \times N$ and employing $1 \times 1$ convolution. The output is shown in Figure 14.1 as $d256 fN$ $k1$, which indicates output maps of dimension (d) $256 \times 512$, $N$ feature maps $(f)$ and kernel dimension $(k)$ of $1 \times 1$. The next convolution layer uses $3 \times 3$ kernels and outputs $f = 32$ feature maps. This is followed by a max pooling step that reduces the map dimensions to $128 \times 128$, and the next convolution layer outputs 64 feature maps using $3 \times 3$ kernels. After three further max pooling and convolution layers, the outputs of the "Encoder" stage are 128 feature maps of dimension $16 \times 16$.

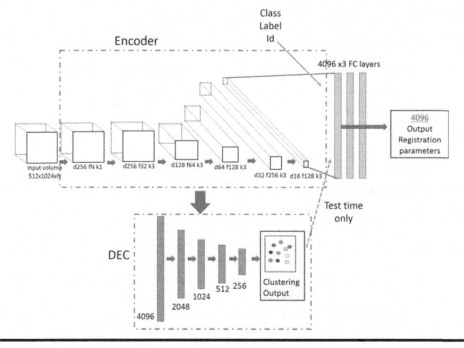

**Figure 14.1  Architecture of our proposed network for AMD classification and severity estimation. A regression network for image registration and deep embedded clustering network are combined to achieve our objectives.**

The Encoder output is used in two ways. The first branch is the input to the DEC network (green boxes depicting fully connected (FC) layers) that outputs a cluster label indicating severity score. The second branch from the Encoder is connected, along with the input volume's disease label, to a FC layer (orange boxes) having 4,096 neurons. It is followed by two more FC layers of 4,096 neurons each, and the final output is the set of registration parameters. The "Class Label id" (disease label of input volume) and the Encoder output are combined using a global pooling step. The motivation behind combining the two is as follows: We are interested to register, for example, a normal volume to the normal atlas. The ground truth registration parameters of a normal volume correspond to those obtained when registering the input volume to the normal atlas, and we want the regression network to predict these parameters. Feeding the input volume's actual disease label guides the regression network to register the image to the corresponding atlas.

## 14.2.4 *Training Stage Implementation*

The entire dataset is divided into training (70%), validation (10%) and test (20%) folds for each class. The DEC parameter initialization closely follows the steps outlined in Xie et al. (2016). The regression network is trained using the input images, their labels and the corresponding registration parameters. We augment the datasets 150 times by rotation and flipping, and obtain their registration parameters with the corresponding atlas. In the first phase of training, only the regression network is trained using mean squared error (MSE) loss for 50 epochs to get an initial set of weights. Subsequently, the DEC is trained using the output of the Encoder network. After training is complete, we cluster the different volumes and observe that 97.8% of the normal patients are assigned to clusters 1–3; 97.5% of DME cases are assigned to clusters 4–7, while 97.2% of AMD cases are assigned to clusters 8–10. Thus, the following mapping between image labels and cluster labels are obtained: normal $\in$ {1, 2, 3}, DME $\in$ {4, 5, 6, 7} and AMD $\in$ {8, 9, 10}.

## 14.2.5 *Predicting Severity of Test Image*

When a test image comes in, we first use the trained DEC to predict the cluster label, which apart from providing disease severity on a scale of (Xie et al., 2016) also gives the image's disease class. The disease label is then used to predict the image's registration parameters to the corresponding atlas. Depending upon the desired level of granularity of disease severity, the number of clusters can be varied to identify different cohorts that exhibit specific traits.

## 14.3 Experimental Results

We demonstrate the effectiveness of our algorithm on a public dataset (Rasti et al., 2018) consisting of OCT volumes from 50 normal, 48 dry AMD and 50 DME patients. The axial resolution of the images is 3.5 μ-m with scan dimension of 512 × 1024 pixels. The number of B-scans varies among 19, 25, 31 and 61 per volume in different patients. The dataset is publicly available at http://www.biosigdata.com. For all registration steps, we used a grid size of 16 × 16 × 16. The number of predicted grid parameters is $16^3 = 4,096$. All reported results are based on 5-fold cross-validation.

### 14.3.1 Registration Results

The output registration parameters from our method are used to generate a deformation field using B-splines and compared with outputs of other registration methods. For the purpose of quantitative evaluation, we applied simulated deformation fields and use different registration methods to recover the registration field. Validation of accuracy is based on mean absolute distance (MAD) between applied and recovered deformation fields. We also manually annotate retinal layers and compute their 95% Hausdorff distance (HD 95) and dice metric (DM) before and after registration. Our method was implemented with Python and Keras, using SGD and Adam with $\beta_1 = 0.93$ and batch normalization. Training and test were performed on a NVIDIA Tesla K40 GPU with 12 GB RAM.

Table 14.1 compares results of the following methods: (i) Reg–DEC: our proposed method; (ii) $Reg_{NoDEC}$: Reg–DEC using only the registration without additional clustering; (iii) VoxelMorph: the method of Balakrishnan et al. (2018); (iv) FlowNet: the registration method of Dosovitskiy et al. (2015); (v) DIRNet: the method of de Vos et al. (2017); and (vi) Reg–k-means: replacing DEC with k-means clustering. Our method outperforms the state-of-the-art DL-based registration methods.

**Table 14.1  Image Registration Results from Different Methods**

| | Before Registration | Reg–DEC | Reg$_{NoDEC}$ | After Registration Reg–k-means | DIRNet | FlowNet | VoxelMorph |
|---|---|---|---|---|---|---|---|
| DM (%) | 78.9 | 89.3 | 85.9 | 84.8 | 83.5 | 87.6 | 88.0 |
| HD$_{95}$ (mm) | 12.9 | 6.9 | 8.4 | 8.7 | 9.8 | 7.5 | 7.4 |
| MAD | 13.7 | 7.3 | 8.9 | 10.3 | 9.1 | 8.6 | 7.9 |
| Time (s) | | 0.5 | 0.4 | 0.6 | 0.5 | 0.6 | 0.6 |

Time indicates computation time in seconds.

## 14.3.2 Classification Results

Table 14.2 summarizes the performance of different methods on the test set for classifying between normal, DME and AMD. Results are also shown for CNN-based classification networks such as VGG-16 (Simonyan et al., 2014), ResNet (He et al., 2016) and DenseNet (Huang et al., 2016), three of the most widely used classification CNNs and the multiscale CNN ensemble of (Vincent et al., 2010) that serves as the baseline for this dataset. Our proposed method outperforms standard CNN architectures, thus proving the efficacy of combining registration with clustering for classification tasks. It also shows Reg–DEC's advantages of lower computing time and fewer training parameters.

## 14.3.3 Identification of Disease Subgroups and Explainability

Besides predicting a disease label and severity score, our method provides explainability behind the decision. For a given test image and its predicted registration parameters, we calculate its $l_2$ distance from each of the ten cluster centers to give us a single value quantifying the sample's similarity with each disease cluster. Let the sample $s$ be assigned to cluster $i \in [1, 10]$, and let the corresponding $l_2$ distances of $s$ to each cluster be $d_i$. We calculate a normalized value:

$$p_d = \left| \frac{d_i - d_1}{d_{10} - d_i} \right| \tag{14.2}$$

where $p_d$ gives a probability of the test sample reaching the highest severity score. It is also a severity score on a normalized scale of [0, 1]. Scores from multiple visits help to build a patient severity profile for analyzing different

**Table 14.2  Classification Results for AMD, DME and Normal on the Test Set Using Different Networks**

| | Reg–DEC | VGG 16 | ResNet 50 | DenseNet | DEC | k-means | MultCNN (Xie et al., 2016) |
|---|---|---|---|---|---|---|---|
| Sen | 93.6 | 91.7 | 92.5 | 92.6 | 89.5 | 85.7 | 92.5 |
| Spe | 94.3 | 92.8 | 93.6 | 93.5 | 90.6 | 86.8 | 93.4 |
| AUC | 96.4 | 94.1 | 95.2 | 95.3 | 91.9 | 87.7 | 95.2 |
| Time (h) | 4.3 | 16.7 | 12.4 | 13.6 | 2.5 | 0.5 | 15.1 |

Time indicates training time in hours.

factors behind increase or decrease of severity, as well as the corresponding rate of change. The rate of severity change is an important factor to determine a personalized diagnosis plan. $p_d$ is different from the class probability obtained from a CNN classifier. The classifier probability is its confidence in the decision, while $p_d$ gives the probability of transitioning to the most severe stage.

Tables 14.1 and 14.2 demonstrate Reg–DEC's superior performance for classification and registration. To determine Reg–DEC's effectiveness in predicting disease severity of classes not part of the training data, we train our severity prediction network on normal and AMD images only, leaving out the DME-affected images. We keep the same number of clusters (i.e., 10) as before. Since there are no DME images and number of clusters is unchanged, assignment of images to clusters is different than before. In this case, 96.4% of AMD images are assigned to clusters 8–10 which is a drop of 0.8% than the previous assignment, while 96.5% of normal samples are assigned to clusters 1–3 which is a decrease of 1.3%.

We see fewer images in clusters 4–7 although the majority of original assignments of normal and AMD cases are unchanged. When we use this trained model on the DME images, we find that 96.9% of the images are assigned to clusters 4–7, a decrease of 0.9% from before. The above results lead to the following conclusions: (i) Reg–DEC's performance reduces by 0.9% for DME and maximum of 1.3% (for Normal images) when DME images were not part of the training data. This is not a significant drop indicating Reg–DEC's capacity to identify sub-groups that were not part of the training data. (ii) Using k-means clustering does not give the same performance levels demonstrating that end-to-end feature learning combined with clustering gives much better results than performing the steps separately. Reg–DEC accurately predicts disease severity even though there is no standard severity grading scale. Severity scale also identifies sub-groups from the population with a specific disease activity.

Figure 14.2 first and second columns, respectively, show AMD images accurately classified by Reg–DEC and DenseNet. The arrows highlight regions of abnormality identified by clinicians. Ellipses (in first column) show the region of disease activity. The length of major axis quantifies magnitude of displacement of the corresponding grid point, and the orientation indicates direction. The local displacement magnitude is proportional to disease severity, while the orientation identifies the exact location. The second column shows the corresponding CAMs obtained from DenseNet (region highlighted). Although the CAMs include the region of

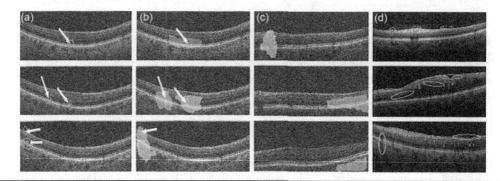

**Figure 14.2 Example of misclassified images. White arrows show positions of diseased activity in AMD images. (a) Predictions by Reg–DEC and quantification of disease activity; (b) CAMs by DenseNet; (c) normal images inaccurately classified as AMD by DenseNet with CAMs; (d) DME images correctly classified by Reg–DEC. The circles are proportional to disease severity.**

disease activity, it does not localize it accurately and is spread out, nor does it output a measurable value. By dividing the displacement magnitude with the distance between the grid points, we get a value very close to $p_d$. The advantages of our registration-based method are obvious since it pinpoints abnormality and quantifies it in terms of displacement magnitude and angle.

Figure 14.2 third column shows examples of normal images that were rightly classified by Reg–DEC but incorrectly classified as AMD by DenseNet. The shaded regions highlight disease activity as identified by DenseNet, which is erroneous since there are no abnormalities here. Reg–DEC does not show any localization of pathologies in these examples. The fourth column shows examples of DME that were rightly identified by Reg–DEC, despite not being part of the training data, along with ellipses showing localized regions of disease activity. They were assigned to clusters 4–7, respectively. The CNNs trained to classify AMD and normal would mostly classify the second and third image as diseased, while the first image was usually classified as normal because of its similar appearance to some normal images. Thus, our method identifies different patient cohorts despite those not being part of the training data.

## 14.4 Conclusion

We propose a method to predict disease severity from retinal OCT images despite there being no labels provided for the disease severity. CNN regressor predicts registration parameters for a given test image which are undergo clustering to output a disease severity scale and a disease probability score in addition to the classification label (diseased or normal). Experimental results show our proposed method achieves better registration and classification performance compared to existing approaches. We are able to identify distinct patient cohorts not part of training data. Our approach also provides explainability behind the classification decision by quantifying disease activity from the registration parameters.

# References

Balakrishnan, G., Zhao, A., Sabuncu, M., Guttag, J. (2018). An supervised learning model for deformable medical image registration. In: *Proceedings of CVPR*. pp. 9252–9260.

de Vos, B., Berendsen, F., Viergever, M., Staring, M., Isgum, I. (2017). End-to-end unsupervised deformable image registration with a convolutional neural network. In: arXiv preprint arXiv:1704.06065.

Dosovitskiy, A., Fischer, P., Ilg, E., et al. (2015). Flownet: Learning optical flow with convolutional networks. In: *Proceedings of the IEEE ICCV*. pp. 2758–2766.

Graziani, M., Andrearczyk, V., Mller, H. (2018). Regression concept vectors for bidirectional explanations in histopathology. In: *Proceedings of MICCAI-iMIMIC*. pp. 124–132.

He, K., Zhang, X., Ren, S., Sun, J. (2016). Deep residual learning for image recognition. In: *Proceedings of the CVPR*. pp. 770–778.

Huang, G., Liu, Z., van der Maaten, L., Weinberger, K. (2016). Densely connected convolutional networks. https://arxiv.org/abs/1608.06993.

Mahapatra, D., Ge, Z., Sedai, S., Chakravorty, R. (2018). Joint registration and segmentation of xray images using generative adversarial networks. In: *Proceedings of MICCAI-MLMI*. pp. 73–80.

Pereira, S., Meier, R., Alves, V., Reyes, M., Silva, C. (2018). Automatic brain tumor grading from MRI data using convolutional neural networks and quality assessment. In: *Proceedings of MICCAI-iMIMIC*. pp. 106–114.

Rasti, R., Rabbani, H., Mehri, A., Hajizadeh, F. (2018). Macular OCT classification using a multi-scale convolutional neural network ensemble. *Transactions on Medical Imaging*, 37(4), 1024–1034.

Simonyan, K., Zisserman, A. (2014). Very deep convolutional networks for large-scale image recognition. CoRR abs/1409.1556.

Sokooti, H., de Vos, B., Berendsen, F., Lelieveldt, B., Isgum, I., Staring, M. (2017). Nonrigid image registration using multiscale 3D convolutional neural networks. In: *Proceedings of MIC-CAI*. pp. 232–239.

Son, J., Shin, J. Y., Kim, H. D., Jung, K. H., Park, K. H., Park, S. J. (2020). Development and validation of deep learning models for screening multiple abnormal findings in retinal fundus images. *Ophthalmology*, 127(1), 85–94.

The insight segmentation and registration toolkit. www.itk.org.

Vincent, P., Larochelle, H., Lajoie, I., Bengio, Y., Manzagol, P. (2010). Stacked denoising autoencoders: Learning useful representations in a deep network with a local denoising criterion. *Journal of Machine Learning Research*, 11, 3371–3408.

Xie, J., Girshick, R., Farhadi, A. (2016). Unsupervised deep embedding for clustering analysis. In: *Proceedings of ICML*. pp. 478–487.

Zhou, B., Khosla, A., Lapedriza, A., Oliva, A., Torralba, A. (2016). Learning deep features for discriminative localization. In: *Proceedings of CVPR*. pp. 2921–2929.

## Chapter 15

# Application of Artificial Intelligence in Thyroidology

Johnson Thomas
*Mercy Clinic Endocrinology*

## Contents

## 15.1 Introduction

Thyroid dysfunction is one of the most common endocrine diseases. About 4.7% of the United States population has undiagnosed thyroid disease (Garmendia Madariaga, Santos Palacios, Guillén-Grima, & Galofré, 2014). Thyroid nodules could be present in up to 67% of the population (Ezzat, Sarti, Cain, & Braunstein, 1994). Increased incidence of thyroid nodules has been attributed to increased use of imaging modalities and improvement in imaging technology (Singh, Singh, & Khanna, 2012). Technological improvements in ultrasound including elastography, 3D ultrasound (Liang et al., 2019) and quantitative ultrasound (Goundan et al., 2019) have been used to improve the diagnostic accuracy. Computer-aided diagnosis software that can automatically detect different features in the thyroid nodules and generate a report has been cleared by the FDA (Lu, Shi, Zhao, Song, & Li, 2019). Similarly, artificial intelligence (AI) algorithms have been used in the diagnosis and management of thyroid diseases. One of the first papers using AI in the diagnosis of thyroid disease was by Sharpe et al. in 1993. They used a multilayer perceptron trained by back-propagation and a learning vector quantization network to investigate the robustness of these models on noisy diagnostic data. In recent years, most of the AI research in thyroidology has been focused on the diagnosis and management of thyroid nodules. Initial approaches used texture analysis to classify thyroid ultrasound images. Later, AI techniques such as machine learning (ML) and an advanced form of ML, deep learning (DL) algorithms were used. In this chapter, we discuss the use of AI in thyroid imaging, cytopathological diagnosis of thyroid nodules and molecular markers. The use of wearable devices and generative adversarial networks in thyroidology is also discussed in this chapter.

## 15.2 Ultrasound Image Classification

At present, when a thyroid nodule is detected on ultrasound, either a radiologist or endocrinologist reviews the images and assigns a probability of it being cancer based on one of the prevalent classification systems. Most popular classifications systems are ACR-TIRADS (Tessler et al., 2017) and the American Thyroid Association's (ATA) classification (Haugen et al., 2016). For example, if the thyroid nodule appears to have irregular margins along with microcalcifications and increased blood flow, then based on ATA classification, this nodule has a high probability of cancer. These are very subjective classification systems (Choi, Kim, Kwak, Kim, & Son, 2009). This subjectivity results in inter- and intraobserver variations. When different radiology and endocrinology groups applied these systems in their respective practices, they got widely varying results. These systems are also designed to capture most of the cancerous nodules, which in turn results in many non-cancerous nodules being labeled as suspicious for malignancy. Because of this, every year, millions of people around the world undergo thyroid biopsy.

To avoid subjectivity, we could use AI algorithms. Researchers have been using different techniques ranging from logistic regression to convolutional neural networks (CNNs) to classify thyroid nodules. In 2014, Zhang et al.

used a multivariate binary logistic regression model to classify subcentimeter thyroid nodules (Zhang, Zhang, Fu, Lv, & Tang, 2014). Their model had a negative predictive value of 85.6% and a positive predictive value of 66.4%. In another study, Chang et al. compared the performance of radiologists and the performance of a computer-aided diagnostic system for classifying thyroid nodules. They used support vector machines with parameters optimized using a grid search to create a binary classification system (Chang et al., 2016). Their model had better accuracy when compared to radiologists. Radial basis function neural network created by Wu and colleagues used features extracted from the ultrasound images by radiologists to classify nodules (Wu, Deng, Zhang, Liu, & Chen, 2016). Their algorithm achieved a sensitivity of 92.31%. But all of these models used input variables that are subjective. Hence, these models did not resolve the issue of subjectivity.

Later generations of models used CNNs to classify thyroid nodules directly from ultrasound images. GoogLeNet model was used by Chi and colleagues from Canada to classify thyroid nodules from an open-access database (Chi et al., 2017). As the complexity of AI models increased so did the accuracy. An article published in *Radiology* journal in 2019 claimed that their deep learning model matched the performance of radiologists (Buda et al., 2019). Another study published in 2019 combined molecular markers and ultrasound images to classify thyroid nodules into nodules with high and low genetic risk (Daniels et al., 2019).

In the future, AI models will aid in the risk stratification of thyroid nodules and eventually decrease the subjectivity in this field. An explainable AI image analysis model that can be incorporated into an existing workflow with a negative predictive value comparable to fine-needle aspiration is needed to achieve uptake by physicians.

## 15.3 Applications in Cytopathology

The first published use of AI in thyroid cytopathology was in 1996 and titled, "Potential of the backpropagation neural network in the morphologic examination of thyroid lesions" (Karakitsos, Cochand-Priollet, Guillausseau, & Pouliakis, 1996). The authors used 26 features from thyroid cells to create the neural network. The accuracy of the system was 98%. Later, the same authors improved the algorithm and tested it on 198 patients to achieve an accuracy of 97.7% (Karakitsos, Cochand-Priollet, Pouliakis, Guillausseau, & Ioakim-Liossi, 1999). In 2004, Ippolito et al. (2004) combined clinical and cytological data from 453 patients with intermediate cytology and used an artificial neural network (ANN) to distinguish between benign and malignant nodules. Of the 453 patients, 371 patients were included in the training set and 82 in the testing set. They concluded that ANN had higher sensitivity and specificity in discriminating between benign and malignant nodules when compared to standard criteria.

Differentiating follicular adenomas from follicular carcinomas is challenging. If one cell crosses the capsule of the nodule, it could be considered as cancer instead of a benign adenoma. Shapiro et al. used nuclear features and chromatin texture as input variables for an ANN (Shapiro et al., 2007). Their model was able to accurately differentiate adenoma from carcinoma with an accuracy of 87%. Ozolek et al. tried to tackle the same problem using optimal transport-based linear embedding for segmented nuclei and showed that their method could outperform standard numerical feature-type methods (Ozolek et al., 2014). Recently, CNNs have been used to classify thyroid cytopathology images. In a study conducted in India by Sanyal et al., CNNs were able to identify papillary thyroid cancer with high precision (Sanyal, Dr, Barui, Das, & Gangopadhyay, 2018). They used images from two different microscopes to account for real-life circumstances and cropped the area of interest. Later, these images were used to create a model in TensorFlow. In a study titled, "Deep convolutional neural network VGG-16 model for differential diagnosing of papillary thyroid carcinomas in cytological images: a pilot study", Guan et al. used multiple patches to train the model (Guan et al., 2019). When tested on 40 nodules, this VGG-16 model achieved an accuracy of 97.6%.

One of the challenges in cytopathology analysis is the need for manual segmentation of the area of interest. A huge portion of the slide may have non-relevant areas. To address these shortcomings, Dov et al. used a two-step fully automated classification system using whole slide images (Dov et al., 2019). In the first step, the area of interest is automatically identified and cropped. In the second step, this cropped picture is fed into a CNN to classify the image. Seven hundred and ninety-nine slides were used for training. The trained model was tested on 109 slides. This system had an area under the curve comparable to human experts. AI algorithms could reduce the limitations of traditional cytopathology and histopathology techniques. AI could flag areas of interest, like an area with capsular invasion for the pathologists to verify. An algorithm like this will decrease the chance of misdiagnosing a follicular carcinoma along with decreasing the workload for the pathologist. There exists a need for prospective multicenter trials in the future to validate these algorithms before being used in clinical practice.

## 15.4 Molecular Diagnosis

Fine needle aspiration of thyroid nodule does not always yield a definitive diagnosis. If there are not enough thyroid follicular cells, it could come back as non-diagnostic. Other potential non-definitive results include atypia of undetermined significance, follicular lesion of unknown significance, follicular neoplasm, suspicious for follicular neoplasm and suspicious for malignancy (Cibas, Ali, & of the Science Conference, 2009). Before the advent of molecular markers, many of these nodules were sent for surgery. But now, aspirates from these nodules could be sent for molecular diagnosis. Afirma® thyroid FNA analysis uses an ensemble machine learning model to classify thyroid nodules from the molecular analysis information (Hao et al., 2019). Another test, Thyroseq, uses a tree-based classification algorithm for indeterminate thyroid nodule classification (Mallick & Harmer, 2018).

## 15.5 Wearables

Wearable devices are ubiquitous now, making it easy to capture real-time medically relevant data. Capturing heart rate variations from wearables have been very helpful in identifying atrial fibrillation. A recent study published in *the New England Journal of Medicine* described how 419,297 participants were recruited to monitor their heart rate using the Apple watch (Perez et al., 2019). According to this study, only a few percentages of the recruits received an alert regarding their heart rate, of which 34% of participants were diagnosed with atrial fibrillation.

Similar to the atrial fibrillation trial, Lee et al. (2018) used Fitbit to monitor the heart rate of patients with hyperthyroidism. Their study showed that the increase in heart rate by 11 beats per minute was positively correlated with a rise in free thyroxine level. The authors concluded that data from wearable could help in the management of patients with hyperthyroidism. In the future, data from wearables could be fed to AI algorithms to predict individual patient's responses to antithyroid medications. This could help in the early titration of medications.

## 15.6  Generative Adversarial Networks

Generative adversarial networks (GANs) are AI algorithms that can produce synthetic data from a given distribution of data (Goodfellow et al., 2014). GANs have been used to create art (Elgammal, Liu, Elhoseiny, & Mazzone, 2017), to mimic speech (Bińkowski et al., 2019) of a person and to create fake videos (Korshunov & Marcel, 2019). Given enough data from different classes, GANs can generate artificial data that mimics the original data distribution in each class. In healthcare, GANs have been used to generate artificial medical records to boost predictions from electronic health records (Che, Cheng, Zhai, Sun, & Liu, 2017). GANs were used to generate synthetic medical records in the hope of protecting the patient's privacy (Choi et al., 2017). Noise reduction in a low-dose CT scan was also made possible by GANs (Wolterink, Leiner, Viergever, & Išgum, 2017).

Lack of large medical image datasets makes it harder to use supervised learning. Yang et al. used GANs to address this shortcoming by using dual-path semi-supervised conditional generative adversarial networks for classification of thyroid nodules in ultrasound (Yang et al., 2019). Another application of GAN is the virtual staining of histopathology slides. Traditionally, staining of medical tissue is a cumbersome and time-consuming process. Rivenson et al. used GAN to create a label-free virtual staining method for tissues including thyroid (Rivenson et al., 2019). GANs can also be used to train label generating AI algorithms. For example, ultrasound images of thyroid nodules generated by GAN can be tagged with different features likes microcalcification, irregular border and hypoechogenicity. These tagged pictures could be used to create an AI model to generate tags for unseen thyroid ultrasound images. Figure 15.1 depicts synthetic ultrasound thyroid nodule images created by the author.

## 15.7  Discussion

The art of medicine is not always precise or consistent. Hence, it is difficult to reproduce medical research. This is especially true for medical AI research. We need prospective trials to evaluate medical AI models. AI model created in one health system may not work well when used in a different setting. Hence, external validation is essential before deploying a model. Even though there is a lot of research articles on the application of AI algorithms in thyroidology, none of them are used widely in clinical practice other than the ones used in molecular markers. This could be due

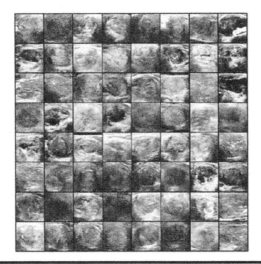

**Figure 15.1    Synthetic images of thyroid ultrasound images created using generative adversarial networks (GANs).**

to difficulty in implementing AI software into the current clinical workflow. Another reason could be due to regulatory hurdles. Not every AI researcher can afford setting up clinical research that meets regulatory standards. Media hype regarding the promise of medical AI might also dissuade prospective physician users. Educating physicians and other stakeholders involved in the implementation of AI, ideal use case scenarios, realistic advantages and disadvantages of the AI and possible error mitigation strategies might improve the uptake of this technology into the day-to-day medical practice.

Most AI algorithms are black boxes. Black box algorithms do not allow physicians to understand the reason behind a particular output by an AI model. Decisions made by the AI model could be explained by demonstrating feature importance, Local Interpretable Model-Agnostic Explanations (LIME), layer-wise relevance propagation, class activation maps and similar image search. AIBx is an image similarity model created by the author with built-in explainability (Thomas & Haertling, 2020). Given a test ultrasound image, AIBx will output similar images with the corresponding diagnosis. Explainable AI models are needed to gain the trust of the physicians and regulators. AI tools in thyroidology can act as decision support tools for physicians. These tools can also be very valuable in resource-poor developing countries where medical experts are not readily available. Ultimately, AI tools in thyroidology could decrease the cost of healthcare, decrease subjectivity and improve the quality of care. AI will become an integral part of the diagnosis and management of thyroid disease in the not so distant future.

# References

Bińkowski, M., Donahue, J., Dieleman, S., Clark, A., Elsen, E., Casagrande, N., … Simonyan, K. (2019). High fidelity speech synthesis with adversarial networks. *ArXiv Preprint ArXiv:1909.11646*.

Buda, M., Wildman-Tobriner, B., Hoang, J. K., Thayer, D., Tessler, F. N., Middleton, W. D., & Mazurowski, M. A. (2019). Management of thyroid nodules seen on US images: Deep learning may match performance of radiologists. *Radiology*, 292. doi: 10.1148/radiol.2019181343.

Chang, Y., Paul, A. K., Kim, N., Baek, J. H., Choi, Y. J., Ha, E. J., … Kim, N. (2016). Computer-aided diagnosis for classifying benign versus malignant thyroid nodules based on ultrasound images: A comparison with radiologist-based assessments. *Medical Physics*. doi: 10.1118/1.4939060.

Che, Z., Cheng, Y., Zhai, S., Sun, Z., & Liu, Y. (2017). Boosting deep learning risk prediction with generative adversarial networks for electronic health records. *2017 IEEE International Conference on Data Mining (ICDM)*, 787–792.

Chi, J., Walia, E., Babyn, P., Wang, J., Groot, G., & Eramian, M. (2017). Thyroid nodule classification in ultrasound images by fine-tuning deep convolutional neural network. *Journal of Digital Imaging*. doi: org/10.1007/s10278-017-9997-y.

Choi, E., Biswal, S., Malin, B., Duke, J., Stewart, W. F., & Sun, J. (2017). Generating multi-label discrete patient records using generative adversarial networks. *ArXiv Preprint ArXiv:1703.06490*.

Choi, S. H., Kim, E.-K., Kwak, J. Y., Kim, M. J., & Son, E. J. (2009). Interobserver and intraobserver variations in ultrasound assessment of thyroid nodules. *Thyroid*. doi: 10.1089/thy.2008.0354.

Cibas, E. S., Ali, S. Z., & of the Science Conference, N. C. I. T. F. N. A. S. (2009). The bethesda system for reporting thyroid cytopathology. *American Journal of Clinical Pathology*, *132*(5), 658–665. doi: 10.1309/{AJCPPHLWMI3JV4LA}.

Daniels, K., Gummadi, S., Zhu, Z., Wang, S., Patel, J., Swendseid, B., … Eisenbrey, J. (2019). Machine learning by ultrasonography for genetic risk stratification of thyroid nodules. *JAMA Otolaryngology–Head & Neck Surgery*, 1–6. doi: 10.1001/jamaoto.2019.3073.

Dov, D., Kovalsky, S., Cohen, J., Range, D., Henao, R., & Carin, L. (2019). Thyroid cancer malignancy prediction from whole slide cytopathology images. *ArXiv Preprint ArXiv:1904.00839*.

Elgammal, A., Liu, B., Elhoseiny, M., & Mazzone, M. (2017). Can: Creative adversarial networks, generating "art" by learning about styles and deviating from style norms. *ArXiv Preprint ArXiv:1706.07068*.

Ezzat, S., Sarti, D. A., Cain, D. R., & Braunstein, G. D. (1994). Thyroid incidentalomas. Prevalence by palpation and ultrasonography. *Archives of Internal Medicine*, *154*(16), 1838–1840. Retrieved from https://www.ncbi.nlm.nih.gov/pubmed/8053752

Garmendia Madariaga, A., Santos Palacios, S., Guillén-Grima, F., & Galofré, J. C. (2014). The incidence and prevalence of thyroid dysfunction in Europe: A meta-analysis. *The Journal of Clinical Endocrinology & Metabolism*, 99(3), 923–931. doi: 10.1210/jc.2013-2409.

Goodfellow, I., Pouget-Abadie, J., Mirza, M., Xu, B., Warde-Farley, D., Ozair, S., … Bengio, Y. (2014). Generative adversarial nets. *Advances in Neural Information Processing Systems*, 2672–2680.

Goundan, P., Korpaisarn, S., Smith, J., Rohrbach, D., Mamou, J., Patel, H., … Lee, S. (2019). MON-571 the performance of an advanced ultrasound technique, quantitative ultrasound, compared to conventional ultrasound in the evaluation of thyroid nodules. *Journal of the Endocrine Society*, 3(Supplement_1). doi: 10.1210/js.2019-MON-571.

Guan, Q., Wang, Y., Ping, B., Li, D., Du, J., Qin, Y., … Xiang, J. (2019). Deep convolutional neural network VGG-16 model for differential diagnosing of papillary thyroid carcinomas in cytological images: A pilot study. *Journal of Cancer*. doi: 10.7150/jca.28769.

Hao, Y., Choi, Y., Babiarz, J. E., Kloos, R. T., Kennedy, G. C., Huang, J., & Walsh, P. S. (2019). Analytical verification performance of afirma genomic sequencing classifier in the diagnosis of cytologically indeterminate thyroid nodules. *Frontiers in Endocrinology*. doi: 10.3389/fendo.2019.00438.

Haugen, B. R., Alexander, E. K., Bible, K. C., Doherty, G. M., Mandel, S. J., Nikiforov, Y. E., … Wartofsky, L. (2016). 2015 American Thyroid Association Management guidelines for adult patients with thyroid nodules and differentiated thyroid cancer: The American Thyroid Association guidelines task force on thyroid nodules and differentiated thyroid cancer. *Thyroid*, 26(1), 1–133. doi: 10.1089/thy.2015.0020.

Ippolito, A. M., De Laurentiis, M., La Rosa, G. L., Eleuteri, A., Tagliaferri, R., De Placido, S., … Belfiore, A. (2004). Neural network analysis for evaluating cancer risk in thyroid nodules with an indeterminate diagnosis at aspiration cytology: Identification of a low-risk subgroup. *Thyroid*. doi: 10.1089/thy.2004.14.1065.

Karakitsos, P., Cochand-Priollet, B., Guillausseau, P. J., & Pouliakis, A. (1996). Potential of the back propagation neural network in the morphologic examination of thyroid lesions. *Analytical and Quantitative Cytology and Histology*, 18, 494–500.

Karakitsos, P., Cochand-Priollet, B., Pouliakis, A., Guillausseau, P. J., & Ioakim-Liossi, A. (1999). Learning vector quantizer in the investigation of thyroid lesions. *Analytical and Quantitative Cytology and Histology*, 21, 201–208.

Korshunov, P., & Marcel, S. (2019). Vulnerability assessment and detection of deepfake videos. *The 12th IAPR International Conference on Biometrics (ICB)*, 1–6.

Lee, J. E., Lee, D. H., Oh, T. J., Kim, K. M., Choi, S. H., Lim, S., … Moon, J. H. (2018). Clinical feasibility of monitoring resting heart rate using a wearable activity tracker in patients with thyrotoxicosis: Prospective longitudinal observational study. *JMIR MHealth and UHealth*. doi: 10.2196/mhealth.9884.

Liang, X. W., Cai, Y. Y., Yu, J. S., Liao, J. Y., Chen, Z. Y., & Wang, N. N. (2019). Update on thyroid ultrasound: A narrative review from diagnostic criteria to artificial intelligence techniques. *Chinese Medical Journal*. doi: 10.1097/CM9.0000000000000346.

Lu, Y., Shi, X. Q., Zhao, X., Song, D., & Li, J. (2019). Value of computer software for assisting sonographers in the diagnosis of thyroid imaging reporting and data system grade 3 and 4 thyroid space-occupying lesions. *Journal of Ultrasound in Medicine*, *38*(12), 3291–3300. doi: 10.1002/jum.15065.

Mallick, U. K., & Harmer, C. (2018). *Practical Management of Thyroid Cancer: A Multidisciplinary Approach*. Retrieved from https://books.google.com/books?id=6f1uDwAAQBAJ.

Ozolek, J. A., Tosun, A. B., Wang, W., Chen, C., Kolouri, S., Basu, S., ... Rohde, G. K. (2014). Accurate diagnosis of thyroid follicular lesions from nuclear morphology using supervised learning. *Medical Image Analysis*. doi: 10.1016/j.media.2014.04.004.

Perez, M. V., Mahaffey, K. W., Hedlin, H., Rumsfeld, J. S., Garcia, A., Ferris, T., ... Turakhia, M. P. (2019). Large-scale assessment of a smartwatch to identify atrial fibrillation. *New England Journal of Medicine*, *381*(20), 1909–1917. doi: 10.1056/NEJMoa1901183.

Rivenson, Y., Wang, H., Wei, Z., de Haan, K., Zhang, Y., Wu, Y., ... Ozcan, A. (2019). Virtual histological staining of unlabelled tissue-autofluorescence images via deep learning. *Nature Biomedical Engineering*. doi: 10.1038/s41551-019-0362-y.

Sanyal, P., Dr, T. M., Barui, S., Das, A., & Gangopadhyay, P. (2018). Artificial intelligence in cytopathology: A neural network to identify papillary carcinoma on thyroid fine-needle aspiration cytology smears. *Journal of Pathology Informatics*. doi: 10.4103/jpi.jpi_43_18.

Shapiro, N. A., Poloz, T. L., Shkurupij, V. A., Tarkov, M. S., Poloz, V. V., & Demin, A. V. (2007). Application of artificial neural network for classification of thyroid follicular tumors. *Analytical and Quantitative Cytology and Histology*, *29*, 87–94.

Sharpe, P. K., Solberg, H. E., Rootwelt, K., & Yearworth, M. (1993). Artificial neural networks in diagnosis of thyroid function from in vitro laboratory tests. *Clinical Chemistry*, *39*, 2248–2253.

Singh, S., Singh, A., & Khanna, A. K. (2012). Thyroid incidentaloma. *Indian Journal of Surgical Oncology*, *3*(3), 173–181. doi: 10.1007/s13193-011-0098-y.

Tessler, F. N., Middleton, W. D., Grant, E. G., Hoang, J. K., Berland, L. L., Teefey, S. A., ... Stavros, A. T. (2017). ACR Thyroid Imaging, Reporting and Data System (TI-RADS): White paper of the ACR TI-RADS committee. *Journal of the American College of Radiology*. doi: 10.1016/j.jacr.2017.01.046.

Thomas, J., & Haertling, T. (2020). AIBx, artificial intelligence model to risk stratify thyroid nodules. *Thyroid*. doi: 10.1089/thy.2019.0752.

Wolterink, J. M., Leiner, T., Viergever, M. A., & Išgum, I. (2017). Generative adversarial networks for noise reduction in low-dose CT. *IEEE Transactions on Medical Imaging*, *36*(12), 2536–2545.

Wu, H., Deng, Z., Zhang, B., Liu, Q., & Chen, J. (2016). Classifier model based on machine learning algorithms: Application to differential diagnosis of suspicious thyroid nodules via sonography. *American Journal of Roentgenology.* doi: 10.2214/AJR.15.15813.

Yang, W., Zhao, J., Qiang, Y., Yang, X., Dong, Y., Du, Q., … Zia, M. B. (2019). DScGANS: Integrate domain knowledge in training dual-path semi-supervised conditional generative adversarial networks and S3VM for ultrasonography thyroid nodules classification. *International Conference on Medical Image Computing and Computer-Assisted Intervention,* 558–566.

Zhang, M., Zhang, Y., Fu, S., Lv, F., & Tang, J. (2014). Development of a logistic regression formula for evaluation of subcentimeter thyroid nodules. *Journal of Ultrasound in Medicine.* doi: 10.7863/ultra.33.6.1023.

*Chapter 16*

# Use of Artificial Intelligence in Sepsis Detection and Management

Neha Deo and Rahul Kashyap

*Mayo Clinic*

## Contents

## 16.1 Background

In the United States, 750,000 people are diagnosed with sepsis every year (Bansal et al., 2018), accounting for 250,000 deaths (Harrison et al., 2015) and 51% of total ICU admissions (Bansal et al., 2018). Sepsis is a complex disease with an even more complex management and treatment process. Diagnosis of sepsis consists of suspected or proven infection and systemic inflammatory response syndrome (SIRS). Delay in diagnosis places a burden on the healthcare system, costing close to 15.4 billion dollars annually

(Bansal et al., 2018). Advanced detection can help mitigate these challenges by allowing for earlier diagnosis (Harrison et al., 2015). Furthermore, initiating early treatment would have a significant impact on mortality rates and alleviate the strain on healthcare resources allocated to sepsis treatment (Bansal et al., 2018).

## 16.2 Sepsis Prediction

Sepsis and septic shock being complex disease entities require scanning through the large scale of data to make as a diagnosis. It often gets delayed which could be detrimental to patient outcomes. Machine learning algorithms (MLAs) could greatly benefit patient outcomes by detecting potential sepsis shock (Shimabukuro et al., 2017). MLAs can synthesize information from different variables and utilize patient data to predict specific outcomes (Nemati et al., 2018). Earlier diagnosis and utilization of sepsis bundles could lead to lower mortality rates and improve patient care (Bansal et al., 2018). MLA systems can improve the timeliness of treatment intervention by alerting the treatment team before the onset of sepsis symptoms (Bansal et al., 2018).

Most electronic health record (EHR) alert tools are score-based, relying on certain criteria to be met diagnosis (Barton et al., 2019). However, MLA is customizable. Providers can use the system to monitor specific patient measures such as lactate levels and blood pressure (Harrison et al., 2015). MLAs can provide an early diagnosis with high specificity and sensitivity which could be very beneficial in the critical care setting (Shimabukuro et al., 2017).

## 16.3 Sepsis Detection

Early detection of sepsis is integral to effective treatment and improved patient outcomes (Harrison et al., 2015). Compliance with bundled sepsis protocols can reduce patient mortality and improve care (Giannini et al., 2019). MLAs have the potential to relieve the burden on healthcare resources via ongoing monitoring of the patients' risk for sepsis (Nemati et al., 2018). With machine learning systems, clinicians can monitor patient outcomes without the need for constantly being at the bedside (Nemati et al., 2018). As MLAs function as an early alert system, many healthcare providers will be able to provide prompt care well in advance (Bansal et al., 2018). There is also evidence pointing to the utilization of MLA's in the non-ICU setting that resulted in earlier and more frequent treatment interventions in septic patients (Harrison et al., 2015).

MLAs help streamlines patient care by providing notifications only when necessary. Most healthcare professionals are often burdened with more than 50 notifications a day from EHR systems and emails (Giannini et al., 2019). This could inadvertently lead to individuals avoiding or ignoring their alerts (Giannini et al., 2019). However, MLAs can also decrease alarm fatigue by providing alerts only when necessary (Nemati et al., 2018). High sensitivity and specificity can be expected from most MLA systems that monitor key vital signs related to sepsis shock (e.g., high lactate levels, blood pressure) up to 48 hours in advance, so healthcare professionals can expect that alerts will only occur in exceptional circumstances.

A current challenge exists is that MLAs that monitor for sepsis may be alerting healthcare professionals too early (Bansal et al., 2018). A response that may occur hours in advance may result in the provider choosing not to provide treatment – especially if the patient is not exhibiting physical signs of sepsis. Furthermore, a single alert may not be enough to incur a response from the healthcare team (Giannini et al., 2019). It is unclear whether an alert system or a dynamic scoring system would be more effective in notifying healthcare professionals (Giannini et al., 2019).

## 16.4 Sepsis Treatment

Delayed treatment of sepsis can lead to higher mortality rates in patients (Harrison et al., 2015); however, early antibiotic therapy can improve patient outcomes (Nemati et al., 2018). The development of MLAs with high sensitivity and high specificity can improve timeliness in sepsis detection (Bansal et al., 2018). A recent study suggested that after every hour a patient is not administered appropriate antibiotic therapy, their chance of survival decreases by 7% (Shimabukuro et al., 2017). Furthermore, there is literature that suggests that timeliness of antibiotic therapy is a key determiner for sepsis outcomes (Nemati et al., 2018). Thus, early intervention is integral to mortality rates in patients undergoing septic shock. MLA systems can decrease the time between the onset of sepsis and treatment by providing alerting treatment providers promptly (Harrison et al., 2015). There is also an increase in the frequency of treatment interventions in the ICU setting when utilizing MLAs (Harrison et al., 2015).

Noncompliance with sepsis bundles can lead to increases in patient mortality (Barton et al., 2019). However, a team-based approach to sepsis management, coupled with MLA systems to alert healthcare providers before the onset of septic shock, can mitigate this risk (Harrison et al., 2015). Interdisciplinary teams that provide patient care after being notified can lead to the more frequent implementation of compliance bundles (Bansal et al., 2018). The utilization of MLAs also leads to decreases in time to ICU transfer (Giannini et al., 2019). Escalating care for patients suspected of having sepsis can occur sooner, leading to earlier treatment intervention (Giannini et al., 2019). However, it is integral that healthcare providers are informed of the variables that lead to alerts; otherwise, there may be distrust in the effectiveness of the system (Giannini et al., 2019).

## 16.5 Sepsis Outcome

Compliance with sepsis bundles is poor, even with training and educational intervention (Harrison et al., 2015). However, MLAs can encourage the utilization of sepsis bundles by decreasing information overload and mitigating alert fatigue (Harrison et al., 2015). By implementing MLA monitoring in the critical care setting, there is the potential for improved compliance, as well as earlier triage (Bansal et al., 2018). High sensitivity and specificity are integral to more frequent utilization of MLA systems in sepsis care, as frequent false alarms can result in providers feeling hesitant in implementing this technology (Shimabukuro et al., 2017).

There is data suggesting that the utilization of MLA systems in sepsis care results in lower mortality rates (Bansal et al., 2018), earlier antibiotic therapy (Shimabukuro et al., 2017), and can shorten the length of stay in the ICU (Shimabukuro et al., 2017). A study found that in-hospital mortality decreased by 12% with patients who were monitored by MLAs for sepsis recognition (Shimabukuro et al., 2017). When pairing sepsis recognition systems with a sepsis response team, the in-hospital mortality rate (9.4%) was lower than the US average (28.6%) for patients with sepsis (Bansal et al., 2018). Patients that were monitored by MLAs received antibiotics up to 2.76 hours earlier than their counterparts and were observed to have blood culture draws sooner (Shimabukuro et al., 2017). In-hospital length of stay was observed to be shorter in patients monitored by MLA systems (6.31 days) versus those monitored by healthcare professionals only (8.40 days) (Shimabukuro et al., 2017) (Table 16.1).

**Table 16.1 Summary of Studies Included in This Chapter**

| S.N. | Study Title, First Author Name, Year | Study Brief Description | ML Methods | Results | Outcomes/Impact on Healthcare Delivery |
|------|---------------------------------------|--------------------------|------------|---------|-----------------------------------------|
| 1. | Developing the Surveillance Algorithm for Detection of Failure to Recognize and Treat Severe Sepsis, Andrew M. Harrison, 2015 | Developed a sepsis sniffer using an algorithm. Detected severe sepsis and monitored failure to recognize sepsis in a timely manner. Measured sensitivity and the specificity of the sniffer in relation to different variables that are symptoms of sepsis. | Used derivation and validation cohorts to clean computer algorithms. Two reviewers and super reviewers used for disagreements. Retrospective study. | Introducing nine additional variables in addition to low BP and elevated lactate levels did not improve sensitivity or specificity. No lactate and BP measurement within 2 hours of severe sepsis was considered a delay in treatment. | Sniffers can decrease ED time for the treatment of sepsis. Need for an optimized system. The decrease in mortality of severe sepsis if there is more implementation of this system into EMRs. It can decrease information overload and human error. |

*(Continued)*

**Table 16.1 (*Continued*)   Summary of Studies Included in This Chapter**

| S.N. | Study Title, First Author Name, Year | Study Brief Description | ML Methods | Results | Outcomes/Impact on Healthcare Delivery |
|------|------|------|------|------|------|
| 2. | Early Machine-Human Interface around Sepsis Severity Identification: From Diagnosis to Improved Management? Vikas Bansal, 2018 | Measured early sepsis identification using an algorithm, as well as human decision-making when deciding to recruit the sepsis response team. | The set of criteria alerts healthcare professionals of early sepsis. ED nurse determines if actually septic using bundle components. The sepsis team is then activated. | The sensitivity of 100%, the specificity of 96.21%, 34% had accurate sepsis team activation. 53% ICU team contacted before activation. 9.4% in mortality. | Team-based care can improve health outcomes and bundle compliance. Intergroup climate in hospitals leads to poor treatment of the patient. Intentionally creating multidisciplinary teams encouraged cooperation and teamwork. Buy in of sepsis team led to enhanced communication and consensus of responsibilities. Lack of advanced algorithms still requires that a human makes the final decision for sepsis. |

*(Continued)*

**Table 16.1 (*Continued*)  Summary of Studies Included in This Chapter**

| S.N. | Study Title, First Author Name, Year | Study Brief Description | ML Methods | Results | Outcomes/Impact on Healthcare Delivery |
|---|---|---|---|---|---|
| 3. | Effect of A Machine Learning-Based Severe Sepsis Prediction Algorithm on Patient Survival and Hospital Length of Stay: A Randomized Clinical Trial. David W Shimabukuru, 2017 | Determined the effectiveness of the MLA with control versus intervention group. The intervention group used a current program in EHR. Measured improvements in length of stay and mortality rate. | The control group used the current sepsis detector, intervention group used algorithm. Same sepsis treatment. The algorithm used a scoring of 0–100 based on values (low BP, pH, glucose, etc.), a score of >80 triggered a call to nursing. | Significant decrease in length of hospital stay (13 days versus 10.3). ICU LOS was 8.40 versus 6.31. The control group had 16/75 patients for mortality, intervention 6/67. Patients in the intervention group given antibiotics 2.76 hours earlier and blood was drawn 2.79 hours earlier. | Improvement in patient outcomes when using the algorithm. It can prevent septic shock if intervening earlier. Some algorithms have low specificities, which may make clinicians hesitant to implement them into practice. Earlier clinical interventions with the algorithm. |

(*Continued*)

**Table 16.1 (Continued) Summary of Studies Included in This Chapter**

| S.N. | Study Title, First Author Name, Year | Study Brief Description | ML Methods | Results | Outcomes/Impact on Healthcare Delivery |
|---|---|---|---|---|---|
| 4. | A MLA to Predict Severe Sepsis and Septic Shock: Development, Implementation, and Impact on Clinical Practice. Heather M. Giannini, 2019 | The algorithm used three markers for severe sepsis (Harrison et al., 2015) greater than two SIRS criteria, 2) lactate greater than 2.2, and 3) positive blood or urine culture. First group: the algorithm used where it did not alert the healthcare team, the second group received the alert. | Had a silent period where it recorded patient but did not create an alert. During the alert period, an alert was sent to the care team. I asked to perform bedside assessment. Assessed alert's impact on care. Data compared to screen-positive patients to screen negative non-ICU patients. | EWS 2.0 triggered for 7.4% of admissions during the silent period and 7.1% of admissions during the alert period. Silent period – the tool triggered a median of 6 hours and 34 minutes prior to the onset of severe sepsis or septic shock, similar to the alert period (median of 5 hour and 25 minutes. Improvement in lactate testing, administration of IV fluid boluses, and complete blood count or basic metabolic panel testing within 3 hours following the alert. Significant decrease in time to ICU transfer, but no change in the frequency of ICU transfer or median length of stay. | One alert may not have been enough to affect clinical care or outcomes. No clear directions were given to the care team on the sepsis bundle, unclear how to manage patients. Sometimes machine fired when the patient was well before later worsening, may not be an actionable moment (provider will not do anything because nothing seems wrong). Prioritized specificity over sensitivity, the clinical provider was already likely to predict sepsis. |

*(Continued)*

**Table 16.1 (*Continued*)   Summary of Studies Included in This Chapter**

| S.N. | Study Title, First Author Name, Year | Study Brief Description | ML Methods | Results | Outcomes/Impact on Healthcare Delivery |
|------|--------------------------------------|-------------------------|------------|---------|----------------------------------------|
| 5. | An Interpretable Machine Learning Model for Accurate Prediction of Sepsis in the ICU, Shamim Nemati, 2018. | Developed and validated an Artificial Intelligence Sepsis Expert (AISE) algorithm for early prediction of sepsis. Used 65 variables to determine a score. Measured times of variables, such as Tsepsis, Tsofa, and Tsuspicion. | Tsuspicion was a time of suspected infection. The onset time of sepsis (Tsepsis) was a change of more than two on the score (Tsofa) from up to 24 hours before to up to 12 hours after the Tsuspicion. 65 variables from EMR used in MLA. | Septic patients had longer median lengths of ICU stay (5.9 vs. 1.9 days), higher median SOFA scores (5.0 versus 1.7), and higher hospital mortality (14.5% versus 2.9%). Hospital mortality increased as the risk score for sepsis (Tsepsis) increased from 0 to 1. False positives with a score higher than 0.8% also had a higher mortality rate. | AUROC can predict sepsis 4 hours in advance, also when combined with dynamic data. Machine learning can contribute to early detection and prompt treatment EMR alerts to detect sepsis can lead to earlier intervention, earlier antibiotic administration, and improve mortality. Those who had higher risk scores had higher mortality as it measured 65 different variables that led to other complications. Can decrease alarm fatigue |

(*Continued*)

**Table 16.1 (*Continued*)  Summary of Studies Included in This Chapter**

| S.N. | Study Title, First‡ Author Name, Year | Study Brief Description | ML Methods | Results | Outcomes/Impact on Healthcare Delivery |
|---|---|---|---|---|---|
| 6. | Evaluation of a MLA for for up to 48-hour Prediction of Sepsis Using Six Vital Signs Christopher Barton 2019 | Developed a prediction algorithm and analyzed patient data retrospectively. Risk score calculated based on systolic blood pressure, diastolic blood pressure, heart rate, respiratory rate, peripheral oxygen saturation (SpO2), and temperature. 24 and 48 hours prior to onset. | Created an MLA detector using Python XGBoost package. Used area under the receiver operating characteristic (AUROC) as a measure of accuracy. Compared against SIRS, SOFA, MEWS, and qSOFA scores. | The MLA trained and tested on the UCSF data set demonstrated a higher AUROC (0.88) than the SIRS (0.66), MEWS (0.72), or qSOFA (0.60) scoring systems for the same data set. | Created a system that may be more accurate The earlier warning provides time to administer sepsis bundles Heart rate, temperature, and systolic blood pressure, along with age, contributed most to the quality of predictions. |

## 16.6 Conclusion

Current EHR systems provide abundant information to providers; however, this can easily plague individuals with information overload and alert fatigue (Harrison et al., 2015). Sepsis MLA systems allow for earlier recognition of sepsis factors versus relying on human recognition via frequent monitoring of the patient (Bansal et al., 2018). Furthermore, constant monitoring of patients puts a burden on bedside staff, and there is the potential for human error (Harrison et al., 2015). As machine learning systems become more sophisticated and are integrated into EHR, providers can streamline care for their patients. However, we must be careful about the data input for developing these algorithms as GIGO – "garbage in, garbage out" (Msmw, 1979) can leave us with false alerts and increased workload for no/harmful effects on patients and system in general.

## References

Bansal, V., Festić, E., Mangi, M. A., Decicco, N. A., Reid, A. N., Gatch, E. L., Naessens, J. M., & Moreno-Franco, P. (2018). Early machine-human interface around sepsis severity identification: From diagnosis to improved management? *Acta Medica Academica*, 47, 27–38.

Barton, C., Chettipally, U., Zhou, Y., Jiang, Z., Lynn-Palevsky, A., Le, S., Calvert, J., & Das, R. (2019). Evaluation of a machine learning algorithm for up to 48-hour advance prediction of sepsis using six vital signs. *Computers in Biology and Medicine*, 109, 79–84. doi: 10.1016/j.compbiomed.2019.04.027.

Giannini, H. M., Ginestra, J. C., Chivers, C., Draugelis, M., Hanish, A., Schweickert, W. D., Meadows, L., Lynch, M., Donnelly, P. J., Pavan, K., Fishman, N.O., Hanson, C W., & Umscheid, C. A. (2019). A machine-learning algorithm to predict severe sepsis and septic shock: Development, implementation, and impact on clinical practice. *Critical Care Medicine*, 47(11), 1485–1492. doi: 10.1097/CCM.0000000000003891.

Harrison, A. M., Thongprayoon, C., Kashyap, R., Chute, C. G., Gajic, O., Pickering, B. W., & Herasevich, V. (2015). Developing the surveillance algorithm for detection of failure to recognize and treat severe sepsis. *Mayo Clinic Proceedings*, 90(2), 166–175. doi: 10.1016/j.mayocp.2014.11.014.

Msmw. (1979). Can GIGO be eliminated? *Western Journal of Medicine*, 130, 366–367.

Nemati, S., Holder, A., Razmi, F., Stanley, M. D., Clifford, G. D., & Buchman, T. G. (2018). An interpretable machine learning model for accurate prediction of sepsis in the ICU. *Critical Care Medicine*, 46, 547–553. doi: 10.1097/CCM.0000000000002936.

Shimabukuro, D. W., Barton, C. W., Feldman, M. D., Mataraso, S. J., & Das, R. (2017). Effect of a machine learning-based severe sepsis prediction algorithm on patient survival and hospital length of stay: A randomized clinical trial. *BMJ Open Respiratory Research*, 4, e000234. doi: 10.1136/bmjresp-2017-000234.

*Chapter 17*

# Transforming Clinical Trials with Artificial Intelligence

Stefanie Lip
*University of Glasgow*

Shyam Visweswaran
*University of Pittsburgh*

Sandosh Padmanabhan
*University of Glasgow*

## Contents

## 17.1 Introduction

Current treatment guidelines are implicitly based on an "average patient" which ignores the complexity of human pathophysiology that manifests with significant inter-individual differences in treatment response. (Mulder et al., 2018) Randomized controlled trials (RCTs) have been utilized for many years and are often heralded as the "gold standard" for determining the safety and efficacy of treatments. In a conventional RCT, the average effect of a drug is compared to the effect of placebo or other active treatment, by assigning patients to alternative treatment groups and recording outcomes. To prevent selection bias patients are randomized to different groups, which produces distinct trial arms that are made up of patients who are largely similar except for the intervention they receive. This balances any confounding factors, known and unknown, and means that any difference in effects between groups is likely to be true, unconfounded treatment difference. However, RCTs are by no means faultless and can induce a multitude of problems including but not limited to poor patient recruitment and high attrition rates, expensive trial designs and the ever-increasing costs of conducting trials which tend to be large, international multi-centre endeavours.

High-throughput screening, genomic technology revolution and digital innovation are examples where advances in basic science and technology work symbiotically to achieve better, faster and cheaper clinical outcomes. (Doroshow & Doroshow, 2020; Seyhan & Carini, 2019; Zeggini, Gloyn, Barton, & Wain, 2019) However, clinical trials have somehow remained detached from such technological advancements and continue to use archaic protocols. The realization of this lack of technological integration in the clinical trial process has become apparent, and stakeholders are investigating how best to adopt more innovative and dynamic technological programmes including artificial intelligence (AI). Furthermore, the results of an RCT provide no information about the response at an individual patient level; rather, they represent the "average treatment effect" which is calculated from the homogenous group of patients enrolled in the trial. In real clinical practice, significant inter-individual differences in treatment response are evident, and this variation in response to treatment between individuals has been termed "heterogeneity of treatment effects". In addition to the heterogeneity of response, there is the heterogeneity of susceptibility to adverse effects between individuals. This implies that a drug found to be effective on average may display varying effects when prescribed more widely at a population scale. According to the Food & Drug Administration (FDA), roughly only one of ten compounds entering a clinical trial reaches the market, and this along with the high pre-clinical development costs highlights the inefficiencies of the drug development cycle.

Although AI has not yet had a significant impact on clinical trials, AI-based models are helping improve trial design, AI-based techniques are being used to increase patient recruitment and AI-based synthetic data

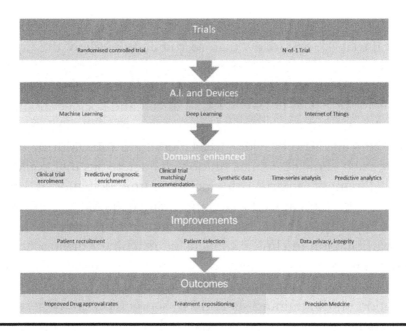

**Figure 17.1    Enhancing and transforming clinical trials with artificial intelligence and machine learning.**

generation are helping overcome privacy barriers to enable secondary analyses and collaborative research. (Harrer, Shah, Antony, & Hu, 2019) Clinical trials are now moving into an era of continuous electronic data collection utilizing devices and techniques, such as wearable sensors, mobile phones, electronic journals and digital imaging. AI and machine learning will be required to efficiently utilize these data. Ongoing data collection and analysis while the trial is being conducted will allow continuous modelling of projected trial results modified to adjust to the patient population actually being enrolled. In this chapter, we describe how AI and machine learning can help improve recruitment and predict dropout, obtain efficiencies in clinical trials execution, and help adapt and inform new clinical trial designs towards improving healthcare outcomes, improving trial success rates, lowering the pharma research and development burden, and enabling precision medicine (Figure 17.1).

## 17.2  Patient Recruitment for Clinical Trials

Patient recruitment takes up one-third of the overall clinical trial duration and represents a major barrier to the successful completion of the trial with a 32% failure rate in Phase III trials attributed to challenges with patient recruitment (Treweek et al., 2010). The adverse consequences and costs of failed clinical trials due to inadequate recruitment highlight the urgent need to identify strategies that could optimize and improve patient enrolment. The known predictors that impact the successful recruitment of patients for clinical trials include age, race, gender, financial and socioeconomic status (SES) and subjective attitudes towards research potentially influenced by family members and care providers (Fletcher et al., 2007; Murthy et al., 2012). Additionally, each clinical trial has unique characteristics that could impact a patient's willingness to participate, including time demands and scheduling, trial type (e.g., randomized trial), and financial incentives (Treweek et al., 2010). Few studies have explicitly attempted to predict the likelihood of patient participation in clinical trials using machine learning. One study, using a gold standard-based evaluation of real-world clinical data and trials, showed a logistic regression algorithm achieved 70.8% precision on 10-fold cross-validation on the training set and 71.5% precision on the test set, significantly better than the baseline predictor that simulated current practice (Ni et al., 2016).

## 17.3 Patient Selection for Clinical Trials

The success of epidemiological studies and clinical trials depends on the selection of the right patients. Rapid and efficient patient selection for clinical trials requires access and interrogation of large electronic medical records which are time-consuming because of the large number of patient records that have to be manually reviewed by investigators. This process is additionally challenging because of variations due to a lack of standards in recording patient information, medical coding mistakes, sparse data or missing details, among other issues. Logical rules that encode trial inclusion and exclusion criteria are widely used to identify patients in electronic medical records; however, they have several limitations including lower accuracy, the need for extensive additional work involving experts and limited reuse in other clinical trials due to the rules being generally trial-specific (Kirby et al., 2016). Automated natural language processing (NLP) methods can alleviate the manual review burden and improve accuracy, but their performance in clinical practice is unclear. Classical machine learning classifiers can automatically learn patterns to identify these patients. However, they still require human expertise to define the most informative feature set for the task.

One example is the NLP- and machine learning-based system – Automated Clinical Trial Eligibility Screener (ACTES) (Ni, Bermudez, Kennebeck, Liddy-Hicks, & Dexheimer, 2019) which automated subject identification for clinical trials and improved the numbers of subjects screened, approached and enrolled by 14.7%, 11.1% and 11.1%, respectively. Although the ACTES achieved an overall performance of 90.3% (micro F-measure), known shortcomings of NLP in understanding language semantics (e.g., word sense disambiguation) and syntax (e.g., assertion detection) resulted in multiple types of false-positive recommendations (Ni et al., 2015).

Consequently, there is a need to explore novel methods that can identify the most suitable set of patients for any clinical trial, independently of the criteria used and with minimal human intervention. Newer deep learning methods promise to improve this process further. One of their greatest advantages is that they can automatically identify the most appropriate features from the raw data and text directly, without the need for expensive manual guidance (Segura-Bedmar & Raez, 2019; Xiong et al., 2019). Nonadherence and dropout in clinical trials can lower study power, reduce the magnitude of treatment effects, and increase trial cost and duration. Machine learning methods have shown promise in predicting treatment discontinuation (Lutz et al., 2018) and in medication adherence (Lee, Kang, Kim, & Son, 2013; Lo-Ciganic et al., 2015). Similar approaches can be used to predict dropout in clinical trials.

## 17.4 Synthetic Data in Clinical Trials

"Synthetic controls" comes from methods developed for website analytics and economics research (Brodersen, Gallusser, Koehler, Remy, & Scott, 2015) where a number of time series that are unaffected by the intervention are optimally weighted according to their fit to the outcome of interest in the period before the intervention, then combined into a composite time series (Abadie, Diamond, & Hainmueller, 2010). Application of synthetic controls method to nationwide administrative databases in Brazil, Chile, Ecuador, Mexico and the United States to evaluate changes in the burden of hospitalizations for all-cause pneumonia associated with the introduction of pneumococcal conjugate vaccines (PCVs) did not detect a decline in all-cause pneumonia in older adults in any country (Bruhn et al., 2017) which had implications on healthcare policies on more widespread use of the vaccine.

Another potential use of synthetic data is in generating synthetic controls or placebo groups for trials. Although a placebo control arm is crucial in clinical trials to determine treatment effects, participants generally do not like the possibility of being placed in the placebo group. One option being explored is the use of synthetic control arms, which are in-silico placebo arms modelled using information that has previously been collected including historical control data, real-world data or the generation of a companion data set from other sources to serve as a comparator. Indeed, the FDA recognizes clinical trials that use this form of hybrid design where real-world data can be used as a basis for external controls.

The second scenario where machine learning can help by generating synthetic data is to overcome the challenges of sharing individual-level data from clinical trials (El Emam, Rodgers, & Malin, 2015). Data sharing requires formal collaboration and extensive data usage agreements between researchers that are time-consuming, with many ultimately resulting in failure. Generative adversarial networks (GANs) have been very successfully used to generate synthetic images in medical imaging, ophthalmology and dermatology (Chi, Bi, Kim, Feng, & Kumar, 2018; Yi, Walia, & Babyn, 2019; Yu et al., 2019) and subsequently extended to electronic health records (Baowaly, Lin, Liu, & Chen, 2019). GANs are deep neural net architectures comprised of two nets, pitting one against the other which in simple terms allows prediction of features given a label in contrast to discriminative algorithms which map features to labels (Goodfellow et al., 2014). A proof-of-concept application to generate synthetic trial data for sharing used GAN with differential privacy recognizing that traditional GAN could learn to create synthetic data that reveals actual participant data (Beaulieu-Jones et al., 2019). They achieved differential privacy by limiting the maximum influence of any single participant during training and then adding a small amount of random noise (Abadi et al., 2016) on the SPRINT (Systolic Blood Pressure Trial) data set (Wright, Whelton, & Reboussin, 2016). The key advantage of using synthetic data from electronic medical records is that they are artificially created and hence do not correspond to real patients and thus do not pose any danger of re-identification. As synthetic data carry attributes similar to actual data, it has value in public use of the information without the hassle of obtaining real data. This proof of concept is promising, and the next steps are resolving a known weakness of GAN's inability to deal with discrete data and testing and validation to ensure accurate implementation.

## 17.5 Trials for Precision Medicine

As noted above, despite the value of RCTs in demonstrating treatment efficacy, in real life these treatments do not work for all similarly. The demand
for more individualized interventions has caused researchers to question
whether traditional RCTs are the best method to evaluate personalized
medicine. One RCT design is the crossover trial design where, rather than
randomization to a treatment arm, patients are randomized to a sequence of
treatments. This is most commonly an AB/BA trial design whereby patients
assigned to the AB group receive treatment A followed by treatment B, and
vice versa for the BA group. The patient takes one treatment for a prespeci-
fied period, followed by the second treatment for the same amount of time.
Appropriate measurable outcomes are recorded, allowing the treatment
effects for the two interventions to be compared. Since each patient receives
both interventions, each patient acts as their own control, which avoids
the problems that arise from the analysis of groups of patients. Comparing
treatment effects within each individual also means there is no opportunity
for confounding due to patient differences. To ensure that the effects of one
drug does not "carry over" to the following treatment period, which would
confound treatment effects, there is often a "wash-out" period between treatments. This is a period in which the patient is not exposed to any intervention, to allow the effects of the first drug to wear off. Crossover trials use the
comparison of two interventions within individuals to establish the effects of
both interventions in the absence of confounding.

An extension of the crossover trial design is the "N-of-1" trial design,
which incorporates the basic elements of a crossover study. Where crossover
studies are used to assess the average treatment effect of a drug in a certain
population, N-of-1 trials are used to assess the individual treatment effect
in a single patient. N-of-1 trials are randomized, multiple crossover trials
which are conducted in a single patient, and are used to determine the most
effective treatment in an individual (Guyatt et al., 1986). N-of-1 studies are a
promising way to advance individualized medicine and a method for gain-
ing insights into comparative treatment effectiveness among a wide variety
of patients. Although N-of-1 trials have generated a lot of interest among
both physicians and researchers over the last 30 years, it is well recognized
that they are more time-consuming and costly than standard care. With
ubiquitous mobile digital devices and advances in AI and machine learning,
the potential of N-of-1 trials is now realizable for personalized medicine.
N-of-1 trials are associated with more intensive data collection, and a large

number of observations collected on a patient require time-series analysis and accommodating serial correlation between measures and possible carryover effects. Machine learning methods are essential for combining and evaluating multiple N-of-1 trials to make population-level estimates (Zucker, Ruthazer, & Schmid, 2010), identification of common characteristics among patients who are ultimately found to respond best to a particular intervention, treatment repositioning and integration of wireless data with electronic medical records.

## 17.6 Conclusion

The application of AI and machine learning can improve clinical trial subject identification, recruitment and retention. Furthermore, they can enable enhanced trial designs for evaluating precision medicine therapies, uncover hidden structure in trial data and lead to novel therapeutic discoveries and treatment repositioning. Generation of synthetic data under differential privacy with deep neural networks offers a technical solution for data sharing and the use of controls without endangering patient privacy.

## References

Abadi, M., Chu, A., Goodfellow, I., McMahan, H. B., Mironov, I., Talwar, K., & Zhang, L. (2016). Deep learning with differential privacy. *Ccs'16: Proceedings of the 2016 Acm Sigsac Conference on Computer and Communications Security*, 308–318. doi: 10.1145/2976749.2978318.

Abadie, A., Diamond, A., & Hainmueller, J. (2010). Synthetic control methods for comparative case studies: Estimating the effect of California's tobacco control program. *J Am Stat Assoc, 105*(490), 493–505. doi: 10.1198/jasa.2009.ap08746.

Baowaly, M. K., Lin, C. C., Liu, C. L., & Chen, K. T. (2019). Synthesizing electronic health records using improved generative adversarial networks. *J Am Med Inform Assoc, 26*(3), 228–241. doi: 10.1093/jamia/ocy142.

Beaulieu-Jones, B. K., Wu, Z. S., Williams, C., Lee, R., Bhavnani, S. P., Byrd, J. B., & Greene, C. S. (2019). Privacy-preserving generative deep neural networks support clinical data sharing. *Circ Cardiovasc Qual Outcomes, 12*(7), e005122. doi: 10.1161/CIRCOUTCOMES.118.005122.

Brodersen, K. H., Gallusser, F., Koehler, J., Remy, N., & Scott, S. L. (2015). Inferring causal impact using Bayesian structural time-series models. *Ann Appl Stat, 9*(1), 247–274. doi: 10.1214/14-AOAS788.

Bruhn, C. A., Hetterich, S., Schuck-Paim, C., Kurum, E., Taylor, R. J., Lustig, R., ... Weinberger, D. M. (2017). Estimating the population-level impact of vaccines using synthetic controls. *Proc Natl Acad Sci USA, 114*(7), 1524–1529. doi: 10.1073/pnas.1612833114.

Chi, Y., Bi, L., Kim, J., Feng, D., & Kumar, A. (2018). Controlled synthesis of dermoscopic images via a new color labeled generative style transfer network to enhance melanoma segmentation. *Conf Proc IEEE Eng Med Biol Soc, 2018*, 2591–2594. doi: 10.1109/EMBC.2018.8512842.

Doroshow, D. B., & Doroshow, J. H. (2020). Genomics and the history of precision oncology. *Surg Oncol Clin N Am, 29*(1), 35–49. doi: 10.1016/j.soc.2019.08.003.

El Emam, K., Rodgers, S., & Malin, B. (2015). Anonymising and sharing individual patient data. *BMJ, 350*, h1139. doi: 10.1136/bmj.h1139.

Fletcher, K., Mant, J., Holder, R., Fitzmaurice, D., Lip, G. Y., & Hobbs, F. D. (2007). An analysis of factors that predict patient consent to take part in a randomized controlled trial. *Fam Pract, 24*(4), 388–394. doi: 10.1093/fampra/cmm019.

Goodfellow, I. J., Pouget-Abadie, J., Mirza, M., Xu, B., Warde-Farley, D., Ozair, S., ... Bengio, Y. (2014). Generative adversarial networks. *arXiv e-prints*. Retrieved from https://ui.adsabs.harvard.edu/abs/2014arXiv1406.2661G.

Guyatt, G., Sackett, D., Taylor, D. W., Chong, J., Roberts, R., & Pugsley, S. (1986). Determining optimal therapy–randomized trials in individual patients. *N Engl J Med, 314*(14), 889–892. doi: 10.1056/NEJM198604033141406.

Harrer, S., Shah, P., Antony, B., & Hu, J. (2019). Artificial intelligence for clinical trial design. *Trends Pharmacol Sci, 40*(8), 577–591. doi: 10.1016/j.tips.2019.05.005.

Kirby, J. C., Speltz, P., Rasmussen, L. V., Basford, M., Gottesman, O., Peissig, P. L., ... Denny, J. C. (2016). PheKB: A catalog and workflow for creating electronic phenotype algorithms for transportability. *J Am Med Inform Assoc, 23*(6), 1046–1052. doi: 10.1093/jamia/ocv202.

Lee, S. K., Kang, B. Y., Kim, H. G., & Son, Y. J. (2013). Predictors of medication adherence in elderly patients with chronic diseases using support vector machine models. *Healthc Inform Res, 19*(1), 33–41. doi: 10.4258/hir.2013.19.1.33.

Lo-Ciganic, W. H., Donohue, J. M., Thorpe, J. M., Perera, S., Thorpe, C. T., Marcum, Z. A., & Gellad, W. F. (2015). Using machine learning to examine medication adherence thresholds and risk of hospitalization. *Med Care, 53*(8), 720–728. doi: 10.1097/MLR.0000000000000394.

Lutz, W., Schwartz, B., Hofmann, S. G., Fisher, A. J., Husen, K., & Rubel, J. A. (2018). Using network analysis for the prediction of treatment dropout in patients with mood and anxiety disorders: A methodological proof-of-concept study. *Sci Rep, 8*(1), 7819. doi: 10.1038/s41598-018-25953-0.

Mulder, R., Singh, A. B., Hamilton, A., Das, P., Outhred, T., Morris, G., ... Malhi, G. S. (2018). The limitations of using randomised controlled trials as a basis for developing treatment guidelines. *Evid Based Ment Health, 21*(1), 4–6. doi: 10.1136/eb-2017-102701.

Murthy, V., Awatagiri, K. R., Tike, P. K., Ghosh-Laskar, S., Gupta, T., Budrukkar, A., … Agarwal, J. P. (2012). Prospective analysis of reasons for non-enrollment in a phase III randomized controlled trial. *J Cancer Res Ther, 8*(Suppl 1), S94–S99. doi: 10.4103/0973-1482.92221.

Ni, Y., Beck, A. F., Taylor, R., Dyas, J., Solti, I., Grupp-Phelan, J., & Dexheimer, J. W. (2016). Will they participate? Predicting patients' response to clinical trial invitations in a pediatric emergency department. *J Am Med Inform Assoc, 23*(4), 671–680. doi: 10.1093/jamia/ocv216.

Ni, Y., Bermudez, M., Kennebeck, S., Liddy-Hicks, S., & Dexheimer, J. (2019). A real-time automated patient screening system for clinical trials eligibility in an emergency department: Design and evaluation. *JMIR Med Inform, 7*(3), e14185. doi: 10.2196/14185.

Ni, Y., Wright, J., Perentesis, J., Lingren, T., Deleger, L., Kaiser, M., … Solti, I. (2015). Increasing the efficiency of trial-patient matching: Automated clinical trial eligibility pre-screening for pediatric oncology patients. *BMC Med Inform Decis Mak, 15*, 28. doi: 10.1186/s12911-015-0149-3.

Segura-Bedmar, I., & Raez, P. (2019). Cohort selection for clinical trials using deep learning models. *J Am Med Inform Assoc, 26*(11), 1181–1188. doi: 10.1093/jamia/ocz139.

Seyhan, A. A., & Carini, C. (2019). Are innovation and new technologies in precision medicine paving a new era in patients centric care? *J Transl Med, 17*(1), 114. doi: 10.1186/s12967-019-1864-9.

Treweek, S., Pitkethly, M., Cook, J., Kjeldstrom, M., Taskila, T., Johansen, M., … Mitchell, E. (2010). Strategies to improve recruitment to randomised controlled trials. *Cochrane Database Syst Rev* (4), MR000013. doi: 10.1002/14651858. MR000013.pub5.

Wright, J. T., Jr., Whelton, P. K., & Reboussin, D. M. (2016). A randomized trial of intensive versus standard blood-pressure control. *N Engl J Med, 374*(23), 2294. doi: 10.1056/NEJMc1602668.

Xiong, Y., Shi, X., Chen, S., Jiang, D., Tang, B., Wang, X., … Yan, J. (2019). Cohort selection for clinical trials using hierarchical neural network. *J Am Med Inform Assoc, 26*(11), 1203–1208. doi: 10.1093/jamia/ocz099.

Yi, X., Walia, E., & Babyn, P. (2019). Generative adversarial network in medical imaging: A review. *Med Image Anal, 58*, 101552. doi: 10.1016/j. media.2019.101552.

Yu, Z., Xiang, Q., Meng, J., Kou, C., Ren, Q., & Lu, Y. (2019). Retinal image synthesis from multiple-landmarks input with generative adversarial networks. *Biomed Eng Online, 18*(1), 62. doi: 10.1186/s12938-019-0682-x.

Zeggini, E., Gloyn, A. L., Barton, A. C., & Wain, L. V. (2019). Translational genomics and precision medicine: Moving from the lab to the clinic. *Science, 365*(6460), 1409–1413. doi: 10.1126/science.aax4588.

Zucker, D. R., Ruthazer, R., & Schmid, C. H. (2010). Individual (N-of-1) trials can be combined to give population comparative treatment effect estimates: Methodologic considerations. *J Clin Epidemiol, 63*(12), 1312–1323. doi: 10.1016/j.jclinepi.2010.04.020.

## Chapter 18

# An Industry Review of Neuromorphic Chips

Deepak Kumar Gopalakrishnan,
Aditya Ravishankar, and Hamid Abdi

*Deakin University*

## Contents

## 18.1  Introduction

Artificial intelligence (AI) has seen growing inputs, research and investments in the last few years. It is believed that AI will enhance the productivity of the healthcare sector qualitatively and quantitatively. All this would be possible because of an AI chip. Chips or integrated circuits on one small board have been around for a while, but the concept of AI on chips is novel and fascinating. The availability of this hardware can accelerate the development of autonomous clinical platforms. This chapter describes these AI chips based on an extensive review of various articles, journals, websites, newsletters and mobile applications.

## 18.2  Overview of AI

AI has been inspired by the human ability to learn, retain the knowledge and use this knowledge later. AI devices are a combination of software and hardware in order to learn and retain knowledge to use in the future. Researchers program devices in such a way that it can read images, texts, audios and videos and retain the knowledge in its database. Once the machine learns, that knowledge can be applied elsewhere. For example, if a system acquires the ability to recognize somebody's face, it can then be used to find them on social media platforms. AI systems need this learning (training) phase which makes them stand out from other systems (Gershgorn, 2017).

The evolution of AI technologies has been taking place at variable speeds based on the medium or type of data to be processed. The ability of pattern recognitions which includes video and images is generally known as "computer vision". The field of natural language processing is known as narrow intelligence, whereas an agnostic approach towards general form of human intelligence is termed as "general intelligence". The rapid advancement of AI technology in the forthcoming years will unveil various machine learning techniques to build a consortium of "general artificial intelligence" methods (Gershgorn, 2017).

## 18.3  AI-Chips

To perform tasks mimicking the human brain, complex calculations are required to be performed within milliseconds. Simulating one second of the human brain requires 82,944 processors. These calculations can be performed efficiently with a proper combination of hardware and the software. The hardware is called AI chip. These are specifically made for machine learning purposes. There have been many start-ups and many giants working collaboratively on making such efficient AI chips.

## 18.3.1 IBM

The idea behind making these chips is to mimic the biological neural structure. So, AI chips are based on artificial neural networks. This can be done in two different manners such as designing a lightweight neural network that consumes less power for processing and others by developing customary co-processors based on AI technology (Tarantola, 2015). IBM has been working on "neuromorphic" chips since 2008. Their chip the building program was named SyNAPSE (Systems on neuromorphic adaptive plastic scalable electronics). In 2015, they unveiled the system called the "True North" system in a three-week training session for academic and government researchers. The chip was produced by IBM in nm collaboration with Global Foundries and Samsung. The chip is said to be 7 nm in size. It was the smallest chip until then. The system/chip was built to run "deep learning" algorithms (Tarantola, 2015). IBM's True North consists of 5.4 billion transistors but uses only 70 mW power. Its power consumption is considerably low as compared to an Intel processor that has 1.4 billion transistors but uses 35–140 W of power (Tarantola, 2015) (Figure 18.1).

True North consists of silicon and germanium in its electricity-conducting channels. IBM has used the new lithography method to print finer circuits. The circuits are around 10,000 times thinner than a human hair. The circuits computing power is expected to double every 18 months. Their next step is to make 5 nm chips, which is even more challenging. Present generation von Neumann computers mimic the functions of the left brain such as the number and symbolic calculations, while the True North chip will perform the activities of the right brain such as sensory and pattern recognition (Modha, 2015).

## 18.3.2 Google

Google has been producing deep learning products since 2015. It published the description of its own deep-learning chip in 2016. The chip uses a TPU (tensor processing unit) (Feldman, 2017). Google's TPU has been built to accelerate the inferencing of neural networks. It is aimed to speed up the

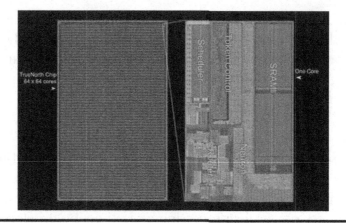

**Figure 18.1   True North chip (Hayward, 2019).**

production phase of the networks that have already been trained for deep-learning applications. In the training phase, Google has been using GPUs. TPU can do a lot of its inferencing at 8 bit rather than 16 or 32 bit which would, in turn, consume less power (Feldman, 2017) (Figure 18.2).

The TPU can perform 8-bit matrix multiplications and can give up to 92 teraops/s. It has 24MiB on-chip memory, 34 GB/s bandwidths. It operates at 700 MHz and uses 40 W of power. The chip is about 28 nm in size. It is estimated that TPU performs 15–30 times faster than NVIDIA's K80 and Haswell's E5–2699 v3. Google estimates that the use of higher bandwidth memory in the TPU would increase its performance by three times (Feldman, 2017).

**Figure 18.2   Google's TPU board (Novet, 2017).**

### 18.3.3 NVIDIA

The idea behind producing AI chips is faster calculations, performance and enhanced outputs. NVIDIA's GPU (graphical processing unit) has been used for deep learning as it can do calculations better and faster compared to other processors (Archer, 2017). NVIDIA's latest Volta series chips are being focused by all AI training data centres. GPUs differ from more traditional CPUs by having hundreds or even thousands of smaller "cores" that can perform small operations, compared to the typically much smaller number of more powerful cores (4–8 in many modern machines) found in CPUs. NVIDIA's Volta series consists of tensor core units. NVIDIA's Tensor cores are specifically designed to be speedy AI system trainers and are 12 times faster than the company's previous series of chips, according to NVIDIA (Archer, 2017) (Figure 18.3).

Specifications of NVIDIA's chips that can be used for high-level computational work and AI are specified in Table 18.1.

### 18.3.4 *Google and Microsoft's Collaboration with AI Chips*

Google and Microsoft have had neural network exchanges between them to keep up with the AI chip race (Quach, 2017). Pixel 2 smartphone by Google had its own AI co-processor chip and its existence wasn't declared publicly because of their incompatibility to any of the smartphone applications. The AI co-processor present in pixel 2 is named as Pixel Visual core which consists of eight image processing units (IPUs) where each IPU core consists of 512 ALUs (arithmetic logic units) with a capacity to process

**Figure 18.3   NVIDIA's Volta (Hayward, 2019).**

**Table 18.1  Specifications of NVDIA's Chips (Hayward, 2019)**

| GPU *Engine Specs* | GEFORCE GTX1080 *1090 TI/1080* | GEFORCE GTX1070 *1070 TI/1070* | GEFORCE GTX1060 *6/3 GB* | GEFORCE GTX 1050 *1050 TI/1050* |
|---|---|---|---|---|
| CUDA cores | 3,584/2,560 | 2,423/1,920 | 1,280/1,152 | 768/640 |
| Base clock (MHz) | 1,480/1,607 | 1,607/1,506 | 1,506 | 1,290/1,354 |
| Base clock (MHz) | 1,582/1,733 | 1,683/1,683 | 1,708 | 1,392/1,455 |
| **Memory Spec** | | | | |
| Memory speed | 11/10 Gbps | 8.0 Gbps | 8.0 Gbps | 7.0 Gbps |
| Standard memory config. | 11/8 GB GDDR5X | 8 GB GDDR5 | 6/3 GB GDDR5 | 4/2 GB GDDR5 |
| Memory interface width | 352/256-bit | 256-bit | 192-bit | 128-bit |
| Memory bandwidth (GB/s) | 484/320 | 256 | 192 | 112 |
| **Additional Information** | | | | |
| Graphics card power | 250/180 W | 180/150 W | 120 W | 75 W |
| Maximum digital resolution | 7,680×4,320 @60 Hz | 7,680×4,320 @60 Hz | 7,680×4,320 @60 Hz | 7,680×4,320 @60 Hz |
| Maximum VGA resolution | 2,048×1,536 | 2,048×1,536 | 2,048×1,536 | 2,048×1,536 |
| Standard display connectors | Dual-Link DVI-I, HDMI 2.0B,3×Display Port 1.4 | Dual-Link DVI-I, HDMI 2.0B,3×Display Port 1.4 | Dual-Link DVI-I, HDMI 2.0B,3×Display Port 1.4 | Dual-Link DVI-I, HDMI 2.0B,3×Display Port 1.4 |
| Multi-monitor | 4 displays | 4 displays | 4 displays | 4 displays |

3 trillion operations/second, and we don't have furthermore details on their technical specifications. The core function of the pixel co-processor chip is to execute machine learning software for image processing within the smartphone by working on the pictures taken by the smartphone's camera (Quach, 2017).

## 18.3.5 Huawei

Huawei has made its own neural processing unit chip and included it in its new phone Mate 10 (Lifestyle, 2017). The Mate 10's Kirin 970 chipset, which the company developed in-house, is the world's first mobile SoC (systems on a chip) to have a dedicated NPU (neural processing unit). Right now, using voice assistants (such as Apple's Siri or Google's Assistant) on other devices requires an internet connection, because the AI is stored in the clouds. But with the Mate 10, the AI is inside the NPU. Huawei reports that it will improve efficiency and speed and will eliminate the need to be connected to the internet. The inclusion of NPU in Huawei Mate 10 has led its camera to identify objects in real-time. For example, if we are taking photos of a plate of food, the camera will know to punch up the contrast to make the colours pop (Sin, 2017).

## 18.3.6 Microsoft

Microsoft revealed its AI chip in a press conference in late July 2017 (Dent, 2017). This comes after Google announced its own TPU chip for AI in 2016. The aim is to create chips for HoloLens-augmented goggles. Microsoft's HoloLens consists of a co-processor on its HPU (holographic processing unit) which is powered by AI. The primary application of HoloLens is to help blind people to identify their family, friends and other lifestyle needs. The silicon part of the AI chip is manufactured in-house by Microsoft which will add power to the HoloLens battery. It will be fully programmable and compatible with different types of deep learning techniques. Tasks such as object and voice recognition can be done fast by flexible AI solution without an internet connection. Apple and Google had also started manufacturing AI processors on their own like Microsoft. Still, HoloLens seems to be the only wearable augmented reality device where AI co-processor forms the core part of the HoloLens which acts as mixed reality devices with its ability to think intelligently (Dent, 2017).

### 18.3.7 Intel

Intel has developed its own neuromorphic chip called Loihi (Mayberry, 2017). It includes digital circuits that mimic the brain's mechanism, making machine learning faster and efficient. A neuromorphic chip mimics the communication between neurons in the human body, using spikes and plastic synapses based on timing. The chip doesn't have to wait for updates from the cloud; it can adapt in real-time. It is up to 1,000 energy efficient compared to typical training systems. Loihi uses fewer resources to complete tasks in comparison with deep learning neural networks (Mayberry, 2017) (Figure 18.4).

### 18.3.8 Apple

Consumers can now use a new technology called "Face ID" to unlock the iPhone X. That's made possible by a True Depth camera system on the front, along with a dual-core Neural Engine on the six-core A11 Bionic chip for real-time facial recognition that looks at 30,000 points on the human face (Ivankov, 2017). It's built to recognize human face no matter whether they are wearing a hat, glasses or sporting a facial beard (Figure 18.5).

### 18.3.9 General Vision

General Vision has manufactured a neuromorphic chip CM1K (General Vision, 2018). Its architecture is inspired by the human brain's architecture. The chip has 1,024 neurons working in parallel and has the capability to learn and recognize patterns in few microseconds. All the neurons receive

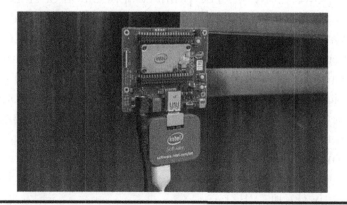

**Figure 18.4   Intel's Loihi (Pratap, 2017).**

**Figure 18.5 Apple's A11 chip (Ivankov, 2017).**

and execute the same instructions in parallel. All the neurons receive patterns at once, either for learning or for recognition. The neurons are trained, and their built knowledge is used in various scenarios. The neurons autonomously decide their own firing threshold. It has a parallel architecture that has been patented and has no controller or supervisor. It works on a frequency of 16–27 MHz and dissipates only 0.5 W. Even though all the neurons work in parallel, they are interconnected to each other in order to make global decisions. All the neurons are connected via a bidirectional bus internally and externally. There are 15 registers on which the simple register-level transfer is based on. There are an optional I2C port and optional digital input bus to broadcast patterns to a simple recognition stage. A daisy chain of CM1K chips is possible, and the neurons in the different chips would communicate with each other in the same manner as they communicate with other neurons on their own chip (General Vision, 2018) (Figure 18.6; Table 18.2).

## 18.3.10 BrainScaleS

The BrainScaleS project was started in 2011 with an aim of understanding the working of human neurons and generates a chip that works like a human brain (Meier, 2012). There were 13 research groups involved in the project headed by Heidelberg University in Germany. The neuromorphic processor was constructed by integrating silicon wafer scales. The silicon wafer scales consist of a number of chips tightly connected to each other and are only 20 cm in diameter. The circuitry contains both analogue and digital circuits. The neurons are analogue, while communication between the neurons and their synaptic weight is digital. One wafer has been built

**Figure 18.6   CM1K chip (General Vision, 2018).**

**Table 18.2   Specifications of CM1K (General Vision, 2018)**

| *Attributes* | *CM1K* |
|---|---|
| Neuron capacity | 1,024 |
| Neuron memory size | 256 bytes |
| Categories | 15 bits |
| Distances | 16 bits |
| Contexts | 7 bits |
| Clock frequency | 27 MHz for a single chip and 16 MHz for a chain of multiple chips |
| I/O | Parallel Bus- 26 lines<br>Serial I2C- 100 and 400 kbit/s<br>Digital input bus – 11 lines for data and sync signals |
| Process and die-size | 130 nm/64 mm$^2$ |
| Electrical | 3.3V I/O Operation, 1.2V core, 260 mA |
| Power consumption | <300 mW at Active mode |
| Package | 100 pin TQFP 14×14 mm package |

on 48 reticles. Each reticle contains 8 HICANN (High Input Count Analog Neural Network) chips. So, there are about 384 chips in a wafer. A HICANN chips size is 5×10 mm$^2$. Each chip contains an ANC (Analog Neural Core) which is the central block along with the supporting circuitry. Each HICANN

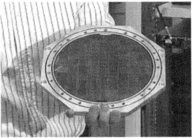

**Figure 18.7  Silicon wafer and aluminium back panel, hexagon silicon wafer (Meier, 2012). The simulations for the chips were run on JUGENE computers and communication between on-wafer neurons was established (Meier, 2012).**

implements 128,000 synapses and 512 membrane circuits. These are grouped to form simulated neurons. The number of neurons depends on the number of synapses configured per neuron. There can be about 196,608 neurons per wafer if all the chips are flawless. The wafer is supported on an aluminium plate that also acts as a heat sink. A PCB board is placed on top of the wafer where all the I/O connections can be made. Several wafer modules can be connected together to make larger systems. The design was done in Heidelberg, and the chip was fabricated in Taiwan (Figure 18.7).

### 18.3.11  APT Group

The APT group in Manchester (four universities and three companies) are involved in the designing and fabrication of the SpiNNaker chip (APT, 2019). The chip consists of 18 ARM968 processors. It has an asynchronous communication infrastructure. The chip has a SpiNNaker directory itself and a 128 Mbyte SDRAM. The chip is globally asynchronous locally synchronous (ALS). It is a multicore system-on-chip. The SpiNNaker chip is $102 \, mm^2$ in diameter (Figure 18.8).

These developments of AI-specific hardware chips have widened the range of artificial intelligence applications across many sectors (APT, 2019).

## 18.4  Application in Healthcare

The availability of AI chips means that healthcare practitioners and researchers can manage interoperable data and accelerate personalized medicine and augmented healthcare delivery (Burt, 2019; IBM, 2019; NVIDIA, 2019).

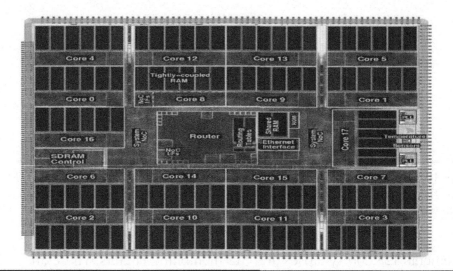

**Figure 18.8    SpiNNaker chip (Group, 2019).**

Importantly, the prowess of AI chips will allow computing closer to the source of data, thus allowing processes such as federated learning, which allows greater protection and privacy of data, and earlier processing of data and detection of diseases (Burt, 2019; NVIDIA, 2019). These possibilities have led to an increasing number of collaborative projects between the chip industry and healthcare institutions. The coming years will showcase the results of these collaborative projects and their impact on healthcare delivery.

## References

APT Group. (2019). *SpiNNaker Project*. The University of Manchester. Available: http://apt.cs.manchester.ac.uk/projects/SpiNNaker/SpiNNchip/ Retrieved October 11, 2019.

Archer, S. (2017). "Nvidia's newest chip has a secret weapon in the AI race (NVDA)". Business Insider. Available: https://markets.businessinsider.com/news/stocks/nvidia-stock-price-newest-chip-has-a-secret-weapon-in-the-ai-race-2017-10-1005455745 Retrieved October 15, 2019.

Burt, J. (2019). *NVIDIA Moves Clara Healthcare AI to the Edge. The Next Platform*. Available: https://www.nextplatform.com/2019/12/02/nvidia-moves-clara-healthcare-ai-to-the-edge/ Retrieved December 10, 2019.

Dent, S. (2017). "The next HoloLens will use AI to recognize real-world objects". Engadget. Available: https://www.engadget.com/2017/07/24/hololens-ai-chip-computer-vision/?guccounter=1 Retrieved October 4, 2019.

Feldman, M. (2017). "Google reveals technical specs and business rationale for TPU processor", Available: https://www.top500.org/news/google-reveals-technical-specs-and-business-rationale-for-tpu-processor/ Retrieved October 4, 2019.

General Vision. (2018). "CM1K". General Vision. Available: https://www.general-vision.com/hardware/cm1k/ Retrieved October 11, 2019.

Gershgorn, D. (2017). *The Quartz Guide to Artificial Intelligence: What is It, Why is It Important, and Should We be Afraid?* Available: https://qz.com/1046350/the-quartz-guide-to-artificial-intelligence-what-is-it-why-is-it-important-and-should-we-be-afraid/ Retrieved October 4, 2019.

Hayward, A. (2019). "Nvidia Volta release date, news and features". TechRadar. Available: https://www.techradar.com/nz/news/nvidia-volta Retrieved October 4, 2019.

IBM. (2019). "Medical labs "on a chip" will serve as health detectives for tracing disease at the nanoscale". IBM Research. Available: https://www.research.ibm.com/5-in-5/nanotech-for-healthcare/ Retrieved December 10, 2019.

Ivankov, A. (2017). "Review: What makes Apple A11 Bionic chip great?" Profulus. Available: https://www.profolus.com/topics/review-what-makes-apple-a11-bionic-chip-great/ Retrieved October 10, 2019.

Mayberry, D. M. (2017). "Intel's new self-learning chip promises to accelerate artificial intelligence". Available: https://newsroom.intel.com/editorials/intels-new-self-learning-chip-promises-accelerate-artificial-intelligence/ Retrieved October 10, 2019.

Meier, K. (2012). *BrainScaleS – Neuromorphic Processors*. Available: http://www.artificialbrains.com/brainscales Retrieved October 11, 2019.

Modha, D. S. (2015). "Introducing a brain-inspired computer". IBM. Available: http://www.research.ibm.com/articles/brain-chip.shtml Retrieved October 4, 2019.

Novet, J. (2017). "Google opens up about its TPU chips for AI". Available: https://venturebeat.com/2017/04/05/google-opens-up-about-its-tpu-chips-for-ai/ Retrieved October 10, 2019.

NVIDIA. (2019). "Healthcare and life sciences". NVIDIA. Available: https://www.nvidia.com/en-us/industries/healthcare-life-sciences/ Retrieved December 10, 2019.

Pratap, K. (2017). "Intel 'Loihi' self-learning AI chip is neuromorphic, mimicking how the brain functions". NDTV. Available: https://gadgets.ndtv.com/science/news/intel-loihi-self-learning-ai-chip-neuromorphic-1756392 Retrieved October 10, 2019.

Quach, K. (2017). "Google and Intel cook AI chips, neural network exchanges – and more", Available: https://www.theregister.co.uk/2017/10/22/ai_roundup/.

Sin, B. (2017). Huawei Mate 10 first impressions: 'intelligent' phone's NPU chip can run AI and an internet-free digital assistant", in Lifestyle, ed. South China Morning Post: Lifestyle. Retrieved October 3, 2019 https://www.scmp.com/lifestyle/article/2115526/huawei-mate-10-first-impressions-intelligent-phones-npu-chip-can-run-ai.

Tarantola, A. (2015). "IBM wires up 'neuromorphic' chips like a rodent's brain". Available: https://www.engadget.com/2015/08/17/ibm-wires-up-neuromorphic-chips-like-a-rodents-brain/ Retrieved October 4, 2019.

## Chapter 19

# Artificial Empathy – An Artificial Intelligence Challenge

Dharmendra Sharma and Balaji Bikshandi
*University of Canberra*

## Contents

## 19.1 Introduction

Artificial intelligence (AI) allows machines to analyse and solve problems utilizing heuristic, stochastic, fuzzy and other computational paradigms including biological principles (Xu et al., 2019). AI can learn from experiential data to automatically model and solve complex problems that may exceed the capacity of humans. AI-based deep learning algorithms have been found in certain instances to be superior to human clinicians in diagnosis, for example, pathologists in detecting the spread of breast cancer (Ehteshami et al., 2017). The current generation of AI systems is widely used in applications that enhance daily human life and those that further sophisticated research. AI and AE researchers could make significant strides in healthcare if AI can generate empathy at appropriate levels to optimize the delivery and effectiveness of healthcare services. Care provision robotics, for instance (as opposed to surgical robots), could ease the current care crisis due to longer life expectancy, the burden of multi-morbidity and shortage of skilled care-provision workforce. But a significant challenge for AI is the possession and deliverance of the human attribute of empathy. In this chapter, we strive to describe the trait of human empathy, analyse the possibility of implementing it using AI, explore the limitations in doing so and briefly discuss the perceivable wide-ranging repercussions of ARTIFICIAL EMPATHY (AE) specifically in the healthcare context while projecting future directions.

## 19.2 Empathy

While we acknowledge empathy as a variably defined term in different domains and contexts, we opine empathy is the quintessentially subjective ability of an individual's consciousness to experience the world of the other person, albeit briefly, and extend compassion. Notwithstanding the difficulty in defining this trait consistently, it is nevertheless, definitely discernible and deliverable by most humans. The deep analysis of this trait invariably leads to philosophy and phenomenology and has a myriad of other complexities – including cultural and religious ones. It is also not clear to us if this attribute is a learned one or is given at its full intensity at birth.

In theatrical and performance art, for example, empathy may mean an analogizing and/or a dialogical endeavour that makes an individual human subject feel the performer's emotions/feelings and be able to reciprocate the same (Rousseau, 1754). In the philosopher Jean Jacques Rousseau's words,

> I perceive two principles antecedent to reason, of which one interests us intensely in our well-being and self-preservation, and the other inspires in us a natural repugnance at seeing any sentient being, particularly a fellow human, perish or suffer. It is from the collaboration and combination of the two principles of which our minds are capable...all the rules of natural law flow.

**(Madumal et al., 2019)**

The trait he eludes to as "antecedent to reason" is perhaps empathy or its primordial source. We take that as the best available description of the concept of empathy.

## 19.3 Enabling Empathy with AI

In our view, empathy is a superior manifestation of human intelligence and in that way could be accommodated by AI. Human intelligence is portrayed, in most circumstances, in an empathetic context. This being the case, it is easily deducible to the reader that such "context-sensitive" AI would be more human and, at least to a significant degree of plausibility, renders itself to be designed using the current Artificial AI tools and techniques.

AI systems could work like automatons, interacting with humans constantly or between themselves. Explainable artificial intelligence (XAI) models could incorporate dynamic interactions to obtain data, respond appropriately and learn to model their future behaviour automatically and transparently (Howarth, 2017). For example, in the healthcare domain, signals/data are constantly generated by patients, and a reasoning system for modelling can draw data for insight analysis. Such systems can provide the fundamental framework to implement AE given the availability of a large amount of electronic medical data from real-time monitoring. XAI models could be designed to discern cognitive, emotional and compassionate parameters (pain, gestures, verbal/non-verbal cues, historical data, specific diagnoses, etc.), in addition to vital physiological data and laboratory data of patients to determine the empathy needed for in a particular care provision situation and deliver it appropriately with verbal and non-verbal methods.

A pioneering study done in Australia by one of the authors of this chapter and a team of researchers, where the concept of acceptability of humanoids in direct clinical care was explored, had garnered significant interest (ANZCTR, 2007; Schwartz, 2019). In this particular study, a commercially available programmable humanoid robot was trained to perform a limited clinical interaction with healthcare professionals in an acute hospital setting. The emphasis being on the nature of clinical communication, the study explored the feasibility of delivering empathy, a clinically pertinent quality, to see if the health professionals (acting as patients) could indeed place trust in such a machine in the position of a healthcare professional (Howarth, 2017; Madumal et al., 2019). While the results of the study are yet to be made publicly available, studies such as this attest to the feasibility of exploring this area further.

## 19.4 Challenges

A fundamental problem is the lack of a universal definition of empathy. For the purposes of this chapter, we limited ourselves to pragmatism by exploring the question of whether this trait could be modelled using machine intelligence to be of use to humanity. "Instead of arguing interminably about the ultimate nature and essence of thinking," as the Philosopher Daniel Dennett wrote to those arguing on the question that Alan Turing posed ("Can machines think?"), "why don't we all agree that whatever that nature is, anything that could pass this (Turing) test would surely have it." (Shanahan, 2015). It was perhaps not necessary to understand the mechanism of thinking in extraordinary detail before designing applications for harnessing the machine thinking ability to human advantage. Resorting to this analogy, we adopted a similar attitude and foresee a parallel trajectory for the possession of empathy by intelligent machines.

The next question is one of the "Authenticity of Artificial Empathy" if exhibited by intelligent machines. There resides a fundamental fallacy in "emulating" a trait that appears to be the epitome of authenticity. Unless machines are "self-actualized," the reader will understand that emulated empathy may not be authentic. And, we wish to steer clear of exploring the concept of machine "self-actualization" or "technological singularity" (Arrieta et al., 2019) in this discourse. Nevertheless, we see applications for artificial empathy which could be of significant benefit to the community and hence directed focus on that aspect more.

Trust in AI decision-making itself is brought to question given the "black box" insularity of many decisions made by intelligent machines. The resurgence of XAI and the design of AE based on such systems can help mitigate this issue, at least to a considerable degree (Stuber, 2019). The absence of validated metrics to quantify empathy exhibited by artificially intelligent machines is a significant deficiency that hinders research progress in this area. Quantifying a subjective parameter is an error-prone task. There had been attempts at devising an "empathy scale," but such endeavours are still in their infancy (AMA, 2019).

## 19.5 Future Direction

Notwithstanding the challenges, artificial empathy could be of significant use to areas such as medicine where care provision requires empathy. Trust levels in AI systems, which are increasing in applications in medicine, could increase with incorporation of AE. Data mining and machine learning algorithms have been quite successful in extracting valuable insights, but little work on their application to model and optimize empathy has been taken so far. This area, no doubt, has enormous potential to develop, and the resulting technology has the potential to empower patients and practitioners alike.

## 19.6  Conclusion

There are only a few discussions that could trigger a deeper sense of curiosity in humans than AE, no doubt. We believe there needs to be a large body of research necessary in this area, urgently. It would amount to stating the obvious to say that a cross-disciplinary collaboration between medical professionals, robots/AI engineers, ethicists, psychologists, sociologists and a myriad of other specialists is a pressing need of the moment to further this research. We believe the future of technology and the societal perception of technology will be transformed forever if empathy can be exhibited by intelligent machines effectively. Research into AE can potentially revolutionize the current computing methodologies as the deeper question of what constitutes intelligence arises if empathy is construed as a form of intelligence. This may lead to a fundamental re-think of the design of computers and artificial intelligent systems to the benefit of mankind at large.

## References

AMA. (2019). *New WMA President Urges Empathy*. Australian Medical Association. Retrieved from: https://ama.com.au/ausmed/new-wma-president-urges-empathy.

ANZCTR. (2007). Clinical skills assessment of a humanoid robot healthcare provider. Australian New Zealand Clinical Trials Registry. Retrieved from: https://www.anzctr.org.au/Trial/Registration/TrialReview.aspx?id=372494.

Arrieta, AB, Díaz-Rodríguez, N, Del Ser, J, et al. (2019). Explainable AI (XAI): concepts, taxonomies, opportunities and challenges toward responsible AI. arXIv.org. Retrieved from: https://arxiv.org/abs/1910.10045.

Ehteshami, BB, Veta, M, van Diest, PJ, et al. (2017). Diagnostic assessment of deep learning algorithms for detection of lymph node metastases in women with breast cancer. *JAMA*. 318(22):2199–2210.

Howarth, C. (2017). Humanoid robot Dr NAO assessing 'patients' in Tasmanian hospital study. Australian Broadcasting Corporation. Retrieved from: https://www.abc.net.au/news/2017-05-10/doctor-robot-on-trial-in-tasmania/8513992.

Madumal, P, Miller, T, Sonenberg, L, & Vetere, F. (2019). A grounded interaction protocol for explainable artificial intelligence. In *Proceeding of the 18th International Conference on Autonomous Agents and Multiagent Systems (AAMAS 2019)*, Montreal, Canada, May 13–17, 2019, IFAAMAS, Retrieved from: https://arxiv.org/pdf/1903.02409.pdf.

Rousseau, JJ. (1754). What is the origin of inequality among men, and is it authorised by natural law (Translated by G. D. H. Cole). Retrieved from: https://www.constitution.org/jjr/ineq.htm.

Schwartz, O. (2019). *Untold History of AI: Why Alan Turing Wanted AI Agents to Make Mistakes?* IEEE Spectrum. Retrieved from: https://spectrum.ieee.org/tech-talk/tech-history/dawn-of-electronics/untold-history-of-ai-why-alan-turing-wanted-ai-to-make-mistakes.

Shanahan, M. (2015). *The Technological Singularity*. The MIT Press Essential Knowledge Series. 272 pp. Retrieved from: https://mitpress.mit.edu/books/technological-singularity.

Stuber, K. (2019). *Measuring Empathy*. Stanford Encyclopedia of Philosophy. Retrieved from: https://plato.stanford.edu/entries/empathy/measuring.html.

Xu, W, Xu, J, He, D & Tan, KC. (2019). An evolutionary constraint-handling technique for parametric optimization of a cancer immunotherapy model. *IEEE Transactions on Emerging Topics in Computational Intelligence*. 3(2). Retrieved from: https://ieeexplore.ieee.org/document/8673711.

# Index

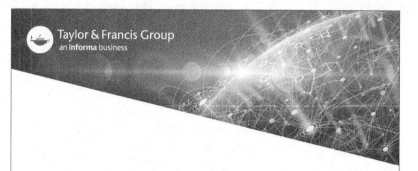

Made in United States
North Haven, CT
25 June 2025

70112662R00193